Your Career

How to Make It Happen

Ninth Edition

Lauri Harwood

Instructor, *Miami University;*
Business Consultant and Trainer, *Cincinnati, OH*

Lisa M.D. Owens

Dean of Learning Sciences, Emeritus, Procter & Gamble;
President, Training Design Strategies LLC

Crystal Kadakia

Founder and Principal, Invati LLC

CENGAGE
Learning·

Australia · Brazil · Mexico · Singapore · United Kingdom · United States

**Your Career: How to Make It Happen,
Ninth Edition**
Lauri Harwood, Lisa M.D. Owens,
Crystal Kadakia

SVP, GM Skills & Global Product Management:
Dawn Gerrain

Product Director: Matthew Seeley

Product Manager: Katie McGuire

Senior Director, Development:
Marah Bellegarde

Senior Product Development Manager:
Larry Main

Senior Content Developer: Anne Orgren

Senior Product Assistant: Diane Chrysler

Vice President, Marketing Services:
Jennifer Ann Baker

Marketing Manager: Scott Chrysler

Senior Production Director: Wendy Troeger

Production Director: Andrew Crouth

Senior Content Project Manager: Betty Dickson

Managing Art Director: Jack Pendleton

Cover images: © Robert Cock/Getty Images;
© Shutterstock/chungking;
© Shutterstock/NAN728;
© Shutterstock/Andrey Popov;
© Shutterstock/Stephen Coburn;
© Money Business Images/Shutterstock

Library of Congress Control Number: 2015948447

ISBN: 978-1-305-49483-1

Cengage Learning
20 Channel Center Street
Boston, MA 02210
USA

Cengage Learning is a leading provider of customized learning solutions
with employees residing in nearly 40 different countries and sales in more
than 125 countries around the world. Find your local representative at
www.cengage.com.

Cengage Learning products are represented in Canada by Nelson Education, Ltd.

To learn more about Cengage Learning, visit **www.cengage.com**

Purchase any of our products at your local college store or at our preferred
online store **www.cengagebrain.com**

Notice to the Reader
Publisher does not warrant or guarantee any of the products described herein or perform any
independent analysis in connection with any of the product information contained herein.
Publisher does not assume, and expressly disclaims, any obligation to obtain and include information other than that provided to it by the manufacturer. The reader is expressly warned to
consider and adopt all safety precautions that might be indicated by the activities described
herein and to avoid all potential hazards. By following the instructions contained herein, the
reader willingly assumes all risks in connection with such instructions. The publisher makes no
representations or warranties of any kind, including but not limited to, the warranties of fitness
for particular purpose or merchantability, nor are any such representations implied with respect
to the material set forth herein, and the publisher takes no responsibility with respect to such
material. The publisher shall not be liable for any special, consequential, or exemplary damages
resulting, in whole or part, from the readers' use of, or reliance upon, this material.

Printed in the United States of America
Print Number: 01   Print Year: 2016

Unless otherwise noted, all items © Cengage Learning.

Contents BRIEF

Contents

Preface

Among the good things in life, a good job doing work you enjoy and building a fulfilling career is one of the best. The single purpose of this book is to help you achieve this goal. You'll find practical, useful, and realistic advice to help you get interviews and job offers and become a valued employee.

Your Career is a journey, and each journey begins with one step out of the front door and into the world. You've likely taken many steps out of that figurative door. Now it's time to map out your journey of many steps so that you can reach a destination of your choice. This textbook can help you choose your next destination—where you can contribute your talents while continuing to strengthen your skills for the next part of your journey. Think of the *Job Search Journey* as one leg of the longer *Career Journey*. You may go on multiple Job Search Journeys throughout your Career Journey.

A successful career no longer needs to be with a single company. However, a successful career is more than a string of jobs. A successful career is one in which each successive job builds strengths and skills to give you greater opportunities to contribute to the world, your community, the company you work for, your family, and yourself.

You are responsible to lead and direct your Career Journey, but many others will provide essential support. Although you will use the Internet to help you find jobs, your most powerful tools are the people you know, the people who know you and your career goals, and the people who are in your Career Network. Start now to build the network of people who will be beside you on your Job Search Journey, the next leg of your Career Journey.

ORGANIZATION OF THE TEXT

As with any journey, it happens one step at a time, and it goes more smoothly if some planning is done before the journey begins. This textbook lays out the Job Search Journey in five phases, with two or three steps for each phase. As you review the table of contents, you will see that each phase is a part, and each step correlates to a chapter in the textbook. The map on page xvi shows the steps and the ultimate destination: the beginning to a successful career.

All along the way, this text provides help during each phase and at each step, in the form of side bars. Each phase starts with advice from two real people. One of these is a career expert and the other is a person who recently went through his or her own Job Search Journey. In addition, each chapter contains:

- motivational statements,
- encouragement to form good work habits,

- a cautionary note,
- typical scenarios that people face,
- advice about your job search online, and
- activities and templates to help ensure a successful journey.

PHASE 1: Prepare for the Journey. This phase is all about getting ready for the journey ahead—both physically and mentally. It's like mapping out a trip. **Chapter 1,** *The Job Search Journey*, introduces the concept of a Job Search Journey as a way to more easily achieve a successful career. It encourages physically preparing systems to file and store the materials needed for this journey, such as educational and work records, samples for a portfolio, information about job openings, and contact information for people who are part of an individual's Career Network. **Chapter 2,** *Know Yourself to Market Yourself*, is about how to market an individual's skills and talents. It leads you, the readers, through a self-analysis of what you have to offer an employer and how to describe it in a way that makes you a desirable employee for the right jobs. **Chapter 3,** *Picture Yourself in the Workplace*, explores different work environments to guide you to look for destination jobs that are more suited to your personality and lifestyle, and explores how to tap into in-demand industries and occupations for a broader array of job openings.

PHASE 2: Create Your Resume. This phase is like packing a suitcase with the essentials for the trip. It focuses on the resume as a primary tool for introductions to prospective employers. When the resume is successfully honed, it is the foundation for job applications, interviews, and communicating the readers' personal brand and character. **Chapter 4,** *Plan Your Resume*, starts by describing how the resume can be used effectively with Warm Introductions—that is, with your Career Network contacts—or with Cold Leads. It goes on to describe what goes into a resume and helps you gather the necessary information. **Chapter 5,** *Write Your Resume*, gives very practical and up-to-date advice on how to write a resume, including what types of words to select (action verbs, keywords, etc.), editing tips, and formatting advice. Together, these chapters help you craft a powerful resume that shares your unique personality and gets employers' attention.

PHASE 3: Apply for Jobs. This phase moves outside the classroom and outside of your head and into the world of work. It's the equivalent of putting money down for travel tickets and packages. **Chapter 6,** *Find Job Openings*, describes how to build a Career Network and use it and other sources to find job openings that are a good career fit. **Chapter 7,** *Write Job Applications*, gives detailed advice and tips for filling out applications, both online and on paper, so that the application is accepted into employers' recruiting systems. **Chapter 8,** *Write Effective Tailored Cover Letters*, describes how to take an extra step, especially for the most desirable jobs, to get your resume noticed. The goal of this phase is to apply for jobs in a way that will lead to interviews.

PHASE 4: Shine at Interviews. With the ultimate destination farther ahead, it's time to explore some places of interest along the way. This phase focuses on the all-important interviews, and stresses the importance of practice and preparation. **Chapter 9,** *Know the Interview Essentials*, gives insight into the employer and recruiter expectations around interviewees' attitude, dress, body language, conversation, and etiquette. With the ground rules established, this chapter goes on to describe actions that attract interviews and methods for keeping the Job Search Journey energized in between these exciting and stressful interviews. **Chapter 10,** *Prepare for Your Interview*, describes the many types of interviews and interview questions, with up-to-date tips on how to succeed all along the way. **Chapter 11,** *Interview Like a Pro*, focuses on the next level of preparation—building confidence through practice, doing homework before each interview, getting physically prepared to climb the summit, and closing the interview on a high note.

PHASE 5: Connect, Accept, and Succeed. Now the destination is in sight. This is not the time to lose energy; rather, it is a time to stay connected and energized until the end goal is reached. Then it's time to enjoy the destination … until it is time for the next journey on a fulfilling lifetime career. **Chapter 12,** *Stay Connected with Prospective Employers*, describes how to follow up after interviews to help snag a job offer. Then it describes how to evaluate job offers and respond professionally—either yes or no thank you—to each offer. **Chapter 13,** *It's an Iterative Process*, helps deal with the realities of rejection and long waits between interviews and offers. **Chapter 14,** *Take Charge of Your Career*, provides up-to-date advice on what to do during the first hours, days, weeks, and months at this new career destination. It wraps up with advice on how to stay for the long term or identify signs that it is time to choose a new destination to further enhance the Career Journey.

APPENDIX A: Succeeding in the Job Search Journey Using Social Media. This section provides a chance to get up to speed on the ever-changing, fast-growing practices surrounding the use of online media for job searches. The American website Glassdoor.com was launched in 2008 to give job seekers a look inside of companies, including compensation and culture. Consider that LinkedIn®, a high-powered job-search and networking site, was launched May 2003. It currently has over 300 million members in over 200 countries. Yet its competitors—Viadeo (50 million members) and XING (10 million members)—might catch up in the next five years. Consider that Monster.com was created in 1999 and, with its Online Career Center (OCC), was the most popular career website on the Internet until 2010, when Indeed.com surpassed Monster.com to become the largest job site in the United States. This appendix, along with the *You, Online* features in every chapter, presents the latest online best practices for each phase of the Job Search Journey.

APPENDIX B: My Career – Making it Happen. These pages pull together the most critical tools and reminders for each phase of the job search journey. Encourage students to tear out these pages and keep them on hand as a quick reference guide whenever they embark on a job search journey during their careers.

NEW TO THIS EDITION

This ninth edition has been significantly updated to reflect the changes in the marketplace, the increasing use of web-based tools in the recruiting process, and the recognition that many jobs are filled without ever getting posted publicly.

In addition, the entire book has been restructured and reorganized for a more logical flow. The five sections of the book correlate to the five parts of the Job Search Journey. Chapters contain fewer, more focused learning outcomes. Each chapter and associated activities build on previous chapters, making the Job Search Journey simpler and easier to digest. Career Action Worksheets are focused on practicing and demonstrating successful mastery of these outcomes.

This edition takes a more upbeat attitude to appeal to Millennials and experienced people who are switching to new careers, while keeping the practical, real-world advice and step-by-step approach that helps students land jobs that are a good career fit.

MindTap for *Your Career* is available with the ninth edition. MindTap is a personalized teaching experience with relevant assignments that guide students to analyze, apply, and elevate thinking, allowing instructors to measure skills and promote better outcomes with ease. A fully online learning solution, MindTap combines all student learning tools—readings, multimedia, activities, and assessments—into a single Learning Path that guides the student through the curriculum. Instructors personalize the experience by customizing the presentation of these learning tools to their students, even seamlessly introducing their own content into the Learning Path. MindTap for *Your Career* also integrates with Pathbrite, guiding students through building their electronic portfolios, which they can access during and after the course.

Beyond the general update and change in tone, overall, there are five highly notable changes, described next. There is a change from a job search cycle to a Job Search Journey, a reorganization of the resume content and the amount of focus on this critical document, the expectation that the Internet is the common approach to job searches rather than a new technique, a view of network building as an excellent approach to find and get jobs, and a new set of advice for making a good start on the new job.

Structural Reorganization

The Job Search Journey

Whereas the eighth edition spoke of a job search cycle, this edition lays out a more personal Job Search Journey in five phases. It does not assume that this is the person's first or only Job Search Journey. The five phases of the Job Search Journey correlate to the five parts of the textbook, and provide a more logical flow: Phase 1, *Prepare for the Journey*; Phase 2, *Create Your Resume*; Phase 3, *Apply for Jobs*; Phase 4, *Shine at Interviews*; and Phase 5, *Connect, Accept, and Succeed*. The first two phases tend toward introspection, organization, and preparation. Phases 3, 4, and 5 move students into the job market, where they search for and apply for jobs, get interviews, evaluate job offers, and—ultimately—start a job that is a good career fit. The steps within each phase correlate to the chapters in each part.

Resume Chapters Reorganized

Formerly in Part 3 of the eighth edition, resume writing content has been moved to Part 2 for a more logical flow, since students must write a resume before they network and look for job leads. Because the resume is a critical document that showcases the job seeker, resume preparation (formerly Chapter 6) has been separated into two chapters about planning and writing a resume. Chapter 4, "Plan Your Resume," focuses on preparing to write and includes two learning outcomes from Chapter 6 in the eighth edition: What Is a Resume? and Plan Your Resume Content, and a new learning outcome: Showcase Your Personal Brand. Chapter 5, "Write Your Resume," now focuses on writing the resume and includes as a new learning outcome, Edit Your Resume, as well as two learning outcomes from Chapter 6 in the eighth edition: Write Your Resume and Format Your Resume. Since most resumes are now combination style (as opposed to strictly chronological or skills-based), the formatting discussion has shifted to the creation of print, web, and plain text resumes. Example resumes now reflect customizing resumes for different job targets instead of highlighting different resume formats.

New and Expanded Concepts

Jobs on the Internet

Every chapter includes a feature, *You, Online*, that addresses use of the Internet and/or social media as part of the job search. In addition, the completely rewritten appendix on social media talks about using the Internet for each of the five phases of the Job Search Journey. Further, the text itself integrates Internet and social media use as part of the natural flow of work during the Job Search Journey, from when to use or not use email to using apps to help with organization and getting to the interview on time.

Your Career Network

While the eighth edition focused on the role of others as primarily a support network, the concept of a Career Network has grown in our society and is embodied in apps such as Facebook, LinkedIn®, and Twitter. This text speaks more to how to build a useful network and use it before, during, and after this Job Search Journey. Throughout each phase the focus is placed on how to build and share personal brand, experience, and career goals with a network of targeted individuals that can provide job leads.

Part 1, Prepare for the Journey

In Part 1, this edition focuses more on the job seeker than on what employers want. By gaining a deeper understanding of what the job seeker has to offer and what his or her personal tendencies are, students will be more likely to conduct a targeted job search where they pursue jobs that they can communicate as a better career fit to employers and therefore increase their likelihood of receiving a job offer. This first part grounds the job seeker by encouraging a clearer self-understanding and enables the job seeker to communicate his or her talents, skills, and qualifications in words that will appeal to the right hiring managers and recruiters.

Chapter 1, "The Job Search Journey," provides an overview of the five phases of the Job Search Journey on which this text is organized. It lays out a new, simplified structure for organizing all those files that are part of a job search and part of this class. All files are in one place that we call the Career Builder Files with three distinct sections: About Me, About Jobs, and Master Career Portfolio. The first two sections (About Me and About Jobs) are draft portfolio sections and allow for clear organization of the many Career Action Worksheets. The Master Career Portfolio section will contain the employer-ready documents such as the master resume, LinkedIn® recommendations, cover letters, and more. Online, these same three sections can be individual portfolios within each student's account.

In the eighth edition, Chapter 2 focused on employer expectations. These expectations are brought to light throughout the ninth edition by prodding the reader to consider many elements from the employer's perspective, thereby building a partnership between employer and employee to achieve common goals. **Chapter 2** in the ninth edition, **"Know Yourself to Market Yourself,"** focuses on clarifying what the job seeker wants, and has to offer, through a series of self-assessments. The eighth edition described a 30-Second Commercial. However, products that sell well have one brand image but many commercials. So the ninth edition moves this concept to a higher level by focusing first on a Personal Brand Statement and then on the creation of a variety of 30-Second Commercials that embody the Personal Brand Statement but speak to different target audiences. This is not only a beneficial and practical approach; it can be thought-provoking and fun.

Given that new types of jobs are coming into being each year, one can no longer target a career job without risking becoming outdated.

Chapter 3, "Picture Yourself in the Workplace," moves beyond the "career targets" discussed in the eighth edition to finding jobs that are a good career fit. This chapter encourages readers to recognize core preferences and interests upon which they can continue to focus as their career develops over time.

Part 2, Create Your Resume

The content of Part 2 in the eighth edition was about networking and finding jobs. In the ninth edition, content has been shifted to Part 3, Chapter 6, "Find Job Openings." In the ninth edition, Part 2 continues the inward look of what the reader has to offer the employer. This is captured in the resume. Chapter 6 from the eighth edition has been split, into the ninth edition, into **Chapter 4, "Plan Your Resume,"** and **Chapter 5, "Write Your Resume."** By focusing an entire chapter on planning the resume, students have a chance to deeply understand the experiences, qualifications, and skills they would like to highlight for prospective employers. Then, by focusing an entire chapter on writing a resume, students and teachers can spend more time on critical grammar skills and the shift to a business writing style.

An entire new section focuses on writing tips. Sample resumes have been updated to reflect current trends and practices, both online and off. The focus is less on format and more on content, telling a story, and keywords, which play a big role in today's software that is used by employers to sift out or highlight potential candidates.

Part 3, Apply for Jobs

While the eighth edition focused on essential job search communications like resumes, job applications, and cover letters, the ninth edition focuses on how to find jobs using a combination strategy that taps into the readers' Career Network and online searches. This is followed by applying for jobs in a customized manner based on a master resume and following up with a customized Job Application Package for those jobs that are an especially good career fit.

Chapter 6, "Find Job Openings," (based on Chapters 4 and 5 in the eighth edition) puts a much greater emphasis on building and using a Career Network (versus the eighth edition's Personal Support System Network) to locate jobs, even before the job opening is publicly announced. New Career Action Worksheets provide guidance for networking. Networking approaches have been updated to reflect today's heavy use of online networking, while continuing to emphasize face-to-face networking.

Chapter 7, "Write Job Applications," focuses on the different sections of a job application and makes the distinction between online and hardcopy job applications. (The eighth edition's Chapter 7, "Job Applications and Cover Letters," has been split into Chapters 7 and 8 for the ninth edition.)

Chapter 8 "Write Effective Tailored Cover Letters," gives more focus to customizing cover letters for those jobs that are great career fits, with the intent of getting noticed among the stacks and lists of resumes. An entire new section addresses writing tips. Another new section provides instructions on addressing a snail mail letter, a skill new to many younger people in this day and age of email.

Part 4, Shine at Interviews

This part continues to focus on interviews. However, the eighth edition centered on how to ask for and get interviews. The ninth edition deemphasizes this topic because so much of this work is done in earlier phases during networking and through applications and cover letters. Instead, the emphasis is placed on practicing for interviews and being prepared physically, mentally, and emotionally. In general, these chapters contain updated advice and tips. **Chapter 9, "Know the Interview Essentials,"** contains content from Chapters 8 and 9 in the eighth edition. **Chapter 10, "Prepare for Your Interview,"** and **Chapter 11, "Interview Like a Pro,"** are based on Chapters 10 and 11 from the eighth edition. The information from the eighth edition about what to do after the interview has been moved to Part 5 in the ninth edition for greater consistency with the Job Search Journey phases.

Part 5, Connect, Accept, and Succeed

Rather than the eighth edition's "Next Steps," the ninth edition emphases three distinct steps: "Connect, Accept, and Succeed." **Chapter 12, "Stay Connected with Prospective Employers,"** describes how to stay connected with employers after the job interview. Next, it addresses how to evaluate job offers to consider the whole compensation package, beyond the wage or salary figure that is offered, to ensure the job seeker fully understands what is being offered. **Chapter 13, "Dealing with Disappointment,"** continues to provide advice on how to deal with rejection notices, but with a more upbeat tone and with encouragement to take positive actions following each rejection. **Chapter 14, "Take Charge of Your Career,"** has been rewritten with all new guidelines for how to successfully onboard to a new job based on the authors' extensive experience with onboarding programs in industry. It also provides practical information on building successful relationships at work, managing one's career, and identifying signs that it might be time to change careers and restart the Job Search Journey.

Appendices

Appendix A. This completely rewritten appendix addresses how and when to use social media throughout each of the five phases of the Job Search Journey. It includes the latest in successful online job search practices, based on leading recruiting resources and suggested approaches by employers.

Appendix B. This all-new appendix pulls together the most critical tools and reminders for each phase of the job search journey, in a convenient packet that can be torn from the book as a quick reference guide.

FOR THE READER: HOW TO USE THIS TEXT

Your Career: How to Make It Happen is more than a text. It is a simulation or practice session for the real event: finding a job that meets your needs.

If you have nearly completed your degree program and graduation is around the corner, use the activities in this text to get you ready for the upcoming Job Search Journey. This text will walk you through every step of the way. Use the early chapters of self-assessment to better understand what elements in your field of study give you the most pleasure and to what kinds of jobs within your field you will most enjoy applying your skills. Use the middle chapters to get peer feedback to help you hone your resume and Personal Brand Statement.

If, on the other hand, you are a few years from graduation, use this text and course as a way to explore your field more broadly. Figure out what you need to add to your life experiences and your portfolio in the next few years to help you land a job that is a good career fit after graduation. Begin now to build your Career Network. You are lucky to be getting a head start on this. Consider practicing to use the Job Search Journey process by applying it as you search for a summer job or internship, or even a volunteer role that will add to your resume.

PHASE 1: Prepare for the Journey
- *The Job Search Journey*
- *Know Yourself to Market Yourself*
- *Picture Yourself in the Workplace*

PHASE 2: Create Your Resume
- *Plan Your Resume*
- *Write Your Resume*

PHASE 3: Apply for Jobs
- *Find Job Openings*
- *Write Job Applications*
- *Write Effective Tailored Cover Letters*

PHASE 4: Shine at Interviews
- *Know the Interview Essentials*
- *Prepare for Your Interview*
- *Interview Like a Pro*

PHASE 5: Connect, Accept, and Succeed
- *Stay Connected with Prospective Employers*
- *It's an Iterative Process*
- *Take Charge of Your Career*

To get the most out of this text, we suggest that you post the Job Search Journey map seen on the preceding page and described in detail in Chapter 1 where you can see it regularly. Then follow these steps for each chapter to maximize your benefits from the text and class:

1. As you start each of the five parts, use the steps in *PLAN for Success* to set you up for success.

2. With each chapter, review the outcomes before you start. When you complete a chapter, confirm that you can accomplish these outcomes by answering the questions in the end of chapter section called *Chapter Checklist*. Each question has a number beside it that tells which outcome section contains the related information, should you want to review the material.

3. Complete the Career Action Worksheets. These give you a chance to practice and get feedback so that you become a pro. Some worksheets will require you to interact with people you do not know. Expect to feel a degree of discomfort. Be brave and get out there to meet new people and expand your Career Network.

4. Take personal notes as you read the features such as *Caution* and *You, Online*. These tips are gifts to you from the authors. Read the Real World Scenarios and strive to answer the questions at the end of each one.

5. Actively incorporate online activities into your Job Search Journey using *You, Online* and the Appendix A. As you complete each chapter, refer to this appendix for related online activities. Search online and find your own resources to supplement concepts in the book.

6. Because the journey is often long, stay inspired. Find your favorite quotes throughout the book. Reread your favorite stories about real-life people and their personal advice to you at the start of each section of the book. Then check your Job Search Journey map to see how far you have come and to remind yourself of the final destination.

7. Tear out the guide provided in Appendix B, *My Career: Making it Happen*, and proactively use it as a quick reference tool throughout your Job Search Journey.

In addition, make sure to create your **Career Builder Files** to stay organized. The detailed instructions for creating your Career Builder Files will help you organize your many career-related documents and notes in an extremely useful system. You will develop this system through a paper system via a binder or portfolio, or alternatively through an online portfolio tool. Through practical, hands-on application, the personal content of the Career Builder Files will motivate you to take on the challenge of the Job Search Journey now and for your entire career.

From your authors, "We wish you lifelong success in your Job Search Journey."

KEY FEATURES

Part Opener Content

Plan for Success

Each Part begins with a *Plan for Success* feature to help students plan specific completion dates for the steps they will accomplish in that part, with a reminder to take into account the other things going on in their busy lives.

PART 1

Prepare for the Journey

PART 1 Your job search is like a journey, and each journey begins with one step out the front door and into the world. Successful job searches tend to have five phases. The first phase, "Prepare for the Journey," begins with organizing for what's ahead, assessing yourself to market yourself more effectively, and visualizing yourself as a successful employee in the workplace.

CHAPTER 1	The Job Search Journey
CHAPTER 2	Know Yourself to Market Yourself
CHAPTER 3	Picture Yourself in the Workplace

PLAN for Success

Most successful people keep a calendar of activities and a running list of tasks they have committed to do. Make *Your Career* a part of your calendar and task list.

- Read the outcomes on the first page of Chapters 1 through 3 and jot down a target date for completing each one. Allow extra time for those that require more than just reading.
- Now make several calendar appointments with yourself to do the readings, homework, and projects for this class.
- Consider your other commitments (other classes, work, home) as you plan to make *Your Career* happen for you!

ADVICE FROM THE EXPERT

With over 20 years of experience in coaching and developing others, Allen Zink has invaluable advice for those starting and growing on their career journey. "The most important aspect of finding a best fit career is to really, truly know yourself. Being honest with yourself regarding who you are, what drives you, and what your purpose is, are critical elements to truly being happy in a career." To understand your strengths and determine your career goals, Allen suggests, "take a little reflection time" and "think about a time when you were operating at your best and consider where you were, who you were working with, what you were doing, and how you were feeling." During that reflection time, define your strengths and goals based on discovering "the sweet spot of things you not only do well, but are passionate about."

Then connect these strengths with a company's need or role. Find a best fit company by considering if "the company's culture, values, and business proposition" align with your values. Also consider "growth opportunities and ways to further develop your skills and capabilities."

When it is time to find the job, Allen says that "networking plays a huge role in the job search!" It's important to have identified your personal brand, the words or statement that describes "how others perceive you or would describe you." Allen suggests asking yourself, "What do I want to be known for? If I could only use one word to describe me, what would that word be?" When you know what you want and who you are, you can "maximize your network" by "giving your contacts something to work with and ultimately to be able to act on." Even though "your contacts typically really want to help you," without clarity, you may not be using your network well. "Always remain positive when interacting with your contacts. Circle back to your contacts periodically and share your progress, as they may continue to have suggestions for you."

Keep positive during the job search by "planning networking meetings with people you are very comfortable with each week to help balance out the more difficult and energy draining meetings with others." It's also important to "celebrate the wins and debrief the losses from an objective point of view." Lastly, stay energized during your job search by "mixing in some activities that you enjoy and finding other people who are currently looking for a new role. It will be comforting to know that your feelings and emotions are normal!"

ALLEN ZINK
Vice President
Senior Development
Consultant, Fifth Third
Bank

Photo courtesy of Liebstadt Portrait Studios.

TALES FROM THE JOB SEARCH

When he was 32, Gabriel Velasco began thinking about changing careers. He had a creative job that he enjoyed at a small television company, shooting and editing news stories and making commercials. Because of his field, videography, Gabriel knew that his career would stall unless he asked his family to move to Los Angeles or New York City, which he didn't want to do.

When Gabriel thought about work he had enjoyed in the past, first in his mind was "helping work" he had done with Habitat for Humanity and the Boulder Sister City Project. He chose nursing because of the challenges and the many career paths for nurses. Four years later, after being a part-time student for one year and a full-time student for two more years, Gabriel is a registered nurse working in a hospital, his first choice of career paths.

Gabriel's advice to anyone entering the job market or choosing a new career is to "prioritize what's important to you, whether it's making a lot of money, making work your focus, or spending time with family and enjoying outside pursuits. You have to consider those things seriously so you can find as much satisfaction and happiness as possible in and out of work."

If you think you may be out of work for a while, Gabriel recommends that you "put your ego in check and be willing to be flexible. Think about taking a job that isn't your first choice, without letting go of your dreams. Network. Be social—you never know where an opportunity is going to arise."

Gabriel has this advice for succeeding at every job: "Do your best at a job no matter what it is. Keep things in perspective as much as possible and don't let trivial matters become weightier than they really are. Each day find some enjoyment in what you do."

**GABRIEL O'NEILL
VELASCO, B.S.N**
Poudre Valley Hospital

Photo courtesy of Gabriel Velasco.

Advice from the Expert

Five real-life profiles that include an HR manager and career coach discuss career management and real-world issues when moving forward on the Job Search Journey.

Tales from the Job Search

Five additional profiles represent job seekers, including a new hire, a mid-career job seeker, and a recently graduated job seeker. They discuss job search issues and solutions to common challenges that students can immediately relate to.

Chapter Opener Content

Learning Outcomes

At the beginning of each chapter, a list of learning outcomes provides a set of concise learning goals. Each learning outcome is addressed in a main chapter heading. Outcomes are also tied to the end-of-chapter worksheets, questions, and activities.

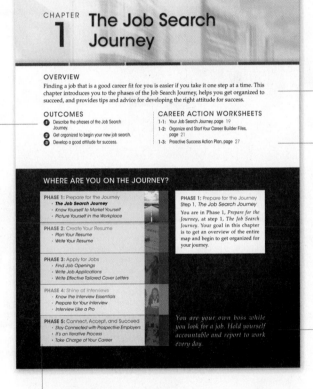

Chapter Overview

List of Career Action Worksheets

A list of the chapter's Career Action Worksheet titles provides a preview, serving both as pre-exposure to the topics and as an aid to help students plan the time they need for this course. Career Action Worksheets are linked to learning outcomes and are introduced within the chapter under the relevant headings.

Motivational Statements

Brief motivational statements at the beginning of each chapter encourage readers to get started on the chapter. Additional motivational statements throughout the chapter encourage students to continue through the end of the chapter.

The Job Search Journey

Upbeat language and achievable, concrete small steps help keep students in a positive frame of mind in the class and on the Job Search Journey. A colorful graphic repeated at the beginning of each chapter helps students recall the steps and track their progress as they work through the course.

Chapter Interior Features

FEATURE BOXES

MAKE IT A HABIT
Start with a Positive Attitude

Your Job Search Journey will be an exciting and challenging time. You will be managing new tasks on top of an already busy schedule, while at the same time feeling the thrill of taking power into your own hands for your future. Every day, make it a habit to reaffirm feelings of excitement and confidence as you move forward on this journey. Post your favorite affirmations in places where you will see them often. Here are a few affirmations to get you started:

- I have the power to succeed.
- I will create happiness and success.
- I can make my own choices and decisions.
- I can choose to make changes in every area of my life.
- I am satisfied that I have done my best.
- I have a plan for the future, and my plan is open to change.
- I will not give up on myself.
- I have the power to succeed. (End your pep talk by repeating the first sentence—it says it all.)

Don't be shy about starting your day with a pep talk. Add your own sentences and repeat them to yourself throughout the day. Forming this habit will help you during challenging times throughout life.

© Infog./Shutterstock.com.

Make It a Habit

This feature spotlights winning behaviors and strategies for growing professionally.

Caution

(This feature (formerly titled Watch Out!). titled *Watch Out!*) alerts students about behaviors to avoid or how to plan in advance for good results.

CAUTION
Take Charge of Your Career Right Now

Many factors in your job search are not under your control, but one thing certainly is—the effort you make to stand out from the crowd every step of the way. To get an edge over other job seekers, (1) set personal goals for this class and for your job search, (2) believe in your drive and commitment to achieve your goals, and (3) use this class and textbook to succeed.

Your Career: How to Make It Happen is filled with practical, realistic advice and actions. When you read each chapter, think about how you can apply the information and advice to your goals and situation. Complete the Career Action Worksheets and be sure to set up and maintain your Career Builder Files. Use the websites that support the textbook.

Set a goal today to use all the resources available to you and to take charge of your career!

© Netfalls - Remy Musser/Shutterstock.com.

You, Online
Positive Support Using Social Networking

Social networking, both online and offline, will be a vital tool in your successful job search. Every chapter of *Your Career: How to Make It Happen* highlights ways to use social networking, specifically social media tools, to enhance your job search. If you were an employer, whose would you look at first: the resume of the job seeker your friend or business acquaintance told you about, or one from the long list of applicants who applied through a job board?

As you start your job search, set a goal to use your social networks to maintain a good attitude for success, to motivate yourself, and to find job leads:

- Post your defined, clear objective for your career goals on your online social media profiles. Make your goals SMART: specific, measurable, achievable, realistic, and time-sensitive.
- Post questions to start conversations with your networks and get Warm Introductions to job opportunities; for example, "Does anyone know someone in this field I could talk to?" and "What qualities do you think make me unique?"
- Stay away from discussing how difficult your job search is in any forum (except in trusted, close relationships). Project an upbeat attitude.

Your social network gives you back what you put into it. It can reinforce your positive outlook—or it can drown you in negativity with well-intended empathy. Use your networks to motivate you and reinforce your own positive thinking.

You, Online

Every chapter includes instruction and tips for using the Internet and social media in the Job Search Journey. *You, Online* (formerly untitled and not in all chapters) connects the textbook to the Internet, both for resources and for the job search itself. Activities guide students to create a LinkedIn® profile, clean up their online social media so they present a professional face to prospective employers, and assess the top-rated online tools for job searches.

Real-World Scenarios

New to this edition: Each chapter now includes one or two real-world scenarios that give insights into how chapter concepts work in real-world situations and pose thoughtful questions that can be great for kicking off class or group discussions in order to personalize the learning.

End-of-Chapter Content

Chapter Checklists

These checklists of questions help students confirm that they have achieved the major goals from each chapter's action steps. These checklists are keyed to the chapter outcomes. Students are encouraged to review a section if they struggle to answer a Chapter Checklist question.

Trial Run

Interactive and role-play activities are provided in *Trial Run* at the end of each chapter. These provide opportunities to practice desired outcomes of the chapter. Each activity requires peer or self-evaluation.

16 | PART 1 Prepare for the Journey

Chapter Checklist

Check off each item you can do. Reread sections in this chapter to help you complete the checklist.

- ☐ Name and explain the phase that best describes where I am today in my Job Search Journey. Name and describe the next job search phase. **1**
- ☐ Plan and organize my job search by collecting and organizing my records and choosing a method to keep track of communications. **2**
- ☐ Describe my plan for further developing and maintaining a good attitude during my Job Search Journey. **3**
- ☐ Put my long-term and short-term goals in writing, with concrete steps to achieve each goal. **3**
- ☐ Describe a few tips to help me manage my time even better during my Job Search Journey. **3**
- ☐ Practice proactive skills that demonstrate a positive attitude and a focus on solving problems. **3**

Critical Thinking Questions

1. What is the value of knowing about the phases and steps for a job search? **1**
2. Why is it important to organize your records for your job search? **2**
3. How will your Career Builder Files help you succeed in your Job Search Journey? What tools will you use? How will you get started? **2**
4. What effects do positive and negative thoughts, images and self-talk have on performance? **3**
5. How would you rate your ability to set goals, manage your time, and be proactive? Would you rate your skills as excellent, good, or needing improvement? What specific actions can you take to stay strong or improve these skills? **3**

Additional Resources

For data files, career resources, and more, visit www.cengagebrain.com.

CHAPTER 1 The Job Search Journey | 17

Trial Run

Get Off to a Good Start

The beginning of your job search is a good time to evaluate some of the skills and attitudes that will help you have a successful journey. Read these statements and rate yourself using the following scale:

Rating Scale: 1 to 4 (1 = not really; 2 = sometimes/somewhat; 3 = usually; 4 = definitely)

_____ A. I tend to be a positive person.
_____ B. I like spending time with positive people.
_____ C. I spend time thinking about my goals.
_____ D. I have a written list of goals with the dates I want to achieve them.
_____ E. When I have something complicated or important to do, I break the task into smaller steps.
_____ F. If something goes wrong, I try to figure out what I could have done differently.
_____ G. If I don't understand something, I'm willing to ask for advice.
_____ H. I tend to keep my files well organized at home and school.
_____ I. I use time management strategies to help me get things done and do them on time.
_____ J. I feel positive about the future.

For your high-scoring statements, consider offering your help to others in these areas.

My high-scoring statements (list from 1 to 3 statements):

Which low-scoring statements do you think will have the most negative effect on you during your Job Search Journey (list from 1 to 3 statements)?

Write a goal for improving in those areas. Find someone—friend, mentor, family member, classmate, instructor—who might be able to help you improve.

My improvement goal:

Who might help me with the low-scoring statements?

Critical Thinking Questions

Critical Thinking Questions encourage students to reflect on each chapter's learning outcomes, and how the students will use those outcomes in the Job Search Journey.

Career Action Worksheets

More than 50 Career Action Worksheets help students apply chapter content and advice to their own unique situations. Extremely flexible, the worksheets can be used individually or in groups, in class or as homework.

Students create personal documents that can be used as they search for jobs, now and in the future. Guided assessments prompt students to consider a good career fit beyond matching skills and qualifications, to include their preferences, personal traits, lifestyle, personal goals, and preferred work style. All this is clearly aimed at helping students find jobs that are a good fit for them and their desired career path.

Self-assessment tools built into the worksheets enable readers to easily evaluate their progress on their Job Search Journey. Students are instructed within the chapter when they should complete each worksheet; the worksheets themselves are located at the end of each chapter.

Career Action Worksheet Callout Boxes

Boxes are placed strategically within the text to suggest at what point the reader can jump to an activity. This encourages student to do a few activities at a time rather than be overloaded with activities at the end.

▶ **CAREER ACTION WORKSHEET**
1-3 Proactive Success Action Plan ❸

Take this time to set goals that inspire and excite you for your Job Search Journey.
My job search goal:

Why is this goal important to me? What will happen if I don't achieve this goal?

Steps I will take to achieve this goal:

Action Steps	Date
1. Schedule time to assemble my Career Builder Files	
2.	
3.	
4.	
5.	

Add your completed work to the "About Me" section of your Career Builder Files.

▶ **CAREER ACTION**
Complete Worksheet 1-1
Your Job Search Journey page 19

SUPPLEMENTAL MATERIALS

For Instructors

Instructor Companion Site

Everything you need for your course in one place! This collection of book-specific lecture and class tools is available online via www.cengage.com/login. Access and download Microsoft® PowerPoint lecture slides, the Instructor Guide, course management forms, and more.

Instructor Guide. Expansive yet focused, the powerful Instructor Guide helps busy instructors create a cohesive learning experience for students.

MindTap

MindTap Career Development for *Your Career: How to Make It Happen*, ninth edition is a personalized teaching experience with relevant assignments that guide students to analyze, apply, and improve thinking, allowing you to measure skills and outcomes with ease.

- Portfolio builder activities your students to build and organize electronic career portfolios, using the online portfolio tool of your choice, that they can access during and after the course.
- Relevant readings, multimedia, and activities are designed to take students up the levels of learning, from basic knowledge to analysis and application. Video animations provide an engaging introduction to chapter topics.
- Personalized teaching becomes yours through a customizable Learning Path built with key student objectives and your syllabus in mind.

For Students

Student Companion Site

Visit www.cengagebrain.com and search for this book to access useful web links and an explanation of common workplace terms.

MindTap

MindTap Career Development for *Your Career: How to Make It Happen*, ninth edition engages and empowers you to produce your best work—consistently. By seamlessly integrating course material with videos, activities, apps, and much more, MindTap creates a unique learning path that fosters increased comprehension and efficiency.

- Portfolio Builder activities guide you to build and organize electronic career portfolios, using an online portfolio tool suggested by your instructor, that you can access during and after the course.
- MindTap delivers real-world relevance with activities and assignments that help you build critical-thinking and analytic skills that will transfer to other courses and your professional life. Video animations provide an engaging introduction to chapter topics.
- MindTap helps you stay organized and efficient with a single destination that reflects what's important to your instructor, along with the tools you need to master the content.

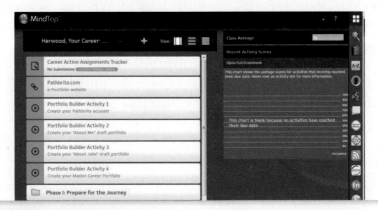

Acknowledgments

The authors are grateful to the people who shared their real-life stories for the profiles. Thank you to Aaron Wang, Allen Zink, D. Lynn Meyers, DedraPerlmutter, Gabriel O'Neill Velasco, Gina Arens, Leslie Kirkland, Lisa Mark, Molly Cramer, and Rene DeAnda.

The authors would like to thank the following people for providing additional insights into our target audience: Ben Palaggo, (Jacob) Eli Thomas, and Anastasia Bandemir.

The authors would also like to thank the people at Cengage Learning, especially our content developer, Anne Orgren, for her guidance, project management, and organization, but even more for her collaboration, responsiveness, and flexibility. Thanks too to Katie McGuire, our product manager, for her leadership, ability to collaborate while making the tough decisions, and handling of the big picture for the ultimate success of the writing team. Thanks to Jack Pendleton for his creative design that reflects his ability to listen to the authors' intent and vision so that it becomes a reality. And a final thank you to our project managers Betty Dickson and Hemalatha Velayutham, who got all the details right for our readers.

REVIEWERS

The authors and Cengage Learning would like to thank the reviewers whose thoughtful comments and analysis helped to guide the development of the ninth edition:

Melba Bolling, Virginia Highlands Community College; Carolyn Carvalho, Kent State University at Ashtabula; Irene Church, Muskegon Community College; Brenda DeLee, Catawba Valley Community College; Rena Doering, San Antonio College; Beth Farnsworth, Bradford School of Pittsburgh; Roger Fulk, Wright State University; Kristin Holmberg-Wright, University of Wisconsin–Parkside; Sandra Johnson, Fortis College; Suzanne Johnson, Copiah–Lincoln Community College; Junnae Landry, Pratt Community College; Theresa Laws-Dahl, Blackhawk Technical College; Lisa Leopold, Middlebury Institute of International Studies; Kris MacDonald, Fortis Institute; Lois McWhorter, Somerset Community College; Nanette Mosser, MedQuest, College; Patricia Riely, Moberly Area Community College; Barbara Sherry, Northeastern Illinois University; Rosalyn Skinner, Dawn Career Institute; Judi Walsh, DeForest Area School District; Kimberlee Weber, East Central College; Casey Wilhelm, North Idaho College; and Peter Young, San Jose State University.

About the Authors

Lauri Harwood

Lauri Harwood is an instructor at the Farmer School of Business at Miami University in Cincinnati. She has been a consulting editor and textbook author for Cengage Learning since 1993. She was a professional writer, instructional designer, and project manager as the former owner of Vandalay Group Inc. and, prior to that, for The Oxford Associates. Lauri has a bachelor of arts degree in English literature from the University of Cincinnati, and a master's degree from Miami University in technical and scientific communication.

Lisa M.D. Owens

Ms. Owens is a learning expert who approaches learning programs in a systemic fashion, applying current best practices emerging from recent neuroscience findings. Following a decade in the engineering field designing chemical plants, recruiting young women engineers, and doing consumer and market research, Lisa shifted into a role as a full-time corporate training manager at Procter & Gamble. In this position, she created P&G's first online global training programs, including a new hire web-based training in 1998 called Experience the Journey. She has also worked on training for P&G interviewers. In 2000, partnering with a P&G recruiting leader, she created the first online internal job posting system for over 80,000 employees and their managers at over 200 sites around the world. Following retirement after 30+ years with P&G, Lisa founded Training Design Strategies LLC (TDS) in 2012 as an avenue to continue doing what she does best: working with the doers and the movers of the world to help them achieve their goals through the power of training. Beyond her current work with several international clients, she is on the advisory board for Ohio University's instructional design certificate program, GC-ASTD's Executive Advisory Board, and CorpU's Leaders-as-Teachers Executive Council. Her publications include the book *Leaders as Teachers Action Guide* (2014, coauthor), *Lo start-up di una Corporate University* (Italian), a series of articles for CorpU on creating Corporate Universities (2007 and 2011), and "Leaders Training" in *Leadership Excellence* magazine (2005).

Crystal Kadakia

Crystal Kadakia is a rising thought leader, invited speaker, and human capital consultant for topics related to the Generation Transition and the Millennial Generation. She started as an engineer for a Fortune 100 company, where she led numerous multi-million-dollar projects and the new hire network, and created a globally standard onboarding program for the engineering function. She then transitioned to a training manager role, where she redesigned the technical training new hire program and rolled it out across the globe. Subsequently, she excelled as a career coach, coaching multiple clients toward finding jobs and new career paths. Today she leverages her unique expertise in engineering, training, coaching, and project management in her consulting firm, Invati. She offers strategic consulting to organizations in order to enable innovation capture and employee engagement so that they can thrive and survive during generation transition. She does this by leveraging Millennial and Generation Z voices and comprehensive case study–based tools to incorporate new workplace trends into organizations. Outside of work, she is the leader of the Human Capital Special Interest Group of her local Association for Talent Development (ATD) chapter. She is also a *Huffington Post* blogger, two-time TEDx speaker, past contributor to *T+D Magazine*, and recipient of numerous ATD awards.

Dedication

To my sister, Rhoda, whose reentry into the workplace has been a model of career development. And to my daughter-in-law, Becky, whose career has helped her live a fuller life.

—Lisa M.D. Owens

To my sister, Sheryl, whose persistence at excelling in her career serves as a good role model for many. To my mother, Rashesha, whose ability to grow a successful career while overcoming her diverse background and facing many challenges inspires me. To my father, Shailesh, whose astronomical aspirations and perseverance to follow his meaningful passions guides me.

—Crystal Kadakia

To my family, Beth Morgan, Lake Brown, and dear grandchild. Also to Lisa M.D. Owens who I trust so much to carry on the legacy of this book in my stead.

— Lauri Harwood

PHASE 1:
PREPARE FOR THE JOURNEY

Prepare for the Journey

PART 1 Your job search is like a journey, and each journey begins with one step out the front door and into the world. Successful job searches tend to have five phases. The first phase, "Prepare for the Journey," begins with organizing for what's ahead, assessing yourself to market yourself more effectively, and visualizing yourself as a successful employee in the workplace.

Photo courtesy of Lifetouch Portrait Studios.

ALLEN ZINK

Vice President
Senior Development
Consultant, Fifth Third
Bank

ADVICE FROM THE EXPERT

With over 20 years of experience in coaching and developing others, Allen Zink has invaluable advice for those starting and growing on their career journey. "The most important aspect of finding a best fit career is to really, truly know yourself. Being honest with yourself regarding who you are, what drives you, and what your purpose is, are critical elements to truly being happy in a career." To understand your strengths and determine your career goals, Allen suggests, "take a little reflection time" and "think about a time when you were operating at your best and consider where you were, who you were working with, what you were doing, and how you were feeling." During that reflection time, define your strengths and goals based on discovering "the sweet spot of things you not only do well, but are passionate about."

Then connect these strengths with a company's need or role. Find a best fit company by considering if "the company's culture, values, and business proposition" align with your values. Also consider "growth opportunities and ways to further develop your skills and capabilities."

When it is time to find the job, Allen says that "networking plays a huge role in the job search!" It's important to have identified your personal brand, the words or statement that describes "how others perceive you or would describe you." Allen suggests asking yourself, "What do I want to be known for? If I could only use one word to describe me, what would that word be?" When you know what you want and who you are, you can "maximize your network" by "giving your contacts something to work with and ultimately to be able to act on." Even though "your contacts typically really want to help you", without clarity, you may not be using your network well. "Always remain positive when interacting with your contacts. Circle back to your contacts periodically and share your progress, as they may continue to have suggestions for you."

Keep positive during the job search by "planning networking meetings with people you are very comfortable with each week to help balance out the more difficult and energy draining meetings with others." It's also important to "celebrate the wins and debrief the losses from an objective point of view." Lastly, stay energized during your job search by "mixing in some activities that you enjoy and finding other people who are currently looking for a new role. It will be comforting to know that your feelings and emotions are normal!"

PLAN for Success

Most successful people keep a calendar of activities and a running list of tasks they have committed to do. Make *Your Career* a part of your calendar and task list.

- Read the outcomes on the first page of Chapters 1 through 3 and jot down a target date for completing each one. Allow extra time for those that require more than just reading.

- Now make several calendar appointments with yourself to do the readings, homework, and projects for this class.

- Consider your other commitments (other classes, work, home) as you plan to make *Your Career* happen for you!

TALES FROM THE JOB SEARCH

GABRIEL O'NEILL VELASCO, B.S.N

Poudre Valley Hospital

When he was 32, Gabriel Velasco began thinking about changing careers. He had a creative job that he enjoyed at a small television company, shooting and editing news stories and making commercials. Because of his field, videography, Gabriel knew that his career would stall unless he asked his family to move to Los Angeles or New York City, which he didn't want to do.

When Gabriel thought about work he had enjoyed in the past, first in his mind was "helping work" he had done with Habitat for Humanity and the Boulder Sister City Project. He chose nursing because of the challenges and the many career paths for nurses. Four years later, after being a part-time student for one year and a full-time student for two more years, Gabriel is a registered nurse working in a hospital, his first choice of career paths.

Gabriel's advice to anyone entering the job market or choosing a new career is to "prioritize what's important to you, whether it's making a lot of money, making work your focus, or spending time with family and enjoying outside pursuits. You have to consider those things seriously so you can find as much satisfaction and happiness as possible in and out of work."

If you think you may be out of work for a while, Gabriel recommends that you "put your ego in check and be willing to be flexible. Think about taking a job that isn't your first choice, without letting go of your dreams. Network. Be social—you never know where an opportunity is going to arise."

Gabriel has this advice for succeeding at every job: "Do your best at a job no matter what it is. Keep things in perspective as much as possible and don't let trivial matters become weightier than they really are. Each day find some enjoyment in what you do."

The Job Search Journey

OVERVIEW

Finding a job that is a good career fit for you is easier if you take it one step at a time. This chapter introduces you to the phases of the Job Search Journey, helps you get organized to succeed, and provides tips and advice for developing the right attitude for success.

OUTCOMES

1. Describe the phases of the Job Search Journey.
2. Get organized to begin your new job search.
3. Develop a good attitude for success.

CAREER ACTION WORKSHEETS

1-1: Your Job Search Journey, page 19

1-2: Organize and Start Your Career Builder Files, page 21

1-3: Proactive Success Action Plan, page 27

WHERE ARE YOU ON THE JOURNEY?

PHASE 1: Prepare for the Journey
- **The Job Search Journey**
- *Know Yourself to Market Yourself*
- *Picture Yourself in the Workplace*

PHASE 2: Create Your Resume
- *Plan Your Resume*
- *Write Your Resume*

PHASE 3: Apply for Jobs
- *Find Job Openings*
- *Write Job Applications*
- *Write Effective Tailored Cover Letters*

PHASE 4: Shine at Interviews
- *Know the Interview Essentials*
- *Prepare for Your Interview*
- *Interview Like a Pro*

PHASE 5: Connect, Accept, and Succeed
- *Stay Connected with Prospective Employers*
- *It's an Iterative Process*
- *Take Charge of Your Career*

PHASE 1: Prepare for the Journey
Step 1, *The Job Search Journey*

You are in Phase 1, *Prepare for the Journey*, at step 1, *The Job Search Journey*. Your goal in this chapter is to get an overview of the entire map and begin to get organized for your journey.

You are your own boss while you look for a job. Hold yourself accountable and report to work every day.

THE FIVE PHASES OF THE JOB SEARCH JOURNEY

OUTCOME 1

Finding a job that meets your needs and uses your talents and skills is a journey. Like most journeys, it starts with YOU deciding to make the journey, planning for it, doing it, and finally reaching your destination, with lots of good stories to tell. Get ready for an exciting journey into your future as you search for your first or next job in your career field.

Your job search can be an exciting journey because:

- There are more options than you might realize
- The journey itself will lead you to know yourself even more
- The journey can lead to a job that will be a major part of your life, affecting how much you are paid, how much time you spend working, and how much you enjoy your time on the job

Exploring career fields and job opportunities will be an important part of your work life not only for your first job, but for your entire career. Career paths are rarely straightforward. Instead, your career path will evolve as you, and your situation, evolve: your interests and passions, your skills and experience, the economy, and your situation in life.

So whether this is your first job search or the start of a new path in your career, you owe it to yourself to get it right. No one will care more about your career than you do. If you are starting a new path in an existing career, review Chapter 14 to see options to grow your career in new ways. Use this textbook and this class to succeed in your job search—and make your career happen.

The **Job Search Journey** (Figure 1-1) has five phases. The five parts of this book correspond to these phases. In each part, you'll find advice and activities to help you succeed in that phase.

Figure 1-1 The Job Search Journey

PHASE 1: Prepare for the Journey
- *The Job Search Journey*
- *Know Yourself to Market Yourself*
- *Picture Yourself in the Workplace*

PHASE 2: Create Your Resume
- *Plan Your Resume*
- *Write Your Resume*

PHASE 3: Apply for Jobs
- *Find Job Openings*
- *Write Job Applications*
- *Write Effective Tailored Cover Letters*

PHASE 4: Shine at Interviews
- *Know the Interview Essentials*
- *Prepare for Your Interview*
- *Interview Like a Pro*

PHASE 5: Connect, Accept, and Succeed
- *Stay Connected with Prospective Employers*
- *It's an Iterative Process*
- *Take Charge of Your Career*

These are the phases and steps of a typical job search. The book is divided into five parts to match these phases, with chapters to address each step. Each chapter starts with this **Job Search Journey Map** as an indicator of what phase and step you will cover in that chapter as you proceed on your journey.

Getting Started

You are about to begin a new job search. The goal of your job search is to find:

- A career field that fits with your skills and interests
- A fulfilling job in your career field that will use your talents
- An employer who will value your work and pay you for it

- A team of people who will be a positive part of your work life

Start now to gather tools that will help you discover your "best fit" career—a career that will be exciting to pursue and that will play to your strengths. If you are already experienced with the Job Search Journey, review Chapter 14 first to understand options to grow your career further.

PHASE 1: Prepare for the Journey. A little prep work understanding your goals makes for a smoother journey, whether you have already chosen your target job title or are still exploring. Get organized, assess your strengths and workplace preferences, explore the breadth of jobs in your career field, and create your first marketing tools in this phase.

PHASE 2: Create Your Resume. Your resume is the image of you that prospective employers will see. Planning and crafting this document takes deep thought and careful work so that you can market yourself effectively.

PHASE 3: Apply for Jobs. Network and research to find job opportunities and openings through Warm Introductions, Career Network meeting, and Cold Leads. Apply by completing your Job Application Package, including job application, resume, and cover letter. Use your resume and cover letter to create a picture for prospective employers that shows how you can fit into their workplace.

PHASE 4: Shine at Interviews. Use strategies for getting interviews, prepare and practice for different types of interviews and interview questions, and write thank-you notes that will help prospective employers remember

you. Be ready for pre-employment tests and follow-up interviews.

PHASE 5: Connect, Accept, and Succeed. Follow up with prospective employers after your interviews to ensure they continue to see you as a prospective employee. Evaluate job offers and decide to accept the job or continue to look for a better job fit. Finally, when you accept a job in your career field, be prepared to shine as you adjust to your new job and begin to grow your career.

 CAREER ACTION
Complete Worksheet 1-1
Your Job Search Journey page 19

ORGANIZE YOUR JOB SEARCH

Now is the time to create systems to organize the information you need on your Job Search Journey. Gathering this information now and making it easy to access quickly will help you be ready to write your resume and job applications as well as meet with people who can help you in your job search and, later, with prospective employers. Think of it as packing your suitcase for a trip.

What's the Difference Between a Job and a Career?

A **job** involves performing a designated set of responsibilities and duties for a specific employer.

A **career** encompasses a series of jobs in the same occupation or profession, either with the same company or with different companies. (*Career, occupation*, and *profession* mean the same thing.)

Your career is your life's work. Your major enables you to follow many different career paths, each with a wide variety of job opportunities. For example, Sandra is studying to become a registered pediatric nurse. She currently works as a licensed practical nurse in a nursing home (her job) and is pursuing a nursing career. Later, she could choose to train fellow nurses or work in a more administrative or management job. This would be a change in her career path toward training or management. Leon works as a security guard (his job) while he studies criminal justice (his major). Although there are other career options with his criminal justice degree, his career goal is to become a federal air marshal or K9 officer.

You can read more about the differences between a job and a career, and what these differences can mean during your working life, in Chapter 14 (page 360).

© Dmitry Kalinovsky/Shutterstock.com.

Career Builder Files is the name for all the records you assemble and organize for your job search. These files have three sections, which are described below. See Figure 1-2 for examples.

- **About Me**: This section contains a collection of records, awards, information about you, your thoughts about jobs and your career, and drafts of your Personal Brand Statement.

- **About Jobs**: Use this section to track job leads, contact information for people you talk to, your research about career fields and job listings, and your draft job applications and resumes.

- **Master Career Portfolio**: In this section, collect documents you will share with others, especially during interviews, such as your final resume and job applications, samples of your work, cover letters, and thank-you notes.

The **Career Action Worksheets** at the end of each chapter will help you gather the information you will need on your Job Search Journey. At the end of each Career Action Worksheet is a reminder to add your work to one of the three sections of your Career Builder Files.

As you pull together your Career Builder Files, both the items recommended here and others that you think are helpful, think about what these documents say about you. What picture do they paint? Where will you best fit into the workplace as you seek your next job as part of your long-term career?

Figure 1-2 Creating Your Career Builder Files

Here are examples of what you might add to your Career Builder Files so that all of your Job Search Journey documents are in one place and easy to find for this leg of your Career Journey. In most cases, you will keep only copies of these documents in your files.

About Me

Records of completion
- Your diploma(s) or degree(s)
- Your transcripts
- Licenses, such as for forklift operation, real estate, or cosmetology

Documentation of Performance
- Performance reviews from past employers or internship managers
- Awards, such as for perfect attendance on the job and in school, academic accomplishments, employee of the month, participation in academic or career-related fairs or competitions
- Letters of recommendation or commendation
- Notes of thanks or praise for previous work and contributions

Samples of Your Work
- Your work, captured as drawings, photographs, website, or video
- Writing samples for dramatic writing, technical writing, or general business writing

Legal or Government Records
- Proof of identity such as a copy of your social security card, birth certificate, passport, visas, and/or immigration forms such as green card or work permit
- Military records such as your discharge papers or military service awards

Personal Assessments
- Career Action Worksheets about you, from this textbook
- Results of recognized self-assessments such as the Myers Briggs Type Indicator or the O*Net Interest profiler at "My Next Move,"

Experiences
- Volunteer work
- Community and school projects
- List of jobs you have held, including your job titles
- Trips you have made that have broadened your life experience
- Notes from Career Network meetings

Your Personal Brand (see Chapter 2)
- Your Personal Brand Statement
- Your 30-Second Commercials

About Jobs

People, Their Contact Information, Title, and a History of Your Interactions
- People in your Career Network, including Warm Introductions (see Chapter 6)
- Recruiters and Career Fair contacts
- Prospective employers, human resource contacts, hiring managers
- People who might provide a good recommendation or reference
- Mentors and advisors
- Professional, trade and industry organizations

Sources of Job Listings
- Websites that list jobs you can apply for, including your username and password
- Location of bulletin boards you can check for jobs
- Publications that provide want ads
- Names and addresses of job and career centers
- Hidden job possibilities, insider tips, and jobs suggested by your network or research

Jobs You Want to Apply For
- List of jobs that are of interest, and their location or source
- List of companies you would like to pursue
- Status of your job application process
- Job descriptions of those positions you will or have applied for

Job Application Documents
- Draft resume (see Chapters 4 and 5)
- Draft job applications and master application data sheet (see Chapter 7)
- Cover letter and customized drafts (see Chapter 8)
- Career Action Worksheets about jobs (at the end of chapters in this textbook)

Master Career Portfolio

Job Application Package (for each company and job that you apply to)
- Resume (all formats, see Chapters 4 and 5)
- Cover letter (see Chapter 8)
- Job application (see Chapter 7)

Recommendations and References (see Chapter 7)

Your 30-Second Commercials (see Chapter 2)

LinkedIn® Profile (a copy of it or your LinkedIn® URL and name) (see Appendix A)

Select Samples of Your Work

Set Up Your Career Builder Files

There are many parts and items to keep track of on your job search, so take the time to set up good systems to organize, store, and track the information you will need. When you need to act quickly, you'll be glad you can find the documents you need to print or photocopy.

How you organize your Career Builder Files will depend on the current format of these documents and your access to the Internet. Choose a system that you are comfortable using and that is secure and available to you at any time.

Some of the documents already exist, or are best stored, on paper. Keep these items in an accordion folder with tabs. Keep the pages clean and neat (no dog hair or coffee stains) and invest in sheet protectors for certificates and other important documents that exist only on paper.

If you have regular, consistent access to the Internet, consider scanning and uploading your documents to a digital notebook or file-organizing website, software, or app, such as Evernote, OneNote, Dropbox, Google Docs, JibberJobber, or StartWire.

Pathbrite (pathbrite.com) is a website specifically designed for building your portfolio. Once you've set up a free account at Pathbrite, you can set up multiple portfolios, add "categories" to organize your content, and choose who can see your portfolios.

Whichever website, software, or app you use to organize your documents, be sure to do these things:

- Organize the documents into folders.
- Use descriptive folder names and obvious file names. Consider creating an index that will make it easy to find files and information, especially for hardcopy files.
- Invest in a flash drive and back up your digital files regularly. (Password-protect the flash drive.)
- Make sure your Career Builder Files are secure and confidential. Don't share your passwords with anyone. If you own a computer, keep your virus protection program up to date. Don't walk away from a computer you use in a public place, such as your school's computer lab. Be especially cautious about visiting questionable websites that could expose your files to computer viruses (such as earn-big-bucks-by-working-at-home sites).
- Back up your files regularly.
- Use password protection to protect your personal information and avoid identity theft.

Once you start applying for jobs and going to interviews, things can move quickly. Organize your Career Builder Files so that you can manage it easily every day. Your email might offer a good option for managing some of your job search information, such as recording people's contact information, tracking which version of your customized Job Application Package you sent to each prospective employer (see Part 3), employer responses, interview details, follow-up requirements, and communications. You can even take notes about your phone conversations and thoughts about a job and then send these notes to yourself in an email.

Be sure to write a descriptive subject line for every email so that it catches the attention of the person you send it to and so that you can find it again.

If your email account is cluttered, or if your email address is not professional, consider opening a new account for your job search and career interactions. Be sure to:

- Use a professional name for your account (for example, nadia.basara@gmail.com, not sk8trgrl@gmail.com).
- Use labels or folders to sort the messages. Think through your organization system. For example, you might sort by company name or by month of your job search.
- Record your username and password in a secure place.
- Check this account every day!

▶ **CAREER ACTION**
Complete Worksheet 1-2
Organize and Start Your
Career Builder Files page 21

Real World Scenario 1-1 Jamie is finishing her associate's degree and has a part-time job. As she starts to look for a full-time job, she realizes that her desk is *very* disorganized. She missed paying a bill for her apartment and finally found it buried under some important class notes she thought she'd lost. (The business cards she'd been looking for since the career fair two weeks ago were also in the pile of paper.) Keeping up with follow-up phone calls for her job search, juggling her class and work schedule, and taking care of her day-to-day needs is harder than she thought it would be. She knows she needs a system to stay on top of everything.

What suggestions do you have for Jamie as she organizes her desk?

⌖ You, Online

Positive Support Using Social Networking

Social networking, both online and offline, will be a vital tool in your successful job search. Every chapter of *Your Career: How to Make It Happen* highlights ways to use social networking, specifically social media tools, to enhance your job search. If you were an employer, whose would you look at first: the resume of the job seeker your friend or business acquaintance told you about, or one from the long list of applicants who applied through a job board?

As you start your job search, set a goal to use your social networks to maintain a good attitude for success, to motivate yourself, and to find job leads:

- Post your defined, clear objective for your career goals on your online social media profiles. Make your goals SMART: specific, measurable, achievable, realistic, and time-sensitive.
- Post questions to start conversations with your networks and get Warm Introductions to job opportunities; for example, "Does anyone know someone in this field I could talk to?" and "What qualities do you think make me unique?"
- Stay away from discussing how difficult your job search is in any forum (except in trusted, close relationships). Project an upbeat attitude.

Your social network gives you back what you put into it. It can reinforce your positive outlook—or it can drown you in negativity with well-intended empathy. Use your networks to motivate you and reinforce your own positive thinking.

DEVELOP A SUCCESSFUL ATTITUDE OUTCOME 3

A Job Search Journey is hard work, and there will be lots of bumps in the road along the way. A positive outlook and positive behaviors can help you stay focused so that you can effectively market yourself to prospective employers.

Maintain a Positive Outlook

Research has shown that a positive outlook can have a powerful effect on personal performance, confidence, and even health. Follow the tips below to stay positive during your Job Search Journey.

Positive Thinking and Behavior

Positive thinking is making a conscious effort to be optimistic and to anticipate positive outcomes. **Positive behavior** is purposely acting with energy and enthusiasm. When you think and behave positively, you guide your mind toward your goals and generate matching mental and physical energy. Use positive self-talk; for example, "I did a good job on that report" or "I can do this." Avoid self-critical thinking such as "I'm really nervous about this phone call." Avoid uncommitted language such as "I'll try." Plan to do it.

Positive thinking actually causes changes in the brain that boost your ability to perform and to project enthusiasm, energy, competence, and confidence—qualities that companies look for when they hire and promote employees. A positive attitude is positively infectious!

Positive Visualization

Positive visualization is purposely forming a mental picture of your successful performance and recalling the image frequently. The act of visualizing the successful performance of a skill or an activity in detail increases learning and skill development.

MAKE IT A HABIT
Start with a Positive Attitude

Your Job Search Journey will be an exciting and challenging time. You will be managing new tasks on top of an already busy schedule, while at the same time feeling the thrill of taking power into your own hands for your future. Every day, make it a habit to reaffirm feelings of excitement and confidence as you move forward on this journey. Post your favorite affirmations in places where you will see them often. Here are a few affirmations to get you started:

- I have the power to succeed.
- I will create happiness and success.
- I can make my own choices and decisions.
- I can choose to make changes in every area of my life.
- I am satisfied that I have done my best.
- I have a plan for the future, and my plan is open to change.

- I will not give up on myself.
- I have the power to succeed. (End your pep talk by repeating the first sentence—it says it all.)

Don't be shy about starting your day with a pep talk. Add your own sentences and repeat them to yourself throughout the day. Forming this habit will help you during challenging times throughout life.

© hfng/Shutterstock.com.

To strengthen your performance, practice visualizing yourself achieving your career goals with confidence and ease.

Strong Self-Esteem

Projecting confidence requires healthy **self-esteem**, a belief in your abilities and your worth. It is easier to project a confident, competent image when you feel good about yourself.

To build and maintain your self-esteem, surround yourself with a positive environment (positive people, activities, hobbies, reading, and entertainment).

Taking care of your body, mind, and spirit also boosts your self-esteem. Looking and feeling your best boosts your confidence, and others are more likely to respond positively to you.

Doing what you love is a constantly changing journey that will last a lifetime.

Set Goals for Your Job Search

Companies stay in business by setting and achieving goals (for example, increased sales, new product development, and lower production costs). Successful job seekers also set goals and work to achieve them. Follow these steps to focus your efforts on achieving your goals.

- **Set long-term and short-term goals.** More ambitious goals such as earning your college degree require more time and are called **long-term goals.** Your **short-term goals** are accomplishments you want to achieve more quickly, such as assembling

CAUTION
Take Charge of Your Career Right Now

© Netfalls - Remy Musser/Shutterstock.com.

Many factors in your job search are not under your control, but one thing certainly is—the effort you make to stand out from the crowd every step of the way. To get an edge over other job seekers, (1) set personal goals for this class and for your job search, (2) believe in your drive and commitment to achieve your goals, and (3) use this class and textbook to succeed.

Your Career: How to Make It Happen is filled with practical, realistic advice and actions. When you read each chapter, think about how you can apply the information and advice to your goals and situation. Complete the Career Action Worksheets and be sure to set up and maintain your Career Builder Files. Use the websites that support the textbook.

Set a goal today to use all the resources available to you and to take charge of your career!

your Career Builder Files. Short-term goals include many tasks that you need to complete to achieve a goal, typically in the next few days or next week.

- **Define your goals clearly in writing.** Experts say that writing down your goals strongly increases your likelihood of achieving them. Written goals increase your sense of commitment, clarify the steps and tasks you need to take, and help you remember important details. Use short, specific statements that you can aim for (for example, "Turn in my college application by August 1"). Avoid vague goal statements such as "I will earn more money this year." To help you clarify vague statements, ask yourself questions that define when, where, why, and how such as "How much money do I need to pay my current bills?" and "What is something I would like to use extra money for?"

- **Define the purpose and benefit of your goals.** Link your goals to a realistic, practical, and specific purpose that benefits you. Then add a stretch goal—something you want and that could become a reality if you challenge yourself. To boost your motivation, set high goals that inspire you, whose results you are really excited to achieve.

- **Develop an action plan, set deadlines, and act.** Divide each goal into logical, progressive steps. Set deadlines and priorities for completing each step. Complete the steps on time.

- **Identify your Career Network.** Examples include your instructors, books that motivate you, and the people who want you to succeed and will encourage you to persevere. Share your goals with others to ensure that you have someone to ask for help when you need it and to increase your sense of responsibility. Identify ways to relax or de-stress when you feel down or overwhelmed.

- **Record your progress.** It may seem simplistic, but a long series of check marks on a list can motivate you by providing a sense of accomplishment. Don't get discouraged if you miss an occasional short-term goal— stay focused on your long-term goal.

- **Reward yourself.** Rewards are motivators. Do something nice for yourself as you progress toward achieving your goals.
- **Evaluate your goals and adjust as necessary.** Evaluate your progress toward achieving your goals. Experiment with new methods if you're not getting the results you want or if circumstances or priorities change your goals.

Here are some templates for goals that you can set.

- Spend _____ hours a day/week finding job leads.
- Apply for _____ jobs each week/month.
- Complete Phase 1 of my Job Search Journey by _____ [date].
- Complete Phase 2 of my Job Search Journey by _____ [date].
- On the first day of each _____ [week/ month], review what I learned from Phases 3 and 4 of my Job Search Journey and adjust my plans based on what I learned.
- Read _____ pages of Chapter 14, "Take Charge of Your Career," every [day/week].

To help you achieve your goals, try some of the time management tips from the next section.

Manage Your Time

Your Job Search Journey may feel like a full-time job. In some ways it is! Even if you are going to school and working, you owe it to yourself to spend enough time on your job search. After all, the job you land will affect where you spend your time, energy, and talents for many years to come.

Time management is an important personal and professional skill. Everyone has 24 hours every day. Successful people learn to make the most of their time by establishing their priorities, setting goals, and using organizational strategies and tools.

- Decide which activities are important and make sure they get done. Plan ahead to avoid doing everything at the last minute.
- Break large projects into small, manageable steps.
- Expect everything to take three times longer than you think it will take.
- Use small amounts of time productively by keeping your task list with you. When you find you have an extra few minutes, take a quick look at your task list and do at least part of a task on your list. Small steps add up!
- Get into the habit of using a planner or calendar (digital or hard copy).
- Make regular appointments with yourself or with a trusted mentor or friend to review your progress and adjust your plans so that you can reach or exceed your personal goals.
- Avoid doing work that makes you feel busy but is not focused on achieving your goals. Cut back on your other commitments or free time if you need to.
- Celebrate when you reach every goal. Do something that energizes you for the next phase of the journey.

Real World Scenario 1-2 Alex knows he needs a better job, but he's overwhelmed by the idea of *looking* for a job. It seems like there are a lot of challenges working against him, including the debt he incurred paying for his family's basic needs while he went back to school. He's worried about how long it may take to find a new job— and it seems like he needed one yesterday. His cousin told him, "Just do it. Start somewhere and see where that takes you." Alex has made that his motto and is moving forward, one step at a time.

What do you think of Alex's motto? Can you imagine your Job Search Journey as a series of small, achievable steps? What resources do you have to feel positive about starting this journey?

Be Proactive

In his world-acclaimed book *7 Habits of Highly Successful People*, Stephen Covey emphasizes that the way people typically approach challenging situations and tasks is a major determinant of their career success.

People who use a **proactive approach** to situations boost their careers by focusing on solving problems, taking positive actions, and taking responsibility for their actions. People who use a **reactive approach** sabotage their success by focusing on problems instead of solutions and by avoiding difficult situations.

Using proactive skills leads to many career benefits, such as positive work relationships, improved work performance, better problem-solving skills, increased motivation, and enhanced self-esteem. Practice your best proactive thinking and behavior while you are on your Job Search Journey.

▶ *CAREER ACTION*
Complete Worksheet 1-3
Proactive Success Action Plan page 27

Chapter Checklist

Check off each item you can do. Reread sections in this chapter to help you complete the checklist.

☐ Name and explain the phase that best describes where I am today in my Job Search Journey. Name and describe the next job search phase. **1**

☐ Plan and organize my job search by collecting and organizing my records and choosing a method to keep track of communications. **2**

☐ Describe my plan for further developing and maintaining a good attitude during my Job Search Journey. **3**

☐ Put my long-term and short-term goals in writing, with concrete steps to achieve each goal. **3**

☐ Describe a few tips to help me manage my time even better during my Job Search Journey. **3**

☐ Practice proactive skills that demonstrate a positive attitude and a focus on solving problems. **3**

Critical Thinking Questions

1. What is the value of knowing about the phases and steps for a job search? **1**

2. Why is it important to organize your records for your job search? **2**

3. How will your Career Builder Files help you succeed in your Job Search Journey? What tools will you use? How will you get started? **2**

4. What effects do positive and negative thoughts, images and self-talk have on performance? **3**

5. How would you rate your ability to set goals, manage your time, and be proactive? Would you rate your skills as excellent, good, or needing improvement? What specific actions can you take to stay strong or improve these skills? **3**

Additional Resources

For data files, career resources, and more, visit www.cengagebrain.com.

Trial Run

Get Off to a Good Start

The beginning of your job search is a good time to evaluate some of the skills and attitudes that will help you have a successful journey. Read these statements and rate yourself using the following scale:

Rating Scale: 1 to 4 (1 = not really; 2 = sometimes/somewhat; 3 = usually; 4 = definitely)

____ A. I tend to be a positive person.

____ B. I like spending time with positive people.

____ C. I spend time thinking about my goals.

____ D. I have a written list of goals with the dates I want to achieve them.

____ E. When I have something complicated or important to do, I break the task into smaller steps.

____ F. If something goes wrong, I try to figure out what I could have done differently.

____ G. If I don't understand something, I'm willing to ask for advice.

____ H. I tend to keep my files well organized at home and school.

____ I. I use time management strategies to help me get things done and do them on time.

____ J. I feel positive about the future.

For your high-scoring statements, consider offering your help to others in these areas.

My high-scoring statements (list from 1 to 3 statements):

Which low-scoring statements do you think will have the most negative effect on you during your Job Search Journey (list from 1 to 3 statements)?

Write a goal for improving in those areas. Find someone—friend, mentor, family member, classmate, instructor—who might be able to help you improve.

My improvement goal:

Who might help me with the low-scoring statements?

This page is intentionally blank.

▶ *CAREER ACTION WORKSHEET*
1-1 Your Job Search Journey ❶

You are on a journey to find your next job (or your first job!) in a career field that you have chosen. As with any journey, it helps to know the parts of the route you will take. Build your understanding of your route by trying this experiment.

1. Without looking in the book, name as many of the five phases of the Job Search Journey as you can remember.

2. Now grade yourself using Figure 1-1 on page 5. How many of the five phases did you remember?

3. Try one more time on a blank sheet of paper. Did your score improve?

4. Most of us get better with practice. Flag Figure 1-1 in your book. Look at the map often to see how far you have advanced on your Job Search Journey.

This page is intentionally blank.

▶ *CAREER ACTION WORKSHEET*

1-2 Organize and Start Your Career Builder Files ②

Start your Career Builder Files. First, choose the location for your files using the following tips:

- Online Options and Considerations
  - o Can give you access to your files from any computer anywhere you have Internet access.
  - o If you use an online file-organizing system like Pathbrite, you can search digitally to find your files relatively quickly. Create three portfolios called About Me, About Jobs, and Master Career Portfolio.
  - o Email is easy to search by name, content, and date. If you use Gmail, you also have access to Google Calendar and Google Drive to organize your documents and appointments.

- Offline Options and Considerations
  - o Some documents, such as a photocopy of your driver's license, may be easiest to keep in hard copy format.
  - o You could use an accordion folder or large three-ring binder, divided into About Me, About Jobs, and Final Portfolio sections. You'll need a three-hole punch or lots of sheet protectors. Create an index that lists the documents behind each tab.

Now, inventory your existing files. In the table on the following page, add the letter, number, or name of the tab in the accordion folder, binder, or online portfolio where each document is stored. For any document you do not have yet, note in the comments section the relevant chapter to refer to for that item. Throughout your Job Search Journey, add files to the appropriate section of your Career Builder Files. Your Master Career Portfolio section will likely be empty at the beginning of your Job Search Journey and will become more complete as you go through each phase.

The following table will become the Table of Contents for your Career Builder Files.

Create an inventory of documents for your Career Builder Files	Need it	Have it	Where I put it	Comments
About Me Section				
Records of completion				
High school transcript				
College transcript				
Diplomas				
Copy of certifications or course completion				
Licenses (especially if related to your field)				
Documentation of Performance				
Awards, such as for perfect attendance on the job and in school, academic accomplishments, employee of the month, participation in academic or career-related fairs or competitions				
Performance reviews from past employers or internship managers				
References (about your skills and performance)				Chapters 4 and 5
Recommendations (about your character), including notes of thanks or praise for previous work and contributions				Chapters 4 and 5
Samples of Your Work				
Your work, captured as drawings, photographs, website, or video				
Writing samples for dramatic writing, technical writing, or general business writing				
Proof of Identity				
Driver's license				
Green card or immigration status				
Military service records				
Social security card				

Create an inventory of documents for your Career Builder Files	Need it	Have it	Where I put it	Comments
Personal Assessments				
Career Action Worksheets about you, from this textbook				
Results of recognized self-assessments such as the Myers Briggs Type Indicator or the O*Net Interest profiler at "My Next Move"				Chapter 2
Experiences				
Volunteer work				Chapter 2
Community and school projects				Chapter 2
List of jobs you have held and your job titles				Chapters 4 and 5
Trips you have made that have broadened your life experience				Chapter 2
Notes from Career Network meetings				Chapter 6
Your Personal Brand				
Your Personal Brand Statement				Chapter 2
Your 30-Second Commercials				Chapter 2
About Jobs Section				
People, Their Contact Information, Title, and a History of Your Interactions (note when and how you met them and keep track of all email and phone conversations; Excel may be a useful tool for keeping a log)				
People in your Career Network, including Warm Introductions				Chapter 6
Recruiters and career fair contacts				Chapter 6
Prospective employers, human resource contacts, hiring managers				Chapters 9 through 11
People who might provide a good recommendation or reference				Chapters 4 and 5
Mentors and advisors				
Professional, trade and industry organizations				Chapter 6

continued

continued

Create an inventory of documents for your Career Builder Files	Need it	Have it	Where I put it	Comments
Sources of Job Listings				
Websites that list jobs you can apply for, including your username and password				Chapter 6
Location of bulletin boards you can check for jobs				Chapter 6
Publications that provide want ads				Chapter 6
Names and addresses of job and career centers				Chapter 6
Hidden job possibilities, insider tips, jobs suggested by your network or research				Chapter 6
Jobs I Want to Apply For				
List of jobs that are of interest, and their location or source				Chapters 3 and 6
List of companies you would like to pursue				Chapter 3
Status of my job application process				Chapter 7
Job descriptions of those positions I will or have applied for				Chapter 7
Job Application Documents				
Your draft resume				Chapters 4 and 5
Draft job applications and master application data sheet				Chapter 7
Cover letter and customized drafts				Chapter 8
Career Action Worksheets about jobs				

Create an inventory of documents for your Career Builder Files	Need it	Have it	Where I put it	Comments
Master Career Portfolio Section				
Job Application Package (for each company and job that you apply to)				
Resume (all formats)				Chapters 4 and 5
Cover letter				Chapter 8
Job application				Chapter 7
Recommendations and References (see Chapters 4 and 5)				
Your 30-Second Commercials (see Chapter 2)				
LinkedIn® Profile (a copy of it or your LinkedIn® URL and name) (see Appendix A)				
Select Samples of Your Work				

Add your completed work to your Career Builder Files as the first page.

This page is intentionally blank.

▶ *CAREER ACTION WORKSHEET*
1-3 Proactive Success Action Plan ❸

Take this time to set goals that inspire and excite you for your Job Search Journey.

My job search goal:

Why is this goal important to me? What will happen if I don't achieve this goal?

Steps I will take to achieve this goal:

Action Steps	**Date**
1. Schedule time to assemble my Career Builder Files	
2.	
3.	
4.	
5.	

Add your completed work to the "About Me" section of your Career Builder Files.

This page is intentionally blank.

Know Yourself to Market Yourself

OVERVIEW

Before you start applying for jobs, take a closer look at what you are marketing about yourself. Consider what differentiates you from others who are applying for these same jobs. Next, develop your personal brand, the one- or two-sentence statement that captures your strengths and goals. Your Personal Brand Statement then becomes the central theme of your 30-Second Commercials and, later, your resume that you use to capture the attention of employers for jobs that are a good career fit for you.

OUTCOMES

1. Take a personal inventory of what you can offer an employer.
2. Start developing your Personal Brand Statement and your 30-Second Commercials.

CAREER ACTION WORKSHEETS

WHERE ARE YOU ON THE JOURNEY?

PHASE 1: Prepare for the Journey
- The Job Search Journey
- **Know Yourself to Market Yourself**
- Picture Yourself in the Workplace

PHASE 2: Create Your Resume
- Plan Your Resume
- Write Your Resume

PHASE 3: Apply for Jobs
- Find Job Openings
- Write Job Applications
- Write Effective Tailored Cover Letters

PHASE 4: Shine at Interviews
- Know the Interview Essentials
- Prepare for Your Interview
- Interview Like a Pro

PHASE 5: Connect, Accept, and Succeed
- Stay Connected with Prospective Employers
- It's an Iterative Process
- Take Charge of Your Career

PHASE 1: Prepare for the Journey
Step 2, *Know Yourself to Market Yourself*

You are in Phase 1, *Prepare for the Journey*, step 2. Your goal in this chapter is to assess yourself so that you know what you have to offer an employer, and to learn to market yourself effectively and concisely with a great Personal Brand Statement and 30-Second Commercials. You will identify what makes you unique and valuable.

You have more to offer employers than you might realize. Just ask someone else! Often, we are our own worst critics. Take time to see your strengths.

TAKE A PERSONAL INVENTORY

It is time to put together a personal inventory of what you have to offer an employer. When you see it all together, it will be easier to identify what is unique about you and what sets you apart as the preferred job applicant. You have already started your inventory as part of assembling the About Me section of your Career Builder Files. In Chapter 2, you will gather information about yourself that will help you learn how to market yourself. In Phases 3 and 4 of your Job Search Journey, you will learn how to share this information with prospective employers. This information includes your:

- Education and professional training
- Work experience, skills, and accomplishments
- Transferable skills, such as your time management and communication skills

The more information you collect, the better, because you will see patterns that you may not have seen before. Look for those things that create the unique combination that describes you.

Your Education and Training

Start by using Career Action Worksheet 2-1 to list your education and training: the name of the school, dates you attended, and your degree or certificate; your career-related courses, skills, and organizational activities; your accomplishments and achievements; and any scholarships, awards, or recognition you received.

Use your own notes, records, and memories to create your inventory. Then go deeper by asking people who knew you at the time to look at the worksheet and help you add to it. They may be able to see value in some things that you might take for granted or have forgotten. Be sure to ask your current instructors and classmates.

As you think about your accomplishments, include your specific contributions and what it took for you to achieve success. Consider these examples:

- Helped the other members of the math team in preparation and practice testing, resulting in winning the competition
- Voted treasurer of the senior class because of my strong organizational skills and experience using Microsoft® Excel
- Won Indoor Archery National championship, Intermediate class, as a result of hours of practice three times a week, diligently following the advice of my coach, and learning to keep my equipment in top shape

---

Real World Scenario 2-1 Anisha listed her educational experiences and decided to get some classmates' input. After all, they knew the "real" Anisha. Mike took one look at her list and immediately asked, "Where's the sociology project we did last year, about the health concerns of students?" As a paralegal student, Anisha hadn't thought of including this project, but as she talked about it with Mike, she realized how much work she'd done, from helping decide what questions to ask, to interviewing several students, to creating a spreadsheet to record all the responses. This project was definitely going on her list!

What's a project you spent significant time on? What skills did you develop that you can document in your Career Builder Files so that you can highlight them at a networking event or job interview?

▶ *CAREER ACTION*
Complete Worksheet 2-1
Education, Training, and Activities
Inventory, page 43

Your Work Experience and Skills

The next step is to use Career Action Worksheet 2-2 to list your work and other relevant experience. Along with the dates and places, list your duties, accomplishments and achievements; the skills and knowledge you developed; and any recognitions or commendations you received. Include internships, cooperative education placements, military career, and volunteer work such as community service projects.

 CAREER ACTION

Complete Worksheet 2-2
Experience and Skills Inventory, page 47

Your Job-Specific Skills

Job-specific skills are the skills and technical abilities that are needed to perform a particular job. For example, using accounting software to prepare a customized balance sheet for a client is a job-specific skill for a bookkeeper. Realigning brakes is a job-specific skill for an auto mechanic. Operating diagnostic equipment is a job-specific skill for a medical sonographer. See Figure 2-1 for more examples.

Employers expect job applicants to have key job-specific skills so that they do not have to provide as much on the job training. You might be required to take a test or demonstrate that you know how to use a software application or specialized tools and equipment.

Your Achievements

Be specific about your achievements when you describe your job-specific skills and duties. For example, "raised 20% more in contributions over previous year" or "my final report was showcased in the organization's newsletter." Your past successes are the best indicator of future successes, so be ready to share this information with prospective employers.

Figure 2-1 Examples of Job-Specific Skills

> **Licensed practice nurse:** Take blood pressure, give injections, apply dressings, give CPR, notate a patient's chart
>
> **Administrative professional:** Use MS Office, manage calendar for others, proofread, run copy machine, type 40 wpm
>
> **Carpenter:** Frame a house, use a power drill, read and follow building codes, set up scaffolding, read blueprints
>
> **Truck driver:** Drive a tractor-trailer truck, use GPS, perform routine vehicle inspections and maintenance, assess load stability
>
> **Electrician:** Read technical diagrams, install lighting systems, identify electrical problems, repair and replace wiring, use power tools
>
> **Cosmetologist:** Provide cosmetic consulting, apply hair color and highlights, give manicures and pedicures, know and follow state regulations
>
> **Sound engineer technician:** Operate audio and video equipment, set up and tear down equipment, install equipment in offices and schools, convert audio and video to digital formats
>
> **Computer security specialist:** Install security software, educate users about computer security, monitor networks for security breaches, respond to cyber attacks

Try using the **WHI method** to describe what you have done: what, how, importance. In other words, describe what you did, how you did it, and why the result you achieved was important to the business or organization. Here are some examples:

- A bookkeeper might describe a task as "Balanced books *(what)* using organizational and detail-oriented skills *(how)* to achieve an 'excellent' rating during annual audits *(importance)*."

- A construction supervisor might write, "Supervised a team of framers for the summer *(what)*, leading them *(how)* to deliver ahead of schedule with only one call-back *(importance)*."

CAUTION
Don't Exaggerate Your Credentials

On resumes, employers expect you to write only about the good stuff: you don't showcase your faults or weaknesses. However, there is a fine line between an exaggeration and a lie. Don't cross that line. Even CEOs have been fired for lying on their resume. For example, did you leave college without graduating? Even if you think that one credit hour shouldn't make a difference, it does.

Exaggerating can be a problem too. Suppose you joined DECA and the German Club but only attended one meeting of each club. While technically you could list these clubs, you would be hard-pressed in an interview to say anything truthful if you were asked about your experiences in these clubs.

Don't pad dates to cover gaps in your education and employment; instead, prepare a response to explain the gaps.

Avoid even the "little lies," such as exaggerating your contribution to a team project. Even if your little lie isn't discovered, you still have to live with not knowing if the "real you" could have been hired.

If you practice using the WHI method now, it will help you when you write your resume and cover letters later on in your Job Search Journey.

Your Transferable Skills

Transferable skills, often called soft skills, are abilities that can be applied in more than one work environment—skills that *transfer* from one job to another. Employers pay a lot of attention to a job applicant's transferable skills because they may not provide training on these skills, such as how to manage your time or do basic math or get along with your coworkers. Different jobs emphasize different transferable skills, but most employees would benefit from the transferable skills listed in Figure 2-2.

Consider, for example, a construction supervisor and a bookkeeper. Both must work well with others, manage time, solve problems, read, and communicate effectively.

Figure 2-2 Examples of Transferable Skills

Ability to follow directions	Negotiating and resolving conflicts
Ability to work independently	Paying attention to detail
Adaptability and flexibility	Planning and managing multiple tasks
Analytical skills	Problem-solving skills
Communication skills	Reading and writing
Coping with deadline pressure	Public speaking skills
Leadership ability or potential	Teamwork and collaboration
Math skills	Time management

Figure 2-3 Examples of Demonstrating Transferable Skills

School/Volunteer Activity or Part-Time Job	Transferable Skill This Activity Demonstrates
Receiving an A in a business writing course …	Shows workplace writing skills
Being elected treasurer of the student government …	Shows that you are trusted and have financial skills
Selling the most advertisements for a soccer tournament program …	Shows that you have marketing skills and persevere at tasks
Receiving a perfect attendance award …	Shows that you are dedicated and reliable
Receiving positive comment cards from several customers …	Shows that you have good interpersonal and customer service skills
Participating in a committee to solve a campus parking problem …	Shows that you have experience working with others to solve problems
Working on a school or community newspaper …	Shows that you are accustomed to deadline pressures

All of these are transferable skills. Both employees will be competent in these areas, even though framing a house and balancing a set of books (a job-specific skill for each field) are not related. See Figure 2-3 for ideas about how you can use your activities and experiences to demonstrate that you have developed a transferable skill.

Employers know that employees who have strong transferable skills are more likely to adapt to new situations and roles. Also, a job-specific skill in one career field might be a transferable skill in a different field. For example, typing 40 words per minute (wpm) is necessary for an administration professional and is a bonus for a lab technician who enters lab results into the computer. For each job you apply for, review and adjust your job-specific skills list to indicate that you know what is required for the job. Then add the transferable skills that might be a bonus for that particular job opening.

Identifying your transferable skills is especially important if you have limited work experience or if there are many applicants for a job opening. Think hard about the transferable skills you have developed and demonstrated in your school and volunteer experiences. These "soft skills" may seem unrelated to your job goals, but they help you build valuable transferable workplace capabilities that you can use to market yourself to employers.

Figure 2-4 Examples of Job-Specific Skills Used as Transferable Skills

Welding skills: Be a welder, weld inspector, or welding equipment salesperson

Teaching or mentoring skills: Teach in public or private schools, provide training to others in a workplace or design training for a workplace, design or deliver online education, manage others

Healthcare experience and skills: Be a nurse, lab tech, senior companion, online training designer for healthcare workers, healthcare inspector

Engineering skills: Be an engineer, project manager for technical work, sales tech, government inspector, specifications writer, technical witness for court and insurance cases

Cosmetology skills: Work at a salon or spa, sell cosmetics to shoppers or to stores, work for a magazine or company that provides reviews of cosmetics, apply makeup for theater, movie, or TV shows

Real World Scenario 2-2 Emilio works as a radiology technician but has started to be interested in medical equipment sales after interacting with the sales representatives who call at the clinic. As Emilio thinks about his experience as a radiology technician, he realizes that he has several transferable skills that will help him in sales. He has the technical background and knows the equipment from the technician's perspective better than the sales reps, in some cases. Positive feedback from patients speaks to his customer service skills. He also has fundraising skills from raising money for the community garden.

What are your strongest transferable skills, and how will they help you in different jobs and careers you've considered?

Some of your transferable skills are simply a natural outcome of who you are. They define you. Are you, by nature, punctual? Friendly? Intensely focused? Curious? These natural qualities can be strengths on the job and are qualities that an employer will value. Complete Career Action Worksheet 2-3 to help you inventory your personal qualities.

▶ *CAREER ACTION*
Complete Worksheet 2-3
Personal Qualities Inventory, page 49

The success you achieve in one area of your life is a good indicator of the success you will achieve in other areas.

Tools for Deeper Self-Assessment

Many self-assessment tools and resources are available to help you assess your career interests and values and match the results not only to appropriate careers but also to groups of jobs within a career field. A self-assessment tool can provide insights that can be a powerful aid when you write your Personal Brand Statement (page 36). You can find self-assessments through:

- **Your school's career services counselors**. These counselors can help you take aptitude and interest tests and guide you to information about career fields and jobs in your local job market. The career center may have a license for self-assessments that charge a fee.

- **Government websites**. All levels of government have a strong interest in assuring that employers can find employees and that job seekers know what skills are needed in today's workplace. Explore federal government websites such as the Bureau of Labor Statistics' *Occupational Outlook Handbook* (bls.gov/ooh) and O*NET Online (onetonline.org), as well as your state's employment website.

▶ *CAREER ACTION*
Complete Worksheet 2-4
Self-Assessments and Career Planning, page 51

DEVELOP YOUR PERSONAL BRAND STATEMENT AND 30-SECOND COMMERCIALS

OUTCOME 2

Now that you have completed your personal inventory, you are ready for the next step: using the information you collected to develop your **Personal Brand Statement**, a summary of the benefits you offer to an employer. This power-packed statement describes YOU: it's a tagline or slogan for marketing yourself. You can use it in conversations and interviews, and you can use this finely crafted statement in your resumes and cover letters and as

MAKE IT A HABIT
Build Greater Self-Awareness

Strong candidates for a job can talk convincingly about their strengths, of course—and they can also demonstrate how a so-called weakness can actually be a strength for a particular job. They do this by focusing on specific skills and personal traits they have.

To be able to communicate about yourself positively and effectively, you have to know yourself! Self-awareness is defined as understanding one's own knowledge, abilities, skills, and personality. To build your self-awareness, think about the process and skills you use to stay organized and accomplish a task or larger project on time—while you are doing the work. Take the time to reflect afterward on what made the project successful. For example, suppose you are going to host a party for your parents' thirty-fifth anniversary, with out-of-town guests, a video of their lives together, a catered dinner, and a DJ. What skills would you need to use to plan and host a great party?

Learn how to reflect on the things you do well— and learn from the things that don't go as planned. Look at your work objectively and think about what you did well. Practice accepting compliments graciously and speaking confidently about your achievements. These habits will help you prepare for interviews later on in your Job Search Journey.

© Danie Nel/Shutterstock.com.

part of your online presence. See "Showcase Your Personal Brand Statement Online" on page 37. It is also the foundation of your 30-Second Commercials.

A strong Personal Brand Statement showcases your strong points and differentiates you from other job applicants. It will be a central theme of your "marketing campaign" to find and get the "best fit" jobs in your career field. Do not settle for the first statement you write. Many people hone their Personal Brand Statement over several weeks as they get new ideas for describing themselves and what they have to offer. You may want to talk to people who know you well to see what they think are your unique strengths. Here is one way to create your Personal Brand Statement:

Step 1: Start with a word or two that describes **you**. Think of things that people say about you or that come naturally to you. For example, you might be a thinker, doer, innovator, educator, caring person, organizer, actor, designer, or salesperson.

Step 2: Next, jot down phrases that describe how you do things or what you are known for. For example, you might be known for delivering results despite challenges, balancing multiple priorities, knowing the right flavor combination, having an eye for color, helping the team work together in harmony.

Step 3: List a few of your personal traits. Think about traits that set you apart from others in the way you do things or the way you approach other people. Examples include doing things with speed, thoroughness, kindness, gentleness, or logic. The personal qualities in Career Action Worksheet 2-3 can help you make this list.

Step 4: Weave the words in Steps 1, 2, and 3 together to create a few lines that describe you. Try out lots of combinations. Change the words and phrases until you feel that the statement describes **you**.

Think of your Personal Brand Statement as your "secret sauce." It describes the ingredient you bring to the team and the workplace. Do you spice things up? Tone things down? Blend with the recipe? Add a splash of color? Are you the specialty spice for specific recipes? Or the go-to spice for every dish? Try to capture those things that you uniquely bring to the table—and that others will want. See the examples in Figure 2-5.

Your Personal Brand Statement should be directly or indirectly connected to your field of study or career field. If you don't see the connection between your statement and what an employer would need, talk to your friends and family members or to a school counselor. Take the first example in Figure 2-5. A person who is a harmonizer and helps people get along together would be great as a team member or team leader in a wide variety of jobs. The "best fit" careers link a person (their interests, preferences, skills, and personal traits) and their work. Your Personal Brand Statement is a way to help you see this link more clearly so that you can convince prospective employers that you are the right person for the type of job you want. Use Career Action Worksheet 2-5 to develop your Personal Brand Statement.

 CAREER ACTION

Complete Worksheet 2-5
Develop Your Personal Brand Statement, page 53

Prepare Your 30-Second Commercials

Think about getting hired as "making the sale." In this case, you and your capabilities are the product. You complete the sale by telling prospective employers what you can uniquely bring to their company that is of

Figure 2-5 Examples of Personal Brand Statements

I am ...
- A harmonizer who helps people get along together.
- A healthcare worker who wants to increase joy among those who struggle to find it.
- A highly competitive individual who likes to win at everything I do.
- A history nut who wants to help everyone know state and local history and understand how our city got to where we are.
- A futurist who applies new technology to make things better and faster.
- A person who sees beauty everywhere and tries to capture it in ways that others will appreciate.
- A researcher who appreciates the challenge of discovering how things fit together.
- A persuasive salesperson with a passion for matching products with people's needs.
- A teacher at heart, whose passion is to help other people be the best they can be.
- A technically minded person who enjoys a wide variety of technical problem-solving challenges.
- A welder who is expert at matching the right welding rod and electrode for every job, whether for sheet metal or aerospace construction.
- An entrepreneur who helps businesses succeed and expand.
- A lover of the outdoors who likes to help people challenge themselves and stay safe.
- A person who loves to keep things organized.

⌕ You, Online

Showcase Your Personal Brand Statement Online

Your Personal Brand Statement, when written well, serves as "bait" to "hook" the people you network with into a conversation about your current goals. Make your Personal Brand Statement visible in as many places as possible online. Consider using your Personal Brand Statement in these places:

- As your email signature to close every communication you send
- In the About section of your Facebook profile
- As your Twitter tagline
- In your LinkedIn® summary
- In your standard bio when posting blog posts

For more ideas about using your Personal Brand Statement online, see the Networking with Social Media Appendix A, page 383.

value to them. When you can describe how your capabilities will benefit an employer, you are more likely to spot job openings and land jobs that are a good career fit for you. Your Personal Brand Statement is the core of what you are selling.

To help make the sale, incorporate your Personal Brand Statement into several 30-Second Commercials that you can use in a conversation or interview. A 30-Second Commercial is a "clincher" speech that highlights your strongest qualities and shows how they will benefit the employer. Each commercial will be slightly different depending on who you are talking with and what that person is looking for. Be careful, though: when you tailor your commercial to your listener, make sure that you are still marketing something you can deliver. See "Do Not Exaggerate Your Credentials" on page 32.

Your 30-Second Commercials will be useful in many situations, such as networking events, practice and real interviews, and thank-you notes. You can draw from a commercial for 45-second and even 15-second "spots."

Drafting Your 30-Second Commercials

Career Action Worksheet 2-6 will help you create several 30-Second Commercials. Here is a description of the steps:

Step 1: Personal Brand Statement. Write your Personal Brand Statement at the top of a sheet of paper or key it into a document. This statement is the core of your message, so you should keep it in front of you as you draft your commercial.

Step 2: Education and Skills. Write a brief summary of your education, experience, and skills that equip you to do a specific job successfully.

Step 3: Employer Needs. List several things you think an employer would need from an employee like you. Beyond experience and skills, there are several things that all employers need, for example, employees who can follow directions, work well with others and on their own; who are careful and accurate and will not make too many mistakes; and who are flexible, trustworthy, and dependable. Before you draw up your list, learn what employers in your career field seem to be looking for. Read job descriptions and talk with your mentor or people who work in the field. O*Net Online (onetonline.org) has up-to-date, survey-based feedback from many employers in the same career fields about jobs in that field, including the skills, interests, and work styles employees need to have.

Step 4: Put it all together. Draft your 30-Second Commercial so that in a few sentences, you describe who you are, what your education and skills are, and how you will meet an employer's needs. The examples in Figure 2-6 can help you get started. Like Nicole and Brad, you should craft a different commercial for each prospective employer. A good 30-Second Commercial will emphasize different elements of who you are and what you can offer that make you the ideal person for a specific job.

Find a job you love and you will never have to work a day in your life.

—*Confucius*

Figure 2-6 Examples of 30-Second Commercials

Example 1: Nicole
Personal Brand Statement: I am a teacher who cares deeply for teenagers and the struggles they go through on their life journey.
Education and Skills: I have a bachelor's degree in education from Central University. I did my student teaching in the eleventh grade at a downtown school where half the students were recent immigrants who did not speak English as their first language. I developed and taught a successful curriculum for beginning composition with an 85% pass rate (high for this school).

Employer's Need	Nicole's 30-Second Commercial
A public school in the inner city that wants someone who understands the challenges in this environment and will stay for at least two years	I am a teacher who cares deeply for teenagers and the struggles they go through on their life journey. My education degree from Central University prepared me well for student teaching in the inner city of Hanover, where half of my students were recent immigrants who were learning to speak English. My passion for helping them helped me relate at their level. Together we achieved an 85% pass rate for basic composition, something that is nearly unheard of at this school. Several students and their parents gave me gifts and thanked me for being their teacher. I would like to make a similar impact at your school.
A private school that seeks teachers who can create curriculum that meets new standards	My education degree from Central University prepared me well for developing curriculum for inner-city high school students. It wasn't easy to teach basic composition to EOL students, but I did it and got praise from my staff teacher as well as from the students. I look forward to the challenge of writing and delivering curriculum to meet the needs of your students because I care deeply about teenagers and their success at this point in their life journey.
A suburban school that wants excellent teachers for its college-bound students	My bachelor of education from Central University plus my own high school education at a premier high school have prepared me to deliver a high-quality program at your high school. While your students are very different from the inner-city students I worked with when I did my student teaching at Hanover High School, I've seen that high schoolers face similar challenges no matter what their economic status: the challenge of discovering who they are and what they will do with their lives. I look forward to helping your students discover these things about themselves in the context of developing their academic skills.

Figure 2-6 *(continued)*

Example 2: Brad

Personal Brand Statement: Creating something from a few pieces of wood, some hardware, and stain still makes me happy. Seeing customers smile when they see my work makes it all that much better.

Education and Skills: I have an associate degree in carpentry from Monty Tech, have passed the U.S. Green Building Council's LEED Green Associate exam, and have a license to practice carpentry in the tri-state area. I've built high-end furniture for family members, and I put myself through school working summers and weekends as a framer.

Employer's Need	Brad's 30-Second Commercial
A home builder who builds for high-end clientele and wants employees who are flexible enough to do framing and high-end cabinetry	Working with wood is the best thing in the world, in my mind. I've framed houses to put myself through school. And I've build high-end furniture for family members as gifts. I got my LEED Green Associate certificate because I like using the most environmentally friendly materials and design practices. I would like to work on your team and with your customers. In my experience, they are the kind of people who will appreciate taking care of our world, one piece of wood at a time.
A remodeling firm that wants carpenters who do a good job and keep the customers happy so that the firm gets good reviews and repeat business	When I can work with wood, it's a good day. When I can create something from wood that others appreciate, it's a great day. I appreciate your company's focus on cabinetry, and I look forward to making your customers happy. My associate degree in carpentry and my LEED Green certification, plus my experience building high-end furniture as gifts for my family, have helped me build the skills I need to do a great job for you and your customers.
A furniture-building company that needs dependable workers who consistently show up for work so that customer furniture orders are delivered on time	It's so nice to know that there is a company where I could work with wood every day. I enjoy cutting, sanding, shaping, fitting, gluing, and staining wood. My associate degree from Monty Tech has taught me how to work with wood so that what I make not only looks great today, but will last for your customers for decades to come.

Figure 2-7 shows the outline of a 30-Second Commercial and shows how Shane delivered his commercial at a professional meeting. Shane's conversation with Lillian probably lasted more than 30 seconds, but notice how Shane uses examples that focus on the employer's needs and that emphasize his results-oriented accomplishments and his transferable skills. Because his outline is short and to the point, he can hone in on the information that will interest Lillian and convince her to take a closer look.

 CAREER ACTION
Complete Worksheet 2-6
Create Your 30-Second Commercials, *page 55*

Figure 2-7 Outline and Delivery of a 30-Second Commercial

Outline	Delivery
Job target: Sales representative with Axion Group, an office technology company	**Shane** (reading Lillian's name tag with her company name): Hi, I'm Shane Bradley. You're with Axion Group? I read about the opening for a sales representative in the office technology solutions group, and I think I'd be a good fit.
Personal Brand Statement: I'm an IT technician and sales consultant who enjoys designing customized systems that help businesses run more efficiently.	**Lillian**: Nice to meet you, Shane. What's your background?
Experience: Four years developing small business solutions at Computer Logistics, Inc.	**Shane**: I've been with Computer Logistics' small business solutions group for four years. I have hands-on experience in customized solutions, and I have an associate degree in information technology and a certificate in business management.
Education: Associate degree in information technology and certificate in business management	**Lillian**: Do you think you can make the transition from a small business to consulting with Fortune 1000 customers on enterprise-wide solutions?
Achievements: Received "excellent" customer performance ratings at Computer Logistics	**Shane**: I do. I recognize that there are differences, and I've wanted to move to larger-scale solutions for a while. I keep up with the industry, and I'm strong on the technical side and the sales side. Selling any technical solution is a team effort, and I've been called the ultimate utility player.
Voted Most Helpful Clerk by customers at Ralston Pharmacy	**Lillian**: That group has a reputation for being tough on new hires. They throw you into the deep end, and it's up to you to sink or swim.
Increased school newspaper revenues by 20% as advertising assistant	**Shane**: The listing says that the reps are on the road about 25% of the time, and that sounds great. You're right, but my career network is only a phone call or LinkedIn® message away. And my family has gradually moved away from this area, so I'd jump at the chance to relocate to help turn around an underperforming district.
Related Job Skills and Preferences: Business math	**Lillian**: Do you have a business card?
Business computing (hardware, networking, data storage, cloud computing, off-the-shelf and proprietary software)	**Shane**: Here it is. My LinkedIn® profile has more details. May I give you a copy of my resume?
Enjoy travel; open to relocation	**Lillian**: Could you email it to me? Here's my card with my email address. It was nice meeting you, Shane.
Transferable skills: Strong communication and interpersonal skills; highly organized	**Shane**: Likewise. You'll have my resume tomorrow, Lillian. Thanks again. It was great talking with you.

Chapter Checklist

Check off each item you can do. Reread sections in this chapter to help you complete the checklist.

- ☐ Document my education, work experience, job-specific skills, and transferable skills. ❶

- ☐ Identify my personal qualities so that I can build some of them into my Personal Brand Statement. ❶

- ☐ Research online self-assessments to help me better understand myself so that I can market myself. ❶

- ☐ Say my Personal Brand Statement out loud. I can read it for now, but eventually I will want to memorize it so I can more easily and comfortably talk to employers about who I am and what I have to offer them. ❷

- ☐ Be prepared to make the sale by delivering at least one polished 30-Second Commercial that emphasizes my qualifications and includes either a WHI statement (what, how, importance) or a measurable accomplishment. ❷

Critical Thinking Questions

1. Why is it important to assess and document your education, work experience, skills, and accomplishments? ❶

2. How are job-specific skills different from transferable skills? Give three examples of each. ❶

3. Why is it useful to identify your personal qualities? ❶

4. Why is it important to be able to talk about your strengths confidently? ❶❷

5. Describe at least three ways you can use your Personal Brand Statement. ❷

6. How is a 30-Second Commercial different from a Personal Brand Statement? ❷

7. Why do you need just one Personal Brand Statement and several 30-Second Commercials? ❷

Additional Resources

For data files, career resources, and more, visit www.cengagebrain.com.

Trial Run

My Dream Job

After you complete Career Action Worksheets 2-5 and 2-6, do this activity with a partner or group.

Pretend you are on a game show and the host asks you to describe yourself. Use your Personal Brand Statement to introduce yourself.

Briefly describe your dream job. Then imagine telling the recruiter at My Dream Job Company why you are the ideal person for this job. You have 30 seconds to make your case.

1. What is the job called?

2. Briefly describe the job:

3. Write your 30-Second Commercial for your dream job, then say it aloud.

4. Now imagine that you are making a YouTube video commercial. Deliver your commercial again, out loud, using your best body language and delivery.

5. If you can, videotape yourself delivering your commercial!

▶ *CAREER ACTION WORKSHEET*
2-1 Education, Training, and Activities Inventory ❶

Complete the sections of this inventory that apply to you: (1) High School Inventory, (2) Post-secondary Education Inventory, and (3) Seminars and Workshops Inventory. Be as thorough as you can. You will use this information again in Part 2 when you plan and write your resume.

HIGH SCHOOL INVENTORY

Name of School: _____

Address: _____

_____

Dates of Attendance: _____ to _____ Date of Diploma: _____

Grade Point Average: _____

Career-Related Courses: List the career-related courses you completed.

Career-Related and Organizational Activities: Describe your involvement in school, extracurricular, community, and other activities (examples: clubs, sports, organizations, volunteer work).

Career-Related Skills: List the skills you developed through you classes and other activities. Include job-specific skills and transferable skills (examples: using MS Office, calculating numbers, using specific tools/equipment, working on a team, persuading others).

Achievements and Awards: List (1) special accomplishments and achievements and (2) awards, recognition, or honors you received in school and through other activities (examples: selected to perform in musical production, second place in marketing competition, award for perfect attendance). Summarize praise you received from instructors, classmates, and others.

POSTSECONDARY EDUCATION INVENTORY

Complete one form for each postsecondary school (beyond high school) you attended. Duplicate the form if you attended more than one postsecondary school.

Name of School: _____

Address: _____

_____

Dates of Attendance: _____ to _____ Date of Diploma: _____

Grade Point Average: Overall: _____ In your area of study: _____

Career-Related Courses: List the career-related courses you completed.

Career-Related and Organizational Activities: Describe your involvement in school and extracurricular activities, in professional or other associations or organizations, in community activities, in volunteer work, and in other activities.

Career-Related Skills: List the skills you developed through your classes and other activities. Include job-specific skills and transferable skills (examples: preparing oral and written communications, marketing, analytical skills, persuading and leading others, working as a team member).

Achievements and Awards: List (1) special accomplishments and achievements and (2) awards, recognition, or honors you received in school and through other activities. List any scholarships you earned. Summarize praise you received from instructors, classmates, and others.

SEMINARS AND WORKSHOPS INVENTORY

Name of Seminar/Workshop: _____

Offered by: _____ Date(s): _____

Career-Related Concepts or Skills I Learned:_____

Name of Seminar/Workshop: _____

Offered by: _____ Date(s): _____

Career-Related Concepts or Skills I Learned: _____

Name of Seminar/Workshop: _____

Offered by: _____ Date(s): _____

Career-Related Concepts or Skills I Learned: _____

Add your completed work to the "About Me" section of your Career Builder Files.

This page is intentionally blank.

▶ CAREER ACTION WORKSHEET

2-2 Experience and Skills Inventory ❶

Duplicate the worksheet for each position or project (cooperative work experience, internship, volunteer/paid work experience, military experience) and complete the sections that apply to your situation. Specific and detailed information will help you create your Personal Brand Statement and 30-Second Commercials. You will also use some of this information in your resume.

POSITION (or ACTIVITY) TITLE _____

Name of Organization/Committee _____

Address _____

Phone Number _____ Salary (if paid experience) _____

Circle Type of Experience: (1) Cooperative (2) Volunteer (3) Internship (4) Paid Work

Dates of Employment or Involvement _____

Manager Name/Title _____

JOB DUTIES AND RESPONSIBILITIES

Career-Related Skills

Job-Specific Skills

Transferable Skills

Accomplishments and Achievements. Describe your accomplishments in this position using the WHI (what, how, importance) method (examples: reduced order processing time by 15% by developing more efficient processing methods that enabled the company to take more orders; named employee/volunteer of the month because of punctuality and being helpful to customers; supervised evening shift of five employees independently and allowed the senior manager to take a vacation).

Praise Received. Summarize praise received from managers, coworkers, committee members, and customers.

Job Transition. Why did you stop working here?

Performance rating from manager (circle one):

Excellent   Very Good   Good   Needs Improvement   Poor

Career Builder Files. Add any evidence of your skills, accomplishments, and praise to your Career Builder Files (examples: written performance appraisal, job description, certificate for attending a workshop).

Add your completed work to the "About Me" section of your Career Builder Files.

▶ *CAREER ACTION WORKSHEET*
2-3 Personal Qualities Inventory ❶

Use this worksheet to identify your strongest personal qualities and work performance traits. These characteristics will help you as you craft your Personal Brand Statement and 30-Second Commercials. Remember, there are no wrong answers when you are defining what is important to you.

Rate yourself on each item by circling high (H), average (A), or low (L).

Add characteristics not listed here that you would give yourself a high rating for.

Respond to the statements at the end of this worksheet.

Personal Quality/Work Performance Trait	Your Rating (High, Average, Low)		
Dependable/responsible	H	A	L
Hard worker	H	A	L
Flexible	H	A	L
Creative	H	A	L
Patient	H	A	L
Perseveres	H	A	L
Punctual	H	A	L
Takes initiative/resourceful/self-starter	H	A	L
Diplomatic	H	A	L
Intelligent	H	A	L
High energy level	H	A	L
Works well with a team	H	A	L
Sets and achieve goals	H	A	L
Plans, organizes, prioritizes work	H	A	L
Outgoing personality	H	A	L
Ability to handle conflict	H	A	L
Optimistic	H	A	L
Realistic	H	A	L
Enthusiastic	H	A	L

(continued)

(continued)

Personal Quality/Work Performance Trait	Your Rating		
	(High, Average, Low)		
Confident/high self-esteem	H	A	L
Willing to take on new assignments	H	A	L
Orderliness of work	H	A	L
Attention to detail	H	A	L
Ability to manage time well	H	A	L
Honest, high integrity	H	A	L
Ability to multitask	H	A	L
	H	A	L
	H	A	L
	H	A	L
	H	A	L

Highlight the five high-rated items that you best describe you.

Describe five examples of how you have used or demonstrated some of these high-rated qualities and traits in the past.

For each of your top five high-rated items, describe why an employer might want to hire a person with this quality or trait.

Add your completed work to the "About Me" section of your Career Builder Files.

▶ *CAREER ACTION WORKSHEET*
2-4 Self-Assessments and Career Planning ❶

Complete a self-assessment about your career interests and/or your personal traits. Start with the O*Net Interest Profiler, a self-assessment tool, by visiting www.mynextmove.org and clicking the "Start" button in the "Tell us what you like to do" box. You can also explore your state's employment website. Consider using the free online version of the mini Myers-Briggs Type Indicator quiz and/or the Keirsey Temperament Sorter. (Your school's career center may have a license for self-assessments that require a fee.)

List at least two things you discovered after taking a self-assessment.

Explain why your career choice is a good match with your personality and interests.

Add the results of the online self-assessments to the "About Me" section of your Career Builder Files.

Add your completed work to the "About Me" section of your Career Builder Files.

▶ *CAREER ACTION WORKSHEET*
2-5 Develop Your Personal Brand Statement ❷

Use the information in Career Action Worksheets 2-1 to 2-4 to answer these questions.

1. What one or two words describe what you do in general terms? (examples: thinker, doer, innovator, educator, caring person, organizer, actor, designer, worker)

2. What are you known for? (examples: delivering results despite challenges, balancing multiple priorities, being driven to finish tasks, knowing the right flavor combination, having a eye for color, helping the team work together in harmony)

3. What sets you apart from your peers? (examples: speed, thoroughness, kindness, gentleness, logic)

Weave these words into a short statement that describes you in a way that is appealing. See the examples in Figure 2-5 on page 36.

Share your statement with two people whose point of view you respect and value. Ask them these questions:

- Does this statement describe me accurately? How could I improve it?
- Can you think of situations when you have seen me demonstrate this statement?
- If I were to write another statement, what characteristics should I include?

Rewrite your Personal Brand Statement based on what you learned from these discussions.

Add your completed work to the "About Me" section of your Career Builder Files.

This page is intentionally blank.

▶ *CAREER ACTION WORKSHEET*
2-6 Create Your 30-Second Commercials ❷

Challenge yourself to write three 30-Second Commercials. Follow these steps for each commercial. Do your work on a blank sheet of paper or in a text file on a computer.

Personal Brand Statement: Write your Personal Brand Statement at the top of the page or key it in at the top of the file.

Employer Needs: List skills and traits an employer or interviewer might need or want. You can find these right now by searching online for a few job postings that you might be interested in. You can ignore the location; simply read these real job postings and pick three or four things the employer needs that match your strengths. (examples: excellent communication and interpersonal skills; ability to work collaboratively in a team environment and independently; high level of energy and drive to accomplish goals; strong PC skills, including MS Word, Excel, and PowerPoint)

Education and Skills: Briefly summarize your education and skills that relate to the employer's need.

Draft the Commercial: Describe how you can meet the employer's need, backing up that statement with your education and your experience, work performance, and accomplishments. Where possible, use data—numbers or percentages—to describe your successes. Be your authentic self. "Sell" only what you can deliver.

Make It Concise: Review your draft and find ways to shorten it. Ask others for ideas and input.

Practice: Practice delivering your commercial out loud for several prospective employers. The goal is not to memorize it word for word, but to have the best words ready in your head when you need them. Strive to sound enthusiastic about what you offer and about your qualifications.

Save your best commercials in your Career Builder Files. As you prepare for interviews, scan these and practice ways to tailor your commercials for each job interview.

Repeat this exercise with two other employer needs (#3 above).

Add your completed work to the "About Me" section of your Career Builder Files.

When one of your 30-Second Commercials is complete enough to share during an interview or important networking meeting, add it to the "Master Career Portfolio" section of your Career Builder Files.

This page is intentionally blank.

Picture Yourself in the Workplace

OVERVIEW

Chapter 3 expands your perspective of where you might find a best fit job and helps you consider how differences between one company and another impact your career success and personal fulfillment.

OUTCOMES

1 Recognize differences in workplace cultures.

2 Explore career fields and workplace possibilities.

CAREER ACTION WORKSHEETS

WHERE ARE YOU ON THE JOURNEY?

PHASE 1: Prepare for the Journey
- *The Job Search Journey*
- ***Know Yourself to Market Yourself***
- *Picture Yourself in the Workplace*

PHASE 2: Create Your Resume
- *Plan Your Resume*
- *Write Your Resume*

PHASE 3: Apply for Jobs
- *Find Job Openings*
- *Write Job Applications*
- *Write Effective Tailored Cover Letters*

PHASE 4: Shine at Interviews
- *Know the Interview Essentials*
- *Prepare for Your Interview*
- *Interview Like a Pro*

PHASE 5: Connect, Accept, and Succeed
- *Stay Connected with Prospective Employers*
- *It's an Iterative Process*
- *Take Charge of Your Career*

PHASE 1: Prepare for the Journey

Step 3, *Picture Yourself in the Workplace*

You are in Phase 1, *Prepare for the Journey*. Your goal in step 3 of this phase is to explore career fields. In the exploration process, you will assess yourself to better understand what you want from a job and what you have to offer an employer. Ultimately, this will help you better market yourself for a best career fit job.

Picture yourself on the job. Not just on the first day, but doing the everyday work. Most jobs are one part wonderful and two parts drudgery. That's why they call it WORK. When you can envision a real day-to-day workplace, and see yourself smiling in that future, then you have a goal. That is the job you want to find.

RECOGNIZE DIFFERENCES BETWEEN WORKPLACES

In the last chapter, you did some self-assessment to see what you had to offer an employer and how you could package this and market yourself. Now let's consider what you are looking for in an employer that will help meet your career desires.

Lifestyle Difference

Consider Sara, Chris, and Jason. Each was graduating with a degree in accounting, but each landed in very different job situations. During a small group exercise in their Career Search class, they noticed that accounting jobs fell into different groups. There were jobs with corporations, small firms, and government agencies. There were jobs related to taxes, payroll, billing, and finance.

Sara was interested in advancing in her career so that one day she could be a manager of others, so her mentor encouraged her to spend more time looking for and applying to accounting positions for corporate and government job openings. In these roles, she would learn from others, work hard to excel, and have opportunities to be a manager within three to five years.

Chris, on the other hand, was more interested in a job that was stable and would allow him to spend time with his family. So Chris avoided jobs related to taxes and payroll because these jobs have big end-of-the-month and tax season periods that often require overtime for people working in the finance and accounting departments.

Jason wanted to be adventurous and travel. He eventually found a job working for a company that does audits of other company's books across the United States. He had to work as an apprentice for two years and take additional certifications paid for by the company. It was all worth it to him to be able to be in San Francisco this month, in Minnesota next month. He was rarely home, so he shared an apartment with a friend. His costs were low, and he could save for that sports car he always dreamed of having.

What lifestyle are you looking for? Look at Career Action Worksheet 3-1, "Career Lifestyle Preferences to Consider." Do you want to jet around the country or stick to one place? Do you need defined hours or a flexible schedule to meet responsibilities with children or aging parents. Or do you prefer long hours and possible overtime? Do you need insurance or education payments to get an advanced degree in the future?

As you read job listings, try to read between the lines to determine what the company or your employer will need from you if you apply for and get this job. If you are not certain, make a list of questions and try to get answers. You could network with an employee of that company or research the company online using sites like Glassdoor.com that gather ratings of companies from employees who work there.

Take time now to think through what you really need. As you begin your job search, look for those things that will best fit with your desired lifestyle. By pursuing companies that best fit your lifestyle, you will be more excited throughout the Job Search Journey, and that excitement will be noticed and rewarded by prospective companies.

> ▶ *CAREER ACTION*
> **Complete Worksheet 3-1**
> Career Lifestyle Preferences to Consider, page 71

Preferences on the Job

Most of us think simply about getting a job with fair pay, healthcare benefits, and a nice manager. If you think a little deeper, you are more likely to find jobs that will bring you greater satisfaction.

Unlike Sara, Chris, and Jason, Trevor did not get the advice he needed to help him think deeply about his needs. Trevor wanted to change careers. He was dispirited and wanted to get out from being a fast-food restaurant manager, a job that had him leading and motivating his team but also had him working at all hours of the week. He wanted an 8 a.m. to 5 p.m. job doing computer work. He graduated from night school with high honors in computing and landed a great job with a local software firm. However, once he was in the new job, he quickly discovered that his new work was very solitary. Not only was he lonely during the day, but he had not thought about what to do to fill his evening hours.

Within a year, Trevor started a new job search. This time, he knew more about what he needed to be happy at work and in life. He moved to a larger firm, where he did computer software repairs with a team of software experts. He also began volunteering with Meals on Wheels and joined a sailing group. Now he is more satisfied with life, both on the job and after hours.

 CAREER ACTION
Complete Worksheet 3-2
Job Environment Preferences, page 73

Culture: Yours and Theirs

What type of organization or company do you want to work for? Here are a few things to consider:

- Size
- Location of headquarters
- Diversity of employees
- Mission, values, and purpose

Size

Small businesses are the heart of the American economy, large companies make a big impact, and midsize companies have room for growth (*Forbes*, "Three Things Mid-size Companies Do Better," http://www.forbes.com/sites/forbesinsights/2012/04/20/three-things-mid-size-companies-do-better/.). Small companies have small staffs and may rely heavily on a few employees, often asking them to do things outside their normal job that broaden their skill set quickly. Midsize firms are likely to reinvent themselves every five years or so and may ask you to reinvent yourself and grow with them. Large firms tend to have more well-refined procedures and policies simply to manage the large number of employees, products, customers, and government requirements. All three types of companies can have good jobs to offer and can be good places to work. The question is, where will you find your best fit job? Are you willing to deliver what this size company will need?

Headquarters

The location of the headquarters provides one clue to the reputation and culture of the company. A company based in Sweden (for example, IKEA) or Japan (for example, Toyota) is likely to have a different view of hierarchy, work standards, and procedures than, say, a company based in the Midwest or New York City. For example, European firms tend to have great vacation policies, but demand hard work and long hours at other times. Japanese firms tend to value relationships before execution when it comes to decision making, and this can cause culture shock for some U.S. citizens. A company with a Midwest culture might emphasize politeness and friendliness, while a company in New York City could be faster paced. Think about the impact the company's culture will have on you. Will you fit in, will you grow and develop, or will you feel stress as a result of the culture in which you spend your time while you are working?

Diversity of Employees

Try to find clues about the diversity of employees within the company. Ethnic diversity may be mentioned on the company website. For example, some companies post blogs and articles saying that ethnic diversity is something they value because diversity helps them achieve their business goals. You can also do other research online. For example, *Fortune* magazine publishes an annual list of the 100 Best Companies to Work For. You might be surprised by the names of the companies that show up on this list! Do the research and then think about how you will fit in.

The Mission, Values, and Purpose

Most company websites state the company's purpose, values, goals, and/or mission statement. Be sure to read these, not only so that you are prepared for an interview but also so that you can decide if this is the type of company you want to be associated with. Which company mission statement appeals to you more: "Combines aggressive strategic marketing with quality products at competitive prices...." or "Provides the best to enable business to excel"? These mission/values/purpose statements may seem like just nice words on a page, yet they provide insight into what is important to the company and how the culture and work environment are on a day-to-day basis. In the first example, employees are likely working in a competitive, sales-driven environment, where performance is measured by reduced costs and increased sales. In the second example, employees may be measured by less tangible business goals such as training hours completed or customer service quality goals. Make sure there is a fit between what enables your productivity and the company's approach to business.

The Employer/Employee Relationship

There is a two-way relationship between companies and employees. This relationship is a big commitment for both parties.

Companies rely on employees to operate their business, produce high-quality products or services, meet the needs of customers, and help make a profit. Companies invest a great deal of time and money in training, developing, and paying workers. In the United States, costs for employees commonly double or triple the cost of the goods a company sells.

Employees invest considerable time and energy in performing their job duties every day. They expect to be paid for their work; have a safe, healthy work environment; be given the equipment and supplies they need to do their jobs; and have an immediate manager who provides just enough direction and support to do the job. Many employees also seek additional training and development on the job so that they can improve their skills.

For the relationship to be successful, the expectations of the company and the expectations of the employee must be met. Be prepared to do your part to understand what is needed of you. Then use the skills you developed—academic, technical, interpersonal, communication—to deliver the job. One company was known for making sure that the relationship was clear and that expectations worked both ways. At the bottom of every paycheck statement were these words: "Now we are even."

Real World Scenario 3-1 Carol is excited and proud to be graduating this year. She is the first person in her family to graduate with more than a high school degree. It took a lot to achieve this goal. When considering a workplace, she wants a company that will support her as she strives to achieve her life dreams. She has a lot of outside commitments and looks for a company and role that will provide flexibility. She wants to continue growing, so she is looking at companies with strong mentorship programs and maybe an education program. Carol knows that she is a persistent person and good at leveraging all her resources to achieve her goals. She believes her personality will be a good fit with a company that values hard work, diversity, and transparency.

What company programs and cultural traits do you feel support your personal values?

▶ *CAREER ACTION*
Complete Worksheet 3-3
Employer/Employee Relationship,
page 75

Workplace Behavior and Conduct

Within each company's culture, there are expectations for employee conduct, and there are workplace rules that must be followed. Typical expectations include the following:

- Be courteous to others—customers, workers, your boss—no matter your own mood
- Be productive, punctual, and reliable
- Follow health, safety, and security rules
- Behave ethically, and especially follow the company code of conduct

↘ You, Online

Social Profiles: It's a Two-Way Street

Companies today have expectations regarding your social media presence. As a part of their recruiting process, many companies search applicants on Google and review existing social media profiles such as on Facebook. Be prepared! Review and update your social media profiles before starting your job search. Google yourself and see what the search results show! Remove references to inappropriate behavior and make sure your profiles demonstrate ethical attitudes.

This is a good time for you to do some homework about prospective companies as well. Many companies have a presence on social media. Review LinkedIn®, Twitter, and Facebook profiles of companies you are interested in, as well as their official websites.

Courtesy

Use your network to get the inside scoop on the expected professional behavior before you go for an interview. You will learn more when you are on the job. Here are some examples:

- In many workplaces, there are rules against employees dating and in all workplaces, sexual harassment is illegal.
- Always treat the customer with respect, no matter what.
- Represent the company well when talking to people outside the company.
- Watch out for unwritten rules. For example, be aware of the proper way to address people, such as in some restaurants, where the senior cook prefers to be called chef. There are lots of rules for talking with managers. Proper etiquette is especially important when navigating the hierarchy, especially related to suggesting changes, expressing your desires, and meeting with upper management without your immediate manager's agreement.

You can learn more about cultural norms and unique workplace manners by observing others and seeking advice from trusted coworkers.

Productivity

A strong work ethic and an inner drive to do a good job goes a long way toward a successful career. Here are ways you can demonstrate a strong work ethic. Consider starting to practice these things now, in your current work or school environment, if you are not doing so already:

- Proactively set goals, preferably with your manager, and persistently meet these goals.
- Make sure you understand assignments, know what success looks like, and stick with tasks until they are finished, even when you have little or no supervision.
- Develop efficient work processes and check your work before you turn it in.

Respect Diversity

An ethical organization is committed to diversity. The ethical employee:

- Understands that the world is diverse and that it will continue to grow more diverse in the future

- Accepts and respects diversity in all people—diversity of ethnicity, race, gender, age, physical ability, and lifestyle

- Understands that there is no place in the workplace for telling or listening to jokes that have racial, ethnic, gender, or lifestyle overtones

The workplace should be an inclusive space. Diversity is about learning from others and showing respect for everyone.

© Huntstock/yes/Disability Images.

Health, Safety, and Security

To protect the company and its employees, the company puts in place many health, safety, and security regulations. Some of these are government or other regulatory requirements. Others are requirements from the company's insurance company. Other rules are just common sense or are based on company experience. Breaking any of these rules might cause the company to be fined, or doing so could cause damage to people, equipment, and/or the environment.

Why Teams Work

Teamwork plays an important role in the workplace. It leads to a more productive as well as a more pleasant work environment. Teamwork benefits both employees and companies. Here is how good teamwork looks:

Collaboration. People work together and support one another to achieve team goals.

Communication. Coworkers share information freely to help each other perform effectively.

Sharing strengths and resources. Team members apply themselves willingly. When one member lacks certain skills, another team member is there to fill the gap.

Better decisions and solutions. A team can generate more discussion, ideas, and solutions than a single individual can. Each member adds a unique point of view.

Quality. Team members take pride in the team effort and ensure that each member gets what he or she needs from other team members to turn out the best possible work.

© Monkey Business Images/Shutterstock.com.

© Vladimir Wrangel/Shutterstock.com.

CAUTION
Be Careful with Sensitive Information

At one time or another, every employee has access to sensitive company information or knows things about the company that are not intended to be made public. Be as careful with company information as you are with your personal information. Information your boss shares with you might be confidential, so do not divulge it without permission.

Here are some examples of common actions employees take to secure sensitive information:

* Password-protect confidential documents.

* Do not leave your computer with open documents on the monitor. Close the files before you leave your station.

* Never leave sensitive documents out on your desk for passersby to see.

* When you leave work for the day, store sensitive documents in a locked file cabinet.

* If you use a laptop, password-protect the system. Use a security cable or put your laptop in a locked drawer to avoid it being stolen.

* Keep your company smartphone in a safe location. Use a sign-on password to protect the data, just in case the phone is stolen.

Security rules also serve a purpose. Be sure to wear your company identification badge as required and be cautious about losing it or loaning it out. This also applies to computer equipment and passwords or security codes. Protect the company by protecting its security. Don't be like the intern who left a company computer unsecured in his car. It was stolen. The thieves got access to customers' personal data. It cost the company money to fix the issue and created a lot of bad press and a loss of trust with its customers.

Ethical Expectations

Ethics are guidelines or accepted standards about what is right or wrong. **Business ethics** is the application of ethical principles in a business environment. The principles apply to individual employees and to the entire organization. Many companies publish their code of ethics online. When you start work, the company may ask you to sign a statement saying you agree to follow these ethical guidelines. Many companies ask all employees to reread and sign these guidelines annually as a general reminder of expectations. Ethical guidelines are good for you and for the business. Ethical guidelines may touch on legalities and company policy, and they are listed to provide full disclosure about how the company operates. Guidelines often include the following:

* Keep accurate, honest records and accounts.

* Follow local, state, and federal laws.

* Treat employees equally without regard for their sex, age, ethnicity, race, religion, physical ability, or lifestyle.

* Be trustworthy. Conduct business honestly.

As an employee, being honest and ethical includes the following:

- Give a full day of work. This includes showing up on time, not taking long breaks, and not conducting personal communications (text, phone, or Internet use) during work time.

- Do not steal or borrow from your employer. This starts with not taking office pens or copy paper and includes being trustworthy with money and financial matters.

- Be a trusted team player. For example, don't take credit for a coworker's idea or leave the dirty work, like a jammed printer or copier, for your coworkers.

- Be honest. If you make a mistake, own up to it quickly. Be especially honest on your resume by not exaggerating your qualifications, age, or experience.

Consider the job applicant who indicated on her resume that she was fluent in Spanish. Imagine her dismay when the interviewer spoke to her in Spanish until he realized that she didn't understand what he was saying!

Code of Ethical Business Conduct

Everyone associated with Hershey is expected to follow Hershey's code of conduct: "All employees, officers, and directors must act according to the principles set forth in our Code. We expect everyone working on our Company's behalf, including consultants, agents, suppliers, and business partners, to adhere to our ethical standards. We may never ask a third party to engage in any activity that violates these standards."

The Hershey Company's entire code of conduct is 44 pages in English. You can read it online in the language of every country where Hershey does business. Here is the high-level overview in English.

OUR COMMITMENTS We have each made a commitment to operate ethically and to lead with integrity. This commitment is embedded in the Hershey values. Our Code of Ethical Business Conduct ("Code") shows us how to uphold this commitment as we interact with the various groups that have a stake in our Company's success.

OUR COMMITMENT TO FELLOW EMPLOYEES We treat one another fairly and with respect, valuing the talents, experiences and strengths of our diverse workforce.

OUR COMMITMENT TO CONSUMERS We maintain the trust consumers place in our brands, providing the best products on the market and adhering to honest marketing practices.

OUR COMMITMENT TO THE MARKETPLACE We deal fairly with our business partners, competitors and suppliers, acting ethically and upholding the law in everything we do.

OUR COMMITMENT TO STOCKHOLDERS We act honestly and transparently at all times, maintaining the trust our stockholders have placed in us.

OUR COMMITMENT TO THE GLOBAL COMMUNITY We comply with all global trade laws, protecting our natural resources and supporting the communities where we live, work and do business.

Source: The Hershey Company. "Code of Ethical Business Conduct," page iii. Web. Accessed 17, September, 2014. http://www.thehersheycompany.com/about/conduct.asp".

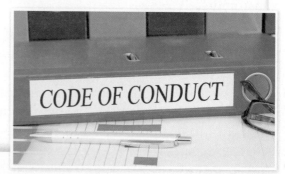

Note that many companies run credit checks on job applicants. A good personal credit rating is a sign that an employee knows how to manage money. A poor credit score is a sign that an employee is financially irresponsible or takes financial risks. So consider fiscal responsibility even before you get that job.

Ethical decisions boil down to this: Do the RIGHT thing. Because of the consequences, doing the right thing often takes courage. If you don't know the right thing to do, that's a clear sign that you should talk with an immediate manager or trusted mentor.

> ▶ *CAREER ACTION*
> **Complete Worksheet 3-4**
> Internet Research on Corporate Codes of Ethics, page 77

EXPLORE CAREER FIELDS AND WORKPLACE POSSIBILITIES ② OUTCOME

Your education is a major factor in determining the industry or field in which you will work. Whether you are just starting out or getting close to graduation, you can view career fields and your field of study more broadly to open up a wider range of job opportunities. Job possibilities that match your skills and education are likely to be found in a broad range of workplaces. Figure 3-1 shows a few examples.

In-Demand Industries and Occupations

At any given time, certain industries are growing, while others are declining. If you can link your chosen field and an in-demand industry, you may find more job openings. For example, can you tap into the burgeoning movie-making industry in the Atlanta area? This industry needs more than actors, directors, and camera crews. They need costumers, computer specialists, set builders, electricians, and more.

Since the 1990s, the U.S. economy has shifted from a goods-producing economy to an economy based on service occupations. The U.S. Bureau of Labor Statistics (BLS) employment projections show, as of this writing, that service-providing industries are expected to add approximately 14.5 million new jobs by 2018. See the CareerOneStop website at http://www.careerinfonet.org/ for up-to-date information about in-demand jobs as reported by the BLS.

A few significant projections include that jobs in the medical field are likely to continue to increase due to the aging population and the increase in the number of medical research breakthroughs. Jobs related to computer and Internet security are likely to continue to rise with increasing use of the Internet and the unending existence of thieves.

Look also for information about the number of jobs in any given field. Especially note if the number of job openings is increasing versus previous years. These career fields are more likely to have more opportunities.

Figure 3-1 Common and Possible Job Environments

Education	Most Common Job Environments	Possible Job Environments
Nursing	Hospitals, medical offices	Clinics at schools and industrial settings, healthcare research, medical insurance
Construction	Residential and commercial construction, remodeling	Set building for movies and theater, specialty shipping container construction, building maintenance supervisor, industry in-house construction team
Historian	Schoolteacher, museum	Librarian, corporate archivist, researcher, media fact checker, publications reviewer or writer

MAKE IT A HABIT
Expand Your Perspective

When exploring workplaces, many people make the mistake of believing that what they have experienced in the past or the knowledge that they currently have defines the possible opportunities they can obtain in the future.

On the contrary, the world of work is continually changing based on economic, political, and societal changes, on both a global and local level. New work policies are being adopted that allow more flexibility for employees, management styles are changing to be more team oriented, and the type of work continues to evolve. Here are some tips to continually expand your perspective:

- Focus on what careers you can do or workplaces you can find instead of what you can't do or can't find.

- Make a habit of questioning your own understanding of your field, including questioning what you've learned from your professors, instructors, and career center.

- Avoid making assumptions. Check your assumptions against the latest facts and data.

Those who challenge their perspectives find more unique and positive opportunities than those who limit themselves by what was possible in the past.

Real World Scenario 3-2 John had originally chosen the field of welding technician because he enjoyed working with his hands. Nearing completion of his degree, he was glad to find that the BLS *Occupational Outlook* showed that welding is a growing field. This reassured him that he had chosen the right field. However, the BLS information also showed that welding technicians were more in demand in some places than where he lived. He decided he would try to find a job in his local area first, and, if absolutely necessary, to look for jobs in other areas even if he had to move to a different state.

Have you looked at the projections for your field? What factors influence the ability to find a job easily and successfully in your field?

As human beings, we tend to seek out varying levels of status, certainty, autonomy, relatedness, and fairness. Seek a job that can provide these elements at a level that you find satisfying.

Online Resources for In-Demand Careers

The U.S. Departments of Education and Labor have developed extensive online and print resources for exploring careers, with additional information about in-demand industries and fast-growing occupations.

One great example is CareerOneStop. To help promote fast-growing industries and help job seekers research careers, the U.S. Department of Labor maintains the CareerOneStop website at careeronestop.org.

This site is designed to provide information on high-growth, in-demand occupations, including average compensation (wages or salary plus benefits) and information on the skills and education needed to attain those jobs. CareerOneStop is updated annually to ensure that it reflects current hiring trends.

These online resources—the most comprehensive guides on the Internet—should be a destination for every job seeker who is actively exploring career information.

▶ *CAREER ACTION*
Complete Worksheet 3-5
Internet Research on In-Demand Careers
page 79

Hidden Jobs

Most people know how to find jobs in the obvious places. Accountants search among accounting firms or accounting departments. Computer techs might look to computer repair or sales companies. Teachers look for jobs at schools. However, there are hidden jobs that you can find.

There are two types of hidden jobs: those that are never posted or advertised and those that are obscure niche jobs. See Chapter 6 to learn more about finding jobs before they are posted by tapping into your Career Network. Niche jobs are found by looking for jobs in unexpected places.

Here is one way to broaden your thinking. Using the Internet, search for a list of companies in your area. The Better Business Bureau often has a good list, as does the Yellow Pages. Now choose five companies and start brainstorming how you might fit in that company. For example, an accountant might find a job with a lawn cutting service that needs help with billing, accounting, and maybe even taxes and scheduling. Or a biologist might find a job with a microbrewery that needs help in the laboratory with managing and running beer chemistry analysis. Likewise, a psychologist could land a job with a medical insurance company counseling clients with special situations.

Think about your hobbies and interests that go beyond your career choice. Maybe you can combine your interests and career. A person interested in outer space, but with a career in computer hardware repair, could focus his or her job search on companies that build aircraft or that supply products for the U.S. Air Force and NASA. A person with education in carpentry and an interest in art can become the managing supervisor responsible for packing art for shipping at a museum or art warehouse. If you are involved in a club related to your interests, talk to other members for more ideas about jobs that combine your career and interests.

Here are a few more examples. Brandon's chosen career is in biology, and he is fascinated with food. He started searching for jobs in laboratories that work with food products, food production, and food inspection. Megan chose a career in teaching and had an interest in religion. She focused her search on teaching roles at parochial schools, nursery schools run by religious organizations, and the seminary in her town. She also explored teaching at high schools that offered classes in comparative religion.

Be excited about the possibilities. Your excitement and the resultant energy will be helpful as you continue on your Job Search Journey. By considering your goals for lifestyle, company culture, and job skills—as well as your personal values—you can uncover a much larger pool of jobs that more closely match your needs and interests.

▶ *CAREER ACTION*
Complete Worksheet 3-6
Exploring Possibilities for Hidden Jobs,
page 81

Chapter Checklist

Check off each item you can do. Reread sections in this chapter to help you complete the checklist.

☐ List some of the lifestyle differences I might experience if I take a job with one company versus another, such as a large, midsize, or small company; or a government, corporate, or not-for-profit organization. **①**

☐ Describe the type of things I prefer when working on a job. Consider the physical atmosphere, the emotional atmosphere, the people, and the level of challenge on the job. **①**

☐ Describe how I can learn about the differences in culture between prospective companies. **①**

☐ Considering that the relationship between employee and company is a fair exchange, make a list of what I can give your company (beyond spending time), and what my company might give me in return (beyond a salary or paycheck). **①**

☐ Describe why ethical behavior at work is valuable and important for both me and my company. **①**

☐ List the types of jobs that I originally thought I was qualified to do. Now add to that list at least three additional jobs based on my research. **②**

☐ List what I might be qualified to do in one of the growth industries or in-demand occupational fields. **②**

Critical Thinking Questions

1. The employer/employee relationship works both ways. Brainstorm some responsibilities the chapter did not list for both the employer to the employee and the employee to the employer. **①**

2. People can grow their skills and experience; however, personality and interests are not as changeable. Your particular personality and interests will be an asset for some jobs and a hindrance for others. For what types of jobs will your personality and interests be an asset? A hindrance? **①**

3. Who else is affected when an organization acts unethically? Who is affected when an employee acts unethically? List at least three groups and explain how each group is affected by unethical actions by a employer and an employee. **①**

4. Why is it important to consider growth industries when exploring careers and thinking about your job prospects? **②**

5. What is the value of considering jobs that are outside of the growth industries and job markets common for your career field? **②**

Additional Resources

For data files, career resources, and more, visit www.cengagebrain.com.

Trial Run

That's Entertainment! Relationships

Working alone or with a partner, watch a movie or television show centered on a workplace (such as a hospital, an office, a police station, a laboratory, a restaurant, a television station, a hair salon, a coffee shop, a school, or another workplace). Identify and discuss the employee/employer relationships in the movie or TV show that you watched. Then select one character who is an employee. Evaluate that employee on the expectations and skills listed below. For each item, provide an example to explain how the character earned the score.

Rating Scale: 1 to 4 (1 = poor; 2 = okay; 3 = good; 4 = exceptional)

Meets employer's expectations   Score: _____

Example:

Is reliable   Score: _____

Example:

Is prompt and timely   Score: _____

Example:

Performance on the job   Score: _____

Example:

Demonstrates a positive attitude   Score: _____

Example:

Behaves appropriately for this workplace   Score: _____

Example:

Demonstrates thinking and problem-solving skills   Score: _____

Example:

Demonstrates communication and teamwork skills   Score: _____

Example:

Demonstrates technology-related skills
(for example, using technology, equipment, and medical skills)   Score: _____

Example:

Shows a strong work ethic   Score: _____

Example:

Is appropriately attired and groomed for the job   Score: _____

Example:

What advice would you give the character to improve his or her score in any areas of weakness? How could the person improve workplace competencies to be successful on the job and in the future?

▶ *CAREER ACTION WORKSHEET*
3-1 Career Lifestyle Preferences to Consider ❶

For each item below, mark how important each lifestyle preference item is to you and your job, and jot down your thoughts on why.

My Lifestyle Preferences	Level of Importance			My Thoughts (such as *why* you chose this answer or your experience related to this topic)
	High	Medium	Low	
Stability: My job isn't expected to change much.				
Security: This company will always be here for me, and I will be able to work here for a long time.				
Purpose: This job helps me be part of something bigger to help the world or other people.				
Independent: When I work, I can do it my way with minimal direction.				
Entrepreneurial: I have a large amount of ownership and ability to innovate and implement new ideas. I will take risks to find new markets, products, and profit.				
Competence: I have the chance to do good work every day and improve my skills with experience and training.				
Challenge: This job gives me tough problems and issues that I can solve using my skills and knowledge.				
Balance: When I I leave the job, I can leave it behind and focus on my life outside of work.				
Advancement: I have the opportunity to advance to manage more people and business.				
Flexibility: I have the ability to define how I get the results of the work, including when and where I best work.				

List your two most important career lifestyle preferences, and describe why these are important to you.

1.

2.

Jot down your thoughts about what types of industries or jobs might provide this lifestyle.

Add your completed work to the "About Me" section of your Career Builder Files.

▶ CAREER ACTION WORKSHEET
3-2 Job Environment Preferences ❶

For each item below, mark how much of this job environment item you would like in your workplace and jot down your thoughts on why.

Description of Job Environment	None 1	2	Some 3	4	A Lot 5	My Thoughts (such as *why* you chose this answer, or where you have seen or experienced this environment)
The Work						
Predictable, structured						
Free to do good work (minimal supervision)						
Intellectually stimulating, contemplative						
Work with people (versus things)						
Hands-on work						
Work with data or ideas (versus people)						
The Interaction with People						
Work together in harmony						
Work together in healthy competition						
Lively, energetic (versus quiet, calm)						

continued

The Emotional Nature						
High risk, edgy						
Get-it-done						
Sense of completion						
Long-term goals						
Creative						
High pressure						
Cutting-edge technologies or thinking						
The Physical Environment						
Orderly and aesthetically pleasing						
Relaxed, easygoing						
Changes regularly						
Lively, upbeat, energized						
Outdoors (versus indoors)						

Jot down your thoughts on a few types of jobs or industries to avoid, based on what you don't want in a job environment.

Jot down your thoughts on a few types of jobs or industries that could provide you with a job that somewhat matches your preferences.

Add your completed work to the "About Me" section of your Career Builder Files.

▶ CAREER ACTION WORKSHEET

3-3 Employer/Employee Relationship ❶

Think about a successful employer/employee relationship you have experienced or observed. List the expectations for the job.

Employer's Expectations	Employee's Expectations

Why was it a successful relationship?

Now think of an unsuccessful employer/employee relationship you have experienced or witnessed. Describe the expectations for the job.

Employer's Expectations	Employee's Expectations

In your opinion, was there a mismatch of expectations? How could the situation have been improved or avoided?

Add your completed work to the "About Me" section of your Career Builder Files.

This page is intentionally blank.

▶ CAREER ACTION WORKSHEET

3-4 Internet Research on Corporate Codes of Ethics ❶

Use the Internet to find and report on two organizations in your career field that have posted their codes of ethics on their websites.

Example: Search words are "marketing" + company's or organization's name + "ethics" OR "code of conduct." Read the web link that is associated with the company's website. OR go to the company website and, if there is a search field, type in "ethics."

Career Field: _____

Organization 1: _____

What are the key topics covered in the code of ethics?

Organization 2: _____

What are the key topics covered in the code of ethics?

Both Companies

How are the codes of ethics different? Are the differences significant? Explain.

Summarize the code of ethics for this career field.

Based on its code of ethics, which organization would you rather work for? Why?

Add your completed work to the "About Me" section of your Career Builder Files.

▶ *CAREER ACTION WORKSHEET*

3-5 Internet Research on In-Demand Careers ❷

Use the CareerOneStop website to research two in-demand jobs that interest you. Write a brief summary of your findings in the areas provided here.

Occupation 1

Job Title:

Description:

Tasks:

Skills:

Median salary:

Education required:

Technology skills required:

Occupation 2

Job Title:

Description:

Tasks:

Skills:

Median salary:

Education required:

Technology skills required:

Add your completed work to the "About Me" section of your Career Builder Files.

This page is intentionally blank.

▶ CAREER ACTION WORKSHEET

3-6 Exploring Possibilities for Hidden Jobs ❷

Your Career Field: _____

List companies in your area in the first column, then use the right column to brainstorm about careers and jobs you might not have considered. See page 65 for examples.

Companies in your area	Brainstorm, then write down how you might use your skills in this company

Other interests you have that are outside of your career	Brainstorm, then write down how you might combine this interest with your career

In-Demand Industries	Brainstorm, then write down how you might use your skills in this industry

Add your completed work to the "About Me" section of your Career Builder Files.

This page is intentionally blank.

PHASE 2:
CREATE YOUR RESUME

Create Your Resume

PART 2 Learn how to plan and write winning resumes that capture prospective employers' attention and lead to interviews.

LISA MARK

MA Career and College Counselor, Employment Coach

Photo courtesy of William Mark.

ADVICE FROM THE EXPERT

Your Career Direction LLC

After 20 years in the recruiting industry, Lisa Mark launched her business, Your Career Direction. Her coaching and counseling practice helps students, underemployed recent graduates, and professionals discover and achieve their career direction. Her services include step-by-step career exploration, interview preparation, resume review, networking skills, and more.

From her extensive experience with resumes, Lisa emphasizes marketability over simply cataloging job history and says that "an effective resume is not a data dump of job responsibilities. It is a marketing document that presents your information in a professional, engaging and easy to read manner." One of the most common errors Lisa sees are "resumes that only list job responsibilities and lack accomplishments, are without any personal style, or make claims without specific facts to back up statements."

Previously, as a corporate recruiter, her process included "a quick scan of about 40 seconds, scanning the top, looking for a Professional Summary, then Job Titles, Company Names and technical skills, and career or industry related keywords. A second read was about 2–3 minutes and included business applications experience and depth of knowledge." She also comments that she "screened OUT rather than IN" using the job requirements. As a result, "the process was very objective." English errors also count significantly. Lisa says a resume with "one typo, maybe" would get an interview; however, "two, definitely not."

On the subject of cover letters, she again emphasizes the importance of sharing your personality, professionalism, and confidence. "The cover letter can be thought of as an appetizer to the main course, which is the resume. If the starter is tasteless, one would have no appetite for the entree."

When sending resumes to job posting sites, Lisa warns job seekers to be sure to apply in a timely fashion. "When using Internet posting sites, apply within 1–3 days of their posting. Understand that listings on aggregator sites such as Indeed are already 7–11 days old by the time they're posted." Lisa recommends that "niche sites are best, as are jobs posted on LinkedIn®, LinkedIn® Groups and Craigslist right now." Applicants can increase their chances greatly by applying directly to companies via company websites or networking.

Lastly, if looking for help with writing your resume, Lisa cautions you to do your research. "Only hire a professional who has knowledge of the current job market and the job search process. Be wary of 'free' resume writing scams and those who market themselves solely as 'Resume Writers' who will lack the comprehensive expertise most job seekers need in order to produce an effective resume."

PLAN for Success

Most successful people keep a calendar of activities and a running list of tasks they have committed to do. Make *Your Career* a part of your calendar and task list.

■ Read the outcomes on the first page of Chapters 4 and 5 and jot down a target date for completing each one. Allow extra time for those that require more than just reading.

■ Now make several calendar appointments with yourself to do the reading, homework, and projects for this class.

■ Consider your other commitments (other classes, work, home) as you plan to make *Your Career* happen for you!

TALES FROM THE JOB SEARCH

Abstract Coder

After a long career in pharmaceutical sales, Leslie felt it was time for a change. Because she felt burned out and wanted to shift to a more personally meaningful career, she sought additional education and achieved the Certified Professional Coder certification in the medical billing and coding field. However, she found the right education wasn't enough to land a job in her new career direction.

So she looked for assistance in writing her resume. She says having assistance helped her "identify my key skills and abilities and write my skills to fit the requirements of the job" as well as "write my accomplishments and how they will benefit a prospective employer." Talking to an expert helped her gain an objective outside perspective and display her history in an engaging way to prospective employers.

LESLIE KIRKLAND
CPC

After revising her resume, she received compliments from interviewers on her resume, including that her "resume was easy to read and understand." She also felt her resume "grabbed your attention."

She also used LinkedIn® during her job search and used her resume to create her profile. "I updated my entire profile for the job search," she said. She also went one step further to build her credibility and asked for recommendations. "My old manager wrote me a recommendation as well as a former client."

The best piece of advice Leslie received about resumes is to "keep it simple and remember it's a sales tool to sell yourself." Leslie finally landed a job in the medical billing department at a local hospital and feels one huge step closer to having a meaningful career.

4 Plan Your Resume

OVERVIEW

Creating a winning resume takes effort but will pay off when you are applying for jobs. Your resume must be organized, written, and formatted so that it represents your personal brand and passes screening by software, and by recruiters and Human Resources personnel. Chapter 4 helps you plan and gather the right information for each section of your resume and describes alternative uses for your resume.

OUTCOMES

1 Identify the purpose and role of a resume.

2 Describe the main sections of a winning resume.

3 Showcase your Personal Brand Statement using your resume as a foundation.

CAREER ACTION WORKSHEETS

4-1: Collect the Right Information, page 101

4-2: Resume Outline, page 103

4-3: Your Qualifications, page 105

4-4: Your Work Experiences, page 107

4-5: Organize Your Experience, page 109

WHERE ARE YOU ON THE JOURNEY?

PHASE 1: Prepare for the Journey
- *The Job Search Journey*
- *Know Yourself to Market Yourself*
- *Picture Yourself in the Workplace*

PHASE 2: Create Your Resume
- **Plan Your Resume**
- *Write Your Resume*

PHASE 3: Apply for Jobs
- *Find Job Openings*
- *Write Job Applications*
- *Write Effective Tailored Cover Letters*

PHASE 4: Shine at Interviews
- *Know the Interview Essentials*
- *Prepare for Your Interview*
- *Interview Like a Pro*

PHASE 5: Connect, Accept, and Succeed
- *Stay Connected with Prospective Employers*
- *It's an Iterative Process*
- *Take Charge of Your Career*

PHASE 2: Create Your Resume
Step 1, *Plan Your Resume*

You are in Phase 2, *Create Your Resume*, at step 1, *Plan Your Resume*. Your goal in this chapter is to understand the sections and purpose of a resume and to gather the right information to write your resume.

Resumes that win are planned. Nothing is typed without thought put into it—just as you should think before you speak, in the virtual world you must think before you type.

WHAT IS A RESUME?

A **resume** is a brief document, typically one or two pages, that details your qualifications for a particular job target. It is a record of your relevant work experience and education, and it is a tool for showcasing your personal brand to prospective employers and getting job interviews. Your resume is an evolving document that you will revise and rewrite as your experience and career goals change over time. Along with a strong networking strategy, a good resume is your key to getting an interview. (See Chapter 6 for more on job targets.)

The Role of Resumes in Warm Introductions versus Cold Leads

As you network or conduct Career Network meetings as described in Chapter 6, you generate a Warm Introduction to a prospective employer. Your Warm Introduction, that is, one of your networking contacts, can speak on your behalf and introduce you to opportunities, even if an official job listing doesn't exist. Warm introductions expect you to follow up by sending your resume after your initial meeting. Your resume can then be passed on to the prospective employer, along with personal comments from your networking contact about your interaction.

When your Warm Introductions pass on your resume, you get the added benefit of people who not only speak on your behalf to employers but who also can provide more personal information that simply doesn't appear in a written resume or submitted job applications. The format of your resume plays a very important part in making your Warm Introductions feel proud to pass on your resume to their colleagues and managers. Often, job seekers build great rapport in person but then write an average or inconsistent resume. It's important to provide a resume that your contacts feel confident to pass on to their organizations.

If you learn about a job opening through an online job board or application process, this is called a **Cold Lead**. Cold leads don't have a warm-bodied person who can intercede on your behalf. Consider the following steps that a typical large organization uses to process resumes received from job listings or Cold Leads and how they determine which applicants to interview:

1. Resume scanning software scans the many resumes received and stores the contents in a database for analysis, distribution, and retrieval. The software searches each resume for keywords and phrases that indicate a match with job requirements. The software flags resumes that appear to be a good fit.

2. Human resources staff members or external recruiters review the resumes selected by the software program. Resumes of the most qualified applicants are forwarded to departmental hiring managers. The other resumes are stored for future consideration and are typically deleted after six months.

3. The hiring managers review the resumes and choose applicants to interview based on the applicants' qualifications and whether they appear to be a good fit with the department's needs.

By the end of Phase 2 of your work in this book, you will have an effective resume that can be used in both Warm Introductions and Cold Leads.

Winning Resumes

Employers are always looking for the best match between their needs and applicants' qualifications when they select just a few people to interview. Your resume needs to compel the reader to want to learn more about you and to contact you for an interview. Try to get

Diana asked for feedback on her resume from a recruiter who mentioned that she needed more industry keywords. Diana did some research and made some updates. She also practiced verbally using the keywords when describing her skills and work experience. At her next Career Network meeting, she made sure to mention her experience in the context of these keywords. She was happy to be copied on an email sent to the contact's manager that stated, "Diana is very knowledgeable and up to date on the challenges and skills we need. Her resume is attached and shows experiences that I think would potentially make her a great fit with our company."

How can you improve your resume as a tool to be used in both Warm Introductions and Cold Leads?

as many Warm Introductions as you can. The more methods you use to build personal connections with a prospective employer, the more likely you will be contacted for an interview.

A compelling, winning resume often does the following:

- Introduces elements of your Personal Brand Statement and 30-Second Commercial that you developed in Chapter 2

- Tells a story, concisely and in compelling language; at a glance, a reviewer should be able to get a feel for your personal brand, strengths, and accomplishments

- Quickly shows that you have the qualifications for the job and can meet the employer's needs

- Contains keywords and phrases designed for resume scanning software and human reviewers

- Offers a professional image and an example of good written communication skills

A successful resume generates interviews for both Warm Introductions and Cold Leads.

PLAN YOUR RESUME CONTENT

Writing a great resume typically does not happen on the first try, and you want to write a great resume, one that gets you interviews. You begin by planning and developing a master resume that you can customize for different job listings, relationships, and events. In this section, you will learn about the most common organizational structure and sections used in resumes today.

Your goal is to create a professional-looking document that can be skimmed quickly for key information and read critically to reveal impressive details. You do not have to include everything. In fact you should NOT include everything! It is more important to be purposeful and focused on the top three or four things you want prospective employers to know about you and your experience. This shows your ability to articulate your strengths clearly and your respect for the employer's time.

In this chapter, you will gather your resume information and create a plan for what to include. In Chapter 5, you will write your resume.

In most situations, your resume is part of an Job Application Package that could include a cover letter, online social networking profile, recommendations, and a business card. Packages work well to get attention for both Cold Leads and Warm Introductions. Part 3, "Apply for Jobs," discusses using your Job Application Package to help you find job openings and apply.

▶ *CAREER ACTION*
Complete Worksheet 4-1
Collect the Right Information, page 101

Organize Your Resume

The way you organize your resume sections and details helps an employer quickly identify your most important skills, qualifications, and experience. The most common resume organization combines a focus on skills and timeline of work experience. For an overview of the sections and general layout, see Figure 4-1.

This resume organization style places equal emphasis on two key sections: the Qualifications section and the Work Experience section. The first two sections of the resume are your Contact Information and Professional Profile.

The *Qualifications* section highlights key skills that are relevant to your job target. The goal of this section is to support your personal brand by concisely identifying strengths, skills, and capabilities. The Qualifications section can contain a bulleted list of the skills you believe you have that set you apart from other applicants. Make it concise. Describe each of your skills using just three to five words.

In the *Work Experience* section, describe the timeline of your work experience in a way that shows both how your career has developed and how you have progressively built your skills. List each position you have held, starting with the most recent and going in reverse chronological order. Include the start and end dates, and stress your major accom-

plishments in each position. Avoid repeating details that are common to several positions. Be sure to describe results that were important to the organization; do not just list the tasks that you did.

The last two sections are the *Education* and *Optional* sections. View Figure 4-2 on page 90 for an example of the overall recommended organization of a resume. Learn more about each section of the resume in the next section.

> ▶ *CAREER ACTION*
> **Complete Worksheet 4-2**
> Resume Outline, page 103

Your Resume Sections

The following sections will fulfill the resume needs of most job seekers. Modify the section headings to best fit your experience and qualifications.

Contact Information

At the top of your resume, list your name, phone number, and email address. Follow these tips:

- Do not use the heading *Resume* or *Contact Information*. The contact information is the only section of a resume that does not have a heading.
- Center justify the information.
- Use the name you are best known by, such as Michael Hardesty, not Michael J. Hardesty III.
- Choose whether you want to include your mailing address. If you are applying for jobs locally, include your address below your name. If you are applying out of city or state, consider whether you expect the prospective employer to pay relocation expenses. If yes, include your address. If not, it may be wise to exclude your address.

Figure 4-1 Resume Outline

- Contact Information
- Professional Profile
- Qualifications
- Work Experience
- Education
- Optional Sections
  - Related Experience
  - Military Service

Figure 4-2 Sample Resume Layout

Note that the
1st statement is a clear
Employment Goal
and 2nd statement is a
strong Personal Brand
Statement related to the
Employment goal

✔ No more than 8-10
bullet points
✔ Contains Industry
keywords
✔ Contains both techni-
cal and transferable
"soft" skills
✔ Try to keep concise:
3-5 words per bullet
point

Note how Kimi
includes her volunteer
experience as work
experience because it
has significant relevant
soft and technical skills

Note the format: the
basic responsibilities
are listed first, then
the bullet points focus
on above and beyond
results Kimi achieved.

Kimi Okasaki

148 Barrister Street • Tucson, AZ 85726
(520) 555.0136 • kimi.okasaki@email.com • linkedin/in/kimi.okasaki

Professional Profile

Seeking Administrative Assistant position at mid-size organization. Detail-oriented professional with exceptional customer service, communication, and relationship building capability.

Qualifications

- Skilled Presentation, newsletter, and report designer
- Advanced software skills in MS Office,

- Adobe Acrobat, FTP, and Quickbooks
- Database design and maintenance using Access and Oracle

- Keyboarding at 75 words per minute
- Proven external relationship builder

Experience

Community Volunteer, Tucson, AZ   December 2009 to December 2011

Served as a volunteer in various roles for three well known organizations that contribute significantly to the community.

- **National Diabetes Foundation.** Reduced fundraising reporting time by 50% by developing and customizing Excel spreadsheet report to track three fund-raising activities
- **Secretary-Treasurer, Valley Elementary School Parent-Teacher Organization.** Designed and published monthly electronic newsletters for organization using MS Publisher.

  Passed yearly CPA audits with excellence through tracking of budget in QuickBooks Pro.

- **Meals on Wheels.** Developed and maintained Access database for survey responses from 1,200 participants.

Katz Department Store, Tucson, AZ   March 2009 to December 2010
Department Supervisor, Part-time.

Perform basic supervisor responsibilities, manage inventory, and meet target sales goals.

- Attained highest part-time sales volume through personalizing customer interactions
- Trained 4 new sales clerks who achieved target sales goals by end of first month using good coaching skills
- Had <5% losses on computing daily cash receipts, balancing registers, and coordinating weekly deliveries by using detailed organization systems and strategies

Value Variety, Tucson, AZ   Summers 2008, 2009
Sales Clerk

- Given positive feedback as a provider of complete customer service in sales and returns.

EDUCATION

Associate of Applied Science, A.S.A., 2012, Westfield Community College, Tucson, AZ
Major: **Administrative Office Technology**, GPA 3.6

- Provide one reliable phone number. Put the area code in parentheses to indicate that it is optional depending on where the user is calling from. (While it's on your mind, listen to your voice mail greeting. Do you state your name as you use it in your job search? Does your greeting sound professional?)

- Use an email address that won't get tossed out by an employer's spam filter. An address such as john.waters@email.com is professional and appropriate. Sk8trBoy@ email.com is not.

- Consider including your LinkedIn® URL or personal website URL if you have space.

- Omit a fax number. Fax machines have been largely replaced by email. If a prospective employer wants to fax a document later in the interview or hiring process, you can provide a number then.

- Avoid crowding your contact information, but also avoid making it so prominent that the rest of the resume looks compressed. Size 12 font should be the maximum used.

- If your resume is two pages, put your name and page number at the top of the second page. Include your email address and LinkedIn® URL if space permits, but do not repeat all of your contact information.

See Figure 4-3 for examples of how to format contact information.

Professional Profile

The *Professional Profile* is a two-sentence section that states your job target or objective and the Personal Brand Statement that you developed in Chapter 2.

The job target or objective:

- Can be stated as a job title or the type of work desired. For example: Medical Laboratory Technician; Office Manager for a travel agency.

- Can reflect the needs and skills stated in the job listing. For example: Health Information Technician position requiring the ability to perform detailed clerical tasks, to change priorities quickly, and to communicate well; Server position in an exclusive restaurant where knowledge of international cuisine is an added value.

- Can include one or more of your most important job-specific skills and areas of specialization. For example: Information Systems Analyst I position in a financial environment requiring system design, programming, investigation, reporting skills.

In large organizations, human resources professionals and the organization's resume scanning software will use your job target to know which job opening you are applying for.

The second statement is the Personal Brand Statement you developed in Chapter 2. Recall that your Personal Brand Statement showcases your greatest strengths, top transferable

Figure 4-3 Contact Information Examples

Appropriate Formatting	Inappropriate Formatting
Michael Hardesty (871) 424-9873 781 Right Road Iowa City, IA 52246 mhardesty@gmail.com linkedin.com/in/michaelhardesty	Michael J. Hardesty III (871) 424-9873 (home) (871) 547-2434 (cell) Iowa City, IA 52246 greathire@gmail.com

Figure 4-4 Examples of Well-Written Professional Profiles

Note how both of these examples follow the format discussed: Job target followed by the Personal Brand Statement.

Example 1: Gain employment as a master chef at a four star restaurant. Experienced master chef that excels in a high-stress, multiple-priority environment and adds new creative energy and flavor with knowledge of international cuisine.

Example 2: Seeking to serve as a welding technician in the utilities industry. Detail-oriented welder known for not only fixing the problem, but identifying additional needs with a strong passion for customer satisfaction.

skills, and personal qualities that you bring from your varied experiences and achievements throughout your career journey. This statement should clearly distinguish you from other applicants for the job. This statement typically remains the same for each job application, though you can choose to highlight different transferable skills for a specific job. See some examples in Figure 4-4.

Qualifications

The *Qualifications* section is a bulleted list of skills that ties together your work, volunteer, and education experience into a cohesive picture to highlight why you are the ideal candidate for the job. Limit yourself to the top 8 to 10 skills. Each skill should be described in no more than three to five words. Keep in mind that you will have to prove in the remainder of the resume that the qualifications you listed are valid. Because this section is a focal point for employers, use it to emphasize specific and relevant skills, capabilities, and related accomplishments such as the following:

- **Experience** in a specialized field and/or specialized skills. This would include tangible skills like Balancing Ledgers, Top Rated at Customer Service, and Precision Welder.

- **Transferable skills**. Briefly describe how the skills gained on previous jobs are relevant to the current job target. This would include soft skills such as Project Management, Customer Service, Strategic Decision Making, and Marketing Material Design.

- **Software skills**. Most jobs require use of software. If appropriate for the position you are applying for and your experience, list several applications you can use and your level of expertise with each. If your list is long, consider grouping the applications into categories labeled Master, Intermediate, and Basic, or by types of software with just a few examples of each. Employers today assume basic computer skills such as typing and word processing or keyboard skills, so if possible, don't list these. Instead, highlight knowledge you have in specialty applications such as Adobe Photoshop, Wordpress, or SAP. (Better yet, set aside time during your job search to take free online tutorials to increase your skills.)

- **Language skills**. Many employers value employees who can communicate in more than one language. If English is not your first language, list your first language as one in which you are fluent. For example: Multilingual: Fluent in English and Spanish, limited conversational French, and reading-only Italian. You can also list TOEFL scores for any language, be it your first or adopted language.

Alternate titles for the *Qualifications* section are Qualifications Summary, Skills Summary, and Career-Related Skills; or, for business and technical careers, Core Competencies. Regardless of the name, spend time crafting a list of concise statements of your skills that let the employer know you are capable of doing the job.

Look back at your completed Career Action Worksheet 2-2 and Career Action Worksheet 2-3 to review your qualifications, skills, and key personal traits. List them in order of importance as they relate to your job target. For example, if you are applying for a position with a doctor's office, start with skills you have learned in your medical courses and your emergency medical volunteer work.

Format the Qualifications section as a bulleted list to draw attention to each item. In the appropriate section of your resume (Work Experience, Education, and/or Related Activities), provide proof of the qualifications you have listed in the Qualifications section.

 CAREER ACTION

Complete Worksheet 4-3
Your Qualifications, page 105

Work Experience

In the *Work Experience* section of a resume, list the jobs you have held, starting with the most recent one, and go backward. Follow these steps to create a well-written summary for each of your work experiences:

1. First, list your job title and dates of employment.

2. On the next line, list the name of the organization.

3. Starting on the third line, write a brief results-oriented description of your basic job responsibilities in one to two sentences.

4. Then create bullet points that focus on what you accomplished above and beyond the base expectations. Follow these tips for writing strong bullet points:

   - **Use the WHI method to provide consistent structure.** In Chapter 2, you learned the WHI method: *what* you did, *how* you did it, and its *importance*. Each bullet point should describe a single achievement using the WHI method. In a single sentence, describe the importance of the achievement you made using quantifiable business results, describe what the task was, and end with how you specifically contributed or delivered the result.

   - **Measurable examples.** Give specific, measurable examples of your accomplishments—such as increased sales,

---

MAKE IT A HABIT
Keep Your Skills Inventory up to Date

During your job search and throughout your career, you will want to update your inventory of skills. Get into the habit of reassessing your skills and accomplishments twice a year. As you develop new skills and gain more experience, training, and education, your goals will change or expand.

Repeating the self-analysis activities in this chapter at turning points in your career will also help you identify your skills and see where you could strengthen your skills to set you apart from other job applicants. You can then seek the training and experience you need to help ensure that you will continue to be an asset to employers and will grow in your career.

decreased costs, and reduced errors—ideally with a percentage, a specific dollar figure, the number of items sold, and so on. For example: Increased sales by 45% through skillful negotiation and sales ability with automotive clients. Note the use of WHI. The *what* and *importance* are combined in the statement "Increased sales by 45%"; the remainder focuses on the *how*.

- **Your role in teamwork.** If you worked as a part of a team and do not have a specific result attributed to you as an individual, state your role on the team, what the team's result was, and what you specifically did to aid in achieving the team's result.

- **Highlight promotions or multiple jobs with same employer.** If you have held increasingly more responsible jobs with one employer, show this to demonstrate your reliability and your ability to learn and achieve on the job. List only new responsibilities and accomplishments for each promotion or job title.

- **Little work experience.** If you have little work experience, list your part-time and summer work, internships, school projects, volunteer work, and community involvement. Even if the title does not relate directly to your job target, emphasize the transferable accomplishments and skills you developed.

See Figure 4-5 for an example of well-written and organized work experience.

All your examples should demonstrate work experience, transferable skills learned, and initiative. Employers consider these qualities real pluses, particularly for entry-level applicants. Furthermore, they demonstrate work ethic, an important quality discussed in Chapter 3.

Review Figure 4-2: Sample Resume Layout on page 90 one more time. This time, pay close attention to the language used in the *Professional Profile, Qualifications, and Work Experience* sections and how well they follow the guidelines you just learned.

> ▶ **CAREER ACTION**
> **Complete Worksheet 4-4**
> Your Work Experiences, page 107

Figure 4-5 Work Experience Example

Job Title
Parking Garage Cashier

Employment Dates
Jan-Jun 2014

Employer Name
University Parking Services

Basic Job Duties
Process payments at university parking garage

Above and beyond achievements using WHI format

- Successfully learned cashier process in less than 3 days by observation, trial, and reviewing manuals

- Recognized for 0 missed days, excellent attendance, and on-time behavior by managing schedule well

Education

List your education in reverse chronological order (most recent first). List the technical schools, colleges, and universities you have attended, the years of attendance, and the degree(s) you earned. Include relevant certifications, specialized training, and seminars.

If your overall GPA or your GPA in your concentration area is high and you graduated with honors, include this information on your resume.

Optional Resume Sections

Add the following sections if they are appropriate for your situation.

Related Experience

Use this section to highlight other experience that relates to your job objective. Include activities such as memberships, awards, and leadership positions earned in professional or trade associations; honorary groups; and social, service, and school organizations. Use similar formatting as in the Work Experience section. For the bullet

Real World Scenario **4-2** Louis knew the job target he was going for: marketing specialist. However, when he looked at his recent college experience, he wasn't sure what he was bringing to the table and how to "wow" prospective employers. He reviewed his previous part-time jobs and school projects to find common themes and inspiration. As he thought back to his experiences, one thing he began to notice was that he was typically the one who had the "creative eye." He recalled that on numerous occasions, people would listen to him and follow his lead when it came to design elements. To help him plan his *Professional Profile* and *Qualifications* sections, he made a list of the themes he found.
What themes related to your work style and strengths have you noticed from your experiences?

points, highlight the role and key projects you were involved in.

Instead of the heading Related Experience, consider a heading that may be more appropriate for your achievements and

© Tyler Olson/Shutterstock.com.

CAUTION
Never Lie or Stretch the Truth on Your Resume

If you can't prove it, it doesn't belong on your resume.

It is *never* acceptable to lie or stretch the truth about your work experience. Employers can and do verify facts on your resume (including degrees, job titles, and dates of employment) and will contact your references. If you are caught in a lie,

you will gain a bad reputation and will have no chance of being hired.

Even if you get away with a lie and are hired, the truth has a way of coming out. When your employer discovers the truth, you can be fired.

experiences, such as Awards and Honors, Volunteer Work, Community Service, Certificates, Activities, or Professional Associations.

Military Service

Include any military experience that is relevant to your job target, emphasizing relevant training, responsibilities, and accomplishments. Highlight any rapid progressions, significant promotion(s), and special commendations.

Consider listing your military record in its own section if it is significant; you can also list it in the Work Experience section. Translate any military jargon into terminology that your readers will understand—and that showcases your relevant qualifications. Make sure to define acronyms and focus on the skills you learned, instead of the specific tasks. Many civilians cannot relate to or understand specific military tasks but can easily understand leadership, strategic decision making under pressure, teamwork, and other skills as being important to the workplace.

Personal Information

In most cases, resumes should not include personal information such as your age and marital status. Fair employment laws prohibit employers from requesting such information. Do not include your photograph; to avoid charges of discrimination, many employers will not consider a resume that includes a photo. The only exception to this rule is a position that requires a certain appearance, such as modeling.

If your job target is in the field of nutrition, physical fitness, or sports and you want to provide relevant information about your own health consciousness, fitness level, or suitability for an active job, do so in a Related Experience section with the name Activities and Awards or something similar. In that section, you can list hobbies and/or accomplishments such as these:

- Completed two marathons in 2011
- Finalist in Eat Your Veggies Recipe Competition, Charleston WV, 2011
- Cofounded running team at Northside Montessori, 2010

SHOWCASE YOUR PERSONAL BRAND

Your resume is the foundation for the many tools used to find job leads and apply for jobs. Getting your resume right allows you to solidify your message to prospective employers and repackage it for multiple uses.

Gather Information

How can you get your resume right? Now that you understand the purpose and sections of the resume, start collecting the right data as you begin writing. Follow these strategies as you gather information:

- **Organize and prioritize.** As you review the Career Action Worksheets, note which experiences, skills, projects, and capabilities have the most "wow" factor.

- **Revise language.** Do your descriptions present your experience in the best, most concise way? Take time to draft more powerful language.

- **Collect evidence.** For the experiences and skills you want to highlight, find any related documents or presentations. Use these to help remind you of important details that you can add to your resume.

Group your best information for each section. When you gather and organize the right information, writing the resume is a faster, easier process.

> ▶ *CAREER ACTION*
> **Complete Worksheet 4-5**
> Organize Your Experience, page 109

References

When you are selected for a job interview, your prospective employer will likely check your references. A job **reference** is a person who can and will vouch for your capabilities, skills, and suitability for a job. References are typically people who have been your instructors and coaches in school or your managers or coworkers in volunteer and paid work environments.

Identify people with whom you have a good relationship and who can confirm (from first-hand observation) your performance on the job, in school, or in other activities. Relatives and classmates are not appropriate references.

The more references you have available, the better prepared you will be for your job search. Many employers request three references they can contact before making a job offer. With a large list of references, you can use the most helpful references for each job you interview for. For example, if one of your references knows someone at a company you are targeting, you can use that person as a reference when you apply for a job there. If you are qualified to work in two career fields, such as retail sales and accounting, ask people in each field to be your references.

Do not assume that a person will agree to be a reference for you. Always ask (and get) permission before using anyone as a reference. Ask if it is okay to share their email and/or phone contact information with employers.

Your references do not belong on your resume. It is unnecessary to state "References available upon request." However, make sure to plan ahead! Make a list of your references' names, titles, and phone numbers and take it to interviews. To protect your references' privacy, do not put your references' names or contact information on your resume or a job application. A typical reference sheet is available on the companion website for this textbook.

Set Up Your LinkedIn® Profile

Make a plan to put your resume on LinkedIn®. As a starting point, create a username and fill out the basics of the profile. The LinkedIn® profile wizard guides you step

Get Effective Recommendation Letters

Written letters of recommendation are an impressive addition to your Job Application Package. Ask the people who agree to be a reference for you and who are most enthusiastic about your job performance, qualifications, skills, and/or abilities if they are willing to write a recommendation letter.

You are more likely to get a positive answer if you can give the person written starter information for the letter. Give the person your resume and a summary of strengths or skills you would like them to cover so that they have concrete information to work with.

File your recommendation letters in the Master Career Portfolio section of your Career Builder Files.

by step through the process. Later, you can experiment with different language to see what resonates most with your network connections.

Also consider asking for recommendations. As part of your plan to create a LinkedIn® profile, plan to ask for recommendations. Receiving a recommendation is similar to receiving a reference except that the former is published and viewable to anyone as part of your LinkedIn® profile. It is considerate to give your network connections at least two weeks to write a recommendation.

For more information on using LinkedIn®—including step-by-step instructions—during your Job Search Journey, view Appendix A.

Align Your Business Card

This is a great time to prepare for networking to find job leads. It often takes seven to 10 business days to print and receive business cards. Using your business card during networking shows professionalism and can be another place to showcase your personal brand. Sites like Vistaprint and Moo offer a variety of business card templates. View the inspiration gallery at Moo to get some ideas for how to make your business

Figure 4-6 Sample Business Card

Front

Kimi Okasaki

**Your detail-oriented, relationship building
Administrative Assistant**

(520) 555.0136
kimi.okasaki@email.com   linkedin/in/kimi.okasaki

Back

Highlights

• Newsletter and Communication Management
• Connector and Relationship Builder
• Access, Oracle, and Quickbooks Experience

card impactful. Also consider the examples shown in Figure 4-6.

By now, you should understand the value of a resume for use with both Warm Introductions and Cold Leads. You should also understand the sections of a resume and have organized your information enough to begin (in Chapter 5) writing this all-important part of your Job Application Package.

You, Online

Building Your LinkedIn® Profile

LinkedIn® was launched in 2003 with the mission of being a place where members can showcase their professional identity and gain insights into the professional world. Today it is the job seeker's most useful social media tool. According to JobVite's 2013 Social Recruiting Survey, 78 percent of recruiters have hired through a social media. Of those hires, 92 percent have come from LinkedIn®.

If you don't have a LinkedIn® profile, create one today. You can use your resume as the starting point for building your profile:

• Copy and paste your Professional Profile into the Summary section of your LinkedIn® profile. Expand further if you would like.
• Copy and paste your job experience by Adding Positions under the Experience section of your LinkedIn® profile.
• You can also add Awards and Honors, Education, Organizations, and Skills to your profile.

For more details and ways to use LinkedIn®, refer to Appendix A.

Chapter Checklist

Check off each item you can do. Reread sections in this chapter to help you complete the checklist.

- ☐ Describe how to use my resume differently with Warm Introductions and with Cold Leads. **①**
- ☐ Know the requirements for a winning resume. **①**
- ☐ Describe the overall layout and sections of a resume. **②**
- ☐ Understand the format and content needed for each section of the resume. **②**
- ☐ Gather the appropriate information from my Career Builder Files to prepare for writing my resume. **③**
- ☐ Request references from the right people in my network. **③**
- ☐ Start building my LinkedIn® profile. **③**
- ☐ Plan to order business cards. **③**

Critical Thinking Questions

1. Why are Warm Introductions more effective than Cold Leads? **①**
2. What characteristics of your resume are reviewed by software programs when you pursue Cold Leads? **①**
3. Why is having a Professional Profile recommended over a simple Objective statement? **②**
4. What skills should be highlighted in the Qualification section? **②**
5. What is the purpose of the bullet points in the Work Experience section? **②**
6. Why is it important to be purposeful about the experiences and strengths you highlight on the resume? **②**
7. What other ways can you use the information in your resume to showcase your personal brand? **③**

Additional Resources

For data files, career resources, and more, visit www.cengagebrain.com.

Trial Run

Review Online Resumes

A good way to get started on creating a resume is to review sample resumes online. However, these samples are only guidelines and are not intended to be used as shown. They are intended to be evaluated, revised, reorganized, and reformatted to fit a job seeker's skills and career objective.

Search the Internet for free sample resumes in your career area. Choose one that is relevant to your job target and evaluate it. Listing the changes needed to make the resume better fit your qualifications and experience and to fit the guidelines in this chapter.

Copy and paste the text of the sample resume into a word processing file and make the necessary revisions.

Edit the revised resume for mistakes and typos. Pair up with a classmate and exchange resumes for peer editing.

Evaluate resumes on the following elements:

Rating Scale: 1 to 4 (1 = not really; 2 = sometimes/somewhat; 3 = usually; 4 = definitely)

_____ A. The Objective or Professional Profile includes the job title or required abilities specified by the employer.

_____ B. Qualifications contain keywords that match requirements for the job.

_____ C. Qualifications are relevant to the stated job objective. Major strengths are included. Each job listing contains the employer's name and address (city and state) and job title.

_____ D. Each job listing describes responsibilities and specific, measurable accomplishments.

_____ E. Job descriptions use power words and keyword nouns that support the objective.

_____ F. If work experience is limited, relevant paid and nonpaid internships and volunteer or other pertinent activities are included.

_____ G. The applicant emphasizes courses, internships, degrees, certificates, and so on that best support the objective.

_____ H. The overall GPA or GPA in the concentration area is included (if impressive).

_____ I. The applicant emphasizes involvement in professional and other organizations that support the job objective.

_____ J. Relevant awards, achievements, and offices held are included.

_____ K. The overall design is appealing.

_____ L. The resume tells a personal, compelling story.

_____ M. The content is correct (grammar, spelling, and punctuation).

▶ CAREER ACTION WORKSHEET
4-1 Collect the Right Information ❶

Use the checklist below to collect all the right files from your Career Builder Files for planning your resume. Read through them and update if needed.

- ☐ CAW 2-1 **Education, Training, and Activities Inventory**
- ☐ CAW 2-2 **Experience and Skills Inventory**
- ☐ CAW 2-3 **Personal Qualities Inventory**
- ☐ CAW 2-5 **Develop Your Personal Brand Statement**

List below other information you want to collect and read before you begin writing your resume.

This page is intentionally blank.

▶ *CAREER ACTION WORKSHEET*
4-2 Resume Outline ❷

You are about to create your draft resume.

PART A: Create an outline—resume sections and headings only—for your resume using this worksheet (here or on the product website) or on a word processing document.

PART B: Fill in as much of your information as you can from the documents you collected in Career Action Worksheet 4-1. Don't fill out the Qualifications or Work Experience sections yet. You will focus on these critical sections in later worksheets.

Name _____

Mailing Address _____ (Optional)

Email Address _____ LinkedIn® URL _____

Phone Number _____ Website URL _____

PROFESSIONAL PROFILE (*State your current employment target and the Personal Brand Statement you developed in* Chapter 2.)

QUALIFICATIONS (*Use terms and keywords that are related to your target job to describe your capabilities and accomplishments.*)

WORK EXPERIENCE (*State your accomplishments in measurable terms whenever possible. Start with the most recent job and list each job in reverse chronological order, ending with your earliest work experience. If you have little actual work experience, list internships, volunteer work, and school projects in this section. Adjust the headings as needed, for example, substituting the school, class, or organization name in place of company name.*)

Company Name _____

Dates of Employment _____

Job Title _____

Company Name _____

Dates of Employment _____

Job Title _____

Company Name _____

Dates of Employment _____

Job Title _____

Company Name _____

Dates of Employment _____

Job Title _____

EDUCATION (*If you have attended more than one school, list the schools in reverse chronological order—the most recent one first. Do not list high school if you have higher-level schooling, unless the high school is considered very prestigious.*)

Name of School	Major(s)/ Minor(s)	Overall GPA GPA in concentration area	Degree(s)/ Certificate(s)	Years Attended
_____	_____	_____ _____	_____	_____
_____	_____	_____	_____	_____
_____	_____	_____	_____	_____

RELATED ACTIVITIES/EXPERIENCE (*Include internships, volunteer work, service clubs, organizations, tutoring, class projects, honor groups, internships, leadership positions, awards and honors, associations and memberships, and so on. List the name of the program or organization and the dates you were involved. Briefly summarize your experience, accomplishments, and activities.*)

MILITARY SERVICE (*List branch of service, highest rank, training, areas of specialization, major duties, skills and knowledge developed, honors, location of service, and discharge status.*)

Add your completed work to the "About Jobs" section of your Career Builder Files.

▶ *CAREER ACTION WORKSHEET*
4-3 Your Qualifications ❷

PART A: Create an initial list of your strengths that could be included in the Qualifications section. Select strengths that you believe would set you apart from other applicants and/or uniquely define you.

List 10 to 15 areas in which you have expertise and then summarize each area concisely in three to five words.

Strength, Capability, or Expertise Area	Concise Three- to Five-Word Description
Example: For an administrator—Looking at large amounts of data and organizing it so it is easy to read	Logical Visualizer of Data
Ex. For a sales professional—Talking to people in a way that makes them feel comfortable to tell me their real problems	Empathetic, Persuasive Marketer
1.	
2.	
3.	
4.	
5.	
6.	

continued

continued

7.	
8.	
9.	
10.	
11.	
12.	
13.	
14.	
15.	

PART B: Revise the outline of the resume you created in Career Action Worksheet 4-3 to include your qualifications.

▶ *CAREER ACTION WORKSHEET*
4-4 Your Work Experiences ❷

PART A: Practice writing your work experience using the WHI format. Choose three previous experiences, either work experiences or experience from a school project or organization if you have little work experience.

Example:

Department Supervisor, Part-Time

Katz Department Store   March 2012 to December 2012

Perform basic supervisor responsibilities, manage inventory, and meet target sales goals.

- Attained highest part-time sales volume through personalizing customer interactions
- Trained 4 new sales clerks who achieved target sales goals by end of first month using good coaching skills
- Had <5% losses on computing daily cash receipts, balancing registers, and coordinating weekly deliveries by using detailed organization systems and strategies

Create three bullets for each work experience using this formula:

Achieved (important result) _____ for (project or organization) _____ by (how did you do it) _____

Work Experience #1:

Job/Role Title: _____

Organization Name: _____

Basic Job Duties or Assigned Task: _____

- Achieved _____ for _____
  by _____

- Achieved _____ for _____
  by _____

- Achieved _____ for _____
  by _____

Work Experience #2:

Job/Role Title: _____

Organization Name: _____

Basic Job Duties or Assigned Task: _____

- Achieved _____ for _____
  by _____

- Achieved _____ for _____
  by _____

- Achieved _____ for _____
  by _____

Work Experience #3:

Job/Role Title: _____

Organization Name: _____

Basic Job Duties or Assigned Task: _____

- Achieved _____ for _____
  by _____

- Achieved _____ for _____
  by _____

- Achieved _____ for _____
  by _____

PART B: Revise the outline of the resume you created in Career Action Worksheet 4-3 to include your work experiences.

▶ CAREER ACTION WORKSHEET
4-5 Organize Your Experience ❸

PART A: Look at each of your work and related experiences collected in Career Action Worksheet 4-1, Career Action Worksheet 4-2, and Career Action Worksheet 4-4 in greater detail. Identify which achievements you would like to highlight for each work experience and put them in order by "wow" factor. Note any evidence you have to support the achievement. Evidence can be presentations, reports, positive feedback received, and so on.

Work Experience 1: _____(Job title)

Project Achievement 1: _____

    Evidence: _____

Project Achievement 2: _____

    Evidence: _____

Project Achievement 3: _____

    Evidence:_____

Work Experience 2: _____(Job title)

Project Achievement 1: _____

    Evidence: _____

Project Achievement 2: _____

    Evidence: _____

Project Achievement 3: _____

    Evidence:_____

Work Experience 3: _____(Job title)

Project Achievement 1: _____

    Evidence: _____

Project Achievement 2: _____

    Evidence: _____

Project Achievement 3: _____

    Evidence:_____

Add your completed work to the "About Jobs" section of your Career Builder Files.

PART B: Revise the resume outline you started in Career Action Worksheet 4-2 to include all of your work experiences, in chronological order. Each bullet point under each experience should be prioritized by what you want the employer to see first and written using the WHI format. Later, when you are preparing for interviews, your list of evidence will help you collect the right documents to take to an interview so that you have physical evidence to support your achievements as you discuss them with an interviewer. **You should now have a first draft of your resume**.

Add your updated first draft resume to the "About Jobs" section of your Career Builder Files.

Write Your Resume

OVERVIEW

Now that you have gathered the right information, Chapter 5 shows you how to transform the evidence of your experience, skills, and achievements into an effective resume that tells a personal story. Use the activities in this chapter to prepare and evaluate a resume draft, revise it, and format your print and plain text resumes. You will then be ready to apply for jobs through both Warm Introductions and Cold Leads.

OUTCOMES

1. Write your resume.
2. Edit your resume.
3. Format your resume for web and print.

CAREER ACTION WORKSHEETS

WHERE ARE YOU ON THE JOURNEY?

PHASE 1: Prepare for the Journey
- *The Job Search Journey*
- *Know Yourself to Market Yourself*
- *Picture Yourself in the Workplace*

PHASE 2: Create Your Resume
- *Plan Your Resume*
- **Write Your Resume**

RESUM

PHASE 3: Apply for Jobs
- *Find Job Openings*
- *Write Job Applications*
- *Write Effective Tailored Cover Letters*

PHASE 4: Shine at Interviews
- *Know the Interview Essentials*
- *Prepare for Your Interview*
- *Interview Like a Pro*

PHASE 5: Connect, Accept, and Succeed
- *Stay Connected with Prospective Employers*
- *It's an Iterative Process*
- *Take Charge of Your Career*

PHASE 2: Create Your Resume
Step 2, *Write Your Resume*

You are in Phase 2, *Create Your Resume*, at step 2, *Write Your Resume*. Your goal in this chapter is to write a powerful, effective resume.

You are the expert on yourself. What could be easier than writing about something you know about very well? It's up to you to decide how to show the best of yourself

WRITE YOUR RESUME

Once you have determined the appropriate sections and gathered all the data for your resume, the next step is to thoughtfully write each section. Your goal is to demonstrate convincing evidence of your experience, highlight your unique personality, and provide a concise, cohesive picture of what an employer should expect of you as an employee. You will learn the following strategies to write a powerful resume:

1. Be purposeful.
2. Use specific examples.
3. Use action verbs.
4. Use keywords strategically.

You will then edit and format your resume and by the end of this chapter, you will have a resume you can be proud to use as you apply for jobs in Phase 3 of your Job Search Journey.

Think about the different sections of a resume (Chapter 4). Each of the four strategies can be used in each section. For example, you can use action verbs in both the Qualifications section as well as when discussing your Work Experience. Consider how each strategy can be applied to each section of your resume. Start by writing your Professional Profile, and apply each of these four strategies.

▶ **CAREER ACTION**
Complete Worksheet 5-1
Write a Stronger Professional Profile, page 133

Be Purposeful

Don't include in your resume every task you were ever assigned to do. Instead, be purposeful about what you will include—and more importantly, what you will exclude—

Real World Scenario 5-1 Ben was struggling with writing his Professional Profile. He felt like there was so much he could say about his strengths and experience that it was difficult to be concise. He wanted to demonstrate how hard and fast he worked by listing all the things he does at his current part-time job. His advisor reminded him that he should focus on the most important things and look for what words could be eliminated. So Ben brainstormed with a few friends to come up with a general description of what he does that would tell the reader that he works hard and fast. He was happy with his final statement: "Works with sufficient speed and excellence demonstrated by the reduction in his shift team size by one person compared to other shift teams."
How can you describe your strengths in a powerful, concise statement?

---

from each section. Review the draft resume you created through the Career Action Worksheets in Chapter 4. For example, if you are targeting a job for a career in accounting, you probably don't need to mention the marketing display design skills you've picked up in your retail jobs, but you might want to include the organization, prioritization, and customer service skills.

For each of your Work Experiences and Related Experiences (education, volunteer, organization, etc.), select just three to five bullet points of the most relevant, impactful experiences that showcase your skills and strengths. As you purposefully choose your bullet points, look for common themes in skills, strengths, and capabilities. Do certain skills come up in multiple work or project experiences? List these skills and strengths and compare them to what you included in Career Action Worksheet 2-2. These skills and strengths form a great start to a purposefully created Qualifications section, especially because you know they are supported by Work Experience examples.

Remember, this is a time for you to craft what you want a prospective employer to see of your history. You can craft this story to highlight successes you've had in both school and work and separate your achievements from mundane, ordinary tasks. That is what will help you stand out from other applicants!

> ▶ *CAREER ACTION*
> **Complete Worksheet 5-2**
> Revise Your Qualifications List, page 135

Use Specific Examples

Once you know what examples you will focus on and highlight for the Work and Related Experience sections, use specific terms to describe your accomplishments. Notice how the specific statements below are more impactful:

General/Vague	Specific
Reduced costs significantly	Reduced costs by 20%
The leading producer	Top producer of 30 employees

The most persuasive resumes describe the applicants' accomplishments with numbers, percentages, and dollar amounts to emphasize how the accomplishments can meet the prospective employers' needs. Use numbers whenever possible to enhance the credibility of your achievements.

It also helps to describe how those results were achieved. Notice how the numbers and further explanation in the example below strengthen the accomplishments further:

- Processed more orders than any other member of the 10-person work team

- Processed 40% more orders than any other member of the team of 10 by creating an efficient process and by leveraging organizational skills

Remember the WHI format you learned in Chapters 2 and 4: **What** you did, **How** you did it, and the **Importance**. Use the WHI format as you finalize the Work Experience section of your resume. It may help to review Career Action Worksheet 4-4.

> ▶ *CAREER ACTION*
> **Complete Worksheet 5-3**
> Strengthen Your Work Experiences, page 137

Use Action Verbs

Review what you've written so far for your Professional Profile and Work Experiences. For each bullet point, have you used action verbs? **Action verbs** suggest a *state of powerful motion* in comparison to "Being" verbs that suggest a *state of existence* (*am, is, are, was, were*).

For example, for a nurse position, try saying "saw patients" instead of "patients were seen." Taking it a step further, try using powerful action verbs such as "provided care to patients," not "saw patients" or "patients were provided care." Action verbs show that you take initiative, and they convey a stronger image of your achievements and contributions. Notice how both examples below use quantifiable results, but the second example with active verbs is more impactful.

- With 95% confidence, statistical data was analyzed by using Excel software

- Analyzed and reported statistical data at a 95% confidence level using Excel software

By using action verbs, you call the reader's attention to the actions and skills you are demonstrating through your experience.

Another type of verb to avoid are "Helping" verbs such as *have, had, may,* or *might.* For example, say "managed" instead of "have managed." Helping verbs sound weaker and can hurt your credibility. They imply you have done something in the far away past, instead of still having a skill today.

Figure 5-1 has a list of common action verbs. Select verbs that convey your qualifications most *powerfully.* Look at the bullet points you wrote using the WHI format. Now, look at the verbs you used. Are there more powerful, active verbs you can use?

Compare the first two examples below and notice the use of more specific action verbs in the second example.

Okay: **Started** inventory tracking system, saving time and increasing efficiency

Stronger: **Designed** and **implemented** inventory tracking system, saving time and increasing efficiency

Designed and *implemented* clearly describe the applicant's scope of responsibility and convey a greater sense of accomplishment. Here are two more strong examples:

Strong: **Raised $55,000** and **organized** and **trained** volunteers for citywide elder-help campaign

Strong: **Reduced** final ballot processing time by 25% by coordinating school's student body elections

Use Keywords Strategically

Resume scanning applications are used by employers to narrow down the number of resumes they receive. The applications

Figure 5-1 Examples of Resume Action Verbs

accomplish	conduct	evaluate	manage	prove	select
adapt	consolidate	examine	monitor	provide	sell
administer	control	execute	motivate	publish	serve
advise	coordinate	expand	negotiate	purchase	setup
analyze	create	expedite	obtain	raise	solve
approve	customize	forecast	operate	rate	specialize
arrange	delegate	formulate	order	recommend	start
assemble	deliver	generate	organize	reconcile	streamline
assess	demonstrate	guide	originate	record	strengthen
audit	design	handle	overhaul	redesign	structure
budget	detect	identify	oversee	reduce	study
build	develop	implement	participate	reorganize	summarize
catalog	diagnose	improve	perform	repair	supervise
change	diagram	increase	plan	report	support
clarify	direct	inspect	prepare	represent	teach
coach	discover	install	present	research	test
collaborate	distribute	instruct	process	resolve	track
collect	draft	integrate	produce	respond	train
communicate	earn	introduce	program	review	update
compile	edit	investigate	promote	revise	upgrade
complete	eliminate	lead	propose	schedule	validate
compute	establish	maintain	protect	screen	write

© iQoncept/Shutterstock.com.

CAUTION
Save It for the Interview

Be careful not to put yourself out of the running for an interview by placing something unnecessary on your resume. It is not necessary to volunteer negative information about yourself. For instance, if you were fired from a job, do not indicate this fact on your resume. If necessary, discuss it during an interview, where you will have an opportunity to explain the situation.

Likewise, reserve any discussion of salary, wages, or compensation until you have had adequate opportunity to discuss your qualifications in an interview. Placing a monetary requirement on a resume could eliminate you from a job or seriously weaken your negotiating position. If employers ask for and insist on your compensation expectations, use broad numbers (the mid-thirty thousands, for example) and indicate that this is negotiable. Look at Chapter 10 to learn more about answering difficult questions.

look for **keywords**—terms that represent the qualifications the company has programmed the software to search for. The software searches for applicants with the required skills, knowledge, and capabilities for a position.

Employers will also search for these keywords when they read resumes. Think of keywords as the magnets that pull employers' attention to your resume. Strive to include as many appropriate keywords in your Professional Profile, Qualifications, and Work Experience sections as possible.

Keywords specify attributes that qualified applicants must have. Appropriate keywords for your job target include industry terminology and specific words or short phrases that are in job descriptions and ads.

Review the websites and publications of companies and professional associations in your career field to identify relevant keywords. These words describe employer-valued qualifications. Use the following list of sources to help identify appropriate keywords to include in your resume.

- Job listings and descriptions for positions you are considering (print or online)
- Websites of employers you are considering
- Government publications such as the *Occupational Outlook Handbook* (print or online)
- Job titles
- Skills and specialties
- Education, certifications, licenses, and course work
- Computer/software/hardware skills and specialized tools
- Industry buzzwords, jargon, and acronyms
- Professional associations in your field (check their websites, publications, and meetings)

Include keywords throughout your resume and repeat critical keywords. The more keywords the resume-search software identifies, the more likely it is that your resume will be

You, Online

Internet Resources

Just as no two resumes are the same, resume guidelines vary widely and are constantly changing. The Internet is a rich resource for staying on top of resume trends and locating additional resume writing and formatting suggestions. As you continue to revise and fine-tune your resume, use your favorite search engine to:

- Research resume strategies.
- Find answers to specific resume questions.
- Search for writing and formatting guidelines.

- Find examples of power words and industry keywords.
- Access sample resumes, content ideas, and templates from different careers.
- Locate resume consulting services.
- Find resume-posting sites and services.
- Investigate quality sites that offer useful resume development advice. See the links at the companion website.

Well-established sites like Indeed, Monster, CareerBuilder, and About also have helpful articles related to resume writing strategies.

selected and you will be considered for an interview.

Employers may use different terms in their search criteria, so use synonyms for keywords (for example, *budget* as a synonym for *forecast* and *supervisor* for *manager*). Include the abbreviation and the full name of your degree, as in *B.A.* and *Bachelor of Arts.*

Resume-search programs typically seek nouns. For example, in searching for AutoCAD drafters, the software may look for nouns (and

noun synonyms) such as *CAD, engineer, AA degree, certified drafter, Computer-Aided Drafting, AutoCAD, wiring diagrams,* and *physics.*

Figure 5-2 has examples of typical keywords used to select resumes to fill two positions.

> ▶ **CAREER ACTION**
> **Complete Worksheet 5-4**
> Resume Action Verbs and Keywords, page 139

Figure 5-2 Sample Keyword Search Terms

Position Title	Sample Keywords	Position Title	Sample Keywords
Accountant	CPA, audit, accounting, accounts receivable/payable, statistics, spreadsheet, finance, systems training, computer, database, team player, B.B.A. Accounting, accurate, project leader, customer relations, accounting database, tax code, ethics, Sarbanes-Oxley compliance, data integrity	Web-based training developer	e-learning, WBT, instructional design, distance learning, synchronous, asynchronous, ADDIE, training, project management, Lectora, Flash, Sharepoint, Dreamweaver, CourseBuilder, Centra, SCORM, Section 508, DeBabelizer, Director, Captivate, Acrobat, LMS, SABA, SumTotal, Illustrator, Photoshop, PageMaker, Persuasion, Fireworks, Premiere, Sound Forge, Movie Maker, Javascript, SQL, Lingo

EDIT YOUR RESUME

By now, you should have completed the second draft of your resume. Now it's time to review, clean up any errors you see, and learn how to customize it for particular job listings.

Common Grammar Mistakes to Avoid

The worst feeling is to spend hours writing a resume only to be rejected by missing typographical errors. Grammar mistakes are easy to make and easy to avoid with adequate proofreading. Make sure to look out for the following common errors:

Homophones

Homophones are words that sound the same but have different spellings and meanings. Here are some common homophones to watch out for when you write your resume:

- Two, To, and Too—*Two* refers to the number; *To* is a preposition usually expressing direction or motion toward a place, person, or time; *Too* is an adverb meaning additionally.

- Their and There—*Their* refers to belonging to them; *There* refers to in or to a place.

- A lot and Allot—*A lot* refers to a large quantity or extent; *Allot* refers to distributing something between people or groups. *Alot* is not a word.

Possessives versus Contractions

One of the most common resume grammar mistakes made by job seekers is confusing words of possession and words that are simply contractions of two other words. Here are some examples:

- Your and You're—*Your* is a possessive meaning something that belongs to you. *You're* is a contraction of *you* and *are*.

- Its and It's—*Its* is a possessive meaning belonging to him or her. If you can replace *it* with *him* or *her*, there is no need for an apostrophe. *It's* is a contraction for *it is* or *it has*.

- They're, Their, and There—*They're* is a contraction for *they are. Their* is a possessive meaning belonging to them. Again, *There* refers to a place.

In general, be careful when you use apostrophes. Besides incorrect use of contractions, make sure you are not making a plural word, such as *employees*, into a possessive term incorrectly, such as *employee's*.

Inconsistent Tense

Use the past tense only for previous jobs or positions, and use the past tense consistently. Never write about a current job experience using the past tense. Switching between tenses like *managed* to *managing* to *manage* appears unprofessional.

Misspelled Words, Abbreviations, and Capitalization

Always use spell check. Then proofread to make sure spell check caught all the errors and didn't mistakenly switch *you're* for *your*. Remember to stay away from abbreviations, even when they are career specific, unless it is a term you know is used industry wide. Nothing dilutes an accomplishment for a reader like not knowing what it was because an acronym was used as a descriptor. Have a consistent use of capitalization throughout

Real World Scenario 5-2 Cara had been over her resume again and again. She was sure it was right. The night before the interview, she printed out a few copies to take with her. She looked at this version so that it would be fresh in her mind. Suddenly she noticed that she had made two errors! She had misspelled the company name with an *ie* rather than an *ei*, and she had used *too* instead of *to*. She quickly fixed both mistakes and was thankful that, despite the errors, she was still getting an interview. She would give the interviewer and any new job leads the new version of her resume and hopefully get a job.

How could Cara have avoided the errors?

MAKE IT A HABIT
Proofread, Proofread, Proofread

Make it a habit to proofread all your documents and make sure you are following grammar rules. The slightest grammatical error can make you appear unprofessional and unqualified for the job. Use these tactics to help you catch any errors:

- Print important documents such as cover letters and resumes, and review with a red marker to highlight any errors.
- Read text aloud and listen for any errors or awkward sentences.
- Ask someone else to review your work.

Stay cautious and don't forget to proofread all your communications.

© Pixsooz/Shutterstock.com.

your resume. Only capitalize pronouns and the first word of each sentence or phrase.

Review your draft resume with these grammatical rules in mind.

Be Clear and Concise

Even for companies that use resume scanning software to select the most promising resumes, deciding which applicants to interview is time consuming. You can expect most recruiters to do a 30- to 60-second scan of your resume. Presenting an easy-to-read, clear, concise message and format is critical for making the most of the limited time your resume will receive. Follow these rules and tips to keep your resume concise:

- **Use phrases**, not complete sentences, and omit *I, me,* and *my.* The reader knows the resume is about you.
- **Be focused and concise.** Eliminate wordiness and complexity by focusing each section, bullet, or line on just one idea. If using full sentences, keep them short!
- **Eliminate articles *the, a,* and *an.*** Instead of saying "balanced the budget," simply say "balanced budget."

A resume for a recent graduate should be one full page. If you have extensive work experience, two pages are acceptable. In this case, use logical page breaks and repeat the current heading at the top of the next page followed by "(continued)" so that the reader can follow the flow.

Customize Your Resume

Do not send the same resume to every prospective employer. A customized resume is more effective at showing how you meet the requirements for this job listing and can increase your chances of getting an interview.

Start with your master resume, the one you are working on in this class. Make sure it is as perfect as you can get it. Ask others to review it and give you feedback, then revise it. Using this final **master resume**, customize it for specific job titles, job listings, and employers.

- Customize the Job Objective statement of your *Professional Profile* section for different job targets and industries.
- Customize your list of *Qualifications* based on the skills and requirements described in the job listing.

- Prioritize bullet points based on relevance to job listing responsibilities and skills in the *Work* and *Related Experience* sections of your resume.
- Use keywords throughout your resume that match the terms in the job listing.
- Use appropriate industry terminology.

Figure 5-3 shows excerpts from a resume for a service manager position along with changes made to customize the resume for a position as an automotive insurance adjuster. Notice how the same person can show how he or she is qualified for different jobs by purposefully choosing what to share about his or her experience and qualifications. (For a side-by-side comparison of a resume customized for two different jobs, view Figure 5-8 on page 128–129.)

When the jobs you are applying for are quite similar, the adjustments may be minimal. If you are applying for different types of jobs in a similar industry or if you are applying to jobs in two or more career fields, you will need to revise your resume to fit each new job target. Try these steps to make it easier to customize your resume.

1. Open a copy of your master resume in a window on the left side of the screen.
2. On the other half of the screen, use your browser to read about the new career field and read several job listings, including listings for jobs you are not considering.
3. Compare your resume against the industry terminology for the new field.
4. Highlight text in your resume that you can modify and then paste the new terminology in your resume where appropriate.
5. Look for ways to increase the number of keywords that match the career or job.

For example, you might list different courses you have taken if a course title includes a keyword that you cannot use when describing your work experience. A teacher who is applying for jobs as a corporate trainer would use the terms *trainer, instructor, presenter,* and/or *facilitator* instead of *teacher.*

 CAREER ACTION
Complete Worksheet 5-5
Create Your Draft Master Resume, page 141

Figure 5-3 Customized Resume Example

"Before"	"After"
Objective: Service manager in multiline dealership	**Objective:** Insurance adjuster in automotive collision repair industry
Auto Repair Customer Service Scheduled appointments, performed pre-inspections, achieved upgrade sales on 95% of accounts, quoted estimates, wrote work orders, performed post-repair inspections, explained statements to customers, and increased referrals from customers by 40%	**Modified to Focus on Claims Management** Scheduled client appointments, determined mechanical and auto body damages within 45 minutes, negotiated repairs with clients and insurance companies, prepared job documentation (pictures, work orders, billing), performed post-repair inspections, and explained statements
Parts Management Managed ordering and stocking of mechanical and auto-body parts inventories, selected suppliers and negotiated vendor discounts that averaged 25% to 30% below wholesale, reconciled shipping invoices to billing statements, and approved payments	**Modified to Focus on Cost Containment** Obtained clients' permission to use appropriate aftermarket and/or rebuilt parts on 95% of jobs; located replacement parts; negotiated price, delivery, and discounts, averaging 25% to 30% below wholesale; returned unused parts for credit; reconciled billing discrepancies; approved payments

Keep Track of Your Resumes

Unless you get very lucky and are offered the first job you apply for, you will develop several versions of your resume during your job search. For example, you may need to change the job objective, emphasize different skills and capability in the Qualifications section, or add specialized keywords. You may also have different formats of the same resume, such as a pdf file and a Word document. The information between different formats must match. You need a system that keeps all versions in sync so that you can respond quickly and accurately to job listings.

Develop a naming convention for each customized Job Application Package (Chapter 7). To be organized and able to respond to job listings quickly, for each job you apply for, create a folder on your computer (and/or on a flash drive reserved for your job search and Career Builder Files). Keep a copy of the job listing, any versions of the resume you used, the cover letter (Chapter 8), copies of all emails related to your application, and—if you get an interview—your interview notes and the text of your thank-you letter. If you are keeping an online portfolio through a service like Pathbrite, you may want to create a separate portfolio for each job listing.

© Elena Elisseeva/Shutterstock.com.

FORMAT YOUR RESUME

Now that you have reviewed the content, grammar, and language used in your resume, pay attention to the format. Up to this point, you may have been using a word processing program. However, when you submit your resume, you may not have a choice about the file type, especially online. You need to be ready with the following resume formats:

- **Microsoft® Word's .doc or .docx file format**—.doc or .docx is currently the best format to use as you create and edit your resume. It may also be requested as the preferred file format for online applications because it is easier for resume scanning software programs to search for keywords.

- **Adobe Acrobat's .pdf file format**—.pdf is the best format for emailing or otherwise sharing your resume because it shows only the finished product without all the formatting and editing that you did.

- **Notepad's .txt file format**—.txt files have no formatting (no bullet points, tables, bold font, etc.) and are used to copy and paste your resume data directly into online application fields.

Print Resume

You'll want your print resume—that is, a printed, word-processed resume—designed to be:

- Visually appealing
- Delivered by one of these methods: regular mail, in person, attached to an email message, or uploaded into an online application
- Capable of being scanned accurately into a resume database

Using your word processing program to make edits, review the Formatting Dos and Don'ts on pages 121–122. After you have drafted and formatted your print resume, print it out and review it again, paying careful attention to every detail. Mark areas for improvement and then revise it.

To save your final version, simply click *Save*. To save your final resume in .pdf format, click *Save As* and select *.pdf* from the file type drop-down menu.

Creating a Plain Text Resume

You also need a **plain text resume,** a text file (.txt file) that has no formatting (no bold, no tables, no bullets, etc.). The main purpose of this text file is to serve as the source file for copy and paste online applications.

- At some sites, you paste the entire plain text resume into one text field.

- At other sites, you paste sections of the resume into labeled text fields such as "Work Experience 1" or "Education."

Other sites use the headings in your resume to fill in fields automatically; you then check each field and correct any errors (for example, if the program puts your job duties in the skills field). Start with the final version of the print resume you are using to apply for a job. Then follow these steps to create your plain text resume.

1. Save the print resume as a .doc file with a different name.

2. Format the file so that it will convert to a clean .txt file:

   a. Replace bold text with all caps and bullets with hyphens.

   b. Remove the tabs and start every line at the left margin.

   c. If your resume has two pages, delete the page break and the header at the top of the second page.

3. Save the "stripped down" Word file as a .doc file and a .txt file. Close both files.

Formatting Dos for Print Resumes

- Use the whole page effectively. Space sections to fill the entire first page with an attractive layout framed by one-inch margins on all sides.

- Create a visual hierarchy in each section. Draw attention to headings by using larger text font as well as bold and italicized text to emphasize items. Do not use all capitals, however, because this gives your resume an alarming tone and feel.

- Use a standard font. Keep the font size between 11 points for body text and 14 points for headings.

- Place the most important information at the top left of the page or section—where readers naturally begin reading.

- Use bulleted lists instead of paragraphs.

- Be simple and consistent. Format the same elements the same way.

- Use one space after periods and add a line break between sections and experiences.

- Use color sensibly. For example, try dark blue for the contact information and section headings. Experiment with color before you send your resume, and don't make color a "feature."

- Print your resume on a laser printer on one side of white or cream-colored paper. If the paper has a watermark, print with the watermark facing up and toward the reader.

Formatting Don'ts for Print Resumes

- Don't use the headings *Resume* or *Contact Information* at the top of a resume.

- Don't use excessive decorative fonts and formatting. These elements look unprofessional and do not scan well.

- Don't crowd the text to fit everything on one page. Check your writing again and see where you can be more concise. If the text still doesn't fit, end the first page at a logical stopping point near the bottom of the page. If a section carries over, repeat the heading on page 2 (for example, *Education, continued*).

- Don't use a newsletter layout or multiple columns. Scanning software assumes that the text reads from left to right across the page in one column.

- Don't adjust the spacing between characters. Use standard left-margin alignment for body text. (Headings can be centered.)

- Don't use formatting that can blur or corrupt the scanned image. Avoid the following:
  - Light-colored text
  - Shadow effect
  - White text on a black background
  - Boxed text
  - Vertical lines (you can use a single horizontal line as a separator between sections if you leave enough space above and below the line so that it doesn't touch any letters)

- Don't fold or staple the resume. (Creases and staple marks can cause scanning errors.)

- Don't print page 2 on the back of page 1; use two sheets of paper attached with a paper clip.

4. Open the folder with the .txt file and double-click the filename to open it. Windows opens the .txt file in the text editor program Notepad. *Do not open the .txt file in Word.* Check the format of the .txt file to make sure you didn't miss anything when you formatted the .doc file in Step 1.

5. If necessary, add blank lines to make the resume more readable. Notepad ignores automatic line breaks in the .doc file and displays paragraphs, such as a description of job duties, as one continuous line of text that runs off the screen. Divide these long lines into lines of 65 characters, including spaces, by inserting a hard return at the end of each new line.

6. Always finalize the *format* of a plain text resume (and cover letter) in Notepad, not in Word. To keep both versions of the current resume in sync, make *text changes* in the formatted print resume and re-create the unformatted .doc file and .txt file.

Look at the sample plain text resume in Figure 5-5 on page 125.

 CAREER ACTION
Complete Worksheet 5-6
Create Your Plain Text Resume, page 143

Your Resume Online

Today, many online sites offer the capability for you to create your own resume-based website. This resume format is more flexible than the others because it supports more sophisticated elements, such as animated graphics, sound clips, and video clips. Web resumes can also be creative sales tools for people who want or need to display their artistic abilities, such as photographers, artists, singers, models, architects, and graphics and computer specialists. Note that a web resume should be used in addition to—not as a substitute for—your print and plain text resumes. Figure 5-9 on page 130 is the first page of a web resume.

In Chapter 4, you began to create your LinkedIn® profile. Now, using your final resume, update all the sections of your profile, including the Summary, Work Experience, Education, and Related Experiences sections. For instructions and details on how to create a web resume site and use your LinkedIn® profile, refer to the Appendix.

Congratulations! You have completed a big part of the Job Search Journey. Now that you have created your resume, you are ready to apply for jobs and proceed to Phase 3 of the Job Search Journey.

Sample Resumes

The following sample resumes are on pages 124–130:

Print Resumes for Different Career Targets

- Figure 5-4: Sample Resume, Private Security Guard
- Figure 5-5: Sample Resume, Health Information Technician
- Figure 5-6: Sample Resume, Registered Environmental Technician

Resumes in Other Formats

- Figure 5-7: Plain Text Resume, Registered Environmental Technician
- Figure 5-8: Web Resume, Art Teacher

Customized Resumes

- Figure 5-9: Side-by-Side Comparison of Customized Resumes

Figure 5-4 Sample Resume Private Security Guard

Thomas' professional profile highlights important competencies in a personable way.

Although he uses more than 3-5 words, he limited the total number to 3 to highlight the most impactful qualifications.

Notice his use of the WHI format and action verbs.

He highlights the broad criminal justice experience. He gained. He places emphasis on safety and security procedures by listing them as the first job duty.

He emphasizes his conflict resolution and interpersonal skills, which are important qualifications for security guards. He also describes his ability to complete and submit essential paperwork.

Although part-time, this position gave him practical experience in a variety of common security guard tasks.

Note the Optional Section Thomas included. Because security guard positions can have several certification requirements, he lists his training, certificates, and licenses with dates to show that they are current. He uses industry keywords and stresses safety, fitness, and security.

THOMAS STANLEY

tom.stanley1066@email.com   linkedin.com/in/tomstanley1066
(716) 555.2457   123 Forest Drive, Springfield, NY 14201

Professional Profile

Private Security Guard position requiring ability to perform safety, security, and surveillance procedures. Observant, careful individual with up to date license, known for excellent communication and interpersonal skills.

Qualifications

- Well trained and certified through multiple training avenues
- Practical experience in closed-circuit video surveillance and switchboard operations
- Experienced in working with juvenile offenders

Relevant Work Experience

Buffalo Juvenile Justice Center, Buffalo, NY   September 2014–November 2014
Juvenile Corrections Intern
Monitor and enforce security at facility.
- Monitored and ensured safety and security of 50 juvenile detainees.
- Successfully enforced facility safety and security rules including managing 3 conflicts
- Escorted juvenile offenders to classes, counseling sessions, and work-release programs.
- Conducted security checks, searches, and pat downs

Erie County Sheriff's Department, Hamburg, NY   Summer 2012, 2013
Assistant Supervisor, County Fairgrounds Grounds and Maintenance
Supervised groundskeeping and maintenance crew of eight work-released juveniles for the County Sheriff's Department.
- Quickly resolved multiple worker disagreements and scheduling issues using training in conflict resolution techniques
- Evaluated work crew weekly and submitted thorough and timely paperwork to the Sheriff's Department

Baker Sporting Goods, Buffalo, NY   April 2011–May 2012
Security Guard, Part-time
Monitored customers and employees to maintan internal and external loss-theft control.
- Conducted closed-circuit video surveillance of store and building exterior.
- Recognized for swift response to employee and customer security and safety requests.
- Identified new security actions through submission of daily loss prevention reports.

Certifications and Training

- New York State Security Guard License, 2011
- Carrying Concealed Weapons License, 2010
- First Aid and CPR Certification, 2007
- Physical Fitness Specialist, 2008
- Fire Prevention and Safety Training, 2009
- Burglary Prevention Training, 2009

Education

Crown Community College, Associate of Applied Science, 2014
Major: Criminal Justice   GPA: 3.75

Figure 5-5 Sample Resume Health Information Technician

SONYA REID

2332 Clovis Boulevard • Savannah, GA 31401 • (912) 555.0109
Sonya_reid@email.com • linkedin/in/sonya_reid

PROFESSIONAL PROFILE

Health Information Technician position requiring the ability to perform detailed tasks, change priorities quickly, and communicate well. Excellent customer service rep and team member, known for helping people feel at ease and working efficiently.

QUALIFICATIONS

- RHIT, Registered Health Information Technician, 2014
- Family practice receptionist, 1.5 years
- Awarded Superior Service Certificate twice
- Five-month internship as assistant to Health Information Technician, Community Hospital

> She emphasizes her Technician certification by placing it first because it is a primary requirement for the job she is seeking. Notice that all bulleted qualifications are repeated elsewhere in Sonya's resume to highlight her most important qualifications and to catch a human reader's attention.

EDUCATION

Associate of Science, A.S., 2014, Savannah College of Georgia, Savannah, GA
Major: **Health Information Technology**, GPA 3.6
Related Courses and Skills
Medical Terminology • Clinical Classification Systems • Health Information Management
Health Delivery Systems • Health Data • Introduction to Health Law and Ethics
Human Disease Mechanisms • Health Care Reimbursement • Alternative Health Care Settings
Business Communications

> Sonya puts her education and certification first because she knows employers will place more importance on this area.

CERTIFICATION

Registered Health Information Technician, 2014

EXPERIENCE

Community Hospital, Savannah, GA   January 2014–May 2014
Clinical Intern

Shadow Health Information Technician and assist in basic duties.

- Reduced Health Information Technician's workload by 25% by end of internship in reviewing and assigning diagnosis codes and DRGs and coding Medicare/Medicaid billing items.
- Abstracted appropriate information and retrieved medical records from records department using appropriate procedures.

> Sonya includes her internship under work experience and uses the WHI format to demonstrate the capabilities she has gained.

Family Practice Partnership, Savannah, GA   July 2012–December 2013
Evening Receptionist2
Manage patients' needs and reception area.

- Provided cheerful, efficient service to patients; awarded Superior Service Certificate in 2012 and 2013.
- Checked in patients, obtained insurance and billing information, and pulled charts for nurses.
- Copied requested records for transport to other medical offices.

Figure 5-6 Sample Resume Registered Environmental Technician

ERIKA ALLEN

10173 Jeffrey Street • Hoboken, NJ 07030
(551) 555.8229 • eallen@email.com • linkedin.com/in/erikaallen

Professional Profile

Award-winning Registered Environmental Technician with A.S. in Environmental Sciences and OSHA Certification. Extensive knowledge of federal and state regulations with demonstrated technical writing abilities.

Core Competencies

- Soil and groundwater sampling and soil vapor extraction
- Environmental site mapping and assessment
- Technical writing and reporting

- Mapping and data entry
- GIS, AutoCAD, Microsoft Office 2010 (expert user, Word and Excel)

Relevant Work Experience

Environmental Technician
Envirocorp, Burlington, NJ   January 2013–Present
Survey sites and conduct environmental assessments. Oversee drilling, excavation, well installation, and remediation systems. Conduct soil and groundwater sampling

- Successfully participated in 20+ environmental site assessments that identified risk areas and possible mitigation plans
- Prevented major breakdowns with remediation systems through implementing good operation and maintenance procedures
- Monitored drilling, excavation, and installation for 3 wells that were completed with no safety incidents
- Presented data, technical reports, and maps to leadership using Word, Excel, GIS, AutoCAD for strategic decision making purposes

Soil and Water Extraction Technician
Environmental Consultants, Inc., Oakwood, NJ   April 2010–December 2012
Conduct soil and groundwater sample testing.

- Completed laboratory tests on water samples in accordance with schedules set by supervisor
- Collected and preserved soil and groundwater samples
- Used Microsoft Word and Excel to record historical research and perform data entry

Education

A.S. in Environmental Science
Ocean County College, Toms River, NJ   May 2010
GPA 3.8

Certifications and Training

RET – Registered Environmental Technician - Certification from National Environmental Health Association 2010

Emergency First Response - Primary and Secondary Care 2009

OSHA Health & Safety Training - 40-hour course 2011; 8-hour refresher course 2013

Awards

Three-time recipient of Envirocorp Safety Recognition Award – 2012, 2013, 2014

Side annotations:

Erika uses the heading Core Competencies instead of Qualifications and includes skills that are often required in Environmental Technician positions. She uses industry keywords that she found in job descriptions.

Erika uses the heading Relevant Work Experience and omits other jobs she has held. She uses the WHI format to show advancement and increased responsibility in her experience. She uses industry keywords and abbreviations that resume scanning software and employers will recognize, and she uses action verbs to describe her job responsibilities.

She includes dates to show that her training and certifications are recent and up-to-date.

Erika is well aware that safety is prized in the environmental industry. Because her awards are measurable proof of her commitment to safety and excellence on the job, she creates a separate section to highlight these awards.

Figure 5-7 Plain Text Sample Resume Registered Environmental Technician

ERIKA ALLEN
10173 Jeffrey Street • Hoboken, NJ 07030
(551) 555.8229 • eallen@email com • linkedin com/in/erikaallen
Professional Profile
Award-winning Registered Environmental Technician with A.S. in Environmental
Sciences and OSHA Certification. Extensive knowledge of federal and state
regulations with demonstrated technical writing abilities.

Core Competencies
* Soil and groundwater sampling and soil vapor extraction
* Environmental site mapping and assessment
* Technical writing and reporting
* Mapping and data entry
* GIS, AutoCAD, Microsoft Office 2010 (expert user, Word and Excel)

Relevant Work Experience
Environmental Technician
Envirocorp, Burlington, NJ
January 2013–Present
Survey sites and conduct environmental assessments. Oversee drilling, excavation,
well installation, and remediation systems. Conduct soil and groundwater sampling
* Successfully participated in 20+ environmental site assessments that identified risk
areas and possible mitigation plans
* Prevented major breakdowns with remediation systems through implementing good
operation and maintenance procedures
* Monitored drilling, excavation, and installation for 3 wells that were completed with
no safety incidents
* Presented data, technical reports, and maps to leadership using Word, Excel, GIS,
AutoCAD for strategic decision making purposes

Soil and Water Extraction Technician
Environmental Consultants, Inc., Oakwood, NJ
April 2010–December 2012
Conduct soil and groundwater sample testing.
* Completed laboratory tests on water samples in accordance with schedules set by
supervisor
* Collected and preserved soil and groundwater samples
* Used Microsoft Word and Excel to record historical research and perform data entry

Education
A.S. in Environmental Science
Ocean County College, Toms River, NJ
May 2010
GPA 3.8

Certifications and Training
RET – Registered Environmental Technician - Certification from National
Environmental Health Association 2010

Emergency First Response - Primary and Secondary Care 2009

OSHA Health & Safety Training - 40-hour course 2011; 8-hour refresher course 2013

Awards
Three-time recipient of Envirocorp Safety Recognition Award – 2012, 2013, 2014

Figure 5-8 Web Resume Art Teacher

THE SHORT STORY

"I found I could say things with color and shapes that I couldn't say any other way–things I had no words for."

Georgia O'Keeffe

Enthusiastic, creative, and talented art teacher with ability to foster student curiosity, creativity, and self-discipline in a positive learning environment. Collaborative educator with outstanding interpersonal and communication skills complemented by strengths in interactive learning and differentiated instruction.

WORK EXPERIENCE

Long-Term Substitute Art Teacher

John F. Kennedy Middle School, Riverside, CA
September 2011-June 2012

Designed and implemented interactive lesson plans and units and educated on proper methodologies and techniques. Evaluated each student's progress and adjusted lessons accordingly.

- Initiated first after-school Art Club to provide students with additional opportunities to further their creative capabilities and explore new mediums.
- Selected and matted 120 pieces of student artwork for exhibition at prestigious art gallery show.

Student Teacher

J.P. McCaskey High School, Lancaster, PA
January-April 2011

- Raised student awareness and appreciation of the arts through creative lesson plans and teaching methods.
- Provided small-group instruction in basic jewelry making, water colors, acrylics, and etching.

Entrepreneur / Metalsmith

Judy's Jewelry Designs (www.judysjewelry.com), Riverside, CA

Figure 5-8 Web Resume Art Teacher *(continued)*

2009-Present

Started small business to manufacture unique sterling silver and bead jewelry. Created business plan and marketing plan, prepared budget, and purchased tools. Traveled throughout region and country to display and sell jewelry at juried craft shows and exhibitions.

- Collaborate with individual customers to design and create custom jewelry.
- Network with boutique owners, customers, and juried craft shows to promote designs.

EDUCATION AND CREDENTIALS

Certification: Art—California and Pennsylvania Permanent K–12

Bachelor of Science in Art Education, 2011
Kutztown University, Kutztown, PA

Jewelry Technician Certification, Revere Academy of Jewelry Art
San Francisco, CA, 2011

CONTACT

See what you like? Get in touch with me:

Email

Phone

Location

Figure 5-9 Side-by-Side Comparison of Customized Resumes

DONITA SILVA

Donita.silva@email.com linkedin.com/in/donita.silva
1247 Madison Rd Columbus OH 43216 (614) 555.5225

	Resume 1: Accounting Systems Auditor	Resume 2: Information Systems Analyst
Note the different focus for the Professional Profile: the job objective is customized.	**PROFESSIONAL PROFILE** Accounting Systems Auditor I	**PROFESSIONAL PROFILE** Information Systems Analyst I position in a financial environment requiring system design, programming, investigation, reporting skills
Note the different qualifications highlighted for the different job objective	**QUALIFICATIONS SUMMARY** • Education in accounting practices and computer systems • Programming competence in C, C++, C#.NET and Visual Basic.NET • Practical experience in EDP accounting applications • Master user: Office 2010, SharePoint 2010, Silverlight 4 • Proven interpersonal skills and team skills in an auditing environment • Experienced in IBM Power Systems, Windows Server 2008, Active Directory, Microsoft Exchange Server 2010, and Novell LAN operations	**QUALIFICATIONS SUMMARY** • Education in computer systems and accounting practices • Proven interpersonal skills and team skills in a financial setting • Programming competence in C, C++, C#.NET and Visual Basic.NET • Practical experience in EDP accounting applications • Master user: Office 2010, SharePoint 2010, Silverlight 4 • Experienced in IBM Power Systems, Windows Server 2008, Active Directory, Microsoft Exchange Server 2010, and Novell LAN operations
	WORK EXPERIENCE	
Donita left the work experience the same. She could have prioritized the bullet points within each experience if there was different relevance or importance for the differing job objective.	**Alexander & Swartz**, Columbus, OH 9/11 to Present **Part-time Assistant Staff Auditor:** Assist in audits of cash, accounts receivable, and accounts payable for midsized firms that use IBM Power Systems. Interface with clients and write audit reports as member of Business Services Assurance and Advisory team.	
	Micronomics Inc., Columbus, OH 6/08 to 9/11 **Part-time Programming Assistant:** Designed, documented, coded, and tested C program subroutines for order-entry system. Achieved 95% average program-accuracy rate on test runs. Cataloged and filed new programs and program patches for company's software library. Used Microsoft Exchange Server 2010.	
	Renton College, Columbus, OH 9/06 to 6/08 **Computer Operator Aide:** Using Windows Server 2008, copied files for backup. Verified accuracy of reports and scheduled print sequences. Implemented schedule changes that improved efficiency of backup procedures by 25%.	
	EDUCATION **Bachelor of Business Administration, B.B.A.**, 2012 Renton College, Columbus, OH Major: Computer Information Systems Minor: Internal Auditing	
She highlighted different Relevant Courses of Study	**Relevant Courses of Study:** • Analysis, and Auditing of Accounting Information Systems • Internal Auditing • Information Systems Auditing • Accounting Applications • Database Management • Advanced Corporate Finance • Cost Accounting	**Relevant Courses of Study:** • System Analysis and Design • Systems Development • Quantitative Analysis • Advanced Programming • Data Communications • Database Systems • Advanced Corporate Finance • Statistical Techniques • Information Systems Auditing

Chapter Checklist

Check off each item you can do. Reread sections in this chapter to help you complete the checklist.

☐ Write a cohesive resume that tells a story and supports my Personal Brand Statement with relevant work experience and qualifications. **1**

☐ Write a clear, concise, attention-grabbing Professional Profile to focus my entire resume. **1**

☐ Use measurable details and accomplishment statements to market myself. **1**

☐ Use appropriate action verbs and keywords to demonstrate that I have the required skills and knowledge. **1**

☐ Edit my resume using proper grammar and eliminating unnecessary information. **2**

☐ Customize my resume to meet the needs of the employer and match my resume to the job description by using specific terms and industry terminology. **2**

☐ Format my resumes in the .doc (or .docx), .pdf, and .txt formats correctly. **3**

Critical Thinking Questions

1. Why is it essential to use action words and industry targeted keywords in a resume? **1**

2. It is important to be selective about what to include in your resume instead of including everything you've done. Why is it so hard for most job seekers to do this? **1** **2**

3. Why is the WHI method such a powerful tool? What can you do if you cannot find quantifiable data to support your skills and experience? **1**

4. What difference do you think it makes to an employer if they see resumes with proper grammar and clean formatting versus ones without? **2** **3**

5. How can you tailor your resume to target a specific job or employer? Give at least three examples from your own resume. **2**

6. Why do you need a plain text resume? What are the requirements for this resume, and how do you create it? **3**

Additional Resources

For data files, career resources, and more, visit www.cengagebrain.com.

Trial Run

Review Online Resumes

To write a powerful resume is a difficult task. As you write your resume, get inspiration by reviewing resumes from your industry or job target. Search the Internet for "Sample Resumes for {Insert your job target here}." Look at the image results and pick three resumes to look at. Specifically focus on the *Work Experience* and *Qualifications* sections. Did they use the WHI approach? Are their examples powerful? Would you believe they are qualified for the job?

Print out these resumes and take out your red pen. Put yourself in the shoes of a recruiter or hiring manager. Evaluate each Work Experience and Qualification for the following characteristics:

1. Wordiness—Do the Qualifications stick to three to five words per bullet point? Are bullet points used? Are there long run-on sentences or unnecessary words included in the Work Experience bullet points?

2. Formatting—Are both sections easy to read? When you skim the resume for 30 seconds, do you get a feel for who the applicant is?

3. Impact—Do the achievements shared indicate that this is a strong applicant for the job? Are the bullet points written as tasks and responsibilities, or are they focused on achievements and results?

4. Overall theme—Do different Work Experiences support one another and the overall Personal Brand Statement? Is there a theme that builds throughout the whole resume about the applicant's strengths and capabilities?

Consider what worked well and what didn't work well in the three resumes you evaluated. Make a list of what you learned that you want to incorporate as you write your resume.

▶ CAREER ACTION WORKSHEET

5-1 Write a Stronger Professional Profile ❶

Copy into a new file the Professional Profile you wrote in Career Action Worksheet 4-2, Resume Outline. Revise it using the following checklist:

- ☐ Used industry-relevant keywords.

- ☐ Strengths are stated in the most concise form.

- ☐ Strengths are supported by your work experience and qualifications.

- ☐ Personal Brand Statement is relevant to your Job Objective.

- ☐ Send your Professional Profile to trusted colleagues, friends, or classmates for review. Ask if they are easily able to understand it and what suggestions they have for improvement. Finalize your Professional Profile using their feedback and what you have learned in this textbook.

- ☐ Update the Summary section of your LinkedIn® profile with your final Professional Profile.

Ensure that these updates are in the "About Jobs" section of your Career Builder Files.

This page is intentionally blank.

▶ CAREER ACTION WORKSHEET

5-2 Revise Your Qualifications List ❶

1. Copy into a new file the Career Action Worksheet 4-3 table with your qualifications. Finalize your Qualifications list for use in your resume by using the following checklist:

   ☐ Have you selected the most important, eye-catching strengths and capabilities? Have you been purposeful and only included the top 8 to 10 strengths?

   ☐ Have you described your top strengths in no more than three to five words?

   ☐ Have you ordered your Qualifications list from most important and relevant to least important and relevant?

   ☐ Have you used industry-relevant keywords?

2. Considering the two different job targets that you selected in Career Action Worksheet 5-1, customize your Qualifications as needed for these different Job Objectives. Update the Skills section of your LinkedIn® profile using these finalized Qualifications.

Ensure that these updates are in the "About Jobs" section of your Career Builder Files.

This page is intentionally blank.

▶ *CAREER ACTION WORKSHEET*
5-3 Strengthen Your Work Experiences ❶

Copy into a new file your Career Action Worksheet 4-4, Work Experiences. Finalize your Work Experiences for use in your resume by using the following checklist:

- ☐ Order your Work Experiences chronologically, starting with the most recent experience first.

- ☐ Follow the correct format: Job Title, Dates of Employment, Company Title, two-sentence job description, bullet points of achievements.

- ☐ Strengthen your WHI-formatted achievements with quantifiable results.

- ☐ Eliminate unnecessary words and acronyms.

- ☐ Use industry-relevant keywords as appropriate.

- ☐ Choose action verbs that are relevant to your Work Experience, using the reference list in Figure 5-1 on page 114 as a starting point.

- ☐ If your work experience is limited, have you included relevant paid and nonpaid internships and volunteer or other pertinent activities?

- ☐ Include any significant school projects, organization work, or other related experiences in this section. Significant projects would include ones where you had significant results, spent a large amount of time, and/or can demonstrate multiple skills using more than one bullet point. If you need only a single bullet point to describe the work, it is probably better to include in an Optional section such as Related Experiences or Organizations.

- ☐ Use your notes from the sample resumes you reviewed to ensure your resume makes the best possible impression.

Ensure that these updates are in the "About Jobs" section of your Career Builder Files.

This page is intentionally blank.

▶ *CAREER ACTION WORKSHEET*
5-4 Resume Action Verbs and Keywords ❶

1. Prepare a comprehensive list of appropriate action verbs and keywords (industry term; acronyms; terms describing your job positions, experience, education, skills, etc.).

2. Use the list on page 113 and the Internet as a primary resource in your research.

3. Print a report with (a) your lists of action verbs and keywords and (b) the resources you used to identify them.

Resources for identifying action verbs and keywords for your resume

- *Your Career: How to Make It Happen* companion website
- Job advertisements and descriptions for positions you are considering
- Websites of employers you are considering
- Government publications such as the *Occupational Outlook Handbook*
- Professional associations in your field (check their websites, publications, and meetings)
- Internet searches on *resume keywords, resume action verbs, resume power verbs,* and *resume power words*
- Online encyclopedias and dictionaries

Add your completed work to the "About Jobs" section of your Career Builder Files.

▶ *CAREER ACTION WORKSHEET*
5-5 Create Your Draft Master Resume ❷

It is time to create your draft Master Resume! Copy your completed Career Action Worksheet 4-2, Resume Outline into a new file for this activity. Make sure you have updated each section with the drafts you created above.

- ☑ CAREER ACTION WORKSHEET 5-1: Write a Stronger Professional Profile
- ☑ CAREER ACTION WORKSHEET 5-2: Revise Your Qualifications List
- ☑ CAREER ACTION WORKSHEET 5-3: Strengthen Your Work Experiences
- ☑ CAREER ACTION WORKSHEET 5-4: Resume Action Verbs and Keywords

When you've updated each section, use the checklist below to edit this file—your draft Master Resume!

- ☐ Ensure you have included and properly formatted all sections, including Education, Related Experiences, Awards and Honors, and any Optional sections.

- ☐ For the Education section, have you emphasized courses, internships, degrees, certificates, etc. that best support your objective? If your GPA is impressive, have you included it (overall or major/minor related to your job objective)?

- ☐ Is the length of the resume appropriate for your level of experience?

- ☐ Is the resume free of all grammatical errors, including incorrect use of homophones, tense, capitalization, contractions, and other common errors?

- ☐ Do you use sentence fragments and omit the articles *the, a,* and *an* and the words *I, me,* and *my*?

- ☐ Is the overall design visually appealing and easy to read?

- ☐ Have you used appropriate fonts; white space; and acceptable enhancements such as bold, bullets, and tabs for indenting? Have you used italics sparingly?

Now give your resume the 30-second skim test. Do you get a feel for who you are as an applicant? Does your eye flow easily toward keywords and strengths? Does your resume tell the story you want it to tell?

Add your completed work to the "About Jobs" section of your Career Builder Files.

NOTE: After review by your instructor, and possibly some final revisions, you can rename this file Master Resume and add this to the "Master Career Portfolio" section of your Career Builder Files.

This page is intentionally blank.

▶ *CAREER ACTION WORKSHEET*
5-6 Create Your Plain Text Resume ❸

PART 1. Convert the print resume you created in Career Action Worksheet 5-5 to a plain text resume. Follow the steps below. You may want to review the sample plain text resume in Figure 5-5 on page 125.

1. Save the print resume you created in Career Action Worksheet 5-5 as a .doc (or .docx) file with a similar name (for example, *MasterResume_plain text source file.doc).*

2. Now save the new .doc file as a .txt file with the same file name. This file will have less formatting. Newer versions of Word create cleaner .txt files, so experiment with the formatting you need to change.

3. Now clean up the .txt file in Microsoft® Word so that it is a usable plain text resume. Use the following checklist:

   ☐ Start every line of contact information at the left margin (no indents).

   ☐ Replace previously bold headings with ALL CAPS to ensure the text still stands out.

   ☐ Add blank lines to emphasize sections as needed. For example, insert two blank lines before the section headings.

   ☐ Replace bullets with hyphens (newer versions of Word convert bullets to asterisks automatically).

   ☐ Format tables as lists.

   ☐ For each company in the employment section, put the dates of employment under the company name.

   ☐ If your resume has two pages, delete the page break and the header at the top of the second page.

4. Save this new "stripped down" Word file as a .doc file. Use Save As to save it again as a .txt file. Close both files.

5. Open the folder with the .txt file and double-click the filename to open it. Windows opens the .txt file in the text editor program Notepad. *Do not open the .txt file in Word.*

   Always finalize the *format* of a plain text resume (and cover letter) in Notepad, not in Word. In the future, if you update or change your resume, you will want to keep the *print* and *plain text* files in sync. To keep both versions of the current resume in sync, make *text changes* in the formatted print resume and create a new unformatted .doc file and .txt file.

6. Check the format of the .txt file to make sure you didn't miss anything when you formatted the .doc file in Step 2. If necessary, add blank lines to make different sections of the resume stand out more. Because Notepad does not wrap text automatically, look for long lines of text that run off the screen. Insert hard returns to divide these long lines into lines of 65 characters, including spaces.

7. Save the .txt file. Repeat these steps to create a new plain text resume every time you modify your print resume.

PART 2. Email your plain text resume to yourself to confirm that the format holds up in email.

1. Open your email program and create a new message addressed to yourself.

2. Select all of the resume text, then copy and paste it into the email message window.

3. In the email subject line, enter a reference number from a job listing you have found.

4. If you have a cover letter (see Chapter 8), create a plain text version and copy and paste it into the email above your resume. Then type a line of asterisks or equal signs under the last line of the cover letter to mark the end of your cover letter and the beginning of your resume.

5. Clean up any odd spacing or other formatting problems.

   Send the message to yourself and check the format of your resume. Repeat this process until your plain text resume comes through as a clean, attractive, and readable document.

Add your completed work to the "Master Career Portfolio" section of your Career Builder Files.

PHASE 3:
APPLY FOR JOBS

Apply for Jobs

PART 3 Learn how to find and apply for jobs that will be a best fit career for you. You will learn how to find jobs using various sources, including through both Warm Introductions and Cold Leads. You will learn how to apply for jobs by filling in job applications and how to write cover letters that get the attention of prospective employers. You'll also learn how to apply for jobs online.

DEDRA
PERLMUTTER

*Certified HR
Professional*

©Jim Calloway Photography.

ADVICE FROM THE EXPERT

JVS Cincinnati Career Network

After 13 years in human resources helping employees navigate the workplace, Dedra Perlmutter changed direction and decided to help job seekers become employees.

The Cincinnati Career Network is not a job placement agency. Clients attend small-group workshops and get one-on-one counseling on any part of their job search. Dedra believes that "it's essential to find a 'go-to person' you feel comfortable with and who will be honest and helpful."

Dedra stresses "the power of networking—everywhere you go!" She emphasizes that networking is about giving and receiving and reminds job seekers to communicate their appreciation to the people they meet. She also promotes "LinkedIn® as an important tool for both job seekers and recruiters."

Dedra advises job seekers that "the interview starts in the parking lot, continues with the receptionist, and doesn't end until you send your thank-you note."

Dedra's most heartfelt advice is to keep reminding yourself that "rejections are not personal! Seek out others who are going through the same thing and share your experiences, disappointments, and successes."

As a free career center, the not-for-profit Cincinnati Career Network has seen an increase in clients since the economic downturn in 2008. "Most communities have an agency like ours. Call the library or United Way to find the one near you—and go!" Dedra knows that every job search is unique and is constantly changing. "Please," she says, "find a counselor who can coach and guide you through the process."

PLAN for Success

Most successful people keep a calendar of activities and a running list of tasks they have committed to do. Make *Your Career* a part of your calendar and task list.

- Read the outcomes on the first page of Chapters 6, 7, and 8 and jot down a target date for completing each one. Allow extra time for those that require more than just reading.

- Now make several calendar appointments with yourself to do the readings, homework, and projects for this class. Consider your other commitments (other classes, work, home) as you plan to make *Your Career* happen for you!

TALES FROM THE JOB SEARCH

RENE DEANDA
MBA Candidate: University of Iowa

Rene DeAnda has a degree in industrial engineering and experience in an engineering and sales environment. He describes himself as "passionate about process improvement and helping others." When it comes to the job search, Rene has had positive experiences with networking, online and offline, to find potential opportunities.

Rene believes networking is important and advises others to "make meaningful connections with people, because you never know what someone else will see in you." In his network, he knows a company owner who "interviews two to three people a week even when he isn't actively hiring for a position. When he meets someone interesting that might match well with his company, he wants to learn more about them."

For offline methods of finding job leads, Rene encourages fellow job seekers to "get outside your comfort zone and meet people in person. You can't rely solely on sitting behind a keyboard and applying for jobs." He also participates in national student organizations, which has led to a broader network for job leads.

Online, Rene heavily recommends LinkedIn®. He says, "Reaching out to people on LinkedIn® with genuine interest about their work will help expand your network." In addition, he uses "Twitter to find job postings and reach out to existing and new contacts." He encourages job seekers to "make use of all online resources that allow you to post a resume and spend time working on a LinkedIn® profile. This will allow you to be more visible to prospective employers and will increase your chances of being contacted without you doing much work."

Rene found the job search may take time, especially to hear back from prospective employers. "I didn't get contacted for interviews for several months, and I would even forget about jobs applied for because it took companies so long to contact me. But then a flood of interview opportunities came in at once, boosting my confidence." Don't give up! He says, "Keep on trying and applying. Be positive, when you begin thinking negatively and feeling down, look back on how far you've come and keep pushing onward."

6 Find Job Openings

OVERVIEW

In this chapter, you will learn how to build a powerful network of people who can give you career advice and serve as Warm Introductions to help you find job openings. You will also learn how to use other strategies to find job openings and learn how to evaluate job openings so that you can focus on the ones that are the best fit for you.

OUTCOMES

1. Networking pays off.
2. Describe strategies for finding job openings.
3. Find job openings that are a good career fit for you.

CAREER ACTION WORKSHEETS

WHERE ARE YOU ON THE JOURNEY?

PHASE 1: Prepare for the Journey
- The Job Search Journey
- Know Yourself to Market Yourself
- Picture Yourself in the Workplace

PHASE 2: Create Your Resume
- Plan Your Resume
- Write Your Resume

PHASE 3: Apply for Jobs
- **Find Job Openings**
- Write Job Applications
- Write Effective Tailored Cover Letters

PHASE 4: Shine at Interviews
- Know the Interview Essentials
- Prepare for Your Interview
- Interview Like a Pro

PHASE 5: Connect, Accept, and Succeed
- Stay Connected with Prospective Employers
- It's an Iterative Process
- Take Charge of Your Career

PHASE 3 Apply for Jobs
Step 1, *Find Job Openings*

Your goal in Chapter 6 is to learn to use and grow your Career Network, develop your strategy for finding job openings, and compare jobs so that you can apply for jobs you are most likely to get a positive response from and are the best career fit for you.

Your network can be a key to a treasure trove of job openings on your Job Search Journey. Pick up a key from everyone you know and start opening doors.

NETWORKING PAYS OFF

Numerous studies have noted that the majority of jobs are found through **networking**—developing relationships with people who can help you find job leads and help with your job search in other ways. The larger your network and the higher the quality of your contacts, the greater your chances are of finding someone who knows about a job that could be a great fit for you. Recall from Chapter 4 that **Warm Introductions** are personal introductions to a prospective employer and possibly a job opportunity, often when a job opening isn't actually posted. Building your Career Network is the best way to get Warm Introductions to job openings.

What Is Your Network, and Why Is It Important?

Who do you know? And who do they know? That is your network. It's obvious to seek help from your close ties, but it is your further connections that often provide great job leads because they travel in different circles. That friend your Aunt Kris always talks about might hold a gold nugget for you on your Job Search Journey.

Every person you meet—friend of a friend, mentor, neighbor, acquaintance, former coworker, classmate, teacher, a job seeker you meet at a career fair, the barista at your coffee shop, a LinkedIn® connection—has the potential to help you in your job search. So treat every meeting—virtual and live—as an opportunity to find a best fit job opening, maybe even before that job is advertised.

Surveys and research on hiring statistics show that more than one third of job openings are filled by job seekers who are referred by a current employee of the company. Employers often see these applicants as the "best fit" for a job since their current employees understand the company well and know what the job requires. This means that you should put effort into finding someone who works at your target employer and create a Warm Introduction with them.

Your network is an important source of job leads. The guidelines in this section will help you get the most from your networking efforts.

Networking Pays Off

Every year about 40 percent of the jobs that get filled are never advertised.[1] Networking can help you find these unadvertised jobs. Through networking, you can also:

- Seek career advice from many people and make them aware of your qualifications and availability

- Get insider information about the industry, trends, and job search and hiring methods in your field

- Get information about specific employers

- Promote yourself and make a good impression

- Practice your communication and interviewing skills

- Seek job leads and get referrals to other people who may be able to help you

[1]Kimberly Beatty. "The Math Behind the Networking Claim." *Jobfully Blog*. 1 July 2010. Web. 14 November 2014.

▶ *CAREER ACTION*
Complete Worksheet 6-1
Where Is Your Network?, page 165

Keep expanding your network. Your network can help you now during your Job Search Journey, and your network can be invaluable in the future when you are on the job.

Identify and Use Your Network

Follow these steps to create, expand, and use your network in ways that will help you find job leads, get interviews, and find your best fit job. Use Career Action Worksheet 6-2, Your Network List, page 167, for Steps 1 and 2.

Step 1: **Create a list and reach out to everyone in your network**—family, friends, former coworkers and classmates, mentors, and other people you know—by phone, email, or in person. Let them know that you are looking for a new job and share your job search goals. For example, you might say, "I'm working on a degree as a geology technician, and my ideal job would combine outdoor work and laboratory analysis. Do you know anyone in this field or industry that can help me learn more?" **Notice that you are not asking for a job or for the name of someone who can give you a job**. You are in the "search" phase of your Job Search Journey, looking for network connections that might eventually lead to an employee-referred job opening. This is the start of your Career Network.

Step 2: **Revise your list.** Check off the people you contact, noting the new connections they give you or if they couldn't help you. Then add the new connections you learned about. Keep track of who referred you to whom. This will help during the next steps, when you contact your new connections and tell them who referred you, and later, when you send thank-you notes and keep them updated about your job search. See "Keep Track of Your Network and Your Leads" on page 154.

Step 3: **Contact your new connections for a Career Network meeting.** Remember, at this step, you are not asking for a job; you are in a listening, learning mode.

- Email: Draft an email requesting 30 minutes of the person's time for the purpose of sharing what they can about your career field. See the sample contact letter in Figure 6-1 on page 151.

- Phone: Before you call anyone, outline what you will say if the person answers the phone and the message you will leave if you get their voice mail. Don't expect to talk right then; ask for a convenient time to call back or meet in person. You should also be prepared to talk with an administrative assistant to set up a time and place.

In-person Career Network meetings are best. Offer to meet at a coffee shop or a local lunch spot where you can sit across from each other without too much noise. Suggest a place and a time that are convenient for your connection. Remember that your connections are **doing you a favor** by helping you with your job search. Don't push to meet in person if they prefer to talk by phone, and change your schedule to accommodate theirs. Always thank them for their time. See the sample thank-you note for this situation shown in Figure 6-1.

Step 4: **Prepare for *every* Career Network meeting.** Prepare a list of questions; see "Good Questions to Ask in a Career Network Meeting" on page 152. Look at your connection's company website before the meeting so that you demonstrate your interest and professionalism by asking a question

Figure 6-1 Sample Contact Networking Letters

Sample Meeting Request

Dear [Mr./Ms. Contact],

I was recently referred to you by Grace Santana of Fairfield Tech. She recommended you as an excellent source of information about the physical therapy field.

I am a student at Fairfield Tech about to begin a search for a position as a physical therapy assistant, and I would welcome the chance to hear your advice about our career field and get your feedback on my qualifications and skills.

Do you have 30 minutes available to talk with me in the next two weeks, either in person or on the phone? Thanks in advance for your insights. I look forward to meeting you.

Sincerely,
[Your name and contact information]

Sample Thank-You Note

Dear First Name [or Mr./Ms. Contact],

Thank you again for taking the time to talk with me today about our career field and my career objectives. I enjoyed hearing about your job at Woodside Physical Therapy, and I appreciate your advice about the upcoming national exam. I'm looking forward to reviewing the online resources you suggested.

As you requested, I have attached my resume. Thank you in advance for your generous offer to give me advice about improving it.

I will be in contact from time to time to keep you updated on my job search. Thank you again for all the valuable information.

Best regards,
[Your name and contact information]

---

or complimenting the company for something it does. Print two copies of your resume and put them in a portfolio or manila folder.

Step 5: Meet with your connection. Here are some strategies and tips for a successful Career Network meeting; be sure to read "Work Your Network" in Outcome 2 on page 156 before your first meeting:

- Call or arrive on time (if you're meeting in person, plan to arrive five minutes early). Punctuality is courteous and shows that you are responsible and prepared.

- Do not start by discussing your specific job goals. Simply let them know you are exploring their field or their employer as a part of your Job Search Journey and want to learn from their experience.

- Ask them about their experience in the field.

- Listen for what employers need, descriptions of the work environment, the terms and language used by professionals in that field, examples of how career paths develop over time, and the process the company uses to fill job openings.

Good Questions to Ask in a Career Network Meeting

Print your questions or write them in a professional-looking notebook. Leave space to take notes during the meeting or phone call. Here are some good questions to ask—but don't expect to ask all of them in 30 minutes. Let the conversation flow naturally, ask deeper questions based on their answers (known as active listening), and watch for cues that the person wants to end the meeting or phone call.

Conversation starters

- What drew you to this career field?

- Is this your first job in this career field?

- How long have you worked at your company?

Job and career questions

- What is your typical workday like?

- Which parts of your job do you find most challenging? Most enjoyable?

- What is the culture like at your workplace/in this career field?

- What is a typical career path at your company?

- What do you wish you had known when you started your career?

- What changes have you seen in this field? What changes do you anticipate?

Career advice

- What advice to you have for someone looking for a job in this field?

- Does my job goal seem realistic and achievable?

- Do you recommend any additional training or certifications?

- What professional or other associations do you recommend joining?

- What publications or websites do you recommend?

- Who else would you recommend I speak with? When I call, may I use your name?

© Dragon Images / Shutterstock.com.

- Talk about your specific job goals toward the end of the meeting. Use your Personal Brand Statement and your 30-Second Commercial.

- Respect the time limits that have been set. Busy employees can't take too much time from their workday.

- Ask if you can share your resume with them. If they say yes, offer a second copy of your resume and ask if they can pass it on to appropriate people in their company. This will be your Warm Introduction to their employer.

- Ask your connections if they can suggest other people who might help you learn more about career paths in your field. Try to get at least two names from every person you meet with so that your network continues to expand exponentially. If your contacts can take the time to introduce you via email to these additional connections, that is ideal. Otherwise, take notes on how to reach these new network connections, either with pen and paper or on your phone.

Never forget the impression you are making when you talk about your job search. Talk about your efforts in positive terms; don't whine about how long you have been looking for a job or how many bills you need to pay. The people who give you leads may be taking a risk with their own reputation, and they expect you to make a good impression on the people they refer you to.

Step 6: **Follow up.** Send a thank-you note or an email within one day after the meeting. You should also follow up with anyone who refers you to a connection and let them know how the meetings went. Your goal is to maintain your relationships and, ideally, get two more connections from every meeting.

Keep your network up to date on your progress, especially if your goals change or become more specific. A well-written thank-you note or email creates a good impression and will remind your connections of your job search. If some new information comes to them, your thank-you note will remind them to share the information with you. See the sample thank-you note in Figure 6-1 on page 151.

 CAREER ACTION
Complete Worksheet 6-2
Your Network List, page 167

Be Workplace Smart

The people you meet while you network should feel that you will represent them well if they refer you to *their* network. Demonstrate that you are a professional who understands and follows the rules of the business world. For example, dress appropriately when you meet with your contacts in person. On voice mail, leave professional-sounding messages that are clear and to the point. Be careful not to put new contacts on the spot by asking personal questions or pushing for insider information that they are hesitant to share. Make sure to thank every person you meet, in the moment that you meet them as well as through a follow-up email.

Throughout *Your Career* you will read about standard workplace expectations. Look through the following list and read about these topics as needed.

- Chapter 4, personal references
- Chapter 4, business cards
- Chapters 5 and 8, writing tips
- Chapter 9, professional dress
- Chapter 9, phone etiquette
- Chapter 9, interview etiquette
- Chapter 11, professional binder or portfolio
- Chapter 12, thank-you notes

Be prepared to make a good impression by learning as much as you can about the situations you may encounter during networking—before you encounter them.

> ▶ **CAREER ACTION**
> **Complete Worksheet 6-3**
> Career Network Meeting Outline, page 169

> ▶ **CAREER ACTION**
> **Complete Worksheet 6-4**
> Hold a Career Network Meeting, page 171

Expand Your Network

Look for opportunities to initiate conversations about your job search. Be friendly and outgoing, and introduce yourself to people. If someone asks how you are doing or what you've been up to, tell them that you're busy looking for a job. Often that is all it takes for other people to ask about the type of job you are seeking. You never know—they just might know someone in your field.

You can also get connections by asking about other people. When you meet new people in social situations, ask what they do for a living and don't be afraid to ask how they found their job and request their advice. In networking, getting job leads is important. Asking directly is typically not as productive as saying something like this:

- What advice would you give me about finding a job in the auto mechanics industry?
- Do you have any advice for finding a job in sports medicine in this area?
- Who would you advise me to talk to about jobs in our field?

This approach focuses on the word *advice* and makes your contacts more inclined to help.

Seek high-quality contacts whenever possible. High-quality for your Career Network means people in your career field, at higher levels, or who know you well. People who already work in your chosen field are likely

---

> **Real World Scenario 6-1** Ralph was feeling frustrated with his job search. He was sticking to his goal of applying for 15 jobs every week, but he hadn't gotten any positive responses from his applications. It was time for a strategy change. He looked at the local Chamber of Commerce website and saw that there were several business events coming up in the next two weeks. He registered and attended an event held in the evening, after his classes and part-time job were over for the day. He had an excellent conversation with the owner of a local business who was looking for more employees. The business owner suggested that Ralph call his site manager to set up a Career Network meeting.
> *What opportunities do you have to get out from behind your computer and in front of a live audience? In addition to live meetings, how can you personalize your online interactions?*

to have more relevant leads. People in high-level positions are likely to have more leads because they are more aware of unadvertised job openings and may be able to connect you directly to the hiring manager. People who have met you in person, or who know someone who knows you well, are most likely to want to take time to help you.

Keep Track of Your Network and Your Leads

Your Career Network can have hundreds of people. Your leads can number in the hundreds too. Keeping track of it all is important so that good contacts and leads do not get away. In Chapter 1, you started to organize your Career Builder Files by collecting and choosing a filing method for information about you and your job search. Now it is time to put that plan into use. Use the About Jobs section of your Career Builder Files and Career Action Worksheet 6-1 to track the following things about your job search network and job leads:

Your Career Network

- **Contact information.** Include the person's properly spelled first and last name, plus as many addresses and other contact information as you can find (email, Twitter, company name, LinkedIn® profile, phone number, etc.).

- **How you know them.** How you came to know this person: by introduction from another connection, from a job fair, from high school, at a networking event, etc.

- **Their connection to your job search.** Why are each of these contacts important to your network? Do they have knowledge of your career field or of local companies you're interested in? Do they have general business connections or a large network of their own? Are they someone who has your interests at heart?

- **Your last interaction and your next interaction.** Keep notes about when you last spoke (date and critical information), and notes about when you next plan to connect. Note if they agreed to provide a Warm Introduction to their employers on your behalf. If you sent a thank-you note, list the date. If you need to update the person after you connect with someone he or she recommended to you, make a note of it.

Your Job Leads

- **Job description or title.** Briefly summarize the lead in your own words so that you can easily remember which job this is. If the job is not yet defined, use something general, such as "biomedical therapy job in Knoxville."

- **Contact information.** Record everything you can, including the name of the company or the recruiter, how you learned about an unadvertised job or where the job is posted, the people associated with this job (employee in the department that has the job opening, human resources person,

office administrator, etc.). List the names here, but keep the detailed contact information with your network contacts list.

- **Interactions list.** Keep good records about every job lead and application (the date of the Career Network meeting, the date of every step in the application and interview process, your notes about how the interactions are going, etc.).

Methods and Tools for Tracking

Here are some options and tips for keeping track of your job search information. You likely have chosen to use a combination of tools (email, Evernote, DropBox, hard copy folders). Revisit your notes from Chapter 1 and, for simplicity, stick to just a few of your favorite tools.

- **Email contact list.** Keep your connections' contact information in your email account with your professional name. If needed, you can export (move and copy) contacts from your nonprofessional email account into your professional account. Typically it is a .vcf file for MS Outlook and a .csv file for web mail like Yahoo or Gmail. Use Google search or the help section of your email account to find instructions for exporting contacts.

- **Spreadsheet.** Create a spreadsheet for tracking the contact information for everyone in your network. Include a column for last name, first name, title, email address, phone number, company name, company website, how you know the person, and the date of your last conversation. Include a "conversation memory" column to describe what you have talked about, including any personal information they shared, such as where they went on vacation last week.

- **Address book.** Buy an inexpensive paper address book for recording some or all of the information you would put in a spreadsheet (above). Treat this little book like you treat your wallet. Don't lose it!

- **LinkedIn®**. LinkedIn® is a very powerful tool to expand your network. If you have a LinkedIn® profile, your LinkedIn® connections should already be part of your list of network contacts. Invite everyone else in your network to connect with you on LinkedIn®. You can read more about LinkedIn® in Appendix A, page 380.

- **Calendar**. Put a note on the calendar for each task you completed and each task you plan to do in the future. Online calendars and calendar apps have alarms to remind you to do tasks. They are also easy to search when you are trying to remember or locate something.

- **Online job tracking service**. Consider using an online job tracking service such as JibberJobber or StartWire to manage your job search (jobs you apply for, contact information, etc.). These services have a free level, but each one has a learning curve.

One more piece of advice: Keep good records of your online searches. All too often, job seekers spot something on the Internet and can't find it again. When you find a good site, use the bookmark function on your browser to save the site and plan to check it regularly for updates.

DESCRIBE STRATEGIES FOR FINDING JOB OPENINGS

The most successful job searches typically start by tapping into your own Career Network. Your network connections can advise you about where to look for jobs, or even tell you about upcoming job openings that are right for you. Other strategies for finding job leads include connecting to professionals and job recruiters through career fairs and other professional events and the traditional searching for job openings in a wide variety of places.

Statistics show that job seekers who use many resources for finding job leads find jobs faster than people who use one or two resources.

Work Your Network

After you have identified your Career Network, you can begin to "work your network" to find information that can lead you to job openings. Here is how to think of it. You've already developed your personal brand, and you practice using this with everyone you meet. You have written your resume and spread your brand everywhere online. Now you're ready to learn from Career Network meetings. At these early meetings, you may learn about other connections who are closer to your career field and target companies. Gradually, you will start meeting with people who can tell you directly about job openings and serve as a Warm Introduction.

The process for each meeting is similar. Use the questions from "Good Questions to Ask in a Career Network Meeting" on page 152 as the starting point for your own questions. Sit down with, or call, someone who is a connection of a connection. Learn about their career and their company. Briefly tell them about your job search goals, using your Personal Brand Statement and 30-Second Commercial. Think of these meetings as practice runs for actual interviews. With each successive meeting, you will likely find that you can deliver your message smoothly in a very short time. During these short meetings, you will learn about a few of the 40 percent of jobs that aren't posted anywhere or will get leads about where to find newly posted jobs. When you apply for these jobs, be sure to mention the name of your connection. Better yet, in addition to your application, request that your connection pass on your resume directly to the HR or hiring manager. Using that person's name may give you a higher chance at getting an interview and, ultimately, the job. (Job seekers who get interviews through personal referrals have about a 30 percent higher chance of being offered the job.) Naturally, you will keep your contacts up to date about your job search because that is the polite way to work with your network connections.

Meanwhile, between your Career Network meetings, continue to fit the other strategies into your schedule.

Get Connected Professionally

The more time you spend with others who work in your career field, the more likely it is that you will learn about job openings and gain valuable information that you can use in interviews and on the job. The earlier you start, the more contacts you will gather. Do not hesitate to start building your network before you are actively seeking a job.

There are both one-time events and ongoing involvement opportunities that allow you to connect with people in your field. Think of these events as pre-interviews and prepare accordingly (look back at Shane and Lillian's conversation on page 40). Prepare conversation starters such as "What brings you here?" or "This location works well for this event." Practice introducing yourself. Set a personal goal to talk with a certain number of people.

Here are some places to connect with people in your field:

- **Attend career fairs**. Career fairs (also called job fairs) are excellent networking opportunities because you can connect with many prospective employers at one time.

- **Attend networking events**. In a typical year, the Chamber of Commerce and other organizations in your area will hold networking events for job seekers. There might be events for veterans, for women, for job seekers in a specific career field, and so on.

- **Participate in professional associations and industry trade groups**. Join and be active in professional, trade, and other relevant associations or groups, many of which offer assistance to job seekers. Nearly every career field has such a group; search for "*career field* trade group" or "*career field* professional association" (for example, "cosmetology trade group" or "cosmetology professional association"). The websites themselves are a valuable source of career information and job leads.

- **Do volunteer work**. Volunteer opportunities can be found in nonprofit organizations that have limited resources. Look for organizations that will likely need your professional skill set. For example, Habitat for Humanity needs volunteers with skills in carpentry, plumbing, and roofing, as well as the less obvious skills of volunteer coordination, meal preparation, accounting, leadership, project management, and many more. Your volunteer contacts can be a wonderful source of networking connections.

- **"Try before you buy."** Consider "practicing" in your career field to gain experience working side by side with people you can learn from. Cooperative education, internships, and volunteer positions are excellent opportunities for networking and may lead to full-time employment. Cooperative education programs place you in a paying job in your field, alternating semesters between school and work. Internships provide a period of supervised work and training in a workplace and are often scheduled during breaks in the academic calendar.

If you are shy or uncomfortable talking with strangers, consider volunteering to work at the registration table, hand out material, or help with other tasks that will help you interact with many people more comfortably. Be ready to exchange business cards and contact information. Take the time after each event to make notes about your conversations and enter the contact and job lead information into your tracking system, as discussed above.

Search for Job Openings

As discussed in Chapter 4, while many jobs are never posted, a very large number of jobs *are* posted, as you can see by searching the Internet and looking at the help wanted ads in your local newspaper's print edition or website. So while you are waiting for your network connections and professional or trade groups to come through for you, get busy—take the search into your own hands and apply to these Cold Leads. Remember the job search goals you set in Chapter 1? Brush them off and use them to help you achieve success in your job search. Now is a good time to revise your goals, as needed, to include goals for using all three job search strategies: working your network, increasing your professional connections, and finding jobs to apply for.

Use this list to make sure you are using all the resources.

- **Online job boards** are websites that post jobs from companies that pay a fee to list job openings. CareerBuilder and Monster are two of the best known job boards, but there are many, many others. Most professional and trade group websites have links to specialized job boards, and you can search for job boards by industry ("environmental job boards," for example). You can also find specialized job boards for summer jobs, internships, jobs on cruise ships, international jobs ("India job board," for example), etc.

- **Physical job boards** are bulletin boards in public places such as colleges, libraries, and stores. While not tech-savvy, these boards focus on local jobs.

- **Employer websites** list available jobs and accept applications. Government agencies and most not-for-profit organizations also have a section on their website for finding and applying for jobs.

© Rawpixel/Shutterstock.com.

CAUTION Dress Like You Have the Job

When you meet with a network contact, dress almost as if it were an interview—professionally and conservatively. Follow these simple tips to make a good impression:

- Be neat. Even the nicest clothes look unattractive when stained, wrinkled, or covered with dog hair.

- Pay extra attention to good hygiene. Simple things make a difference, like using mouthwash and cleaning under your fingernails.

- Avoid revealing or tight clothing such as tank tops, shorts, or low-rise jeans. Showing skin is not appropriate in most workplaces.

- Unless you are applying for a job at the gym, leave the athletic wear in your gym bag.

- Don't accidentally offend someone by wearing clothes with political or religious slogans or advertisements.

- Typically it's best to cover up or downplay body art such as visible tattoos and piercings.

- **Job search engines** scour the web for jobs listed on job boards and employer websites. The most popular job search engines are Indeed and SimplyHired.

- **Job information sites** are set up to connect employers and job applicants. Many are sponsored by government agencies. They include extensive job banks; you can apply online and may be able to post your resume so that employers can find you. The Department of Labor's CareerOneStop (careeronestop.org) has an extensive job information site.

- **Help wanted ads** (also called classified ads) are listed in print and online versions of newspapers and professional journals. Phony ads that require you to give personal information or pay a fee up front are a well-known problem. The more respectable the source, the more likely the ad is legitimate job opening, but be careful.

- **College career centers** have a wide range of services. The staff can help you weed through job listings and find the best jobs to apply for. They can also help with the tasks before you're ready to apply for jobs (personal assessments, resumes, and cover letters) and after you apply (mock interviews, thank-you notes, and customized advice for following up after an interview). Some career centers help students network with alumni in their career field. If you have already graduated, find out what services are available to alumni.

- **Private employment agencies** can be useful for getting considered by a particular employer, especially an agency that works in your field or that has a long-term relationship with a specific employer. Some agencies find employees for companies, while others actually hire the employee and contract him or her to the company. Some charge the employer for finding full-time employees; others charge the job applicant. Research the agency and understand what

you're getting into before you sign a contract. Consider asking one of your connections to read the contract too.

 CAREER ACTION
Complete Worksheet 6-5
Research Job Openings, page 173

 You, Online

Finding Quality Job Leads: Networking in the 21st Century

With so many options to find leads and apply for jobs, it is easy to get overwhelmed. You can submit your resume through Indeed, Monster, LinkedIn®, and the company's website, all for the same job! Savvy job seekers also use social media tools to generate and pursue quality leads.

- Set up email alerts on Indeed or another job search engine to alert you to new job openings. Research shows that applicants who apply within two days of a job listing are more likely to be reviewed and called for an interview.
- Instead of applying through the job search engine, search online for the same job listing on LinkedIn®, Twitter, or the company website. Can you find the name of someone internally who is associated with the posting?
- Connect with an employee through LinkedIn® and try to arrange a Career Network meeting or phone call as soon as possible.
- In your cover letter, refer to any employees you have connected with through social networking.

Your goal is to set yourself apart from the applications that get submitted to online job boards by having a Warm Introduction who knows your personality and initiative. Social media is a great tool to narrow down your job openings to a manageable number, while allowing you to connect warmly with real people. For more information, read the step-by-step social media strategies in Appendix A, page 379.

FIND JOB OPENINGS THAT ARE A GOOD CAREER FIT

Obviously you are not going through all this effort just to accept any job that you happen to find. Instead, you want to focus on finding those jobs that are an ideal best fit career for your personality and preferences, your skills and qualifications, and your interests. Part of your Job Search Journey includes evaluating job openings so that you can spend your valuable time on the ones that are a good career match. You can rate job openings based on how they fit—great, good, poor—and then compare jobs with the same rating to help you focus on the best ones.

Winners in all fields agree: Perseverance is a major factor in their success. When they meet an obstacle, they find a way around it.

Evaluate Your Qualifications for Job Openings

In Part 1 of this book, you spent time thinking about your career goals. In Part 2, you documented your qualifications in your resume. Now it's time to begin to compare job openings to your career goals and your qualifications—to your career goals so that you will gain greater pleasure from your work and to your qualifications so that you are a competitive candidate for the jobs you seek.

Evaluate each job listing and decide if it is (1) a stretch target, (2) a current target, or (3) a contingency target.

1. A **stretch job target** is the hard-to-get "dream job" you would like to have in the near future. It might be in a competitive company or field that does not hire many applicants; it might offer exceptional compensation and benefits, or it might offer a desirable location. Since we are "our own worst critics," it is well worth it to apply for a job higher than you think you can achieve to "test the waters." Be confident and put your best efforts into a great cover letter and resume. You may be more competitive than you realize, and you might even get the job! Even if you are not fully qualified for the job yet, by reaching for these "stretch jobs," you get exposure and experience that can move you toward higher career goals in the future.

2. A **current job target** is a job that is ideal for you right now. It suits your view of your current qualifications and interests, matches your compensation and work environment preferences, and provides a challenging and interesting work situation. You believe you have a realistic opportunity at being hired for such a job. (Just be careful that you aren't underestimating yourself!)

3. A **contingency job target** is your backup plan. You could easily get this job, most likely because you are overqualified. It is a "safe bet." It is not your first choice because it might lack the compensation or work environment that you want, or it might not be in your preferred career area. It offers security by giving you a compensation and the opportunity to develop your workplace skills, but it is usually the job you take when you have exhausted other options. A contingency job should never be the end of your job search. If you are overqualified or unhappy, you can continue your Job Search Journey and eventually leave this job for a better one, but without burning bridges with the contingency employer.

As you evaluate jobs, think about the factors covered in Chapter 3, including your personal preferences, the workplace culture, and the employer/employee relationship.

▶ *CAREER ACTION*

Complete Worksheet 6-6

Compare Jobs to Your Needs and
Qualifications, page 175

Determine the Best Fit for You

Try it now. Complete the first part of Career Action Worksheet 6-6 on page 175 by looking at a handful of job listings that you found and rating each one as a 1 (stretch job target), 2 (current job target), or 3 (contingency job target).

Now look at several of the jobs that you rated as 2, that is, as a realistic job target that fits your current qualifications. How will you compare these jobs? It's no problem if you have 20 or so jobs that are a current career fit. Apply for all of them. However, with your expanding Career Network and good job search practices, your list of job leads and job openings can quickly expand to twice that many. You need a way to sort through the job openings and find the best ones to focus on.

Make a list of the top things that are important to you on a job. Maybe it is compensation at a certain level, or avoiding travel. Using a simple 3, 2, 1 approach, rate each job in each category and sum up the total. For example, if you don't want to work on weekends, give a 3 to the job listings that indicate there is no weekend work, a 2 to the jobs with occasional weekend work, and a 1 to the jobs with regular or significant weekend hours.

After rating each job for the things that are important to you, add up the ratings. The jobs with the highest ratings are the ones you should focus on. If your ratings don't match your "gut feeling," it is time to talk with someone and review what you wrote down as being important. It is common to need to think through "what is important to me?" several times to better understand your own internal motives. Don't hesitate to go through

Real World Scenario 6-2 Diana just completed her first Career Network meeting with someone she met through online networking—and it was great. She had found Erik through LinkedIn® and was intrigued because his job sounded like her ideal stretch job. Although she hadn't heard of Erik's company, what she learned about his day-to-day tasks and the most important qualifications for his job was promising. Even though she didn't meet all the qualifications, Diana had great examples from her current job proving her ability to do the day-to-day tasks and meet similar challenges. Erik gave Diana his department manager's name and email address, and told her to use his name in her email. Diana feels much more confident about applying for a stretch job like Erik's and is ready for her next Career Network meeting.

What qualifications might be negotiable in the jobs you're interested in? How can you learn more about the day-to-day tasks? How can you find similar jobs you might be qualified for?

the process a few times on paper. After all, this assessment is much easier to do in writing than in real life, jumping from job to job.

Make the "Best Fit" Job Openings a High Priority

As you search for job openings and apply for jobs, be aware of the balance between current, stretch, and contingency job targets. It is important to have a few possibilities in each category, but most of your leads should be for jobs in the realistic "current job target" category.

Don't fall into the trap of focusing only on the dream jobs. Likewise, don't fall into the trap of "settling" by focusing only on contingency jobs. This second trap is common when a person lacks confidence or is afraid of failing. If this is you, talk to a trusted friend or ask a career counselor to help you stay focused on jobs that are a good fit for your current qualifications.

MAKE IT A HABIT

Schedule Time to Network

One of the biggest mistakes job seekers often make is focusing their job search strategy on applying to X number of jobs a week through online job boards such as CareerBuilder. While job boards are a critical resource, make it a habit to strategically connect and network with real, live people behind the job listings. When you create your Job Search Journey goals, include time every week for networking activities:

- **Reach out to your connections.** Take time every week to keep your existing connections up to date on your progress, follow up with your new connections, and write introductory emails or make phone calls to new connections.

- **Search for new connections.** Actively consider who could be your next lead-providing resource. Think about people in the "real world" and people you meet online.

- **Schedule Career Network meetings.** Schedule several of these meetings each week or month with people who work in your career field or who can help you in other ways. See Steps 3 through 5 in "Identify and Use Your Network" on page 150.

- **Go to events.** Schedule and attend career fairs and industry events, such as trade shows. Make these a priority on your calendar. See "Get Connected Professionally" on page 157.

- **Find ways to be helpful, and interested.** Many of the people in your network may also be looking for a job. If someone asks for help or information, provide it graciously or explain why you can't (for example, if you don't have a contact at a particular company). Stay in touch by sharing job leads that aren't a good fit for you or by inviting someone to attend a networking event with you. If a connection mentions that she's nervous about a meeting next Tuesday, send her a quick email on Wednesday saying that you hope it went well.

Make it a habit to get out from behind your computer and showcase your personality, qualifications, and professionalism in person.

© tukkata / Shutterstock.com.

Chapter Checklist

Check off each item you can do. Reread sections in this chapter to help you complete the checklist.

☐ Explain the six steps for creating and using my Career Network. ❶

☐ List the people who are part of my network—people who can help me with my job search by providing career advice, job leads, referrals, and other assistance. ❶

☐ Prepare for and conduct effective Career Network meetings with people in my career field. ❶

☐ Plan how I will expand my network to include more people in my career field. ❶

☐ List the three strategies for finding job openings. ❷

☐ List the resources that I plan to use to find job openings in my career field. ❷

☐ Categorize job listings in my career field as stretch, current, or contingency job targets. ❸

☐ Determine the best fit job openings by rating them against my needs and preferences. ❸

Critical Thinking Questions

1. Who is more likely to be helpful in your Career Network: neighbors and friends or people you meet at trade fairs and professional events? Explain your answer. ❶

2. Which of the three strategies for finding job leads is most likely to help you on your Job Search Journey? Why? ❶

3. Why is it so important to be polite and professional in Career Network meetings? On online social media? ❶

4. What are *your* goals for your Career Network meetings? Explain. ❶

5. What barriers do you anticipate in scheduling Career Network meetings? How can you overcome these barriers? ❶

6. How can volunteer work help you in your job search? What are three local organizations that you could volunteer with? ❷

7. Should you take the time to apply for stretch jobs? Why or why not? ❸

Additional Resources

For data files, career resources, and more, visit www.cengagebrain.com.

Trial Run

Role-Play a Career Network Meeting

Use role-playing to practice for your first Career Network meeting. If possible, pair up with a classmate in a related career field. The role-play has four parts:

1. Brainstorm good questions to ask. Print or copy Career Action Worksheet 6-3, Career Network Meeting Outline, on page 169 and fill it in together.

2. Take turns being the job seeker and the network connection, and role-play two meetings. The job seeker asked for the meeting, so he or she leads the role-play. Spend three to five minutes doing each role-play.

3. Evaluate how well each of you did in the role of job seeker.

4. Together, write a thank-you note. See the sample thank-you note in Figure 6-1 on page 151.

When it is your turn to role-play the job seeker:

- Introduce yourself professionally and quickly explain why you asked for the meeting.

- Be professional and courteous.

- Ask two questions from your networking meeting outline in Career Action Worksheet 6-3.

- Ask your connection for additional contact names.

- Thank your connection for her or his time.

Evaluate the job seeker on the following elements:

Rating Scale: 1 to 3 (1 = not done; 2 = done; 3 = well done)

Feedback for Job Seeker (completed by role-play contact)	**Rating (1 to 3)**
Stood up, shook hands, introduced self politely	_____
Asked good questions	_____
Demonstrated knowledge of the career/job	_____
Acted in a professional and courteous manner	_____
Smoothly requested additional contacts	_____
Ended meeting on time	_____
Thanked the connection for his/her time	_____

Job seeker's strengths:

Suggestions for improvement:

▶ CAREER ACTION WORKSHEET
6-1 Where Is Your Network? ❶

Before you start listing all your network connections, think about how you will keep track of everybody. Below, describe how you will track common information about each contact. It might help to review your completed Career Action Worksheet 1-3, Career Builder Files Organization System, on page 27, as well as the options described in this chapter.

Item	Think About This	Describe How You Will Track This
Contact names	Indicate that you have confirmed the spelling of the person's name?	
Social media contact information	Examples: LinkedIn® address, Facebook name, Twitter @name	
Phone numbers	Note if this is a mobile or office phone (it might be okay to leave late-night messages on office phones, but not on mobile phones)	
Physical or mailing address	Mailing address can be different from street location. The company may have multiple buildings or locations.	
Notes	a. How you know each other b. Preferred communication method (phone, email, text) c. Related people (manager, support person, mutual contact)	
History	Example: notes from last discussion, agreements made, date of last meeting, when to reconnect	

Add your completed work to the "About Jobs" section of your Career Builder Files.

This page is intentionally blank.

▶ CAREER ACTION WORKSHEET
6-2 Your Network List ➊

Complete items 1 to 3 now and do item 4 in a few weeks.

1. **List the people who are in your network today**. Use the method you chose in Career Action Worksheet 6-1. How many people are on your list today?

   _____

2. **Evaluate the quality of your network**. Rate how likely each person is to be able to help you in your job search. Add 1 point for each item; each person will have from 1 to 8 points.

   _____ This person is on my list today

   _____ We have met in person

   _____ We are connected on social media (LinkedIn®, Facebook, etc.)

   _____ We have known each other for at least two years

   _____ We stay in touch during the year (via phone, email, social media, in person, etc.)

   _____ We work in the same career field

   _____ He/she works at a company I am interested in

   _____ He/she has a high-level position in the company

3. **Grow your network**. Reach out to at least five of your highest rated network connections and ask them for the names of two people they know who might be able to talk with you. Try to add at least two names for each person you contact. **Important**: You are not asking for the names of people who will give you a job. You are seeking career information and additional contacts.

4. **How many people are in your network now?** _____

Keep repeating Step 3. Continue to grow your network throughout your Job Search Journey. Grow both the number of people and the quality of your contacts.

Add your completed work to the "About Jobs" section of your Career Builder Files.

▶ *CAREER ACTION WORKSHEET*
6-3 Career Network Meeting Outline ❶

Develop a general outline for your Career Network meetings that you can customize for each meeting. Start with the sample questions on page 152 and add questions that are relevant to you and your career field.

Conversation Starters (write at least 2 questions)

Job and Career Questions (write at least 5 questions)

Career Advice (write at least 5 questions)

Add your completed work to the "About Jobs" section of your Career Builder Files.

This page is intentionally blank.

▶ *CAREER ACTION WORKSHEET*
6-4 Hold a Career Network Meeting ❶

Use this worksheet to plan, schedule, and evaluate at least one Career Network meeting. Look back at Steps 3 through 6 in "Identify and Use Your Network" on pages 150–153.

1. **Identify at least two people in your career field.** Ask your college career center staff, instructors, family, and friends to suggest people to contact. Write each person's name, title, company, phone number, and/or email address here:

2. **Call or email the person and ask for a 30-minute meeting to learn about his or her job and discuss your job search.** Schedule a date, time, and place to meet. Outline what you will say in your email or phone call, or the message you will leave, here:

3. **Prepare for the meeting.** Print your questions from Career Action Worksheet 6-3 or write them in a small notebook. Print two copies of your resume. Bring business cards if you have them and a few samples of your work, if appropriate.

4. **Act professionally.** Dress as you would for the job, and plan to arrive a few minutes early. Take notes, but do not let note-taking interfere with the conversation. Do not ask for a job or an interview during these meetings, and end the meeting on time.

5. **Follow-up and evaluation.** After the meeting:

   - **Follow up with a thank-you note or email** and send a note to the person who helped you get the meeting.

   - **Summarize what you learned** and store your notes in your Career Builder Files.

   - **Take the time to evaluate the process**, from greeting the person to saying good-bye. Think about what happened, what was different from what you expected, what went well, and what you would do differently next time.

Be prepared to tell the class about your meeting or write a short summary of the meeting.

▶ *CAREER ACTION WORKSHEET*
6-5 Research Job Openings ❷

Use at least five sources to research job openings (see "Strategies for Finding Job Openings" on page 156). Fill in the table and then answer the questions at the end of the worksheet.

Here are Ibrahim's notes to help you get started. Ibrahim is finishing his associate degree in accounting and volunteers as a bookkeeper for the EMT crew that's based in a nearby fire station. He hopes to find a job where he can combine his degree and his interest in the medical field by doing billing and accounting work at a hospital or medical facility.

Site/Location (or path)	Date of Search	Search Terms	# of Job Openings	Helpful? Y/N
Mercy South Hospital bulletin board	3/14	N/A [not applicable]	3	Yes; met Rita Wagner, head of volunteer services
Mercy South Hospital website	3/14	Accounting Insurance Billing	8 2 6	Yes
SimplyHired.com	3/19	Hospital billing	528	Yes and no; must register to use advanced search to narrow down leads
Saylor College > Career Services > Resources > Career Specific Sites > Accounting	3/13	[name of city] hospital medical	0	No; did other searches too, but most jobs are not local

Save a least five job openings that you can use for Career Action Worksheet 6-6.

Site/Location (or path)	Date of Search	Search Terms	# of Job Openings	Helpful? Y/N

1. Which resource was most helpful? Why?

2. How long did it take to find a job opening that might be right for you? _____

3. What types of sites will you use to expand your search?

4. When will you schedule time to look for more job openings?_____

Add your completed work to the "About Jobs" section of your Career Builder Files.

▶ *CAREER ACTION WORKSHEET*

6-6 Compare Jobs to Your Needs and Qualifications ❸

Use this worksheet to categorize five of the jobs you found in Career Action Worksheet 6-5 as a stretch, current, or contingency job target; then compare two jobs in terms of their fit with your needs, interests, and qualifications. Be prepared to report your findings in a PowerPoint presentation or short report.

List the job title and the company's name for five of the jobs you found in Career Action Worksheet 6-5. Categorize each job as a stretch, current, or contingency job.

Job Title and Company	Stretch, current, or contingency job?
1. _____	_____
2. _____	_____
3. _____	_____
4. _____	_____
5. _____	_____

Compare Two Jobs

Select two jobs above to compare and label them A and B. In "My interests and needs," list five things that are important to you in a job and rate each job on these items. For example, you might list challenging work, close to home, and flexible hours (see Career Action Worksheet 3-1 and 3-2 on your preferences). In "My qualifications," rate how qualified you are for each job.

Rate how two jobs match your interests

(3 = great; 2 = okay; 1 = no match)

My interests and needs	Job A	Job B
1. _____	_____	_____
2. _____	_____	_____
3. _____	_____	_____
4. _____	_____	_____
5. _____	_____	_____

Rate how the same two jobs match your qualifications

(3 = overqualified; 2 = well qualified; 1 = not qualified)

My Qualifications	Job A	Job B
Education	_____	_____
Work experience	_____	_____
Job skills	_____	_____
Transferable skills	_____	_____
Accomplishments and recognitions	_____	_____
Personal values	_____	_____
Personal traits	_____	_____
Other: _____	_____	_____
Total ratings:	_____	_____

Add your completed work to the "About Jobs" section of your Career Builder Files.

Write Job Applications

OVERVIEW

You will be chosen to interview based on the quality and effectiveness of your Job Application Package: resume, cover letter, and employment application. If you carefully completed the activities in Part 2, your resume should be top-notch. This chapter presents tips and activities for completing job applications correctly, followed by Chapter 8 on cover letters.

OUTCOMES

1 Describe how to apply for jobs.

2 Complete a job application correctly.

3 Apply best practices when using preprinted job application forms.

4 Use the suggested steps to apply for jobs online.

CAREER ACTION WORKSHEETS

7-1: Create an Application Data Sheet, page 189

7-2: Create Your References List, page 191

7-3: Complete a Paper Employment Application, page 193

WHERE ARE YOU ON THE JOURNEY?

PHASE 1: Prepare for the Journey
- *The Job Search Journey*
- *Know Yourself to Market Yourself*
- *Picture Yourself in the Workplace*

PHASE 2: Create Your Resume
- *Plan Your Resume*
- *Write Your Resume*

PHASE 3: Apply for Jobs
- *Find Job Openings*
- ***Write Job Applications***
- *Write Effective Tailored Cover Letters*

PHASE 4: Shine at Interviews
- *Know the Interview Essentials*
- *Prepare for Your Interview*
- *Interview Like a Pro*

PHASE 5: Connect, Accept, and Succeed
- *Stay Connected with Prospective Employers*
- *It's an Iterative Process*
- *Take Charge of Your Career*

PHASE 3 *Apply For Jobs*
Step 2, *Write Job Applications*

Your goal in this chapter is to complete job applications accurately and to use key words that grab attention.

When you're doing something tedious, that's when you should check, double check, and triple check before calling it complete.

APPLY FOR JOBS

Throughout your networking, you will encounter many leads for jobs. Some of these leads may be found through job boards, social media sites, print job listings, or directly on a company's website. Once you find a job opening, the next step is to complete the job application using your Job Application Package. Even though you may pass on your resume through a Warm Introduction, you likely will still have to complete a job application. Chapter 7 covers the following topics:

- Completing employment application forms (most of the information is in your resume)
- Applying for a job with a specific employer
- Applying online for jobs posted at career websites and company sites

Many job seekers think of the application as something to get through quickly so that they can get on with the interview. Wrong! Employers are using more and more advanced software to screen applicants based on "best fit" prior to investing time and money on interviewing possible candidates. Employers carefully consider employment application forms, cover letters, and resumes. They use these documents to select interviewees and to weed out people who do not look to be qualified on paper.

Application Forms

Employers design application forms to get the information they consider most important to making hiring decisions. They use the forms to collect the following:

- Consistent information from every applicant so that they can compare applicants accurately and objectively
- Information needed to evaluate an applicant's qualifications, cultural fit, and match with the job (for example, references, years of experience, or specific technical skills)

- Background and legal information needed to make a job offer, such as Social Security number, proof of citizenship or proof of legal right to work in the United States, and information related to affirmative action and equal employment opportunity

Employers use a variety of application formats. The length and complexity of forms vary greatly—from preprinted paper forms to sophisticated online forms. Some applications have questions that require detailed answers. Some employers ask questions that test applicants' knowledge of the job or career field. Treat every question seriously and answer it completely. Applicants who submit incomplete applications with mistakes are the first to be eliminated.

Many employers require online applications. Others scan paper applications and file the information electronically. Applications are searched for information (education, work experience, etc.). If you omit important information, your application may be passed over.

Preparation and Practice

Search the employer's website for an application you can use as a practice version.

Real World Scenario 7-1 Louisa made a great impression at a recent job fair when talking to a recruiter. The recruiter left her a business card and a link to the job application on the employer's site. Louisa was so excited that she went home and filled out the application right away. She then followed up with the recruiter and provided a cover letter and resume, along with the job application in .pdf format. She was sure she had done everything correctly. However, she received a response from the recruiter stating that she had applied to the wrong job posting!

What impact did this mistake have on Louisa's impression as an applicant? How could she have avoided this issue?

If you pick up an application in person and plan to fill it in by hand, take the form home with you; do not fill it in on the spot. Ask for two copies or photocopy the application and fill in a practice form so that you can present your best work.

Following directions is important to employers. Be sure to demonstrate this ability when you apply for a job. Read the instructions carefully and *follow them exactly*. Before you pick up your pen (black or blue ink; fine tip if possible), *read the entire application* to see how sections are related and which sections require more or less detailed answers. Employers judge neatness and completeness of the form, not only the quality of answers.

So that you have all of the information with you when you complete an application, create a plain text Application Data Sheet using Career Action Worksheet 7-1 with all of the information you will need that is not already included in your resume. The sole purpose of the data sheet is for your own use when filling in job applications. Because the data sheet is a plain text file, you can paste text from it into an online application form. This is a good time to pull out the plain text version of your resume that you created in Career Action Worksheet 5-5. You can copy and paste answers from your plain text resume into an online application as needed.

▶ *CAREER ACTION*
Complete Worksheet 7-1
Create an Application Data Sheet, page 189

WHAT IS AN EMPLOYMENT APPLICATION?

This section has guidelines for completing the major parts of a typical application form. Refer to the completed sample application in Figure 7-1 on pages 180–181. Do not leave any section of a form blank. Enter "NA" or "N/A" (not applicable) if a question does not apply to you.

Personal Information

In this section, provide your name, address, contact information, Social Security number, and information about any history with the employer. If the application asks for a current address and a permanent address, repeat your current address in the permanent address section rather than leave it blank. If the form asks for a second phone number, list a phone number where messages can be left. Provide a working email address that you check regularly.

Position Information

List a definite position objective, title, or job requisition number (provided by the employer on the job listing). If you submit your application online, the scanning software will use this information to match your application to the job you are applying for. Moreover, employers are not impressed with applicants who list "anything" as the position desired. This hints of desperation, a lack of confidence, or a lack of focus or direction.

If you can start work right away, enter "Immediately" for Date Available. If you are currently employed, think about the amount of notice you will give (typically two weeks). You may be asked about your available days, hours, or shifts and your willingness to relocate.

The application may also ask how you heard about the position. Mark "Other" and name a referral if you found out about the position through a Warm Introduction.

Education

List all schools/colleges attended, your major, your degree/diploma, and your graduation dates. Figure 7-1 lists one high school and one community college.

Figure 7-1 Sample Employment Application Form

APPLICATION FOR EMPLOYMENT
ABC Company

This application is used in the selection process and both pages <u>must</u> be completed. Attach extra sheets if necessary (references to resumes are <u>NOT</u> acceptable).

APPLICANT INFORMATION

Last Name	First	M. I.	Social Security Number	Home Phone	Alternative Phone
Martinelli	**Elizabeth**	**S.**	**999-00-0088**	**208.555.0106**	**208.555.0170**

Permanent Address – No. & Street	City	State	Zip	Date
6518 Willow Way	**Boise**	**ID**	**83706**	**01/15/--**

Have you previously ☐ applied to OR ☐ been employed by ABC Company? Where and when? **N/A** E-mail Address **emartinelli@provider.net**

Do you have relatives working for the ABC Company? ☐ Yes ☒ No If yes, give names and departments where they work.

POSITION

Position Desired	Salary Desired (per month)
Sales Supervisor	**Negotiable**

Willing to relocate? ☒ Yes ☐ No Do you want ☒ Full-time ☐ Part-time Date Available for Work **Immediately**

EDUCATION

Highest Educational Level Completed:

Name of School	Location	From	To	Degree or Diploma	Major	Minor
High School **Idaho Falls High School**	**Idaho Falls, ID**			**Diploma**		
Community College **Central Community College**	**Boise, ID**	**9/08**	**1/10**	**A.A.**	**Marketing**	
College or University						
Graduate School						
Special Training						

Languages Other Than English (if required in employment announcement):	Speak **Spanish**	Read **Spanish**	Write **Spanish**

EMPLOYMENT HISTORY & RELATED EXPERIENCE List present or most recent experience first. Include armed services experience and volunteer work.

Employer Name **Kevington's Emporium (Part-time)**	Employer Address **3315 Front Street Boise, ID 83705**	Dates (Mo./Yr.) From **12/08** To **Present**

Position Title **Assistant Sales Supervisor**	Supervisor **Charlie Wu**	Phone **208.555.0131** Ext. **125**

Reason for Leaving **Still employed**	Salary: Start **9.00/hr** End **11.58/hr**	No. Hours Per Week: **20**

Duties:

Training, supervising, and scheduling staff of six

Promoted to Assistant Sales Supervisor after only six months

Employer Name **Crown Sportswear (Part-time)**	Employer Address **1800 Orchard Street Boise, ID 83704**	Dates (Mo./Yr.) From **5/08** To **11/08**

Position Title **Sales Clerk**	Supervisor **Connie Pratt**	Phone **208.555.0114** Ext. **418**

Reason for Leaving **Took new job**	Salary: Start **8.50/hr** End **8.50/hr**	No. Hours Per Week: **10-15**

Duties:

Sales, customer service, and design and setup of all merchandise displays

Performed managerial and closing duties for store three nights a week

(continued)

APPLICATION FOR EMPLOYMENT

Employer Name **Value Market Variety (Part-time)**	Employer Address **460 Park Way** **Idaho Falls, ID 83402**		Dates (Mo./Yr.) From **12/05** To **3/08**
Position Title **Salesclerk**	Supervisor **Tevia Levitt**		Phone **208.555.0199** Ext. **420**
Reason for Leaving **Moved to college location**	Salary: Start **7.00/hr** End **8.25/hr**		No. Hours Per Week: **15**
Duties: **Sales, customer service, and inventory stocking tasks** **Selected "Customer Service Employee of the Month" twice in one year**			
Employer Name	Employer Address		Dates (Mo./Yr.) From To
Position Title	Supervisor		Phone Ext.
Reason for Leaving	Salary: Start End		No. Hours Per Week:
Duties:			

REFERENCES

Name	Address	Telephone	Occupation	Years Known
Charlie Wu **(Kevington's Emporium)**	**3315 Front Street** **Boise, ID 83705**	**208.555.0131** **Ext. 125**	**Sales Manager**	**2 years**
Tevia Levitt **(Value Market Variety)**	**460 Park Way** **Idaho Falls, ID 83402**	**208.555.0199** **Ext. 420**	**Supervisor**	**3 years**
Dr. Robert Cornwell	**Business Department** **Central Community College** **8500 College Way** **Boise, ID 83704**	**208.555.0143**	**Professor, Marketing** **and Sales**	**2 years**

ADDITIONAL INFORMATION

ΦAre you currently employed? ☒Yes ☐No   May we contact your employer? ☒Yes ☐No   May we contact your former employers? ☒Yes ☐No

Can you (if accepted for employment) provide proof of your legal right to remain and work in the U.S.? ☒Yes ☐No

A separate affidavit on felony and misdemeanor convictions is REQUIRED to be completed on the attached form.

I hereby certify that all statements on this application are true and complete to the best of my knowledge and belief. If employed, I understand that any untrue statements on the above record may be considered grounds for termination.

Date *01/15/--*   Signature *Elizabeth S. Martinelli*

- If you attended more than one high school, list the most recent one you attended and indicate the year you received your diploma. List your GPA only if it is requested or if it is high.

- If you have attended more than one post-secondary educational institution, list the most recent one first and work back to the first one you attended.

- If necessary, attach a separate list of additional schools you attended.

If the form has a space to list additional information, include items such as subjects of study, research, special skills (such as a foreign language), or other activities; also give examples of your capabilities and activities that relate to your job objective. Emphasizing foreign language skills can be a very valuable asset to prospective employers. If you do speak a language other in addition to English, make sure to highlight this in the appropriate section. Sometimes, the application will specifically ask if you speak other languages. Other times, you may be able to include this information in the Education section or Special Skills section. Summarize the information and use abbreviations if space is tight.

Employment History

List your most recent job first. Most forms ask for the month and year you started and stopped each job. If the application does not have a separate section for military service, list it in your employment history.

Before you fill in the application, decide which information to put in the education section and which to put in the employment section.

References

In Chapter 4, you began to consider who in your network could serve as a reference. Although references are not included in your resume, they are usually requested as a part of the job application. Use Career Action Worksheet 7-2 to create your reference list. Consider the following when choosing references:

- **Right number.:** Provide the number of professional or personal references requested. Employers may ask for three to five references. Find both personal references (people who vouch for your good character) and professional references (people who vouch for your work skills and qualities).

- **Right relationship:** Employers may specify the relationship they would like you to use as a reference. Whenever possible, tie your references directly to your work experience. Most prospective employers value good references from former reputable employers because former employers know firsthand how you performed at work. In Figure 7-1, notice how the first two references are the applicant's coworkers at previous jobs.

  - **Former direct managers:** It is generally better to request a recommendation letter when leaving a job and then keep it in your files. Always try to leave on good terms and stay in touch with previous managers, including keeping contact information current.

  - **Former coworkers:** Again, maintain positive relationships with former coworkers. You never know when they can help connect you to a job or act as a reference.

  - **References not related to work experience:** Consider teachers, members of volunteer organizations, and members of your network who know your skills and capabilities.

- **Permissions:** Remember that you must talk to your references in advance and get their permission to list them on an application. Thank them for allowing you to do so.

MAKE IT A HABIT
Respect Your References

A person cannot be a reference for you without providing a phone number for prospective employers' use. Whether or not you discuss privacy issues with your references, they expect you to guard this information.

When you complete an application and send a copy of your resume, do not include your references' phone number or attach a reference list with their phone numbers. Instead, enter "Upon request" in the field or on the list. A prospective employer will not call your references before meeting you, and you can provide the phone numbers during the interview.

Never include your references' email addresses in an application. When a site will not accept an application without references' email addresses, one job applicant enters "uponrequest@ uponrequest.com" in these fields. She has been selected for phone interviews by employers when she has done this. During the interview, she gives the phone numbers verbally so that the interviewer can include them in the interview notes.

© Tashatuvango/Shutterstock.com.

Watch out for the following when you develop your reference list:

- Use only those references who would recommend you highly from firsthand knowledge and with whom you have a good relationship and regular communication.

- Because legal constraints may restrict your previous employers from giving a reference, ask former coworkers. They may be more willing to give you a recommendation.

- Do not use relatives as references.

- It is inappropriate to use someone you have not spoken to in years as a reference. He or she may not have enough information to provide an accurate view of your qualifications. To maintain your references, stay in touch via an occasional email or phone call with regular updates on your job status and career goals.

Prospective employers will check your previous employers and your references. Previous employers might only confirm your dates of employment, but references may be asked to respond to questions about your attitude, work history, job performance, ability to work with others, and work habits. Coach your references accordingly. You can't control what your references will say about you, but you should give them information about the jobs you seek and the skills required so that they will be able to emphasize your qualifications and abilities.

> ▶ *CAREER ACTION*
> **Complete Worksheet 7-2**
> Create Your References List, page 191

Difficult Job Application Questions

Employers may ask additional questions throughout the application or in an "Additional Questions" section. Consider carefully how to handle challenging questions.

Contacting Your Current Employer

If an application asks permission to contact your current employer, answer yes only if your employer is aware of your job search and approves. Otherwise, protect your current job by answering no.

Legal Status

You will be asked for information that protects the employer if you are hired. You must indicate that you are a U.S. citizen or have the legal right to work in the United States.

Law Violations

If you have been convicted of a felony or misdemeanor (excluding minor traffic violations), you will be asked about the nature of the crime, when and where you were convicted, and the disposition of the case. (Note that you can be asked only about convictions; employers are not permitted to ask if you have been arrested.) Answer these questions truthfully and indicate "will discuss at interview." Your best option is to explain any negative history in person, where you must be prepared to take responsibility for your actions and explain what you learned.

Also, do some research. In your state, depending on the nature of the offense and how long ago it was, you may be able to expunge your record or obtain a Certificate of Good Conduct (for multiple offenses) or Certificate of Relief (for one offense) that can help reduce the legal barriers to employment.

The application will probably inform you that the employer may procure an investigative consumer report on you as part of considering your application. If so, the investigative report could include information about your criminal record, education, credit history, and driving record. Any misrepresentation on your part would be identified, and you would be eliminated from consideration for the job.

Whether or not you have a law violation on your record, you must often indicate whether you are willing to take a drug test.

Reasons for Leaving Prior Job

Answer this question using positive, growth-oriented language. Do not criticize your former employer and do not use reasons that may indicate you may be unreliable or

Real World Scenario 7-2   Danilo recently had been laid off from his job. He needed to find a new job soon. There were several people in his division who were laid off. In his case, it was because he was a good but average performer. He wasn't sure how to talk about his lay off in a positive way. On his application, he decided to be as truthful and positive as possible. He outlined the financial difficulties in his division but did not go into detail regarding his performance. He mentioned that he could discuss this further at the interview if requested. He was sure that his previous manager would still provide a reference because his performance problems had not been serious. He felt comfortable about not going into detail in his job application for this reason.

How can you put a positive spin on any difficult questions you encounter on job applications?

a poor fit for the job. For example, "Seeking advancement" is a positive reason compared to "Company refused to promote me."

Desired Salary

Because salary is such an influential factor in employment, use "negotiable" as the salary desired. Don't risk eliminating yourself before you have a chance to present your qualifications in an interview. Save any discussion of salary until the employer has expressed a definite interest in you. If you are required to enter a salary figure, use the following tips:

- If the position is advertised at a set, nonnegotiable salary, list that figure.

- List a range based on your salary research. Review Chapter 12 for more information on how to research salary ranges.

- If you are not allowed to type a range, pick the midpoint of the range and list that figure.

Sign the Application

Because an employment application is a legal document, when you sign the form or check the box indicating that the information is correct, you literally take an oath that the information you provided is true and accurate. (On a more practical note, unsigned applications cannot be processed. You may lose valuable time—and face—if the company has to take extra steps to ask you to sign your application.)

APPLY FOR A JOB WITH A PREPRINTED APPLICATION

Not every job application requires a cover letter and resume. A preprinted application form by itself may be all you need to apply to a company where many people have the same job (a discount retailer or a national restaurant chain, for example). You may be able to fill in a preprinted application, or you may need to apply online through the company website or at an application kiosk. (See "Apply for Jobs Online" on pages 186–187.)

If you apply in person at a small business, you will probably be given a blank application to fill in by hand. Fill in the application at home and return the completed form with a customized version of your print resume and, optionally, a cover letter. Learn more about cover letters in Chapter 8.

Follow these tips to make the best impression when you apply for a job in person with a preprinted paper job application.

- **Look the part and be ready to interview**. Never visit an employer's place of business without dressing conservatively and looking professional (business casual is fine). You could be invited to meet the manager and even interview on the spot. Be sure you get the manager's full name. Prepare by studying the interview chapters in this book, Chapters 9–11.

- Bring your driver's license or other proof of identification.

- **Come alone and do not conduct any business during your visit**. Do not order food or come to the customer service desk carrying a bag of purchases.

- **Allow enough time for your visit**. You may be asked to take a survey or an employment test, so allow plenty of time for your visit. You do not want to miss out on an opportunity because you have to rush to another obligation.

- **Proofread the application carefully**. The application is your "ambassador"; make sure it represents you well. Check it for accuracy, neatness, completeness, and the quality of your answers.

- **Keep a copy of the application**. Create a filing system for all of your applications. Include a sheet of paper with the manager's name and contact information along with any notes about the application process.

- **Ask to meet the manager when you return the application**. Ask if you can give your application to the manager. Be gracious if the answer is no; ask for the manager's name and the name of the person who takes the application.

- **Keep a copy of the application**. Create a filing system for all of your applications. Include a sheet of paper with the manager's name and contact information along with any notes about the application process.

- **Check back in a week if you don't hear from anyone**. Call or visit if you haven't heard from the company within a week. If you really want the job, go in person and leave a copy of your resume.

▶ *CAREER ACTION*

Complete Worksheet 7-3
Complete a Paper Employment Application, page 193

APPLY FOR JOBS ONLINE

This section describes the basic process of applying for jobs online.

Register with a Career Site

You must register with a career site to apply for the jobs posted there. Registration for job seekers is free because the sites earn their revenue from the fees that employers pay and from advertisements. Some professional organizations charge nonmembers a fee to use their sites. Create a free account using the name on your resume and letter. Create a highly secure password to use at all of them—and don't forget what it is. It's critical to select a strong password because your job application contains a lot of private information such as social security number.

You create a profile when you register, with your contact information, job objective(s), career field(s), and skills and qualifications. Your profile is posted on the site where employers can find it, so use as many keywords as you can.

⌖ You, Online

Applying Using LinkedIn®

LinkedIn® is a unique site because not only is it a professional online social network, it is a job search and application engine as well. You can find out about jobs on LinkedIn® through the Groups feature or using their Job Search tool. Many employers now have the option to use LinkedIn®'s basic job applications form to accept job applications. Some employers may ask you to apply through LinkedIn® and fill out an additional application on the employer's site. LinkedIn® can be your one stop shop for your Job Search Journey, from posting your personal brand and resume, to connecting and finding job leads, to applying for and receiving requests for job interviews.

Submit an Online Job Application

You can fill in most of the fields by pasting in text from the application data sheet you created in Career Action Worksheet 7-1. Employers get a report with the data you enter into the form and the print copies of your resume and cover letter (Chapter 8).

> **CAUTION**
> Save, Save, Save
>
> When applying online, Internet or technical issues can easily derail your application process. You may have spent the time to fill out the full application and at the last screen, run into a page load issue. You may have painstakingly typed in the answer to a difficult question, only to accidentally hit the Back or Refresh button. To avoid the risk of losing your entered data:
>
> - Keep an open Word document or add to your existing plain text document. Copy and paste any new content you are entering into this file throughout the application process.
>
> - If the application site has a "Save Application" functionality, use it frequently.
>
> - Fill out job applications in a place where high-speed Internet is available.
>
> Save passwords and other relevant information in case you need to go back and edit your application. Make sure to create strong passwords.

Figure 7-2 First Page of Application on a Company Website

How did you become aware of this opportunity?

* Source: [--None-- ▼] Referred By: [＿＿＿＿＿]

Other Source: [＿＿＿＿＿]

Applicant Data

* First name: [＿＿＿＿＿] Street address: [＿＿＿＿＿]

* Last name: [＿＿＿＿＿] * City: [＿＿＿＿＿]

Middle: [＿＿＿＿＿] * State/Region: [-- ▼]

* Phone #: [＿＿＿＿＿] ZIP/Postal code: [＿＿＿＿＿]

Mobile #: [＿＿＿＿＿] * Country: [United States ▼]

Email Registration

Your email address will be used as your login name allowing you to return to our website to view your status and update your profile. If you do not have an email address, you can obtain a free account at Yahoo or Gmail. Please make sure that the syntax of your email address is in the following form: *username@ispname.com*

* Email: [＿＿＿＿＿]

Please create your password

* Password: [＿＿＿＿＿]

Re-type new password:

[＿＿＿＿＿]

Resume & Cover Letter

Your resume can be uploaded in any of the following formats: DOC, RTF, PDF, TXT, HTML. Files saved in .DOCX are not currently supported

* Attach resume or CV: (Choose File) no file selected

Cover Letter: [＿＿＿＿＿＿＿＿＿＿＿＿＿＿]

Please indicated the highest level of education **completed**

* Education: [--Please select-- ▼]

Legal Status

Are you authorized to work in the U.S.?

* Work status: [--Please select-- ▼]

Figure 7-2 shows the first page of a job application at an employer's website.

Apply via Email

Some employers ask applicants to apply by sending an email. Put the title or number of the job listing and your name in the subject line.

Use the default email font. In the body of the email, copy your cover letter into the email message. Attach your resume and/or job application as requested in .pdf format.

Before emailing your application to the employer, send it to yourself or to a friend to see how well the documents survive the cyberspace transfer. You may need to modify the spacing and formatting. Always proofread your attachments and the data in the form before you click "Send."

Because no one wants to receive an email with a lot of attachments, do not attach any items from your Master Career Portfolio other than those requested by the employer. Save them for the interview.

Chapter Checklist

Check off each item you can do. Reread sections in this chapter to help you complete the checklist.

☐ Fill out employment application forms accurately with a positive self-representation. **❶**

☐ Identify at least five good-quality references. **❷**

☐ Understand how to answer challenging questions on job applications. **❷**

☐ Be ready for any possibility when applying in person, including an on-the-spot interview. **❸**

☐ Fill out online applications with no issues. **❹**

Critical Thinking Questions

1. What are the possible consequences of not filling out an employment application completely and according to the instructions? **❷**

2. Should you mention a salary figure in an application? Explain. **❷**

3. What are the consequences of choosing the wrong references? **❷**

4. What are the consequences of not notifying your references of their inclusion in your job application process? **❷**

5. How is an online application different from a print application? Describe what you will do differently with each one. Then describe how an employer might use these differently. **❹**

Additional Resources

For data files, career resources, and more, visit www.cengagebrain.com.

Trial Run

Job Application Challenges

Work with a partner. Consider the following tough job application questions and brainstorm answers that would represent an applicant in the best light possible. Write a three- to five-sentence answer or explanation for each question.

1. Why do you want this job?

2. What is your desired salary for this position?

3. Why did you leave your previous employer?

▶ *CAREER ACTION WORKSHEET*
7-1 Create an Application Data Sheet ❶

A preprinted application form requires information that will not be on your resume. Below, you will create an application data sheet. When you fill out multiple job applications, this will allow you to easily copy and paste the information from this application data sheet and your plain-text resume.

PART A: Use this Career Action Worksheet to collect commonly requested information. The textbook companion site has a form for recording the information.

Remember: A completed employment form is an official document, and you can be denied employment or fired if you aren't truthful about the information you supply, including details about previous jobs. Your signature indicates that the information is complete and accurate.

Name		
Street Address		
City		
State		
Zip Code		
Social Security Number		
Email Address		
Phone Number		
Days available to work		
Hours available to work		
If not a US Citizen, Type of Visa and Expiration Date?	Type of Visa	
	Expiration Date	
If Armed Forces:	Specialty	
	Date Entered	
	Date Discharged	
Criminal History	Conviction	
	Nature of Offense	
	State Where Offense Occurred	
	Sentence	

Foreign Language Skills	Language	
	Skill Level	

PART B: Find several job application forms for jobs in your industry, either from online or paper copies from local employers. As you review these applications, find three more items that you can add in the left column of your application data sheet. Then fill in your data on the right.

In addition to your plain text resume, this Career Action Worksheet will allow you to easily copy and paste information into multiple job applications.

Add your completed work to the "About Jobs" section of your Career Builder Files.

▶ CAREER ACTION WORKSHEET
7-2 Create Your Reference List ❷

Review your network and identify the following possible references who you think would be able to vouch for you, professionally or personally:

Relationship	Name	Phone Number Email Address	Agreed?
Former Managers			
Former Coworkers			
Instructors and Other Academic Mentors			
Organization Presidents or Leaders (Volunteer, School, etc.)			

Reach out to these references with an email or phone call and ask if they would agree to be a reference as you continue your job search. This conversation is a good time to bring them up to date on what you're doing and catch up on their activities as well.

Add your completed work to the "About Jobs" section of your Career Builder Files.

This page is intentionally blank.

▶ *CAREER ACTION WORKSHEET*

7-3 Complete a Paper Employment Application ❸

If possible, obtain an employment application form from an employer in your target industry—even one from your target employer. Using an application from your target industry provides the best preparation and practice. If one is not available, search the Internet for "sample job applications." Complete the application for practice and use it as a model when you fill out actual applications for employment.

Add your completed work to the "About Jobs" section of your Career Builder Files.

Write Effective Tailored Cover Letters

OVERVIEW

Use cover letters to encourage hiring managers and recruiters to choose to read your resume and applications out of the stacks of hardcopy and online files they receive. Cover letters help you share your personality during both Warm Introductions and Cold Leads. You've put lots of work into your documents; now take the extra step to encourage people to read them!

OUTCOMES

1. Structure your cover letter.
2. Apply effective writing tips.
3. Customize the content.
4. Describe how to distribute Your Job Application Package.

CAREER ACTION WORKSHEETS

WHERE ARE YOU ON THE JOURNEY?

PHASE 1: Prepare for the Journey
- *The Job Search Journey*
- *Know Yourself to Market Yourself*
- *Picture Yourself in the Workplace*

PHASE 2: Create Your Resume
- *Plan Your Resume*
- *Write Your Resume*

PHASE 3: Apply for Jobs
- *Find Job Openings*
- *Write Job Applications*
- **Write Effective Tailored Cover Letters**

PHASE 4: Shine at Interviews
- *Know the Interview Essentials*
- *Prepare for Your Interview*
- *Interview Like a Pro*

PHASE 5: Connect, Accept, and Succeed
- *Stay Connected with Prospective Employers*
- *It's an Iterative Process*
- *Take Charge of Your Career*

PHASE 3: Apply for Jobs
Step 3, *Write Effective Tailored Cover Letters*

Your goal in this chapter is to design cover letters for your resume and applications that will grab the attention of employers and recruiters.

To get noticed, begin by noticing others first. To encourage others to care about you, begin to care about them first. What you do reflects back toward you.

STRUCTURE YOUR COVER LETTER

It is a good practice to use a Job Application Package when you are prospecting for jobs and when you spot an ideal job opening. A **Job Application Package** consists of the documents needed when applying to a job opening. These documents may include a job application, cover letter, and resume, based on the requirements of the job opening. Additionally, the package may include your business card and copies of a few select samples of your work from your career portfolio.

A **cover letter** is a letter of inquiry or introduction that introduces you to a prospective employer. Your cover letter states your interest in the advertised position or asks about openings in the company. Most important, the cover letter answers the questions every reader has: "Who is this person, and how will this person help us?" and "Should I take the time to look at this resume or application?"

Effective cover letters make an excellent first impression. They are well written and get the reader's attention and interest. Good cover letters provide information that convinces the reader to read the attached resume and offer an interview. An effective cover letter markets yourself, highlights your most important qualifications, and emphasizes how those qualifications can meet the employer's needs.

Cover letters take time to write. Spend your time writing cover letters for two types of jobs: those for which you have a Warm Introduction and those for which you are an excellent match or the job is a stretch or "dream" job, as described in Chapter 6. Your cover letter can give you an edge over other applicants. Your letter demonstrates professionalism and initiative that employers are looking for and indicates that you are serious about this particular job opening. Adding a cover letter to your resume might put your resume at the top of the stack where it will be seen.

There are two types of cover letters:

- **Application cover letter:** Use this when responding to a job listing. State your interest in and qualifications for that job. Attach your application or reference your online application. You can use this for a Cold Lead or a Warm Introduction. (See Figure 8-5, page 209.)

- **Prospecting cover letter:** Use this to ask about possible job openings when none have been advertised. Attach your resume. (See Figure 8-6, page 210 and Figure 8-7, page 211.)

Both types of cover letters are short—one page with 200 to 300 words total—and have similar structures. Figure 8-1 shows a standard cover letter. Additional examples are at the end of this chapter.

Top Part: Address, Date, and Salutation

The top part of the letter is intended to draw attention to your name and provide your contact information. If you type and print a letter, place your name, address, contact information, and the date at the top of the letter. Next, for both email and printed letters, type the employer's name, title, company name, and address. Skip a line, then use a formal salutation or greeting such as "Dear Ms. Och," followed by another blank line.

If you are using email, some of this is already done for you, so you start at the salutation line. See Figure 8-8 for an example of an email cover letter.

Content

Your cover letter content will include three short paragraphs: opening, sales pitch, and close.

Figure 8-1 Structure of a Cover Letter

Your Name as a title or header
Your physical mailing address
Your email address | Phone number with area code

Today's Date

Mr./Ms./Capt./Chef/Dr./Prof./Rev. [last name]
Person's job title
Name of person's company
Street address at the company (or PO Box number)
City, State abbreviation, Zip code of company

Dear Mr./Ms./Captain/Chef/Dr./Reverend [last name],

Content of letter that includes three parts. First and opening line to introduce yourself and explain in a sentence why you are contacting them. (Tips: Use only your name, not Mr., Ms., or Mrs.) Specifically mention a job title if one exists that you are aware of.

Content continues with you marketing yourself by explaining why you are a good fit for the job, or why you would be a good employee at this company. Use your Personal Brand Statement in a way that flows smoothly in the letter.

Content wraps up with a closing that summarizes what you hope to achieve as a result of this letter—a phone call, meeting, email, or reference.

Sincerely,

[your signature]

[your printed name]

Enclosure

Opening

Introduce yourself and state your purpose. Mention by name the position you are applying for if one has been made public. Explain why you are interested in the company or this type of job.

Mention any earlier communications you may have had with the person you are writing to. Also, if you have a contact who knows this person, ask your contact if you can mention his or her name in the letter.

Figure 8-2 is an excerpt from a prospecting cover letter by Kimi Okasaki. You can see the associated resume in Chapter 4, Figure 4-2 on page 90. Kimi mentions Carmine Garduno, a person who is well known to the addressee. Carmine told Kimi it was okay to use her name in this cover letter.

The Sales Pitch

This is the heart of your letter. A sales pitch refers to communication you use to market yourself. It's similar to your 30-Second Commercials. Focus on what you have to offer—your most relevant qualifications for the job. Include two to four results-oriented, bullet point descriptions of capabilities and accomplishments that show how you can benefit the employer and handle the job. These might be restatements of things you have already written in your resume and application. It's okay to use similar wording. Be sure to include

Figure 8-2 Opening of a Prospecting Cover Letter from Kimi Okasaki

Carmine Garduno from the Health Services Bureau recommended that I talk with you about the possibility of your needing an administrative support person with experience in educational and community activities. I am confident that my experience as a volunteer in the Valley Elementary School Parent-Teacher Organization (VES-PTO) and the Diabetes Foundation would be useful in helping you achieve success with your new five-year education and community plan.

elements of your Personal Brand Statement. Be truthful and remember that you must be able to verify these accomplishments during an interview. Express interest and enthusiasm for the job and focus on your strengths, experience, and achievements.

Somewhere in the letter, refer to the job description or something specific you know about the company's activities or requirements. This demonstrates your initiative and interest in the company. It demonstrates that you care enough to do your homework and learn about this company and this job.

Write one to three lines to highlight the qualifications you want to emphasize. See Figure 8-3 for an example. An alternative,

Figure 8-3 Example of Sales Pitch for Use in Cover Letter

Job Requirements	My Qualifications
GPA of 3.0 or higher	I completed an Associate of Science degree, majoring in Information Management Technology, with an overall GPA of 3.5.
Interest in health and disease prevention	Through my volunteer work at the Diabetes Foundation, I learned about the disease prevention techniques your department teaches to day care workers. I am highly motivated by the desire to help families and fight disease.
Community involvement	I am actively involved in community volunteer work and serve as Secretary-Treasurer of the VES-PTO. I use Word and Excel to generate and track correspondence with more than 500 families.

easy-to-read style is to use a bulleted list. As shown in Figure 8-3, the left column lists the key job requirements (quoted exactly from the job listing using the company's language), and the right column describes your matching experience.

The Closing

Ask for a meeting, phone call, or an interview—not a job—and indicate when you would like to connect. State that your resume is attached or enclosed. Then add a courteous sentence that expresses appreciation or thanks. Set a goal on your calendar to follow up by phone or email to check availability and interest. See Figure 8-4 for a good example.

As you write your cover letter, you might feel as if you are repeating some of your resume content. That's all right. Think of the cover letter as a movie trailer with just enough of a preview to encourage them to look at your resume. That's the goal: Write it so that the reader wants to turn the page. This takes practice. Ask people in your network to help you hone your marketing message by reading several versions of the cover letters that you write. Ask them to compare versions and tell you what they like better about one version versus the other, and why. In this way, you can begin to hone your message so it's a real page turner!

Figure 8-4 Example Cover Letter Closing

My resume is enclosed for your review. I would appreciate meeting with you to discuss the possibility of our working together. If you are interested, what does your availability look like for a 30-minute call next week? I would welcome the opportunity to contribute to the exceptional community outreach efforts of the Department of Disease Prevention. Thank you for your consideration.

Your cover letter tells the reader who you are. Be yourself.

The Signature

How you sign your cover letter will depend on the type of cover letter you are sending: printed letter, email message, online form, or an attachment of a word processing file.

For a printed cover letter, after the letter content, skip a few lines, then type a closing phrase such as *Sincerely*, or *Kind Regards* followed by a comma. Leave a few blank lines for your signature. Next type your formal name—the same name that you used at the top of your resume and on your job application. At the bottom of the page, type the word *Enclosure* to indicate that there should be other pages that go with this letter. Next, print your cover letter and sign it with blue or black pen in the space above your typed name.

An email cover letter is similar, but you can skip the word *Enclosure* because emails show that there is an attachment. It is a good idea to mention in the body of the letter that your documents are attached, just in case the email is forwarded to someone without these original attachments. At the end of the email, simply type your name. Lastly, below your signature, you can add additional contact information such as your phone number with area code, your LinkedIn® address, and a link to your web resume if you have one. This is added for the recipients' convenience so that they can contact you quickly. All other contact information will be in your job application and resume. Caution: if you use a standard email signature—a block of text that is appended to the end of your email—for your normal emails, make sure it is appropriate for this use. If not, change it now, or start using an email account that you set up exclusively for your Job Search Journey.

For online forms, there is rarely an opportunity to insert a cover letter. If there is a space for "additional comments," you can insert the content of your cover letter and end by typing your name.

For attachments uploaded to a web page or email, you can either simply type your name or insert a picture of your signature into a cover letter before you upload or attach it. An alternative is to print the cover letter, sign it with a pen, and then scan it as a pdf that can be attached or uploaded. Do a good quality scan so that it is readable. While photos of documents are acceptable in many situations, the business world at the time of this writing still prefers scanned documents.

Your signature represents you. A common mistake is to forget the signature. Be sure to sign your cover letters. This shows the valued traits of attention to detail and pride in your work.

▶ *CAREER ACTION*

Complete Worksheet 8-1, Part 1
Draft of Master Cover Letter, page 215

APPLY EFFECTIVE WRITING TIPS

The way you write will tell the reader about you. Are you a hometown student? A high-end scholar? A hardworking individual? A creative? Your writing should use good English grammar, but it must reflect you. Cookie-cutter look-alike cover letters are not as effective. Here are a few tips.

Tips for Writing Effective Cover Letters

Start by writing a master cover letter. Make it as perfect as you can. A good master cover letter makes it easier to customize every letter for each specific job listings and get great results in less time. Keep in mind the writing tips from Chapter 5, "Write Your Resume." The advice to write clearly and concisely also applies to your cover letters. Here are additional tips:

- **Use a template.** Look online for free, standard cover letter templates. By using a template, you can rely on the template to get the format right so that you can focus on crafting great content.

- **Use your Personal Brand Statement**. You've crafted your story. Now is the time to use it. Be sure your letter does is consistent with your resume. No contradictions! Use a conversational tone and tell a cohesive story or paint a vivid picture of your abilities and experience.

- **Use the three-part structure.** Tell them why you want to connect with them, tell them why they want to connect with you, and close with a direct request to connect and general time, date, and details about how to connect.

- **Be positive.** Share your positive qualities. Project confidence and show interest in the job. Ask friends to see if they can find any negative tone in your cover letter, then delete it!

- **Write clearly and concisely**. Use short sentences, short paragraphs, and short words. It makes it easier for the reader. Then make sure every word counts in your master cover letter.

- **Use specific, measurable terms to describe your abilities**. Avoid overblown or empty words. For example, instead of "My customers really like me," you might say, "My program increased reported customer satisfaction by 35%."

- **Be truthful.** Never misrepresent yourself or encourage a reader get a false impression. Be honest about your education, background, experience, and interests. On the other hand, don't go overboard to tell all your faults and fails. Everyone has them, so drop it and move on. Be positive.

- **Do your research.** Make sure you have researched the company and/or the job enough to make informed comments.

- **Answer the basic three questions.** Write the content so that the reader can quickly answer these three questions: Why are your contacting me? What's in it for me? and What do you want me to do next?

- **Read the letter aloud.** Listening to your cover letter will give you distance from your writing and help you judge the letter from the reader's perspective. Do you sound likable and sincerely interested in working for *this* company? Are *you* convinced to give your application a closer look?

Address the Letter Appropriately

There are several parts to an address and two places you need to use the address.

Parts of an address:

- The recipient's name, spelled correctly
- The correct honorific, such as Dr., Ms., Mr., Lt. Col.
- The recipient's job title
- The company name, and, for larger companies, the department
- The street address or PO Box

Where to use the address:

- On the cover letter
- On the letter envelope if a printed letter and resume package is used

---

MAKE IT A HABIT
Show Off Your Writing Skills

Use your cover letters to show employers that you have business writing skills. Re-read your letter (and get help from your network) until it is concise, articulate, and convincing. An error-free, grammatically correct letter shows that you are conscientious and detail-oriented.

Never allow slang, informal language, or texting abbreviations to sneak into your job search correspondence. Use well-crafted sentences and businesslike language to demonstrate your professionalism and readiness to communicate in the workplace.

You can write more concisely if you avoid clichés, dated expressions, and "inflated" words. Here are some common examples and alternatives:

Clichéd/Dated	Concise	Complex/Wordy	Concise
At this point in time	Now	Advantageous	Helpful
Ballpark figure	Estimate	Attempt; endeavor	Try
Explore every avenue	Explore the options	Equitable	Fair
In a timely manner	On time; promptly	Initiated	Started
In the event that	If	Possess	Have
In the near future	Soon	Proficiency; proficient	Skill; skilled
Last but not least	Finally	Regarding	About
State-of-the-art	Latest	Remainder	Rest
		Timely	Prompt
		Transmit	Send
		Utilized	Used

For an *application cover letter*, the parts of the address may be found in the job listing. For a *prospecting cover letter*, seek the name and contact information through your Career Network, LinkedIn®, or other social media tools.

In many cases, you may not know the name of the person who should receive the letter. Some companies do not accept unsolicited cover letters and resumes. If sent to the human resources department, you may receive a form letter stating that no applications are currently being accepted.

To boost your chances of getting an interview, address a prospecting letter to the person who has hiring authority for the position. Never address your cover letter "To Whom It May Concern." This type of salutation may target your letter for the wastebasket.

With a strong Career Network, you will know the names of people to contact and even have your cover letter and resume hand delivered by some of your contacts. However, if your network does not have the right person's name, consider one of these methods:

- **Call your target employer.** Say that you are researching careers and want to write to the person who specializes in your area. Get the person's full name and title, and verify the spelling and mailing address or email. When you call, introduce yourself and thank the person by name for his or her help. Always say that you are a student or that you are doing research. The person you speak to could help you later, and using names establishes a courteous, friendly tone.

- **Search the company's website** for an organizational chart or contact information. If this is not available, contact the human resources office (if your target employer has one). Ask whether there is an organizational chart you could use for your career planning class or personal research. The chart should provide you with the name of the department head to whom you should address your cover letter.

- **Contact employees**, on LinkedIn® or other social media sites, who currently work for the company and ask if they can direct you to the right person. Because you may not know these people, read their titles carefully and always approach each person with the ultimate courtesy.

If these methods are not effective, ask members of your Career Network to help you devise a workable approach. As a last resort, address the prospecting letter to a hiring manager, department head, or the human resources department and use the address from the company's website.

Consider sending your resume and letter to both the human resources department and the hiring manager in the department in which you are interested in working. Indicate in your letters that you have sent similar communications to each party so that no one gets surprised. In the best case, the two recipients of your letters will talk to each other about you.

Addressing letters appropriately also means using the right format on the envelope. If you are uncertain or have not addressed envelopes very often, go online and research how to do this. Be sure to put the right amount of postage on the envelope. Postage is based on both weight and the size of the envelope. The U.S. Post Office website or someone at the Post Office can help you.

Make it Look Good

Formatting and visual style won't matter if you cut and paste your cover letter and resume information into an online application. However, if you are uploading files or printing and mailing your Job Application Package, the way it looks makes a difference. Remember, your goal is to invite the reader to

Real World Scenario 8-1 As he explored career fields in Phase 1, Evan found several companies he was particularly interested in. They had similar values to Evan, including supporting work/life balance, and challenging projects in areas Evan was passionate about. Evan didn't see any current job openings, so he looked on LinkedIn® for a current employee at the manager level. He prepared a cover letter, detailing the specific values that attracted him to the company as well as his skills and qualifications. He asked to connect with the manager through LinkedIn®. When the manager accepted his invitation, he reviewed the manager's profile and made some adjustments to his cover letter, highlighting that they went to the same school and were part of the same nonprofit organization. He then sent his cover letter with his resume attached through email. *How can you discover more information about prospective employers to use in your cover letter?*

read more. So make it look inviting. Here are some tips:

- **Clean and simple:** A clean and simple style looks easier to read. Use one typeface, one type size, and consistent margins throughout. An exception is to use a different typeface and size for your name at the very top of the letter to draw attention to it.

- **Similar cover letter and resume:** This is a package, so the two documents should look similar. Use similar fonts, color (black is a good type color), and margins throughout. Even use the same paper for both documents if you are printing.

- **Paper and printing:** The best is white or cream-colored 8.5-inch by 11-inch paper with black or dark print. If you choose to use paper that has a watermark, print the letter with the watermark facing up and toward the reader. Use a laser printer, not an ink-jet printer.

- **Consistent information:** Your cover letter and resume, and anything else in your Job Application Package that you send out, must have consistent information. This means that your contact information should be exactly the same on all documents.

- **The page:** Use 1-inch margins and center the letter on the page. Use the standard left-margin alignment. Use one simple, standard font such as Calibri, Arial, Verdana, or Times New Roman, in size 11 or 12 point. Single-space the body text and double-space between paragraphs and sections. Use bulleted lists to break up lengthy paragraphs. Do not write more than one page.

- **Don't use headers:** Employer will not necessarily print out your letter or resume unless you are scheduled for an interview. So if you put information in the document header or footer, there is a chance that the recipient won't see it, depending on the screen view they typically use.

- **Spaces and periods:** Use one space after periods at the end of sentences. Use periods in your degree (B.A. instead of BA).

- **No decorations please:** Don't use excessive underlining, shadows, backgrounds, or colored text. It is simply unprofessional. Avoid distracting or elaborate graphics.

- **Your signature:** Hand-sign every print cover letter. You should sign digital files too. Here are two methods. Print the document, sign it by hand, and scan it as a .pdf document (preferred format). Or, create a .pdf file online—do not scan the .doc file—and use the Adobe Fill & Sign tool to insert your signature. Use the online help instructions to learn how to do this.

- **Letter perfect:** Make the final letter perfect—no errors! Proofread and proofread again!

> ▶ *CAREER ACTION*
> **Complete Worksheet 8-1, Part 2**
> Draft of Master Cover Letter, page 215

CUSTOMIZE THE CONTENT

The recipient of your cover letters should feel as if you took the time and effort to write this letter especially for him or her. This is not hard to do if you start with a good master cover letter and customize small parts for each recipient. The impact can be worth the little extra time. Here are the types of things you should customize.

- **Show your fit with this job**. First, tailor the letter to emphasize your fit with each particular job you are applying for. Edit the text to match the job title and use the same job requirements wording as is listed in the listing. Matching their words is one way for you to begin to show that you can fit in with the people at this company.

- **Get an edge through research**. Demonstrate your knowledge of the company or industry. Use your company research to personalize the letter. Mention your interest in a new or popular product or service; the expansion of the firm; recent accomplishments; the company's reputation (for example, the quality of its products or services, excellent customer service, or community involvement); or a special achievement of the person you're writing to or the company in general. Mention only one thing and keep your praise short.

- **Incorporate specialized terminology** from your industry and job target where appropriate. Be sure to use the terminology correctly.

- **Emphasize how you can meet the employer's needs**. Restating the duties and qualifications in the job listing shows how you meet them. For example, consider an applicant who has the education and work experience to apply for customer support jobs and IT jobs in both the accounting and insurance industries. Each letter (and resume) should use concrete, specific terminology and examples that highlight the writer's qualifications, experience, and education and training in the field (customer support or IT) and the industry (accounting or insurance) of the job opening.

- **Edit the text carefully.** Check every part of the letter, including the date, inside address, salutation, name of the company, and job title. Starting fresh with a master cover letter each time can reduce errors.

Customizing will take time, yet it is a reflection of your genuine interest in the company and the position. Plan accordingly.

> ▶ *CAREER ACTION*
> **Complete Worksheet 8-2**
> Customize Cover Letters, page 217

Real World Scenario 8-2 Deidra applied for a job position that stated the importance of being able to manage multiple priorities and organization skills multiple times throughout the job description and qualifications. As Deidra customized her cover letter, she used a bullet point format. She highlighted three examples of when she had to manage multiple priorities and in some cases, delivered before the deadline or under budget. She included an example from when she successfully managed an important school project deadline and planning a school organization's event. She even considered various formats of her cover letter that would display her organization skills best. *How can you customize your cover letter for your ideal job position?*

DISTRIBUTE YOUR JOB APPLICATION PACKAGE

Once you have customized your master cover letter and job resume for a specific job opening, it is time to send them out. If you are sending an *application cover letter*, be sure to include your completed application in this Job Application Package. Here are several ways you can deliver it:

- Send it via email.
- Upload it to a recruitment website.
- Print it and send it in the mail.

For jobs of high interests, some job seekers use all three delivery methods. In addition, they follow up with additional emails, phone calls, and personal visits, over a period of several weeks or months when appropriate and without becoming a pest.

So how do you choose what delivery method to use first? Consider this: You want to use the method that helps you stand out from the crowd. You also want to use a method that is easiest for the recipient to handle. For example, some companies prefer to use their online system or email with attachments so that they can forward resumes from the human resources department to the hiring manager. Other companies prefer a printed copy and keep just a few physical file folders to hold all the paper resumes in one stack for the manager's review. Ask your network about the normal approach for your industry.

There are a few things to consider for any of these methods. The tips below can eliminate barriers and issues so that people will be able to read your Job Application Package. That's the goal: get people to read the cover letter, turn the page and read the resume, then contact you for an interview!

Printed Cover Letter

- Print on quality print paper and business-size envelopes.
- Check that your printer is printing clearly. If needed, use new ink cartridges or go to a professional printer at a local office supply store or copy shop.

You, Online

Find Job Leads with Twitter

Unlike many other social media sites, Twitter users commonly chat and connect with complete strangers. This is great news for job seekers who are willing to be outgoing and meet others in their industry. A simple search can yield hundreds of people and businesses that hold the same interests and are willing to talk with you.

- Create a free Twitter profile if you haven't already and complete your profile, indicating interest in your industry and career fields.
- Search for people and businesses that are interested and active in your field and follow them.
- Read tweets sent out by select companies to learn what's new with them and whether they're hiring. More and more companies tweet out current job openings.
- Follow experts who are active in your industry, read the articles and information they are tweeting, and ask them for advice.
- Send out tweets about your job-seeking interests.

Twitter users share information and links in real time, so you can often find the most up-to-date information on the web. Search engines have to play catch-up because they need more time to find and index articles.

- Sign your cover letter with a black or blue ink pen. No pencil. (Tip: For a professional look, get the ink flowing before you start your signature by writing on a scrap piece of paper.)

- Properly address the envelope. You can get instructions from the USPS website.

- Put all the pages together and fold them as one. Look online for written or video instructions for how to fold a business letter. Websites such as eHow can help.

- Seal the envelope so that nothing falls out during shipping.

- Be sure to use the right amount of postage. Usually one standard stamp is sufficient. However, if you are including more than a few sheets of paper, go to the post office, where they will weigh your package and tell you how much postage is needed.

- Keep a copy of your letter so that you know exactly which wording you used when the recipient contacts you.

The Online Application with Plain Text Cover Letter

Because you will apply for most jobs through career sites and company websites, your typical Job Application Package will consist of your completed online application and an uploaded file of your cover letter and resume. You may also have an opportunity to upload a business card.

If you are uploading your cover letter, the best approach is to create your customized letter, then save it as a .pdf file. Upload the .pdf file. This type of file has fewer compatibility and viewing problems for uploaded and downloaded files.

Sometimes you may have to paste the core content of your cover letter into an online application. After you customize the text and content, customize the format by removing all the formatting (no bold, no tables, no bullets, no underlines, etc.). Now look for long lines of text and convert them to shorter lines. Long sentences are harder to read without formatting. Some programs cut off long lines and limit the content to a specific number of characters. In most word processing programs, you can do a word or character count before cutting and pasting into the online application.

When you are satisfied with the text of your cover letter, select the content and copy and paste it into the online field. You can skip the top part of the typical cover letter, that is, skip the addresses and salutations. Now scroll within the online field and make sure that all of your text was properly copied into the field. If not, try again.

The Hand-Delivered Job Application Package

If you deliver your Job Application Package in person, put the documents in a large white envelope so that you do not have to fold them. Documents that lie flat on the desk are easier to read and easier to scan into the computer.

Address the envelope to a real person. Print the recipient's address and your return address on labels or directly on the envelope just as if you were going to mail it. Use black ink and print neatly, or use a computer-printed address label and adhere it to the envelope. Next, attach your business card to your cover letter with a paper clip, and place these on top of your resume and application. If your resume is longer than one page, clip the pages together with another paper clip. If you are including a reference list, place this behind the resume. Then add copies of a few impressive items from your Master Career Portfolio. Use only a few items; save some for the interview.

The Emailed Job Application Package

Some employers ask applicants to apply by sending an email with the cover letter and resume attached. Put the title or number of the job listing and your name in the subject line of the email. Attach .pdf files of your cover letter, resume, and application, unless the company specifies a different file format.

Use the default email font. Copy the cover letter content into the email body and attach only your resume and application.

Before you email your application to the employer, try to send it to yourself or to a friend to see how well the documents survive the cyberspace transfer. You may need to modify the spacing and formatting. Make sure you have attached the files you intended to attach! You never want to make the error of saying "View enclosed," only for the reader to find no attachment. Review the following Caution box for other items

you should double-check and remember to include. Always proofread your attachments and the text body before you click "Send." Do not clutter your email with extra attachments from your Master Career Portfolio. Save these for the interview unless these are specifically requested or part of your industry's standard practice.

Some businesses in certain industries block emails that contain attachments. If you are in such an industry, you will need to copy and paste your application and resume into the email. The formatting is likely to look atrocious. In such cases, it might be better to include a link to your LinkedIn® profile or to an online web resume. Your network of people who work in your industry can advise you on standard practices.

© Ashwin/Shutterstock.com.

CAUTION
Did You Forget Anything?

No matter how qualified you are and how well written your cover letter and application are, if you forget something important, you will be viewed as careless and will be unlikely to get the job.

According to a recent Career Builder survey about cover letters, one of the most common errors made by applicants is forgetting to enclose a resume or cover letter in their envelope or neglecting to attach a document to an email message. Before you send an envelope or email, take a moment to make sure all of your documents are enclosed or attached. Don't forget…

Contact information. Always include your phone number and email address. Because applications, cover letters, and resumes can become separated, it is essential that your contact information is on all documents.

The date, salutation, or closing on the cover letter. Use proper business letter format and include all sections of the letter.

The context. Especially for prospecting letters, where a job opening may not exist, make sure you have clearly laid out why you are contacting the reader.

The "ask." Are you clear on what follow-up action you would like the reader to take? Make sure you have told him or her what you would like him or her to do with the information you are sharing.

Your signature. On a cover letter, the signature shows your personal attention. On an application, your signature is required to certify and validate your information.

> ▶ *CAREER ACTION*
> **Complete Worksheet 8-3**
> Master Cover Letter and Job Application
> Package Review, page 219

Other Ways to Use Your Job Application Package

Print your Job Application Package and use it in situations such as these:

- For job interviews, take several copies of your Job Application Package—cover letter, resume, application and a few career portfolio items.

- As a physical "thank-you package" after a phone interview, use a paper clip to attach your handwritten thank-you note to your resume. Slip this into an envelope and send it to the interviewer.

Follow Up with the Employer

After you have sent your cover letter and resume to get a job interview, don't just sit around and wait for the phone to ring. Applicants who follow up to request an update demonstrate initiative and increase their name recognition.

- If you applied by mail, contact the person you sent your application to.

- If you applied through the company's website, contact the human resources department and tell the receptionist which position you applied for (have the reference number when you call) and ask for the hiring manager's name, phone number, and email address.

- If you applied through a career site for a job listing that includes that hiring manager's name, contact the manager directly.

- If you applied for several jobs through a career site or if the job listing did not include the manager's name, decide whether getting the information is the best use of your time.

Keep the conversation or email brief. Here's an example of a phone call:

> Hello, _____. Thank you for taking my call. I'm Jennifer Ortiz calling from Raleigh. I applied for the system support programming job and wanted to make sure you received my resume and job application.

Sample Cover Letters

The following sample cover letters are on pages 209–212:

- Figure 8-5. Sample Application Cover Letter (uses paragraph style for qualifications)

- Figure 8-6. Sample Prospecting Cover Letter (uses the bullet style for qualifications)

- Figure 8-7. Sample Prospecting Cover Letter (uses two-column, comparison-list style)

- Figure 8-8. Sample Email Cover Letter with Resume Inside Body of Email

Figure 8-5 Sample Application Cover Letter

Kimi Okasaki

148 Barrister Street   •   Tucson, AZ 85726

(520) 555.0136   •   kimi.okasaki@email.com   •   linkedin.com/in/kimi.okasaki

April 20, 20—

Mr. George O'Donnell
Office Manager
MegaMall Property Management Company
P.O. Box 555
Tucson, AZ 85726

Dear Mr. O'Donnell:

EXPERIENCED ADMINISTRATIVE ASSISTANT, JOB #4864

Please accept my application for the administrative assistant position advertised on the *Arizona Bugle* website. As secretary-treasurer of the Valley Elementary School Parent-Teacher Organization, I appreciated MegaMall's offer to let us hold our promotional event in the center of the mall last fall at no charge. I would welcome the chance to work in a civic-minded organization.

I am an energetic, detail-oriented person who has strong administrative and computer skills, retail and community service experience, and the ability to work well with others. I have held positions of responsibility in three community organizations over the last three years.

As you can see from my resume, I thrive in a busy atmosphere that involves many different tasks, the opportunity to work with people, the satisfaction of meeting deadlines, and the chance to excel. I would enjoy the opportunity to talk with you about how I can help MegaMall Property Management with its administrative needs. I will call you next week to request an appointment, or you may call me at your convenience at the number above. Thank you for your consideration.

Sincerely,

Kimi Okasaki

Kimi Okasaki

Enclosure

Figure 8-6 Sample Prospecting Cover Letter (Bullet Style)

Kate Foresman

2689 Canyon Avenue
Riverside, CA 92502
(951) 555.0179 | kforesman@email.com
linkedin.com/in/katelouiseforesman

June 29, 20–

Ms. Stephanie Nolan
Manager, Auditing Staff
Nolan Henry O'Leary Public Accountants
1410 Granada Avenue, 7th Floor
San Francisco, CA 94115

Dear Ms. Nolan:

Meagan Gerena at Smythe and Associates indicated that you are interested in hiring an experienced accounting graduate. My degree and special interest are in Accounting/Information Systems. Please consider me for a place on your well-respected auditing team, which the *San Francisco Business Reporter* recently named one of the Top 10 auditing firms in the area.

During the last two years, I have worked for a CPA firm where I developed a wide range of accounting and accounting-related skills. My accomplishments included:

- Received excellent ratings for speed and accuracy as a full-charge bookkeeper with duties such as opening, posting, and closing the books; completing federal and state corporate tax returns; and creating error-free Excel templates used by myself and others.
- Assisted a consultant in upgrading software for a customized accounting system by applying my knowledge of both accounting and IT, to meet in-house needs on schedule.
- Created a procedures manual for operating, maintenance, and troubleshooting situations that can occur between the two operating systems that users say helps them identify and fix problems quickly, resulting in fewer calls to the help-line.

During my senior year at the University of Los Angeles, I led an internship research team. We studied the operations of a local accounting firm and assisted its auditors in the audit of several clients. These experiences cemented my interest in auditing as a career.

I am confident in my ability to make a positive contribution to Nolan Henry O'Leary Public Accountants and am enclosing my resume for your review. I will call next week about your interview schedule, or you may reach me at the contact information above. I look forward to meeting you.

Respectfully,

Kate Foresman

Kate Foresman

Enclosure

Figure 8-7 Sample Prospecting Cover Letter (Two-Column List)

TAYLOR WHITAKER

10806 Delaware Avenue | Camden, NJ 08105
[856] 555.0195 | taylor.whitaker@email.com
Linkedin.com/in/taylor.whitaker

January 10, 20–

Mr. Gary Whaley
District Sales Manager
Computeriferals Company
1 Computer Way
Camden, NJ 08102

Dear Mr. Whaley:

Computeriferals has earned my respect. I have used and repaired peripherals from most of the leading manufacturers in my studies as a Business Systems/Computer Repair major and in my job as a sales representative at ComputerChoice. I know you build quality products, and I want to sell quality products—Computeriferals.

Careful review of my qualifications and the requirements of a sales representative at Computeriferals suggest that I am well qualified for a sales position with your organization.

Your Requirements	**My Experience**
• Ability to handle multiple prospects	• Expanded customer base from 137 to 183 accounts in the past year—a 34% increase
• Proven ability to meet sales goals	• Increased yearly sales from $743,000 to $1,236,000—exceeded goal by 66%
• Ability to expand sales in existing accounts	• Negotiated a new $250,000 service contract for an existing client with five locations
• Strong communication and follow-up skills	• Attained 100% customer retention through a service-first approach and frequent communication

The expanding market for Computeriferals presents an appealing challenge. Even if you have no current sales openings, I would appreciate meeting with you to discuss your requirements. My resume is enclosed for your convenience. I will call next week to request an appointment, or you may reach me at the contact information above. Thank you for your time.

Respectfully,

Taylor Whitaker

Taylor Whitaker

Enclosure

Figure 8-8 Sample Email Cover Letter with Resume inside Body of Email

```
EXPERIENCED ADMINISTRATIVE ASSISTANT, JOB #4864-10                                              [_][□][✕]
File   Edit   View   Insert   Format   Tools   Message   Help
From:     Kimi Okasaki <'kimi.okasaki@email.com'>
To:       'hiring.manager@megamallmanagement.com' <'hiring.manager@megamallmanagement.com'>
Cc:
Subject:  EXPERIENCED ADMINISTRATIVE ASSISTANT, JOB #4864-10
```

Dear Hiring Manager:

Please accept my application for the administrative assistant position advertised on the *Arizona Bugle* website. As secretary-treasurer of the Valley Elementary School Parent-Teacher Organization, I appreciated MegaMall's offer to let us hold our promotional event in the center of the mall last fall at no charge. I would welcome the chance to work in a civic-minded organization.

I am an energetic, detail-oriented person who has strong administrative and computer skills, retail and community service experience, and the ability to work well with others. I have held positions of responsibility in three community organizations over the last three years.

As you can see from my resume below, I thrive in a busy atmosphere that involves many different tasks, the opportunity to work with people, the satisfaction of meeting deadlines, and the chance to excel. I would enjoy the opportunity to talk with you about how I can help MegaMall Property Management with its administrative needs. I will call you next week to request an appointment, or you may call me at your convenience at the number below. Thank you for your consideration.

Sincerely,
Kimi Okasaki
kimi.okasaki@email.com

==

Kimi Okasaki Resume
Kimi Okasaki
148 Barrister Street, Tucson, AZ 85726, (520) 555.0136
kimi.okasaki@email.com, linkedin.com/in/kimi.okasaki

PROFESSIONAL PROFILE
Seeking Administrative Assistant position at mid-size organization. Detail-oriented professional with exceptional customer service, communication, and relationship building capability.

QUALIFICATIONS
• Skilled presentation, newsletter, and report designer
• Advanced software skills in MS Office, Adobe Acrobat, FTP, and Quickbooks
• Database design and maintenance using Access and Oracle
• Keyboarding at 75 words per minute
• Proven external relationship builder

EXPERIENCE
Community Volunteer, Tucson, AZ. December 2009 to December 2015

   Served as a volunteer in various roles for three well-known organizations that contribute significantly to the community.

• National Diabetes Foundation. Reduced fundraising reporting time by 50% by developing and customizing Excel spreadsheet report to track three fundraising activities
• Secretary-Treasurer, Valley Elementary School Parent-Teacher Organization. Designed and published monthly electronic newsletters for organization using MS Publisher. Passed yearly CPA audits with excellence through tracking of budget in QuickBooks Pro.
• Meals on Wheels. Developed and maintained Access database for survey responses from 1,200 participants.

Katz Department Store, Tucson, AZ. March 2009 to December 2010

   Department Supervisor, Part-time.
   Perform basic supervisor responsibilities, manage inventory, and meet target sales goals.
• Attained highest part-time sales volume through personalizing customer interactions
• Trained 4 new sales clerks who achieved target sales goals by end of first month by using good coaching skills
• Had <5% losses on computing daily cash receipts, balancing registers, and coordinating weekly deliveries by using detailed organization systems and strategies

Value Variety, Tucson, AZ. Summers 2008, 2009
   Sales Clerk
• Given positive feedback as a provider of complete customer service in sales and returns

EDUCATION
Associate of Applied Science, A.S.A., 2015, Westfield Community College, Tucson, AZ
Major: Administrative Office Technology, GPA 3.6

==

Chapter Checklist

Check off each item you can do. Reread sections in this chapter to help you complete the checklist.

- [ ] Write an *application cover letter* or a *prospecting cover letter*, depending on the situation. **1**
- [ ] Write a persuasive cover letter that includes the position I am applying for, elements of my Personal Brand Statement that show I am a good fit for the job, and a request for a meeting or interview. **1**
- [ ] Get employers' attention with results-oriented examples in my cover letter. **1**
- [ ] Ask my network for feedback on and assistance with my cover letters and applications. **2**
- [ ] Format cover letters correctly for different methods of delivery such as print, email, online uploads, and email attachments. **2**
- [ ] Tailor my cover letters to specific employers to demonstrate my knowledge of and interest in their company. **3**
- [ ] Distribute a complete Job Application Package **4**
- [ ] Demonstrate initiative by contacting prospective employers after submitting my Job Application Packages. **4**

Critical Thinking Questions

1. When writing a *prospecting cover letter*, what would be different from an application letter and why? **1**

2. When you use the standard business format and protocols for your cover letter, what might this communicate to the prospective employer? What might the employer think of job applicants who do not use the business standard? **1**

3. How can you incorporate your Personal Brand Statement into the cover letter text? Is there a way to craft your letter so that the entire page reflects you and your brand? **1**

4. Think of a probable employer with whom you would like to interview. How can you learn to whom you should address your cover letter? Write the name, title, and address of the person in your answer. **2**

5. What is the value in customizing a cover letter? What do you think are the most valuable three things to customize? Why? **3**

6. There are at least three ways to submit a cover letter to an employer. Which methods are most effective in your industry? Why do you think this? **4**

Additional Resources

For data files, career resources, and more, visit www.cengagebrain.com.

Trial Run

Critically Analyze Cover Letters

For each of the following cover letter excerpts, explain how it fails to meet the guidelines in the chapter. Rewrite the paragraphs to make them more acceptable for an effective cover letter. Use the resume evaluation checklist in the Trial Run in Chapter 4 as a model. (Invent supporting details and evidence as needed.)

- Even though most of my experience is in retail, I think nursing is a field where I could be successful because I am totally into helping people.

- I just love to design computer graphics to enhance specialized publications. It was the only thing I liked about my last job.

- In my volunteer work with Habitat for Humanity, all of my supervisors said that I was one heck of a carpenter. By the age of 5, I was already able to make a wooden birdhouse.

- I'm a talented mechanic, and I really need this job because my rent is expensive.

- Working for Grant Brokerage Company will give me the experience I need to become a certified financial planner. I don't know a lot about the stock market yet, but I'm sure I'll learn quickly on the job.

Working with a partner, use the guidelines in this chapter to create a checklist of 15 criteria for evaluating cover letters. Make sure you include criteria for content, convincing marketing, writing style, addressing letters, formatting, and distribution. Devise a rating scale (for example, 1 to 5) and use your checklist to evaluate a sample cover letter you have written or one from an Internet resource.

▶ CAREER ACTION WORKSHEET
8-1 Draft of Master Cover Letter ❶ ❷

PART 1: Structure Your Cover Letter. ❶ Use this worksheet or the worksheet on the website to organize and outline your master cover letter. Don't try to write a perfect letter at this point; just work on getting the essence of your message on paper. You will refine it later. Use the sample cover letters in Figures 8-5, 8-6, 8-7, and 8-8 for guidance.

Part 1: Cover Letter Outline	
Text for your letterhead: (your name, address, phone number, email address, and LinkedIn® URL)	
Date:	
Inside address: (recipient's name, title, company, and address)	
Salutation: Dear (put a colon after the person's name; use the right honorific such as Ms. or Dr.)	
Paragraph 1 (opening): (include the name of the job position and of a referral if you have these)	
Paragraph 2 (sales pitch): (tailor it to the job listing; where appropriate, use bullets or side-by-side columns to highlight strong job-relevant qualifications; see cover letter examples in this chapter)	
Paragraph 3 (closing): (mention your attached or enclosed resume and request a meeting or an interview; include your phone number and email address if not already provided on this page; thank the reader)	
Complimentary close: (leave enough room for your signature and type your name under it)	Sincerely, _____ (type your name here)

PART 2. Write a Master Cover Letter. ❷ Using your cover letter outline, compose a draft master cover letter. Use a blank sheet of paper or draft it in a new word processing file. Make it concise and courteous. Most importantly, make sure it demonstrates how you can benefit the employer.

Add your completed work to the "Master Career Portfolio" section of your Career Builder Files.

▶ CAREER ACTION WORKSHEET

8-2 Customize Cover Letters ❸

Find two job listings that are similar to ones you might be interested in applying for. Now customize a cover letter for each job. When you are done, you should have three documents: your master cover letter, a cover letter for the first job listing, and a cover letter for the second job listing. Now answer the questions below.

1. About how much of the core content do you estimate you needed to change?

    For the 1st job listing: [ ] some of it? [ ] half of it? [ ] most of it?

    For the 2nd job listing: [ ] some of it? [ ] half of it? [ ] most of it?

2. What types of changes did you make?

    a. For the 1st job listing: [ ] match job listing language?
       [ ] describe why I am a good fit for the job?   [ ] something else?

       (describe)

    b. For the 2nd job listing: [ ] match job listing language?
       [ ] describe why I am a good fit for the job? [ ] something else?

       (describe)

3. Based on having customizing two cover letters, what would you tell a friend or fellow student about how to customize cover letters quickly and effectively to encourage the reader to give them an interview?

This page is intentionally blank.

▶ *CAREER ACTION WORKSHEET*

8-3 Master Cover Letter and Job Application Package Review ❷ ❹

PART 1: Final Master Cover Letter. Working in a Word file, polish the draft of your master cover letter, emphasizing your qualifications and making the content clear and concise. Use a thesaurus or synonym look-up to find words with just the right meaning. Review your cover letter carefully. Remember that, just as with a resume,

IT MUST BE LETTER PERFECT!

PART 2: Outside Review of Printed Cover Letter. Get a final review of your cover letter with the entire Job Application Package in a printed format.

A. **Assemble the package.** When you think your letter is perfect, print the final letter on top-quality paper. Attach your resume and any other additional items that are appropriate for your Job Application Package (e.g., business card, job application, select career portfolio items).

B. **Ask an outside critic**, perhaps someone who is in your Career Network, to comment on how to make your cover letter clearer, better, and more convincing. Get his or her overall impression of your package.

C. **Revise and save.** Decide what changes you will make based on the input you receive. Then make the changes. Save the file using a name that helps you find your final master cover letter.

Add your completed work to the "Master Career Portfolio" section of your Career Builder Files.

This page is intentionally blank.

PHASE 4:
SHINE AT INTERVIEWS

Shine at Interviews

PART 4 Learn how to shine at the most important business meetings you'll ever attend: your job interviews. Learn how to get interviews, prepare for the many types of interviews, showcase your Personal Brand Statement, manage all the questions, and even ask a few questions of your own.

D. LYNN MEYERS

Producing Artistic Director Ensemble Theatre of Cincinnati

© Jim Calloway Photography.

ADVICE FROM THE EXPERT

D. Lynn Meyers has been producing artistic director of the nationally renowned Ensemble Theatre of Cincinnati (ETC) since 1995. The nonprofit ETC recently celebrating its 25th anniversary and is dedicated to the production and development of new plays and of works new to the region.

Lynn values the opinions of each member of her small staff when hiring. She usually interviews four or five people for a staff position and conducts two interviews. After the preliminary interview determines that an applicant is suitable, she says, "We invite the person back to meet the staff they would have contact with on a daily basis." She has passed on qualified applicants who did not interact well with their prospective coworkers or who did not convince her that they had a strong desire for the job.

Lynn researches job applicants online and on social media sites. "Frankly, if we find unprofessional behavior, we take that into consideration," she says. "We always check references—after we meet the applicant—so we know what to ask the person offering the reference."

When faced with two equally qualified candidates, Lynn chooses the person who demonstrates a long-term commitment to be with ETC and a desire to be part of the team. "If we're impressed by someone we can't hire, we keep their application on file. More than once we've called someone back when we added a job opening or needed to replace someone who didn't meet our expectations," says Lynn. She suggests that applicants "should want the job, know why they want it, and be prepared to answer serious questions about their long-term goals."

PLAN for Success

Most successful people keep a calendar of activities and a running list of tasks they have committed to do. Make *Your Career* a part of your calendar and task list.

■ Read the outcomes on the first page of Chapters 9, 10, and 11 and jot down a target date for completing each one. Allow extra time for those that require more than just reading.

■ Now make several calendar appointments with yourself to do the reading, homework, and projects for this class. Consider your other commitments (other classes, work, home) as you plan to make Your Career happen for you!

TALES FROM THE JOB SEARCH

AARON WANG
Management Consultant and Digital Entrepreneur

Aaron Wang graduated with a bachelor's degree in finance and MIS and has had his share of interviews on his fast-paced career path in management and it consulting. He constantly looks for growth opportunities and often lands interviews to accelerate his career. He has modified and perfected his interview strategies over time on everything from body language to impressing in person.

The biggest lesson he has learned is "you've got to put yourself in the shoes of the interviewer and identify the key 'competence' triggers they are looking for." Once you've identified competence triggers such as "specific work experiences, hard and soft skills, difficult situations you've handled, speaking the industry jargon or lingo" then "make sure you tailor all of your responses to hit upon those key triggers wherever possible."

A way to demonstrate your experience is to "ask smart questions that someone less qualified or inexperienced would not have thought of."

When approached with the question about salary, Aaron says, "Be honest about what you want but make sure to emphasize you value the fit, experience, and growth opportunity of the position above all else."

Aaron recommends several tactics to prepare for interviews. To combat nervousness, he suggests, "Create a document with written out responses to various behavioral interview questions and memorize three to five of them. For the 30 minutes leading up to the interview, review your answers by practicing them out loud as if you were speaking to the interviewer."

There's an added benefit if the interview takes place over the phone because "you have the advantage of creating and using a 'cheat sheet' with your interview responses if you are having trouble memorizing them (or talking about them)." Body language for both Skype, video, or in-person interviews should include "sitting straight, leaning forward when making a key point, appropriate hand gestures, making direct eye contact, and flashing a confident, winning smile."

Lastly, follow up after interviews with "a thank-you email detailing exactly why you are a great fit for the position."

CHAPTER 9 Know the Interview Essentials

OVERVIEW

After applying for jobs, it's time to prepare for interviews. In Chapter 9, learn interview preparation basics, how to ask for and get interviews, and how to continue the Job Search Journey even while waiting for invitations to interview.

OUTCOMES

1. Know the key elements of successful interviews.
2. Learn strategies for getting interviews.
3. Stay on the Journey between interviews.

CAREER ACTION WORKSHEETS

WHERE ARE YOU ON THE JOURNEY?

PHASE 1: Prepare for the Journey
- *The Job Search Journey*
- *Know Yourself to Market Yourself*
- *Picture Yourself in the Workplace*

PHASE 2: Create Your Resume
- *Plan Your Resume*
- *Write Your Resume*

PHASE 3: Apply for Jobs
- *Find Job Openings*
- *Write Job Applications*
- *Write Effective Tailored Cover Letters*

PHASE 4: Shine at Interviews
- **Know the Interview Essentials**
- *Prepare for Your Interview*
- *Interview Like a Pro*

PHASE 5: Connect, Accept, and Succeed
- *Stay Connected with Prospective Employers*
- *It's an Iterative Process*
- *Take Charge of Your Career*

Interviews are about the complete package—not just the answers you give.

PHASE 4: Shine at Interviews
Step 1, *Know the Interview Essentials*

Your goal in this chapter is to prepare for interviews by starting now to practice basic interview success skills, learn how to ask for and get interviews, and learn how to keep your Job Search Journey moving forward even while waiting for the invitation to an interview.

KEY ELEMENTS OF SUCCESSFUL INTERVIEWS

No one ever gets a job without having some type of interview. The interview is the doorway that every job seeker must be prepared to walk through on the way to successful employment. Think of it as a very important business meeting—maybe the first one with your new employer. Your goal is to learn about the job and the company. The interviewer's goal is to learn about your abilities and potential. Both of you are evaluating whether you are a good match.

If you have done your homework well, you will know the name of your interviewer, and the interviewer will be aware of your personal brand through your network contact who made you aware of this job opening. The interviewer will likely have looked at your application documents and seen your education, work experience, and qualifications.

The interview is your chance to market yourself as someone who can help the employer achieve its goals. A successful interview has many elements, some of which are more important than you may realize. Your confident attitude is the biggest factor determining your success, and it comes through in many ways, including your appearance, body language, how you speak, and your manners. Your confident attitude comes through in the way you describe your job qualifications and tell examples of your experience. Start practicing now! Demonstrate your confident attitude at every networking meeting and interaction.

Your Attitude–The No. 1 Factor

Attitude is the number 1 factor that influences an employer to hire. Here are some ways you can exhibit a good attitude:

1. **Concentrate on being likable.** As simple as this may seem, research proves that one of the most essential goals in successful interviewing is to be liked by the interviewer. Interviewers want to hire pleasant people whom others will enjoy working with on a daily basis. Many interviewers use this question as a guideline: "If I was stuck in an airport with this person overnight, would I enjoy it?" Build rapport with your interviewer by bringing energy to your interview and smiling. At the end of the interview, ask a question to get to know your interviewer better such as "How long have you worked here? How did you arrive at this company?"

2. **Project an air of confidence and pride.** Act as though you want the position, are capable, and deserve the job—not as though you are desperate. However, do not act as though you already have obtained the job.

3. **Demonstrate enthusiasm.** The applicant who demonstrates little enthusiasm for a job will never be selected for the position. Genuinely show excitement for the role by sharing how you will grow from the job. Show your passion for the career field you have chosen.

4. **Demonstrate knowledge of and interest in the employer.** Saying "I really want this job" is not convincing. Explain why you want the position and how it fits into your career plans. You can cite opportunities that may be unique to the company or emphasize your skills and education that are highly relevant to the position.

5. **Perform at your best every moment.** There are no time-outs during an interview. From the parking lot to the waiting area to the interview room and on your way out, treat everyone courteously, like you would like to be treated. Learn and use the assistant's or receptionist's name. An interviewer often requests this person's opinion of the applicants and hears reactions from others.

6. **Understand that an interview is a two-way street.** Project genuine interest in determining whether both you and the employer can benefit from your employment.

Dress for Success

By the time you have walked in the room and sat down, the interviewer has decided whether you will be considered for the position. One way your attitude is projected is the way your dress. Your image and appearance help determine the all-important first impression you make. That impression may count for as much as 25 percent of the employer's positive or negative hiring decision.

Dress Conservatively

Wear businesslike clothes when you apply for office or professional positions. Review the box in Chapter 6 titled "Caution: Dress Like You Have the Job." You can start planning now by shopping for sale prices on clothes that are appropriate, fit you well, and are comfortable.

Look the Part

If you have an inside contact, ask for suggestions for what to wear and what to expect. A word of caution: Even if an employer permits casual dress on the job or if employees wear uniforms or safety gear, you should still dress formally for an interview to show that you take the opportunity seriously. T-shirts, jeans, tennis shoes, and other casual items may cost you the job. Avoid trying to make a bold statement with your attire. Instead, show that you conduct yourself professionally and dress accordingly.

Use Positive Body Language

Your body language speaks louder than your words. Through our life experiences, we become experts at sending and interpreting nonverbal messages. You may be speaking persuasively, but body language that conveys arrogance, lack of enthusiasm, excessive nervousness, or other negative messages will drown out your words. Start now! Practice confident body language.

> ▶ *CAREER ACTION*
> **Complete Worksheet 9-1**
> Body Language Self-Assessment, page 241

The First 30 Seconds Count

People often form opinions about others within 30 seconds of first meeting them! For this reason, the first 30 seconds can make or break an interview.

Interview and interpersonal communications experts have studied what applicants can do to make a favorable first impression and project professionalism and competence during interviews.

Area	Impact on Interview
Attitude	40%
Image and appearance	25%
Verbal and nonverbal communication	25%
Job qualifications	10%

©iStock.com/wragg.

Appear Relaxed

Your body language will immediately notify an employer if you are overly tense. Be well rested before an interview so that you will be alert and, if possible, exercise by running, stretching, or doing yoga on the day of the interview. Exercise is one of nature's best techniques for relaxing your body and your mind. Try to allocate adequate time in your day—especially during your job search—to do some form of exercise. And be sure to eat something light and healthy before your interview so that you don't feel hungry or tired.

During the interview, occasionally change your position in your seat; this relaxes muscular body tension and breaks the rigid feeling that nervousness can cause. Breathe deeply and don't hurry your movements; this will project confidence and will reduce your anxiety. If a question arises that you cannot immediately answer, pause and take a breath to think about it. If possible, give a genuine smile! It's an effective tension breaker for both you and the interviewer.

If you think you don't have any physical mannerisms or don't know what they are, spend a day watching the body language of the people you interact with.

Develop Assertive Body Language

Concentrate on sending assertive messages with your body language. Your intent is to appear as though you believe that you are the top talent among all job applicants and they are lucky to have you join the company. Assertive body language is relaxed, open, and confident. Your posture and gestures support your words and convey credibility and self-assurance.

- **When you meet the interviewer, give a firm handshake and make eye contact.** This immediately communicates intelligence, competence, and honesty.

- **Walk briskly.** You'll look confident and show that you're ready for the meeting.

- **Sit, stand, and walk with your head up and your back straight.** Good posture conveys that you're composed, respectable, alert, and strong. Slouching conveys that you're bored, disinterested, lazy, or unintelligent. Crossing your arms and legs may be interpreted as being closed or stubborn.

- **Make eye contact.** Making good eye contact is essential to achieving effective communication. It conveys that you really care about what the person has to say. It also conveys confidence, intelligence, competence, and honesty. This doesn't mean that you should glue your eyes to the interviewer; it means that you should look at the interviewer, especially when he or she is talking. Break eye contact at natural points in the discussion. If you are extremely uncomfortable looking directly into the eyes of the interviewer, look at his or her forehead. This gives the impression of looking into his or her eyes. In a group interview, periodically make eye contact with each person. Avoid letting your eyes dart back and forth around the room.

- **Aim for a pleasant, uplifted facial expression.** Occasionally nod your head and gesture to convey agreement and emphasis. Avoid frowning, clenching your jaw, and making other negative expressions.

- **Don't fidget.** Fidgeting is distracting and makes you look nervous, self-conscious, and unsure of your ability to get the job. Keep your hands apart to avoid fidgeting. Rest them on the arms of the chair and keep them still. Keep your hands relaxed, not in tight fists.

- **Watch the interviewer's body language.** The interviewer may lean forward, signaling you to expand on what you are saying. If the interviewer shuffles papers, looks around the room, or gives other nonverbal cues that you should finish speaking, heed the signal. Continue listening and watching to determine whether what you are saying is clearly understood. Retreat from a subject if you observe that it's not being well received.

- **Subtly mirror the interviewer's communication behaviors.** Some people have intense, highly energetic body language and voice qualities, while others are more relaxed. Subtly match your interviewer's style, speed, and tone of voice—but don't overdo it. Do not mirror negative behavior.

Diane just finished interviewing Marcus for a nurse position at her hospital. She was impressed with his answers based on his previous experience concerning how he handles stress, challenges, and multiple priorities. These are all important skills for a nurse. However, customer service and bedside manner are also important characteristics, and Diane was not sure that Marcus would be a good fit. He often looked down when answering questions and had a hesitant, nervous manner. Nurses needed to be able to reassure patients with confidence and positivity. If Marcus wasn't able to exhibit positive behavior during an interview, how would he handle stress with a seriously ill patient? Diane placed Marcus's folder on the "reject" pile, picked up the next resume, and resumed her search for the best fit candidate.

What would have helped Marcus in his preparation for the interview? What unconscious body language do you send out that you would like to change?

Speak Well for Yourself

You're dressed for the part; your positive attitude is shining through; and your body language shows that you're confident, relaxed, and enthusiastic. What's next? Speaking, of course. Even though research shows that body language can carry more influence than words can, you need good verbal communication skills to make a strong case for yourself and to get the information you need.

It's How You Say It

Follow these general tips about voice quality to build on the great first impression you made.

Sound Impressive by Sounding Prepared

- **Identify yourself.** "Hello, this is Brenda Bernstein." Personnel who screen calls are suspicious of callers who don't give their names or state why they are calling. Be straightforward to eliminate any suspicions instantly.

- **Explain why you are calling.** Emphasize your qualifications before you make a request so that your listener has a reason to answer yes. Ask for an interview or use a practiced indirect strategy for getting through to the employer.

- **Get the name of the person who answers.** Ask, "Could I please have your name in case I need to talk with you again?" Write down the name. Using this person's name may make him or her more receptive to helping you.

- **Ask whether it's a good time to talk.**

- **Clarify the details.** Clarify any follow-up activities you are instructed to complete (for example, pick up an application, supply additional information or references, or keep an appointment). Verify the time and place of any meetings and get the correct spelling and pronunciation of the names of the people you will meet.

- **Thank the person you speak to by name.**

- **Use an energetic, pleasant tone of voice** to convey a positive attitude and to enhance your likability. View some TED Talks videos to find a few role models of energetic voices.

- **Modulate your voice.** Don't speak in a monotone or speak too slowly or too rapidly. Speak loud enough to be heard, but not too loudly. Evaluate your tone and speed by recording and listening to yourself as you practice your opening lines and your 30-Second Commercial.

- **Don't slur your words.** Speak distinctly and clearly. No one likes to ask a person to repeat something.

- **Use positive words and phrases.** One of the most important interview goals is to keep the content positive so that the interviewer's final impression is "Yes, this is the person for the job." Use a positive vocabulary and eliminate all negative terms. For example, instead of saying, "I haven't done that exactly," say, "I've done something similar" or "That sounds like something I would enjoy doing."

- **Use proper grammar.** Use correct grammar, word choice, and a businesslike vocabulary, not an informal, chatty one. Avoid slang and never use profanity or derogatory terms. When under stress, people often use pet phrases (such as *like* and *you know*) too often. Ask a friend or family member to help you identify any speech weaknesses you have, and start now to practice good interview language.

It's What You Say

Be clear about your key messages in advance of the interview. Communicate your 30-Second Commercial, how you are a good fit for the job, and how you are interested in learning enough to assure yourself

---

CAUTION
Choose Your Words Carefully

© PathDoc/Shutterstock.com.

Avoid using words and phrases that make you sound indecisive or unbelievable. Eliminate the following credibility robbers from your vocabulary:

- *Just or only.* Used as follows, "I just worked as a waiter" or "I only worked there on a part-time basis" implies that you are not proud of your work or that you don't consider the work meaningful. All work is meaningful; it demonstrates initiative. Leave out these credibility robbers.

- *I guess.* This makes you sound uncertain.

- *Little.* Don't belittle your accomplishments, as in "This is a little report/project I wrote/developed."

- *Probably.* This suggests unnecessary doubt: "The technique I developed would probably be useful in your department." This statement sounds more convincing: "I believe the technique I developed would be useful in your department."

This is a small sample of words and phrases that can diminish your image. Ask members of your support system to help you identify other verbal credibility robbers and to remind you when you use them.

that the company is a good fit for you. Here are some tips you can practice.

- **Start off right by greeting the interviewer by name.** This conveys respect, which enhances your likability. If more than one person is conducting the interview, learn and use everyone's name.

- **State your name and the position you're seeking.** Begin with a friendly greeting, such as, "Hello, Ms. Ong. I'm Bella Reyna. I'm here to interview for the accounting position." Identifying the position is important because interviewers often interview for many different positions. If someone has already introduced you to the interviewer, simply say, "Good morning, Ms. Ong. I'm pleased to be here today."

- **Emphasize how you fit the job.** Near the beginning of an interview, as soon as it seems appropriate, ask a question similar to this: "Could you describe the scope of the job and tell me what capabilities are most important in filling the position?" Listen carefully and jot down a few notes if needed. The interviewer's response will help you focus on emphasizing your qualifications that best match the needs of the employer.

- **Keep the interview businesslike.** Do not discuss personal, domestic, or financial problems.

- **Don't ramble.** Be concise—but not curt—with your replies. Answer questions with required information, adding anything you think is relevant or especially important; then stop talking or ask your own question.

- **Concentrate.** An interview isn't just about talking. Listen to the interviewer carefully to learn important details about the job requirements, the company, and the department so that you can respond appropriately. See "Become a Good Listener" in Chapter 10 on page 258.

- **Come prepared with stories.** Practice giving examples of situations where you used a variety of skills relevant to the job. You should have many of these stories that are so well practiced that they are part of your normal conversation by the time you get to an interview (See Chapter 10 for more on this.) Practice your 30-Second Commercials.

- **Emphasize your strengths—even when discussing an error you made.** Although you want to avoid bringing up past shortcomings, do not try to dodge one that comes out during an interview. Face it head-on and explain what you learned from the experience. If the interviewer asks you about the circumstances, explain briefly; don't make excuses or blame others. You will create a better impression by being honest, candid, and sincere. Remember: The interviewer is human too and has made his or her share of mistakes.

- **Do not lie during an interview.**

- **Be prepared to state why you left a previous job if asked.** Do not speak unfavorably about your former supervisor or company. Interviewers may believe that you would do the same after leaving their companies. Speak only well of others, and stick to facts. Practice this in advance.

- **Focus on your goal.** Keep coming back to the main purpose of the interview: determining how both you and the employer can benefit from your employment. One way is to get feedback from the interviewer by asking such questions as: "Do you think my skills in that area would be helpful to you?" If the answer is yes, you know you're on the right track. If the answer is no or unclear, get clarification on the qualifications needed for the job, and reintegrate your own qualifications while expressing willingness to continue growing on the job.

MAKE IT A HABIT

Practice Assertive Behaviors in Every Interaction

Don't wait until interview day to become a master at your body language, dress, communication capability, and etiquette. Every interaction, from Career Network meetings to connecting with an old friend to discover potential job leads, is an opportunity for you to practice and perfect your professional, confident presence. Often, you don't know how you appear from a third-party perspective and what changes need to be made. If you wait until the interview day, something that could have been modified earlier may become the deciding factor between you and the next top candidate for the job.

- Give your old friends confidence that they can refer you to other businesspeople by amping up your professional presence when you meet with them. Although it may take them by surprise, it will shift their perspective about how serious you are about your job search.

- Wow recruiters, associates and new connections at Career Network meetings and job/career fairs by coming prepared with a confident, assertive approach, including tone, body language, and dress.

- Ask for feedback from those you feel comfortable approaching. Ask questions such as "What could I have done better? Did I seem prepared, confident, and engaging? Was there anything I did that gave you a pause?"

- You can improve your image and approach before you start doing interviews. Sometimes minor changes in your style is all it takes to make a big difference.

Be Aware of Business Etiquette

Business etiquette is the expected professional behavior in the workplace, and it is based on common courtesy, manners, and cultural and societal norms. Etiquette blunders include leaving your cell phone ringer on during a business meeting and using your napkin to wipe your nose during a business lunch.

Your behavior in an interview gives your prospective employer clues to how you will treat clients and customers.

Culturally appropriate business etiquette is important in conducting global business successfully. An unintentional etiquette breach can quickly squash a delicate international transaction. For example, in Asia, presenting a business card using only one hand is considered rude. So brush up on etiquette now by researching the topic as it applies to your industry. You can research online and with people in your network who are in this career field.

GET AN INTERVIEW

If you have been doing Career Network meetings, you have already had pre-interviews. Now it's time to get official interviews that can lead to signed paperwork making you an official employee. To get an interview, ask for one, either directly or indirectly.

Direct Requests for Interviews

First, find out WHO to talk to for an interview, that is, get the name and contact information of a person who would interview you and have authority to offer you a job. If you are working through a recruiter, this part is done for you. Otherwise, a good way to get the name of your interviewer is to ask your networking contact, especially one who already works in the company. Alternately, search online to find the name of a person in the department where you want to work, or the head of human resources (HR) or recruiting. If you can't get a name, contact the receptionist, front desk, or someone at the workplace, either in person or by phone, and request the name of the person you should talk to about an interview for a job.

When requesting an interview, it's best to meet face to face or talk over the phone. Don't write when you can call and don't call when you can make a personal visit. If you can't visit or call, a standard letter or email is appropriate. Tailor your request for an interview to each prospective employer by emphasizing your strengths and experience that are most relevant to the employer's needs. See Chapter 8 on cover letters for more on this topic.

Request an Interview in Person

Requesting an interview by making a personal visit is the most successful method of getting an interview. It is difficult for people to ignore you when you are standing in front of them. If you make a good impression, you have already achieved a major goal in the interview process. Follow these guidelines:

1. **Research the firm** thoroughly beforehand.

2. **Dress for the part.** Dress and groom yourself as though you are going to an actual interview.

You, Online

Find Out the Basics!

Before an interview, learning and being able to speak about the employer is a great way to stand out. With so much information available on the Internet, it may surprise employers if you aren't aware of the basics about the company. You can use social media tools along with the employer's website to research the employer thoroughly before any interaction. Here are some things you should know:

- Formal name, address, locations, contact information, and hours of operation
- Industry; products and/or services, competitors, and customers
- Advertised job openings (with salary ranges)
- Number of employees, departments, and managers
- Corporate culture
- Reputation and history (past successes and challenges)
- News (Have they been in the news lately? Why?)

3. **Be prepared.** Use the Interview Preparation Checklist (see Chapter 11) to make sure you have everything you need, including your resume.

4. **Pay special attention to the gatekeeper** (the person standing between you and the employer). This may be a front-line staff member, an administrative assistant, a supervisor, or a human resources staff member. Actively and courteously seek that person's help.

5. **Present a concise, action-packed version of your 30-Second Commercial;** then request an interview.

6. **Thank your contact by name** for his or her time and consideration.

If you don't get an interview, ask for a referral to another department or company that may need your abilities. Remain courteous and professional throughout the conversation.

Study the example of a request for an interview made during a personal visit to an employer in Figure 9-1. The applicant is applying for an administrative support position in a medical center. Note how he highlights his qualifications, demonstrates his knowledge of the employer and the industry, and expresses his interest in a job—just the right approach.

Request an Interview over the Phone

Your phone communication skills will affect your success throughout your career. You can develop these skills just as you develop any other skill. Your voice is your personality over the phone. You want to use your voice to project confidence and enthusiasm and make a positive impression. Follow these guidelines:

1. **Know why you are calling.** Is your purpose to get the name of the hiring individual? Is it to request information about the position? Is it to request an interview?

2. **Research the firm beforehand.** Get the name of the person you need to contact before you call to request an interview, as suggested above.

3. **Write a script or an outline before you call.** This helps you organize your message, making you sound intelligent and well prepared. List the information you need to obtain from your contact before the phone call ends. Pattern your script after the samples in this chapter and use your 30-Second Commercial.

4. **Don't read from the script during the call.** Practice what you want to say ahead of time until you are comfortable saying it. During the call, use your script or outline as a checklist to guide you from one idea to the next.

Figure 9-1 Sample In-Person Request for an Interview

The Opening. "Hello, Mr. Washington. My name is Stephen Rogowski. My instructor Phyllis Johnston recommends your Information Services Department at St. Mary's Hospital for its well-organized systems design. I recently completed my education at Mesa College, earning two A.S. degrees—one in information management technology and another in medical administrative assisting."

The 30-Second Commercial Excerpt. "My ability to organize and communicate information in an easy to understand way has been a big asset in my previous work. I worked for 18 months as a clerical assistant in the Business Office at Lewis State College while attending school. I'm proficient in Office 2010 and SharePoint software and have my MOUS certification in Office 2010. I operate personal computers, networks, and general office equipment. I also key 70 words per minute and am skilled in English usage."

The Request. "I've developed time-saving methods for creating templates and macros that may be appropriate for your department. Would you have time today for me to review them with you, or would a day next week be more convenient?"

The Close. "Next Tuesday at 10 a.m.? I appreciate your willingness to meet with me so soon, Mr. Washington. I look forward to meeting with you then. Thank you. Good-bye."

5. **Speak clearly and get to the point.** Any long pauses could cause you to be put on hold or transferred to voice mail before you have had a chance to make your pitch.

6. **Don't do anything else.** Listen and respond to the person on the other end of the line. Give the phone call your complete attention. Don't chew gum or drink while talking on the phone.

7. **Stand up, speak directly into the mouthpiece, and smile while you talk.** The muscles used to smile relax your vocal cords and create a pleasant tone of voice. Standing up gives your voice more energy. Start with, "Hello, this is xxx, and I'm calling to …." We are all comfortable saying our own name, so this is a smooth way to get started.

Study the phone request for an interview in Figure 9-2. Note how the applicant incorporates her qualifications, knowledge of the employer and the industry, and interest in the employer.

 CAREER ACTION
Complete Worksheet 9-2
Develop Your Request for an Interview,
page 245

Write a Letter or Email to Request an Interview

If you can't meet or call, use the written word to request an interview. Review the guidelines for preparing and distributing a cover letter in Chapter 8. You may use email and a letter to give extra emphasis to your message and increase the likelihood that your request will be read.

If you don't receive responses from your cover letter and resume within 10 days, reinforce the request through a phone call, personal visit, or, if needed, a one-time follow-up email.

If you call, say that you mailed a letter or email on a specific date and that you are calling to see if it was received and, if a standard letter, who received it. Then ask to speak to that person to discuss your letter. You can also ask about company hiring policies or openings.

Figure 9-2 Sample Phone Request for an Interview

The Opening. "Hello, Ms. Hope. This is Jaleesa Williams. I recently completed research comparing the product quality and service records of computer network manufacturers. I'm impressed with the results XYZ Company has achieved, and I'm interested in learning about a possible sales representative position."

The 30-Second Commercial Excerpt. "I've become fascinated with the impact that service can have on sales. I'm completing my degree in sales and marketing at Fairmount State College and have two years of successful retail sales experience. I also was the advertising assistant for our school paper and increased sales by 18 percent this year."

The Request. "Would it be possible to arrange a meeting with you to discuss your sales goals and how I might contribute to them?"

The Close. "Thank you, Ms. Hope. I look forward to meeting with you next Tuesday, the 18th, at 2:30. Good-bye."

Indirect Strategies for Landing Interviews

Using an indirect strategy is really simply an extension of your networking efforts with the goal of getting an interview rather than more connections. The indirect strategy can create opportunities to meet people in your target company who can arrange an interview for you. To reach an employer, to bypass a gatekeeper, to find the hidden job market, or to get around the office receptionist, consider using the indirect strategy to land an interview.

Get Through to an Employer

When job competition is high, employers are flooded with applicants. In response, they may issue a temporary no-hire policy, which makes personal contact difficult because employees are instructed to notify applicants that no interviews are being scheduled at that time.

Please Leave a *Good* Message

- **Make notes about what you want to say** before you place the call.

- **Have a plan for a conversation if the person** answers the phone.

- **Listen carefully to the person's voice mail greeting.** The person you are trying to reach may be on vacation or may ask callers to send an email instead of leaving a message.

- **Use a pleasant, professional speaking voice.** Your voice IS you to the person who has never met you. Sound confident and helpful; avoid sounding needy or pushy. Encourage the listener so that they want to call you back.

- **Speak slowly.** Speak more slowly than you ordinarily do so that the person can take notes without having to listen to your message more than once.

- **Pronounce your name clearly.** Clearly say your name and spell your name if it is commonly misspelled. For example, "Hello this is Ken Owens, that's Owens with an s."

- **Say your phone number clearly and slowly.** Your listener is writing down your number, so don't mumble or rush. Be sure to give the area code. Remember that many work-place landlines do not have an auto call-back feature, nor do they record the phone number that called.

- **Leave *yourself* the message before you make the real call.** Practice makes perfect, so call yourself from another phone and leave the message on your own voice mail.

- **If you speak English with an accent,** ask a friend to listen to your message and tell you if any parts of it were hard to understand. Speak slowly and clearly. Being able to be understood is much more important than speaking quickly or demonstrating difficult vocabulary.

- **Repeat your name and phone number** at the end of the message. For example, "I look forward to hearing from you. Again, my name is Ken Owens (with an s) at ###."

© auremar/Shutterstock.com.

In a situation like this, use your initiative and persistence. Develop a persuasive reason to contact the person with hiring authority in your target company. See examples below.

While you should not make a direct request for a job during a meeting that is arranged indirectly, you can discuss your experience and abilities. By doing so, you may convince your contact that you would be an asset to the company, which is exactly your intention. Also ask whether the employer may need your skills in the future or if your contact could suggest another company or department that may need someone with your qualifications.

Ask for Professional Advice

One effective indirect strategy is to arrange a brief meeting or phone call with a prospective employer to discuss professional issues and to ask for advice about additional preparation to make you more employable.

Ask About Professional Organizations

Ask for recommendations about professional associations, industry trade groups, and publications in your field. Consider asking the following questions:

- What professional association(s) would keep me informed of industry developments, technological advances in the field, and emerging trends?

- Which professional publications or Internet resources deal specifically with our field?

- Who else could I speak to for further advice on this topic?

Ask for Help with Career Planning

If you have not completed your education or have limited experience related to your target job, ask for help in choosing your course work or with career planning. Your conversation could be similar to this example.

Ask for Help with Your Resume

If you are seeking help in developing your resume into one that employers will not pass over, you can place a phone call to an employer and ask for his or her help in a manner similar to this.

Figure 9-3 Sample Request for Career Advice

"Hello, Mr. Cuervo. This is Cecilia Lee. I'm completing an assignment for a career planning course and would appreciate your assistance with some of my research. I'm seeking opinions from people who are recognized and experienced in the field of (your field).

"My skills are in the area(s) of _____. Could you please help me identify positions in (your career field) for which these skills would be most useful?

"I'd also appreciate your recommendations about any additional course work and preparation I may need."

Figure 9-4 Sample Request for Resume Advice

"Hello, Ms. Pappas. This is Nhon Tran. You've been highly recommended to me by Dr. Ivarsen of the Computer Information Systems Department of Nevada College. I'm developing a professional resume and would very much appreciate your critiquing it."

Develop a Relationship with Your Target Employer

The **gatekeeper** (the administrative support person, receptionist, or human resources staff member) who must screen all job applicants can help, hinder, or ruin your chances of obtaining a job with the company. Because this person's influence on your job search can be considerable, use good diplomacy when communicating with him or her. Follow these guidelines:

- Express respect for the employer, perhaps referring to its reputation for professionalism, reliability, or leadership.

- Find common ground in an effort to establish a good rapport with the gatekeeper. If he or she likes and trusts you, you may learn valuable information about what it is like to work for the company and whether you will fit in.

- If it seems feasible, ask for the person's help in arranging a meeting with the appropriate staff member. Indicate your awareness of everyone's busy schedules and ask the gatekeeper the best time to contact the employer. Ask if you could speak with someone else who can tell you more about your areas of interest.

- Before leaving, thank the person by name for his or her time and assistance.

When making the first contact with a prospective employer, remember that if you are successful in your job search, you will be working with the people you meet. You cannot afford to be ill-mannered, unprofessional, or overbearing with anyone you encounter during the first phone call or step through the door.

Uncover the Hidden Job Market

Numerous studies emphasize that 80 to 85 percent of job openings are never published and that personal searching is required to uncover them. This is the **hidden job market**. It's up to you to make an employer aware of your potential and possibly create a job in the process.

The first step to uncovering the hidden job market is through your job search network contacts. Next, research target employers thoroughly. See the You, Online feature in Chapter 3 "Social Profiles: It's a Two-Way Street" on page 61 for what you should learn. Find out who is in charge of the department that can use your assets. Then analyze how your qualifications can be useful—or even essential—to the employer. The key is to identify how you can provide a useful service or save or make money for the company.

Practice and polish your 30-Second Commercial. Ask a member of your support system to help you by playing the role of your contact and critiquing your presentation. Then present your qualifications for the job or service so convincingly that an employer is motivated to create a job for you. The hidden job market is uncovered through your own ingenuity.

Other Indirect Strategies

Try these tried and true strategies for getting interviews. Refer to additional sources of job leads in Chapter 6.

Go Through the Human Resources Department

If your target employer has a strict policy requiring all applicants to be processed through the human resources department, follow the required procedure. You can

---

> **Real World Scenario 9-2** Lily had created a list of her ideal employers in her area, following the guidelines in Chapter 3. Even though she hadn't seen job openings posted, she knew, through her research, that she could contribute greatly to these companies and would fit well with their culture. Using LinkedIn®, she found the name of a manager in the department where she would like to be hired. She went in person to the office and asked to schedule a meeting with the manager. She casually asked the administrator what it was like working in the department, and she was excited to hear that several people had recently left the department. Although the jobs were expected to be filled internally, this was just the opportunity Lily was looking for. She was able to schedule the meeting and began to prepare to market herself effectively. *What are some conversation starters that will help you discover the hidden job market? What indirect strategies can you use to create interview opportunities?*

expect the first step to be submitting an application, a resume, and a cover letter. If you are selected, you will be invited to a screening interview with a member of the human resources staff. This interview may be in person or over the phone. (The screening interview is covered in Chapter 10.)

If you perform well during a screening interview and you appear to be qualified, you may be scheduled for a departmental interview. If the employer doesn't have an opening in your area, find out how to keep your file active and how you can stay informed about the hiring status for the position.

Use a Private Employment Agency

If you plan to use employment agencies, staffing agencies, or employment contractors in your job search, they will arrange your job interviews. Read the agency's agreement thoroughly to be certain you are satisfied—and comfortable—with their procedures, including interviews.

Request Interviews at Career Fairs

Employers use job fairs to show off their businesses and to actively seek resumes and contacts. Job seekers can meet dozens of prospective employers in one location, so bring several copies of your resume. Ask company representatives about hiring procedures, their opinion of industry trends, and the types of employees they typically hire. Try to arrange a follow-up Career Network meeting with an employer, using the name of the person you meet as your contact. Keep your contact's business card and use it to follow up within the week with a thank-you note or phone call.

Show the interviewer the type of employee you will be. Give solid, to-the-point answers. Ask thoughtful questions and never interrupt.

STAY ON THE JOURNEY BETWEEN INTERVIEWS

Getting interviews can take a long time. The hiring process typically last several months. Don't expect to hear immediately from employers. While getting an interview and a job may be your top priority, recognize and respect the fact that employers have other business to attend to. Make good use of the time while waiting for interviews by advancing your Job Search Journey in other ways. Here are some suggestions.

Get Closer to People in Your Career Field. Look back at the suggestions in Chapter 6 about joining professional groups, taking on internships or cooperative jobs, and

doing volunteer work. This is a great way to get experience and expand your network. You might even run into your prospective employer in the process.

Keep Applying for Other Jobs. Until you have a job offer in hand, your Job Search Journey is not over. Even if you have a possibility or strong lead, do not stop finding and applying for other leads.

Follow Up. Call your target employer regularly, especially if you sense that there has been a favorable change in the job market. Ask whether the employer would consider re-evaluating your qualifications in light of your new experience.

Take Another Job. You may need to take another job while you wait for your best fit job position to become available. This work experience can increase your value. Use the experience to polish your current skills, develop new ones, and establish a reputation as a valuable employee. Then follow up on your best fit jobs every 6 to 12 months.

Check Back Periodically. Call the human resources department to remain informed of the hiring status and to reaffirm your interest. This may help you be first in line for openings.

If you consider more than one company to be a prime employer, don't let one discouragement slow you down. Review the techniques in this chapter and rally your efforts toward your next target. Preparation, practice, action, and perseverance will pay off. Keep at it until you get several interviews, and ultimately, the job you want.

> ▶ *CAREER ACTION*
> **Complete Worksheet 9-3**
> Stay on the Journey While You Wait, page 247

Chapter Checklist

Check off each item you can do. Reread sections in this chapter to help you complete the checklist.

☐ Describe how to start practicing now for interviews by working on my attitude and body language, and what I say about myself. **1**

☐ Prepare to request an interview in person, by phone or in writing, as though it were the start of an actual interview, knowing that a first impression can influence the outcome. **2**

☐ Emphasize my qualifications before I ask for an interview, giving the listener a reason to answer yes. **2**

☐ Prepare a written script or an outline and practice asking for an interview before doing it. **2**

☐ Treat gatekeepers and other staff members courteously and professionally because I know they are often the key to connecting with the hiring authority. **2**

☐ Use my time effectively to continue on my Job Search Journey while waiting for the next interview. **3**

Critical Thinking Questions

1. Which aspects of the job applicant do interviewers focus on the most? Why? **1**

2. How can a job applicant demonstrate a positive attitude during an interview? **1**

3. Why do interviewers respond positively to assertive body language? How can a job candidate demonstrate assertive body language? **1**

4. What negative nonverbal habits are most important for you to eliminate to improve your interview abilities? **1**

5. What method of making a request for an interview do you think will be most effective in your Job Search Journey? Why? **2**

6. What are some advantages to requesting interviews by phone rather than by letter? **2**

7. Why is it important to establish a good relationship with the gatekeeper and other people you meet while you wait to be interviewed? List several strategies you can use to establish good rapport. **2**

8. What could happen when requesting an interview if a job applicant hadn't prepared a 30-Second Commercial? **2**

9. Get creative. Think of an employer you could realistically target for a hidden job market position. What are the needs of this employer based on your research? What special skills and knowledge do you have that represent a hidden job you could perform to meet the employer's needs? **2**

10. If you have already scheduled or completed an interview with one company, why should you keep searching for jobs? Describe what could happen if you had multiple interviews. **3**

Additional Resources

For data files, career resources, and more, visit www.cengagebrain.com.

Trial Run

Request an Interview

You need to be proactive and confident to use the strategies in this chapter successfully. Before you try your approach on strangers, practice with your classmates and support team. Most of these approaches are new, so review the advice as a class to make sure you understand when to apply each suggestion.

Divide into teams of three or four students. Each team creates an interview request scenario and presents it to the class. Discuss types of employers, types of approaches, possible pitfalls, and follow-up. One student can play the role of the employer on the phone or in person, reacting to the request for an interview.

Use these criteria to evaluate each team:

☐ Verbal and language skills (in person, by phone, and in writing requests)

☐ 30-Second Commercial applicable to job

☐ Align with the employer's style (attitude, dress, body language, how you talk about yourself)

☐ Reaction to rejection

Team's Strengths:

Suggestions for Improvement:

▶ CAREER ACTION WORKSHEET
9-1 Body Language Self-Assessment ❶

PART 1: Review the descriptions of nonverbal behaviors and voice qualities and check the box for each item that describes your body language habits. You also can do this Career Action Worksheet with a partner.

Definitions:

- **Assertive body language** is relaxed, open, and confident. It supports your words and conveys competence, self-assurance, caring, and credibility.

- **Passive body language** looks nonenergetic and diminishes your credibility by conveying insecurity, weakness, anxiety, and a lack of self-assurance and competence.

- **Aggressive body language** appears brash and overbearing and sends offensive messages that convey hostility, pushiness, intimidation, and a domineering attitude.

Review your answers and highlight your aggressive or passive habits. In Part 2, list the habits you think are most important to change. Finally, take action to correct these habits and ask others to remind you when you exhibit them.

POSTURE

☐ Comfortably upright	Assertive
☐ Relaxed, balanced	Assertive
☐ Open, not constricted	Assertive
☐ Overly stiff	Aggressive
☐ Arms/legs crossed	Aggressive
☐ Overbearing, intimidating	Aggressive
☐ Wooden, tight	Passive
☐ Slumped shoulders	Passive
☐ Slumped back/spine	Passive

HANDSHAKE

☐ Appropriately firm	Assertive
☐ Connect between thumb and first finger	Assertive
☐ Shake from elbow through hand	Assertive
☐ Held for appropriate length of time	Assertive
☐ "Bone-crushing" grip	Aggressive
☐ Held for too long	Aggressive
☐ Limp	Passive

☐ Shake from wrist through hand	Passive
☐ Held too briefly	Passive
☐ Grasping fingers only	Passive

FACIAL EXPRESSION

☐ Open, relaxed, pleasant	Assertive
☐ Frowning	Aggressive
☐ Moody, sulking	Aggressive
☐ Tight upper lip, pursed mouth	Aggressive
☐ Clenched jaw	Aggressive
☐ Wrinkling forehead	Passive
☐ Biting or licking lips	Passive
☐ Continual smile	Passive

EYE CONTACT

☐ Comfortably direct	Assertive
☐ Staring off; bored expression	Aggressive
☐ Sneering, looking down nose	Aggressive
☐ Direct stare	Aggressive
☐ Constantly looking down	Passive
☐ Blinking rapidly	Passive
☐ Frequently shifting focus	Passive
☐ No eye contact; avoidance	Passive

VOICE QUALITIES

☐ Distinct and clear	Assertive
☐ Controlled but relaxed	Assertive
☐ Warm, pleasant tone	Assertive
☐ Energized; suitable emphasis	Assertive
☐ Too rapid	Aggressive
☐ Too demanding or urgent	Aggressive
☐ Too loud	Aggressive
☐ Arrogant or sarcastic	Aggressive
☐ Dull or monotone	Passive
☐ Whiny tone	Passive
☐ Too soft or too low	Passive
☐ Too nasal	Passive

GESTURES

☐ Natural, not erratic	Assertive
☐ Occasional gestures to emphasize	Assertive
☐ Occasional positive head nodding	Assertive
☐ Open hand (conveys trust)	Assertive
☐ Leaning toward speaker	Assertive
☐ Pointing finger	Aggressive
☐ Hands on hips	Aggressive
☐ Wooden gestures	Passive
☐ Tilting head to one side	Passive
☐ Bringing hand to face	Passive
☐ Nodding head too much	Passive
☐ Fidgeting	Passive

DISTRACTING NONVERBAL HABITS

☐ Drumming fingers	Passive
☐ Use of fillers (*um, uh, you know*)	Passive
☐ Jiggling leg/arm	Passive
☐ Fiddling with hair or glasses	Passive
☐ Fiddling with an object	Passive
☐ Rubbing beard or mustache	Passive
☐ Biting nails	Passive
☐ Scratching	Passive

PART 2: In order of importance, list the negative nonverbal habits you plan to change.

My Goals for Improving My Nonverbal Communication and Voice Qualities

1. _____

2. _____

3. _____

Add your completed work to the "About Me" section of your Career Builder Files.

This page is intentionally blank.

▶ *CAREER ACTION WORKSHEET*
9-2 Develop Your Request for an Interview ❷

PART 1. Read the sample request for an interview on page 233 and write a script or an outline that would be appropriate to use when requesting an interview with your prospective job target(s). Next, determine what would be different if you were making this request by phone rather than in person.

The Opening:

The 30-Second Commercial Excerpt:

The Request:

The Close:

PART 2: Turn to your support system for assistance. Do some role-playing, following the guidelines below. Deliver your request for an interview to someone in your support system. First as if you were in person, and then by phone.

1. Critique your delivery and improve on it. It helps to record your delivery and play it back.

2. Have your helper ask you questions that require more information about your qualifications.

3. Practice responding when your helper makes excuses for not scheduling an interview. (Remember to stay cool and positive, and be courteous to the gatekeeper.)

4. Practice presenting your qualifications persuasively, using your 30-Second Commercial.

5. Practice turning objections into acceptance.

Add your completed work to the "About Jobs" section of your Career Builder Files.

This page is intentionally blank.

▶ *CAREER ACTION WORKSHEET*
9-3 Stay on the Journey While You Wait ❸

While waiting for the next interview request, continue your Job Search Journey. Use this worksheet to discover more jobs that you are qualified to do. Refer to your completed Career Action Worksheets in Part 1 to help complete the following.

1. List the benefits of working in a field related to your career field that may be an untraditional use of your talents.

2. Find and list three jobs that you are currently qualified to do that you have not previously applied for.

3. Describe your action plan for getting closer to people in your chosen career field.

4. Find and list three jobs that you are currently overqualified to do. Describe why you haven't applied for these jobs, and at what point you would apply.

Add your completed work to the "About Jobs" section of your Career Builder Files.

Prepare for Your Interview

OVERVIEW

You can improve your chances of success in an interview if you prepare for different kinds of interviews, practice answering interview questions, learn to ask appropriate questions of your own, and practice good listening skills.

OUTCOMES

1. Prepare for pre-employment tests.
2. Prepare for common interview styles.
3. Prepare answers to typical interview questions.
4. Ask questions that stand out.

CAREER ACTION WORKSHEETS

WHERE ARE YOU ON THE JOURNEY?

PHASE 1: Prepare for the Journey
- *The Job Search Journey*
- *Know Yourself to Market Yourself*
- *Picture Yourself in the Workplace*

PHASE 2: Create Your Resume
- *Plan Your Resume*
- *Write Your Resume*

PHASE 3: Apply for Jobs
- *Find Job Openings*
- *Write Job Applications*
- *Write Effective Tailored Cover Letters*

PHASE 4: Shine at Interviews
- *Know the Interview Essentials*
- ***Prepare for Your Interview***
- *Interview Like a Pro*

PHASE 5: Connect, Accept, and Succeed
- *Stay Connected with Prospective Employers*
- *It's an Iterative Process*
- *Take Charge of Your Career*

Those who prepare show the best of themselves when put to the test.

PHASE 4: Shine at Interviews
Step 2, *Prepare for Your Interview*

You are in Phase 4, *Shine at Interviews*, at steps 1 and 2, prepare and practice and take pre-employment tests. Your goal in this chapter is to prepare and practice for common interview questions and pre-employment tests.

PREPARE FOR PRE-EMPLOYMENT TESTS

Before you are even considered for an interview, you may be asked to take pre-employment screening tests. Some tests are requested only after you have successfully completed a screening interview. To help you feel confident and to do your best, it helps to know what to expect. Here are some common types of tests.

The Personality Test

The **personality test** is the exception to the "do your homework" rule. Because this type of test is usually designed to determine whether your personal and behavioral preferences are well matched to the work involved and company culture, advance study doesn't apply. Technically, there are no wrong answers in these tests. Personality tests can measure, for example, your solitary or social tendencies, your relative need for stability, your preference for efficiency or creativity, your style of goal achievement (flexible or fixed), and your tendency to accept others' ideas or stick to your own. Answer all questions honestly. If your personality doesn't match the culture of the employer, you won't be happy in it.

The Skills Test

If you will be taking a general **skills test,** start to review, practice, and improve your skills today. Try to learn what is covered in advance of the test, for example, grammar, spelling, math, typing or computer skills, or something else. No matter how good your skills are, you can improve them with practice, which increases your employability. Another benefit of polishing your skills is that you'll be able to start your new job with more confidence. However, stop preparing one or two days before you take a skills test. Cramming until the last minute increases anxiety and often results in poorer performance.

The Technical Test

The purpose of a technical test is to find out how much you know about a subject related to your job. Try to get samples of the technical questions that may be asked through the employer's human resources department, other employees in the company, people who have taken the test, and people who have taken similar tests in your field. Libraries, bookstores, and websites may also have sample tests.

If you find sample questions, write out answers to the questions as a way of practicing. The important thing is to be as complete as possible in your answers.

The Computerized Test

The computerized pre-employment test is useful for screening large numbers of applicants because it saves time and other expenses. The test may be general in content, or it may be a skills or personality test.

Typically, you take this test at the employer's site or at an employment agency. You may also be asked to log on to an employer's website and take the test online. You receive instructions on how to use the computerized test program and are given a specific amount of time to complete it. The results are usually scored electronically and generated in a report. They are then analyzed by human resources personnel. The best advice for performing well on a computerized pre-employment test is relax, do your best, and don't try to outwit the test by overthinking the questions.

Taking Employment Tests

Employment testing may be an important factor in an employer's hiring decision. Follow these guidelines to perform at your best:

- Try to find out in advance what will be tested and how. Is it a written, oral, computerized, or combination test? Does it

Take Drug Screening Seriously

Applicants who test positively for drug use or who admit to using illegal drugs may be screened out of the job immediately. Never give flippant answers to questions about drug use. They could be interpreted negatively.

Policies for drug screening vary considerably from one employer to the next. As part of your employer research, find out the drug screening procedures and requirements. Check with employers directly and with people who work for them. Schools' career services counselors often have information about drug testing procedures and may be familiar with the procedures that local employers use.

To protect yourself, before you are tested, report to the employer any prescription or over-the-counter drugs you are taking. Some of these can result in a false-positive test.

©iStock.com/Justin Horrocks.

test technical knowledge, skills, manual dexterity, personality, special abilities, or other job-related capabilities? Prepare accordingly.

- Eat properly before the test and be well rested. A sluggish body and brain can diminish your performance.

- Do some physical exercise or yoga before the test to improve your circulation and your ability to relax and concentrate.

- Arrive 10 minutes early to avoid feeling rushed or tense.

- Ask exactly how much time is allotted for the test. Take your time and don't rush into poor performance.

- Read the test carefully to clarify the instructions and to determine how many points are assigned to each question. If the points aren't indicated, ask the person monitoring the test how the questions are weighted.

- Read each question multiple times to make sure you understand what is being asked. If you have a question, ask the test monitor if possible.

- Ask whether points will be deducted for questions you don't answer. If they will, answer every question. If not, don't spend a lot of time on questions you can't answer easily. (Save those for last.)

- Many tests are objective, often including multiple-choice questions. In true-false questions, extreme statements are frequently false (for example, choices that contain the words *all, never,* or *always*). Moderate statements are often true.

- Double-check to be sure you didn't skip any questions. Because your first response is usually the correct one, don't change answers unless you made a careless mistake.

Real World Scenario **10-1** Jacob was never a good test taker. When he heard his upcoming interview required a basic math test using Excel, he was nervous. The week of his interview, he set aside time every day to practice using sample tests he found on the Internet. He limited his studying to one hour a day and aimed to finish six samples tests prior to the interview. The day before the interview, he took the last sample test in the morning and then decided to relax the rest of the day. Prior to the interview, he reviewed a few notes of the common errors he had made during the sample tests. He took a deep breath and felt calm, knowing he had done the best he could to prepare for the test.

What tactics help you to be calm during times of stress and pressure? How can you apply these tactics when preparing for pre-interview tests and the interview process overall?

- On general math tests, expect some simple addition, subtraction, multiplication, division, fraction, percentage, and decimal problems. Many math tests also include word problems.

- Advanced math tests will be geared to your field (engineering and statistical analysis, for instance). Consult others who have taken similar tests to determine what you should review. Your education and work experience are your primary preparation for advanced math tests.

Once you have successfully completed pre-employment tests, you are on your way to the next steps in your Job Search Journey.

▶ *CAREER ACTION*
Complete Worksheet 10-1
Research Pre-employment Test Types, page 269

PREPARE FOR COMMON INTERVIEW STYLES

Have you ever had a job where you had all the time in the world to finish each assignment or where your department could choose the deadline for an important project? Of course not. Hiring a new employee is no different—the people in charge of finding the perfect person need to work efficiently to fill the empty position. Chances are high that for most jobs, you are competing against a handful of applicants—the very few whose cover letter and resume made the cut. You will be nervous—everyone is—but less so if you know what to expect during the interview and have practiced your answers to the most likely questions. There are two basic styles of interviews that you should be prepared for:

- **Structured**: In these interviews, all the job candidates are asked the same or similar questions. This allows the employee to compare candidates more easily.

- **Unstructured**: These interviews might follow a pattern or outline but can "go with the flow" to get to know the candidate and assess their fit for the company and the job.

You may receive a request to schedule an interview at any time. The request can come by email, standard mail, or phone. In case the request comes by phone, have a businesslike outgoing voice mail message that includes your name, and make sure anyone who may answer the phone knows to answer professionally and take a complete message. If a call comes at an unexpected time, politely ask if the caller can hold for a moment while you move to a quiet location. When you get an interview request, respond promptly with your availability.

In general, for any interview, use the following tips.

1. **Be prepared.** Have a copy of your resume and any other materials you would like to use during the interview. Have paper and pen so that you can write down names and information.

2. **Focus on why you are interested in working for the prospective employer** on the basis of your research and understanding of the employer's products or services, current developments, philosophies, mission and values, and so on. Talk about your qualifications that make you a good fit.

3. **Be professional, courteous, and friendly;** let the caller lead the conversation but ask questions of your own.

4. **Be factual in your answers; be brief yet thorough.** Avoid yes/no answers; they give no real information about your abilities.

5. **If you need time to think about a question, avoid using repetitive phrases to buy time.** Instead, simply say, "Let me think about that."

6. **As the interview wraps up, ask what about next steps.** Tell the interviewer that you are available for a follow-up interviews, if needed. Get an approximate date when you can expect to hear from the company again about this job.

7. **Follow up.** Contact the interviewer one or two days later to say thank you for his or her time, and restate your interest in the position. You can leave this message by voice mail or send an email.

While there are only two basic styles of interviews—structured and unstructured—there are many types of interviews. These vary based on where the interview takes place, who conducts the interview, and the intent of the interview—to screen potential candidates or to make job offers. Get familiar with all these types so that you can recognize which type of interview you are doing and be prepared and relaxed for this all-important meeting.

Screening Interview

Large employers often require applicants to go through a **screening interview** to screen out unqualified applicants and identify candidates—qualified applicants—who will be invited for the next level of interviews. Screening might be done by phone or in person. Screening interviews might be outsourced to recruiting agencies or done by human resources people.

The interviewer may use a rating sheet to evaluate each candidate. Your goal in a screening interview is to be scheduled for the next required interview. Make sure you state your qualifications clearly and concisely. Ask what to expect next, who is responsible for making a hiring decision, and when this decision will be made.

Computer-Based Interview

Computer-based interviews may be part of the application process to screen candidates. The candidate logs onto a password-protected website with instructions on how to complete the interview. The interview may consist of 50 to 100 multiple-choice and true–false questions and be timed, so start the interview only when you can have uninterrupted time. Some programs search for contradictions by asking you the same question several times in different forms; so be consistent in your answers. Some computer-based interviews include open-ended questions that are reviewed by recruitment specialists or managers. Answer questions just as you would in a face-to-face interview. Use correct grammar and strong written communication skills. Emphasize your related skills but don't exaggerate. Be concise, and be positive in your responses. Your goal is to get through this screening process by demonstrating your skills, honesty, and qualifications.

Campus Interview

Campus interviews, generally scheduled through a school's career center, are typically structured screening interviews averaging 20 to 30 minutes. Because the interviewer must evaluate each candidate quickly, you should keep your remarks concise and to the point. Let the trained interviewer guide you through the fact-finding process. Respond concisely without omitting pertinent information about your qualifications. Smile and be pleasant in order to build rapport with the interviewer.

Phone Interview

A **phone interview** is a cost-effective screening technique. For this type of interview, be sure to have a quiet place without distractions. Have all your materials ready—resume, pen, paper, and so on. Stand up, speak directly into the mouthpiece, and smile while you talk. This gives your voice more energy and a pleasant tone. Never smoke, eat, or chew gum while on the phone. Be sure to listen as well as talk. Pay extra attention to articulating your words clearly.

Video Interview

A **video interview** uses two-way video to conduct a "face-to-face" interview over the Internet. Video interviews are used to save money and time for employers. Test your video setup and connectivity in advance. Make sure lighting and sound quality are set up properly. You should have a light in front of you so that your face is not shadowed. Your face should be centered with your chin clearly in the picture. Try to find a plain wall or background to sit in front of so that the background is professional, not distracting. Find a quiet place with no interruption from children, pets,

MAKE IT A HABIT
Collect Your Stories

It takes planning and preparation to be able to discuss your strengths persuasively and explain how they can benefit an employer. Throughout your experiences, consider the positive capabilities and personal qualities your coworkers, managers, instructors, and others have recognized in you. Consider times when you have made a big impact or achievement:

- Examples that demonstrate your organizational skills and orderly mind
- Examples of improved methods of performing tasks
- Examples of motivating people successfully
- Examples of leading a team or being an effective team member
- Examples of effective problem solving
- Examples that demonstrate your creativity
- Examples of handling detailed assignments carefully and accurately
- Examples of being dependable and flexible
- Examples of working independently without regular supervision

Make it a habit to collect stories as they happen during your career.

or phone calls. Dress appropriately, project energy, and maintain eye contact with the camera. Use positive body language and good posture, and avoid fidgeting. Ask if it is okay to take notes, and then do so as needed.

You may want to practice your interview skills using the video conferencing technology available today, regardless of the scheduled interview format. Using two-way video technology such as Skype with a friend or colleague can be a great way to prepare for the real interview. You can also record your interview using iMovie or other recording software and have a small group provide critique.

Behavioral Interview

The **behavioral interview** is based on the premise that past performance is the best predictor of future behavior. The interviewer asks questions aimed at getting the candidate to provide specific examples of how he or she has successfully used the skills required for the target job. This helps the interviewer evaluate the candidate's experience and predict future on-the-job behavior. Take time to prepare for behavioral interview questions, covered later in this chapter. The examples you give about your past success can be useful in most every other type of interview.

Panel Interview

In a **panel interview** (also called a *board interview*), more than one person interviews you at one time. Although this situation can seem more difficult than a simple one-on-one interview, it can play in your favor because you have the opportunity to appeal as a strong candidate to multiple people on the panel. Focus on the person questioning you at the moment, but don't ignore the others. Appearing relaxed and projecting a self-assured attitude is important. Before a board or panel interview, try to obtain and memorize the names of the panel members. During the interview, draw a diagram of the seating arrangement and label seats with interviewers' names. At the close of the interview, shake hands and thank each interviewer by name as you leave. Leave your business card with each person, if possible. A key to success is being personable.

Team Interview

A **team interview**, or **Day Visit** (if conducted on-site), is a series of three to five interviews with different people in the company. The candidate meets individually with each person. The interviewers might be your peers or managers, if you are given

⟲ You, Online

Stay Relevant!

Using social media is a quick way of staying relevant and up-to-date on news about your prospective employers and the industry. Instead of spending hours researching and reading news articles, consider using some social media shortcuts to speed up the process:

- Review the Twitter feed of your prospective employer. Anything exciting on the horizon?
- Visit the site of a news aggregator such as Reddit or Digg. Search for your industry to find headlines quickly.

- Did you know that you can specifically search News on Google? Do a quick search on Google and then narrow the results by clicking on News, located below the Search bar.

Sometimes just knowing the headlines is enough to get a conversation started. For more information on how to research a company in depth using social media, read the Appendix. The next time you're heading out the door to a networking opportunity or interview, take a few minutes to check social media sites to keep yourself sharp!

The Stress Interview

Stress interviews are generally reserved for jobs that involve regular pressure. They are designed to test the candidate's behavior, logic, and emotional control under pressure.

A skilled interviewer may combine some stress techniques with an unstructured interview approach to get a well-rounded picture of your personality. Some techniques used in stress interviewing include (a) remaining silent following one of your remarks, (b) questioning you rapidly, (c) placing you on the defensive with irritating questions or remarks, and (d) criticizing your responses or remarks.

Some stress questions are routinely asked in other types of job interviews—even informal ones. Every job has an occasional crisis situation. An interviewer may also use a stress technique unintentionally. Do not react negatively. Take a deep breath, demonstrate control, and be courteous.

© PathDoc/Shutterstock.com.

the job, so building rapport and leaving a positive, likeable impression is key. Team interviewers often meet before the interview to decide who will cover each topic. The team members may ask a few common questions to give the candidate more than one opportunity to cover a particular topic. After the interview, the team members meet to discuss the candidate's performance and identify the best candidate. Before a team interview, learn the names of the members and, if possible, learn something about their areas of expertise. Use this information to enhance your performance. Be sure to give consistent answers to the individual members' questions.

▶ *CAREER ACTION*

Complete Worksheet 10-2
Research Interview Styles, page 271

PREPARE FOR TYPICAL INTERVIEW QUESTIONS

The core of a job interview is the question-and-answer period. Generally, you should let the interviewer take the lead. Interviewers usually consider a candidate's effort to control the interview to be rude or aggressive.

Questions asked by interviewers generally fall into four categories:

- General information questions
- Behavioral questions
- Character questions
- Difficult or "stress" questions

Start preparing for your own interview by studying the following lists of the most common questions and suggested answers. Keep your Personal Brand Statement and 30-Second Commercial handy while preparing for interviews because these contain the key message and impression you want to leave your interviewer with. Your answers to most questions should continue to reinforce your Personal Brand Statement and 30-Second Commercial.

General Information Questions

General information questions are asked to obtain factual information. They usually cover your skills, work experience, education, interests, and so on.

1. **Why do you want this job?** Be prepared; every employer wants to know the answer to this question.

   Suggested answer: "My skills and experience are directly related to this position, and I'm very interested in this field because _____." Position your answer as a win-win situation: You have skills and talent that will benefit the company, and you have a long-term interest in the position because of your personal development goals. If applicable, relate examples of your experience, education, and/or training that relate to the job you are seeking. Never say that you want the job because of the pay and benefits.

2. **What type of work do you enjoy most?**

   Suggested answer: Play your research card; name three of the top types of tasks that are involved in this job and demonstrate how you are qualified for the position.

3. **What are your strongest skills?**

   Suggested answer: Review your abilities and accomplishments and your 30-Second Commercial to develop your answer. Describe three of your skills that directly relate to those required for the position. Be specific and focused, and avoid overwhelming the interviewer with too much or appearing vague.

4. **Are you a team player?**

   Suggested answer: The ability to collaborate and get work done through others is highly valued in today's workplace, so a positive answer is usually a plus. Give examples of your successful team roles (as a leader, a member, or a partner) from school, previous jobs, volunteer work, or sports, in which you demonstrated the ability to work well with, communicate, influence, and lead others.

5. **What are your long-term career goals, and how do you plan to achieve them?**

   Suggested answer: Emphasize your strengths, state that your goal is to make a strong contribution in your job, and explain that you look forward to developing the experience necessary for career growth. Employers are impressed with employees who show initiative and a desire to learn because they perform better than those who have no plans for self-improvement. Mention your plans to continue your education and expand your knowledge to become a more valuable employee.

6. **Do you have a geographic preference? Are you willing to relocate?**

   Suggested answer: Your research should let you know in advance if this job requires travel. Have your answer ready in advance. If you have no objection to relocating, make this perfectly clear. If you do have objections, be honest in your answer; otherwise, you will no doubt be unhappy in the job.

7. **With what type of manager have you had the best relationships?**

   Suggested answer: "I've had good relationships with all of my managers. Communication is so important; I make sure I understand what I'm supposed to do. That's especially important when I've been given new responsibilities so that we can get off to a good start. I think managers appreciate someone who takes responsibility for his or her job." Then give an example. This is also a good time to use your research on the company culture. For example, if you

Become a Good Listener

You may think of the interview primarily in terms of talking, but listening carefully is just as important. So that you can respond appropriately, you need to listen to the interviewer carefully to learn important details about the job requirements, the company, and the department.

Follow these tips to become a more effective listener:

- Give each question your undivided attention. Don't formulate your response while you are listening.

- Nod as appropriate.

- Repeat or summarize the main ideas.

- Ask questions when you need to clarify what the interviewer means. If you don't understand a question, ask for clarification instead of talking and hoping you answered correctly.

- Listen "between the lines" for the underlying messages.

- Don't argue or interrupt.

- Maintain eye contact (but not too intensely).

- Maintain an "open" position (don't cross your arms or legs; keep your hands unclenched).

- Maintain the same eye level as the interviewer (sit or stand as appropriate).

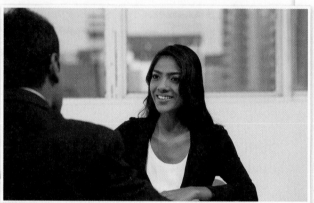

© Stuart Jenner/Shutterstock.com.

are aware that the culture is to work under tight deadlines, share your willingness to work with managers on communicating and delivering results frequently. Caution: Avoid any reference to a bad manager, and instead talk about what type of supervision you prefer.

Behavioral Questions

Behavioral questions probe a candidate's specific past performance and behaviors. The interviewer wants details of experiences that illustrate how you perform or behave on a job or in stressful environments.

To prepare for behavioral interviews, recall scenarios from your experiences that illustrate how you have performed or behaved on the job. Write out examples that demonstrate good performance. Also be ready to describe how you have handled difficult situations.

Students with little work experience should focus on class projects and group situations that illustrate their task performance and interpersonal behavior. These four steps provide a good model for your answers to behavioral questions:

1. Describe the situation. (What)
2. Explain the actions you took. (How)
3. Describe the outcomes. (Importance)
4. Summarize what you learned from the experience. (Insights from you)

This should sound familiar—it's an expanded version of the WHI (What, How, and Importance) model you have been using as you developed your marketing materials and resume! Now, you have a chance to go into the details of the concise story you have already shared and add some new examples, too.

Example: Describe an accomplishment that demonstrates your initiative.

Suggested answer: "While I was working part-time as a computer lab technician for Seattle Technology College, our department received several complaints about service response time. I set a personal goal of answering all troubleshooting calls within 90 minutes. I recorded the exact response time for each call and maintained the goal of a 90-minute response time for one full semester. I was awarded the Customer Service Certificate for this performance. I learned that by making a plan to address an issue, I can be more effective."

Whenever possible, give positive examples that demonstrate measurable achievements. Or when describing a less positive experience, emphasize what actions you took to correct weaknesses or poor performance. By giving specific examples, you establish credibility and believability that can translate into a job offer.

Prior to the interview, practice your stories. You should have at least eight stories describing such things as times where you went above and beyond in completing a task, or used your leadership skills, or handled a difficult situation, or used your talent to contribute to a goal or project. By rehearsing so many examples and stories, you will be ready to answer a wide variety of questions using stories during a behavioral interview. These stories give the interviewer confidence in your answers and can help you earn the job.

You can expect questions such as "Describe the most challenging assignments you've had. How did you handle it?" followed by "Explain what problems you encountered. How did you overcome them?" Some behavioral questions probe for negative experiences. Use the WHI method to frame your answer: **What** you did, **How** you did it, and the **Importance** of the results, then add

Insights you gained, what you learned from the experience, or what actions you took to improve the situation.

As you prepare your stories and examples, be sure to include the following content:

- **Your work skills:** Work-specific skills, such as computer programming, CAD, and medical transcription.

- **Your functional and transferable skills:** Skills used with people, things, or information, such as good communication, organizational, or planning skills. These skills are valuable from one job to another.

- **Your self-management skills:** Personal characteristics such as being a dependable person, a team player, a self-directed worker, a problem solver, or a decision maker.

Review the activities in Chapter 2 to help you prepare for behavioral interview. Your 30-Second Commercial can be used as an answer to these questions, especially if it contains proof-by-example descriptions of your capabilities that are relevant to the job.

Here are some common questions you should be prepared to answer:

1. **Tell me specifically about a time when you worked under great stress.**

   Suggested answer: Be careful to choose a relevant example that would be considered stressful in a work environment, such as working under pressure of time. Quickly describe the elements that made it stressful for you and how you maintained your cool and got the job done.

2. **Describe an experience when you dealt with an angry customer or coworker.**

   Suggested answer: Give an answer that highlights how you value communication and know that conflict can lead to personal growth and opportunity. Discuss your ability to maintain a calm and positive attitude. Your reply also should include how you turned the situation from negative to positive.

3. **Give me an example of your ability to adapt to change.**

   Suggested answer: Choose a time when there was a significant change at work, school, a club, or a volunteer organization. Explain what the change was, and focus on sharing how you quickly and successfully adapted to the change.

4. **Explain what problems you have encountered. How did you overcome them?**

   Suggested answer: Some behavioral questions probe for negative experiences. In responding to these, focus on what you learned from the experience or what actions you took to improve the situation. The intent of the interviewer is to discover how you turn negative situations into positive results.

   Do you see any recurring themes in the suggested answers? Turn negatives into positives and focus on your strengths.

Write the answer to every question you think you may be asked—and every question you hope you won't be asked.

Character Questions

Character questions are asked to learn about your personal attributes, such as integrity, personality, attitudes, and motivation.

1. **How would you describe yourself?**

   Suggested answer: Emphasize your strongest personal attributes and focus on those that are relevant to your target job. Review your capabilities and accomplishments. Examples: "I'm punctual and dependable. At my current job, I haven't been late or missed one day in the last two years." "I get along well with others; in fact, my coworkers chose me to represent them in our company's monthly staff meetings."

Real World Scenario 10-2 Sam sat comfortably in a meeting room, ready for his interview. He was careful to exhibit positive, assertive body language by keeping his hands relaxed in his lap, sitting up straight, and having a smile on his face. He had carefully prepared and practiced eight stories showcasing his strengths, experience, and results. He felt so familiar with the stories because of course they were his life! He was the expert! Regardless of the question asked, he knew he could tailor at least one out of the eight stories to create a great answer. He also had researched the company on Glassdoor and through his Career Network meetings and had questions prepared for the interviewer as well. As soon as the interview ended, Sam knew the preparation paid off when the interviewer said they would get back to him within the week and they were excited to have had the opportunity to interview him.

What are your best stories that are "multiuse" and can be tailored to answer a variety of questions?

Give specific examples of your strengths. Don't just say, "I'm a hard worker" or "I'm dependable." Other leads include "I learn quickly," "I like solving problems; for example ...," "I like contributing to a team," and "I like managing people." Use a relevant example that shows that you know what is important in a work environment.

2. **What rewards do you look for in your career?**

   Suggested answer: Don't make financial rewards your prime motivator. Emphasize your desire to improve your skills, make a valuable contribution to the field, and become better educated. These answers show initiative, interest, and professionalism.

Be Prepared for Silence

Be prepared to handle silence. The interviewer asks you a question, you answer, and the interviewer does not respond.

Interviewers sometimes use this technique to test candidates' confidence and ability to handle stress or uncertainty. Do not retract your statement; just wait calmly. You have no obligation to continue talking if you answered adequately. By doing this, you will pass the "test" and project a mature, confident image. Break a long silence by asking whether the interviewer needs more information or by asking a related question.

You also can use silence. If you are asked a difficult question, answering too quickly without enough thought can be detrimental. You're entitled to think carefully about a question and

to prepare a response. The employer wouldn't want you to solve problems on the job without adequate thought and planning.

Avoid long pauses in a phone or video interview, however. When the interviewer has fewer "clues" about you as a person, long pauses may be perceived as slow thinking abilities.

© pan_kung/Shutterstock.com.

3. **What accomplishment are you most proud of, particularly as it relates to your field?**

   Suggested answer: Relate an accomplishment that shows special effort and initiative. "I recognized the need to improve communications [between two departments]. I designed a questionnaire that was completed by representatives from each department. Management made several of the changes, and communications were improved in those areas."

4. **Do you work well under pressure?**

   Suggested answer: You may be tempted to answer with a simple yes or no, but don't. Yes and no answers reveal nothing specific about you. Don't miss an opportunity to sell yourself.

   Be honest in your answer. If you prefer to work at a well-defined job in an organized, calm atmosphere (rather than one

that involves constant decision making and pressure), say so. Otherwise, you may end up in a job that is a constant source of tension. If you enjoy the challenge of pressure, either in decision making or in dealing with people, make this fact clear.

Keep in mind that a large company may have more than one working environment. For instance, an administrative support job in the customer relations department would likely involve more interactive pressure with the public than a support job in the data processing department.

Difficult or "Stress" Questions

Difficult or **"stress" questions** are asked to understand deeper motivations and identify a possible mismatch between you and

CAUTION
"Tell Me about Yourself"

Sometimes an employer will start an interview by taking a few minutes to establish rapport or make small talk and then say, "Tell me about yourself."

Be prepared to handle this type of interview effectively. Once the interviewer makes this request, he or she comments just enough to encourage you to keep talking. The purpose is to see whether you focus on your qualifications for the job and how the employer would benefit by hiring you. Do not ramble on about your life history; this is a sure way to disqualify yourself on the spot. Ask questions such as "What exactly do you want to know about [my work experience, educational experience, skills, or extracurricular and community activities]?"

© imtmphoto/Shutterstock.com.

Your objective is to highlight your positive qualities (personal attributes, accomplishments, skills, pertinent training, work experience, etc.). After you think you have covered these topics, ask, "Would you like me to clarify or expand on any area for you?" This helps you focus on the information the interviewer wants.

the company, such as being overqualified or underqualified or lacking dependability (if your resume shows many different jobs). They also provide the opportunity for the interviewer to determine whether you are good at making decisions, solving problems, and thinking under stress.

Remaining Cool Under Stress. Take three to five calming deep breaths and tell yourself, "I can do this." After using Career Action Worksheet 10-3, you will be prepared to answer difficult questions. Make sure to rehearse your answers.

However, if you are asked a question that you are totally unprepared for, don't ramble through an answer. Pausing to think is perfectly fine. Use the "That's a good question, let me think about it for a minute" technique. Your goal is to demonstrate that you can handle stress—that you don't just

react, but instead think through the situation and remain composed.

When describing a less positive experience, emphasize what actions you took to correct weaknesses or poor performance, and what you learned from the experience for next time.

1. **Why do you think you are the best candidate for the job?** *or* **Why should I hire you?**

   Suggested answer: Summarize what you believe the important objectives and challenges of the job are. Ask the interviewer for confirmation that you have a good understanding of what the job entails. Then explain how you can handle them. Focus on how you can benefit the employer, citing examples of increasing productivity, saving money, increasing sales, and so on. Summarize your accomplishments, skills, and experience that are pertinent to the job. Then ask, "How does that fit your requirements?" This shifts the focus from you to the interviewer, helping reduce stress for you.

2. **Why do you want to leave your current job?**

   Suggested answer: This question will likely be posed to determine whether you have a problem with your current job. Accentuate the positive—for example, you are seeking a new challenge, you have mastered your present job and are seeking advancement, or you want to work for a company with stability. If you have a problem with your current job or boss, do not discuss it. Do not be specific or emotional in your response to this question. Be prepared by practicing your answer to this question in advance.

3. **Why have you held so many jobs?**

   Suggested answer: Employers like to see a work history that implies stability and dependability. People often have valid reasons for holding numerous jobs that don't necessarily imply immaturity or an inability to commit. Be factual and emphasize that your current goal is to apply yourself to long-term employment and the development of a career. You can also describe the skills you learned from the variety of jobs that will be beneficial on this job.

MAKE IT A HABIT
Savvy Q&A Strategies

- **Pause to think before you reply.** If you're uncomfortable with a question, go back to the familiar. Stress your assets. Use a "thinking pause" to buy time to answer the question well. For example, "Could we return to this question? I'd like to think about it for a moment" or "That's a good question" or "Let me see ..." (This works if you need only a little extra time.)

- **Be candid and honest.** Be realistic when expressing your preferences and dislikes. You won't be happy in a job that isn't a good fit. Honesty also naturally builds trust and rapport.

- **Understand the motive behind the question.** Listen actively when the question is asked and try to answer what they are really looking for. For example, asking about a challenging project is usually not just about the results that were achieved, but what leadership skills and creative thinking you displayed in overcoming challenges.

- **Give appropriate context.** Don't assume the interviewer knows the full background or needs to know all of the details. Practice telling the right amount of relevant background.

- **Fill in the gaps.** If you sense that the interviewer thinks you have an area of weakness, communicate how you plan to eliminate the weakness or round out your qualifications—perhaps by completing research or course work in the area.

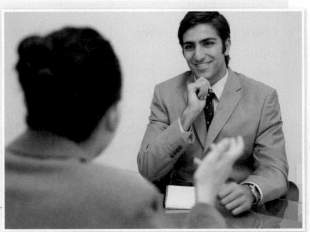

4. **What is your greatest weakness?**

   Suggested answer: Either describe something that is not needed for this job, or a skill that you are working on improving. "My weakest area is foreign language, so I am focusing on a career that is more geared to mathematics at national companies." Or "My weakest area is accounting, so I am taking a course in beginning accounting at the community college. It's going well, and I plan to take the advanced course next semester." The objective is to acknowledge a weakness that is low on the employer's list and to explain your steps to improve or manage the weakness.

5. **Have you ever been fired from a job?**

   Suggested answer: If accurate, use less negative terms such as *laid off, let go,* or *employment ended.* Be honest, but not too specific about the reason for your termination Use phrases such as "the job was not a good long-term fit" or "my career goals no longer aligned with the company goals." Be truthful, yet brief. Briefly describe the situation; explain what you learned from the experience and how you could have handled the experience differently. Take responsibility for past mistakes but end your response on a positive note. Your goal is to give some assurance that the situation will not be repeated.

6. **Does your current employer know you are planning to leave?**

   Suggested answer: If your current employer is aware of this fact, say so. If not—and especially if you depend on your current income—make this clear. Say that you prefer your current employer not be informed of your job search until a firm offer is made and that you will give two weeks' notice before leaving. Consider it a good sign that the interviewer is asking this question—you are probably close to being offered a position.

Explaining Gaps in Employment and Reasons for Leaving a Job

- Use brief, positive phrases to explain reasons for leaving a job and periods of unemployment: "returned to school," "changed careers," "reorganization," "employment ended," "business closed," or "took a position with more responsibility."

- Avoid negative language ("couldn't find a job," "quit," "personal conflict," "fired for no reason") that may lead an employer to question your abilities and judgment.

- If you were fired from a job, be as brief and positive as possible and leave longer explanations for the interview.

- Be prepared to describe what happened using unemotional and professional language.

- Take responsibility for your actions (don't blame others), explain what you learned from the situation, and explain how you could have handled the situation differently.

It may help to write out an explanation, but your best chance of getting a job will come from explaining the situation in person. It also will be essential to have a reference who will give you a solid recommendation.

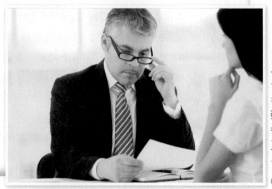

Inappropriate Questions

The interview is going along well, and then it happens: "Do you have any children?" or "How long has your family been in this country?"

On the surface, questions such as these seem innocent enough. Yet the structure and format of the questions may be illegal or, at the very least, inappropriate. When you are in a situation where the person asking the question has the power to decide whether you will get the job, this information can be used to discriminate against you or other candidates.

Questions that focus on age, gender, race, marital status, language, children, criminal record, national origin, religion, or disability are inappropriate in a job interview.

So you've just been asked an inappropriate question. What do you do? How do you respond?

The most effective approach is to answer the question in a polite, honest manner. Don't offer detailed personal information. Instead, steer the conversation back to your ability to meet the employer's expectations, by stating simply "This issue does not affect my ability to perform the job" or "I am confident I will be able to perform the duties of this job."

ASK QUESTIONS THAT STAND OUT

The interview is not only a chance for the employer to learn about you, but for you to learn about them. Treating the interview as a two-way communication process is important because it displays confidence, genuine interest in a best fit match, and preparation. Prepare to ask three to five well-chosen questions to help you learn about the employer, company culture, and position.

Don't ask all of your questions at the end of the interview. Interject them naturally at appropriate intervals throughout the meeting unless you're told you will have the opportunity to ask questions at the end. Keep your questions positive. Also, do not discuss salary until a job offer has been made. The best scenario is to first have the company share the salary range with you before you share your expectations.

Good Questions to Ask

Asking appropriate questions demonstrates interest and confidence, showcases your knowledge, and gives you an active role in the interview. Study the following sample questions carefully; then write your own questions as part of Career Action Worksheet 10-3.

1. **Do you have a training program for this position? If so, will you describe it?**

   Why it works: This question demonstrates interest in the job and a desire to perform it well.

2. **Can you tell me about the duties and tasks of this position in a typical workday?**

   Why it works: The answer will help you better understand the scope of the job and if it is well matched to what you want to do.

3. **May I have a copy of the written job description?**

   Why it works: Getting a job description can help you tie your qualifications to those required for the job in follow-up emails or later interviews. Of course, if the job description was online or you already have it, don't use this one!

4. **Will the responsibilities of this position expand with time and experience on the job? Can good performance in this job lead to opportunities for career growth?**

   Why it works: These answer will help you determine whether this is a dead-end job or whether employee career growth is encouraged.

5. **Can you tell me about the people I would work with? To whom does this position report?**

   Why it works: These answers can help you assess company structure and how you might fit into the company.

6. **Do you need any more information about my qualifications or experience?**

   Why it works: If the interviewer wants more information, you have an opportunity to clear up any misunderstanding or lack of information. It also gives you another chance to run your 30-Second Commercial, once again emphasizing just how well qualified you are.

7. **When will you be making your hiring decision? What does your hiring process and timeline look like? May I call you if I have additional questions?**

   Why it works: These types of questions help you judge when to follow up and will keep the door open for further communication.

Turnoff Questions to Avoid

Following are some questions that are most disliked by employers. Do not ask them; they will make you sound uninformed and diminish your likability.

1. **What does this company do?**

   Why to avoid: You should have done your research well enough to know what the company does. Employers are not looking for employees who know nothing about their business.

2. **How much sick leave and vacation time will I get?**

   Why to avoid: This question gives the impression that you are looking forward to being off of work, rather than on the job. Ask this and other benefits question only before making a final decision about a job offer. Employers understand the importance of major benefits to prospective employees.

3. **Will I have an office?**

   Why to avoid: This suggests that you care more about where you will work than about what you will do.

4. **What time do I have to be at work in the morning? How long do you allow for lunch?**

   Why to avoid: These questions do not project an enthusiastic interest in the work, and suggest that you might have personal business that will distract you from work.

5. **How long do I have to work before I am eligible for a raise?**

   Why to avoid: This question tells the employer that you are more interested in the salary than the job.

▶ *CAREER ACTION*

Complete Worksheet 10-3

Create a Question-and-Answer Planning Sheet, page 273

Chapter Checklist

Check off each item you can do. Reread sections in this chapter to help you complete the checklist.

☐ Prepare for different types of pre-employment tests. ❶

☐ Prepare for different types of interviews. ❷

☐ Focus on responding persuasively to questions about my qualifications and abilities; cite examples of applying my abilities in work, school, and other activities. ❸

☐ Prepare and rehearse responses to typical interview questions. ❸

☐ Anticipate the stress of inappropriate interview questions and practice careful responses. ❸

☐ Prepare and practice responses to stress questions, while being calm and composed. ❸

☐ Prepare and ask appropriate questions. ❹

☐ Avoid asking questions that diminish my likability, including questions that are too direct, questions that my research should have answered, and questions that make me appear immature or uncommitted to the job. ❹

Critical Thinking Questions

1. How can you prepare for the different types of pre-employment tests? ❶

2. How will you benefit from knowing what style of interview your target employer typically uses? ❷

3. What style(s) of interviewing do you expect to be most prevalent in your job search? What techniques do you plan to use to maximize your performance in these types of interviews? ❷

4. What are the candidate's main objectives during the question-and-answer portion of the interview? What are the interviewer's main objectives during an interview? ❸

5. What specific types of questions do you most need to prepare for to be ready for your interviews? List two examples and include the answers you plan to give. ❸

6. How will you handle an illegal or inappropriate question from an interviewer? ❸

7. Why is it important for a candidate to ask some questions during an interview? ❹

Additional Resources

For data files, career resources, and more, visit www.cengagebrain.com.

Trial Run

Find Good Answers to Interview Questions ❸

Divide into teams of four and make sure you have a sheet of paper.

Each person selects a type of interview question (general information, behavioral, character, or difficult/stress) and uses a sheet of paper to write two questions from the lists in this chapter:

- One question on side A.

- One question on side B.

Pass the sheets to the left.

- Take two minutes to write an answer to the interview question on side A.

- When time is up, pass the sheets to the left again and answer the question on side A of the second sheet of paper.

- Do this until each person on the team has answered all four interview questions on side A.

Repeat the exercise with the questions on side B.

When all A and B questions have been answered by each team member, compare answers and discuss which is the best. You can do this by reading each question and the four suggested answers aloud. Critique the answers and decide which one is the best choice or how a combination of the answers would be most appropriate. Be creative.

If possible, have someone record all of the questions and answers and distribute them to the group.

▶ *CAREER ACTION WORKSHEET*
10-1 Research Pre-employment Test Types ❷

Use Your Network Contacts for Research.

Contact at least two companies in your field that are similar to your target employer and arrange a brief meeting with someone at each place to research the company's use of pre-employment tests. Make sure the person understands that this is not a request for an interview. Follow the guidelines for conducting a Career Network meeting in Chapter 6, as well as these steps. During your meetings, ask your contacts to describe the following:

1. Types of pre-employment tests

2. How the test answers are used to select employees

3. What they recommend as ways to prepare for these tests

Take notes of any information you find useful. As always, act professionally and thank the people who help you. Follow up by sending thank-you notes.

Add your completed work to the "About Jobs" section of your Career Builder Files.

▶ *CAREER ACTION WORKSHEET*
10-2 Research Interview Styles ❷

Use Your Career Network for Research.

Contact at least two companies in your field that are similar to your target employer and arrange a brief meeting with someone at each place to research his or her interview style. Make sure the person understands that this is not a request for an interview. Follow the guidelines for conducting a Career Network meeting in Chapter 6, as well as these steps.

1. During your meetings, ask your contacts to describe the style of interviewing they use to evaluate candidates for positions similar to the one you are targeting.

2. Ask what criteria (skills, experience, education, personal qualities) they use to evaluate candidates.

3. Ask for specific examples of candidates' positive and negative actions and comments.

4. Take notes of any information you find useful.

5. As always, act professionally and thank the people who help you. Follow up by sending thank-you notes.

Add your completed work to the "About Jobs" section of your Career Builder Files.

This page is intentionally blank.

▶ *CAREER ACTION WORKSHEET*
10-3 Create a Question-and-Answer Planning Sheet ❷

Record the answers to typical questions you can expect to be asked during job interviews. Also write sample questions you can ask during interviews. Use the suggestions in this chapter and Chapter 9, as well as your 30-Second Commercials and Personal Brand Statement. Tailor your answers to your target job. Emphasize your qualifications for the job at every opportunity. Use positive, action-oriented words.

General Information Questions

Why do you want this job?

What type of work do you enjoy doing the most?

What are your strongest skills?

What are your long-term career goals? How do you plan to achieve them?

Do you think of yourself as a team player? If so, give examples.

Do you have a geographic preference? Are you willing to relocate?

Under what management style do you work most productively?

What is important to you in a company? What do you look for in a company?

Behavioral and Character Questions

What have you accomplished that demonstrates your initiative?

How do you deal with an angry customer or coworker? Describe an experience you've had.

How are you able to adapt to change? Give an example.

How would you describe yourself?

What rewards do you look for in your career?

What accomplishment are you most proud of, particularly as it relates to your field?

What do you think are the most important characteristics and abilities a person must possess to be successful? How do you rate yourself in those areas?

Stress Questions

Why do you think you are the best candidate for this job? Why should I hire you?

Why do you want to leave your current job?

Why have you held so many jobs?

What is your greatest weakness?

Have you ever been fired from a job?

Does your current employer know you are planning to leave?

What kinds of decisions are most difficult for you?

What is your salary range? (Although this is not strictly a stress question, being asked about salary expectations is awkward. Chapter 12 has advice about handling this common question. Hint: Avoid giving a direct answer.)

Questions and Topics to Avoid

List several questions to avoid asking during an interview and explain why the questions are inappropriate.

Q&A Savvy Strategies

Review "Savvy Q&A Strategies" on page 263. List the strategies that are most applicable to your job search. Add others you found through your Internet research.

Your Questions

Review the sample questions in "Ask Questions That Stand Out" on pages 265–266. In your own words, write the questions you want to ask during your interviews. If necessary, ask for help from a member of your support system. Add questions that are pertinent to your job search and goals.

Add your completed work to the "About Jobs" section of your Career Builder Files.

This page is intentionally blank.

Interview Like a Pro

OVERVIEW

To interview like a pro you have to practice like one—mentally, emotionally, and physically. In this chapter, practice describing your ability to do the job through examples and stories, research companies so you can talk their language, prepare physically, and practice a strong close for your interview.

OUTCOMES

1. Develop confidence by participating in practice interviews.
2. Do your homework before every interview.
3. Be physically prepared for the interview.
4. Close an interview in your favor.

CAREER ACTION WORKSHEETS

WHERE ARE YOU ON THE JOURNEY?

The pros practice. Shouldn't you?

PHASE 1: Prepare for the Journey
- *The Job Search Journey*
- *Know Yourself to Market Yourself*
- *Picture Yourself in the Workplace*

PHASE 2: Create Your Resume
- *Plan Your Resume*
- *Write Your Resume*

PHASE 3: Apply for Jobs
- *Find Job Openings*
- *Write Job Applications*
- *Write Effective Tailored Cover Letters*

PHASE 4: Shine at Interviews
- *Know the Interview Essentials*
- *Prepare for Your Interview*
- **Interview Like a Pro**

PHASE 5: Connect, Accept, and Succeed
- *Stay Connected with Prospective Employers*
- *It's an Iterative Process*
- *Take Charge of Your Career*

PHASE 4: Shine at Interviews
Step 3, *Interview Like a Pro*

You are in Phase 4, *Shine at Interviews*, step 3, *Interview Like a Pro*. Your goal in this chapter is to develop confidence and to do your homework before every interview so you are comfortable and natural at interviews.

PARTICIPATE IN PRACTICE INTERVIEWS

While some people may claim that they can walk into an interview and "wing it," do not try to be one of them. Interviews require practice. Because an interview is a dynamic exchange between two people, there will never be a list of "Interview Dos and Don'ts" that works in every situation. Instead, be at your best in every interview by giving yourself these three gifts:

- **Plenty of time** to prepare so that you aren't rushed or stressed the day before the interview
- **A competitive edge** through thoughtful, focused preparation and practice
- **Self-confidence** gained from feeling ready for the interview

If you are asked to come to a job interview, the employer is interested in you. You are the focus of the interview. You will be evaluated on your past successes and mistakes and on your future goals and potential. You will be expected to give concrete examples of your skills and explain how they relate to the requirements for this job.

Any nervousness that you feel about an upcoming job interview is an appropriate response to a situation that will test your interpersonal, social, professional, and verbal and nonverbal skills. Preparation and practice can help you relax. Users of *Your Career: How to Make it Happen* emphasize that doing practice interviews improves their actual interview performance by as much as 100 percent. They say that practice increases their self-confidence, improves the image of competence they project, and reduces their anxiety about the process—all of which improve their performance in actual interviews. Gain these valuable advantages yourself by doing practice interviews.

Real World Scenario 11-1 Out of all the steps in the Job Search Journey, Sara was most scared of the interview. It was easy to stay behind the computer or network at events, but the pressure of making a mistake during an interview after all that hard work was nerve-racking. She decided to reduce her anxiety by scheduling practice interviews, starting with a friend that knew her very well and ending with someone she recently met at a career event. By the end of her practice interviews, she was more confident presenting herself and her strengths to a stranger and had gained valuable feedback. For example, when the "interviewer" asked a question, she learned to listen actively to the question being asked instead of focusing on how she was going to respond. Honing her active listening skills helped her answer questions better and with more confidence and relevance.

What interview strategies do you need more practice in? How can you reduce interview-related anxiety?

Set Up Practice Interviews

Schedule a practice interview with a friend, family member, or acquaintance, preferably someone who is experienced in interviewing, knows you personally, and is comfortable providing impartial, honest, objective feedback. Ask someone else to observe the practice interview and get recommendations from both people—the practice interviewer and the observer—for improving your performance.

If possible, video-record the practice interview. You can use video recording technology such as iMovie or the camera on your phone. You can also use Skype or another video-conferencing technology to practice with a friend. Watching yourself firsthand may be the most valuable performance

Figure 11-1 How You Are Rated During an Interview

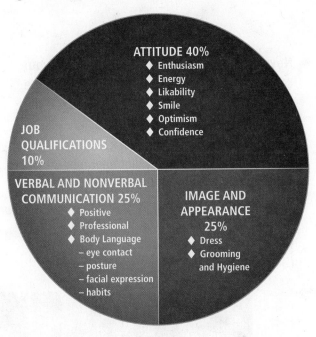

obtain leads that result in jobs. Everyone gains helpful interview experience. When making an appointment for a dress rehearsal interview, do the following:

- Explain that the interview is a course assignment and that you would appreciate the employer's help in completing it.

- Say that you would like the interview to be as realistic as possible.

- Ask what the protocol is for real candidates and follow each step. If there is an application form, pick it up ahead of time and complete it carefully.

- Prepare using your Interview Preparation Checklist (described later in this chapter) and use it appropriately.

When you attend the practice interview, do the following:

- Be dressed and groomed as if this were a real interview. You have practiced this already for your Career Network meetings, as described in Chapter 6.

- Show up for the interview a few minutes early and dressed as if it were a real interview.

- Practice interacting with any "gatekeepers" as described in Chapter 9.

- Ask the person or people who interview you to evaluate your performance and give them a copy of the Interview Critique Form in Career Action Worksheet 11-4.

- Be sure to follow up with a thank-you note. Chapter 12 shows an example thank-you note in Figure 12-1 on page 310.

Remember that your intent is to practice an interview, and that any job offered during a practice interview should come spontaneously from the employer. Asking directly for a job contradicts your request for help in practicing your interviewing skills. If your contact makes an offer or provides leads or suggestions, however, follow up immediately

feedback you can get. Use the Chapter 9 Career Action Worksheet 9-1 to assess your body language and try to improve it.

Figure 11-1 shows the areas that employers consider when they are evaluating you as a possible fit for their company. Practice being a pro in each of these areas.

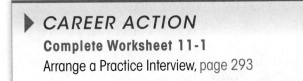

▶ *CAREER ACTION*

Complete Worksheet 11-1
Arrange a Practice Interview, page 293

Interview with Someone in Your Career Field

Once you feel comfortable with your performance in the practice interview, schedule a dress rehearsal interview. This is best done with an employer in your field, but is typically done with a Career Network contact who is working in your career field, or with a recruiter or professional career coach.

Some people receive job offers as a result of dress rehearsal practice interviews; others

MAKE IT A HABIT
Reduce Stress on the Interview Day

Many things can derail you on the day of the interview. Using advance preparation and managing your schedule well can eliminate stress and risk during interview day. Consider the following strategies:

- **Limit the number of interviews scheduled in one day.** After two interviews, a candidate's performance level typically drops. Don't jeopardize your chances of getting a job because you are tired.

- **Know where you are going.** If the interview is in an unfamiliar area, be sure you have directions and know how long it will take to get there. If possible, go to the location a few days before, at the same time of day, to look for construction delays and traffic jams. Alternatively, take public transportation and use the time to relax and rehearse.

- **Never be late for an interview.** Plan your commute to arrive about 10 minutes before the interview in case something goes wrong. If you are early, sit in your car or find someplace else to wait until a few minutes before it's time to go in. Being too early for an appointment may create some awkwardness with the receptionist and/or the interviewer, who may be busy until the time of the interview. Take your cell phone so that you can call the interviewer if you will be late. (Be sure to turn it off during the interview.)

© Michaelpuche/Shutterstock.com.

if you are interested. After each practice or real interview, use Career Action Worksheet 11-3 to do a self-evaluation and make plans for gradually improving your performance over time.

> ▶ *CAREER ACTION*
> **Complete Worksheet 11-2**
> Participate in a Dress Rehearsal Interview, page 295

> ▶ *CAREER ACTION*
> **Complete Worksheet 11-3**
> Summarize and Evaluate Your Interviews, page 297

DO YOUR HOMEWORK BEFORE EVERY INTERVIEW

OUTCOME 2

If you do your homework before every interview, you will give yourself a competitive advantage and be more confident during the interview.

Demonstrate That You Are Interested

You want the interviewer to be interested in you. It helps if you can reciprocate by demonstrating that you are interested in the company. Use these three tips to help you do just that.

Show that you read and understand the job posting or job description. While this seems obvious, you will give yourself a competitive advantage by going through the posting line by line. As you do this, make a note of how your qualifications fit each item or where you are missing skills or requirements that you will need to address. Prepare your example stories to demonstrate that you have these qualifications or transferable skills. Confirm that you know what each word means. If you don't know, ask someone in your network, or, if necessary or if the word seems important, ask the interviewer to explain. Your interest in understanding the company lingo may impress them.

Read the company website. Find out everything you can about how the company started, where they are located, their major clients, products, names of their leaders and owners, and their mission statement and values. Check out Wikipedia, Facebook, and LinkedIn® too for more information.

Search for the company in the news. If you search for the company's name or the name of the CEO, owners, or leaders, you can learn about the current events that are important to the company. You might also look at online reviews, such as Angie's List, Better Business Bureau, Consumer Reports, Best Doctors, the local newspaper, and industry newsletters. While you may see negative press, stick to the positive while being aware of potential areas of concern for the company.

As you learn more about the company, think about ways that you might use your new knowledge during the interview to demonstrate your interest in the company.

▶ *CAREER ACTION*
Complete Worksheet 11-4
Interview Critique Form, page 299

Be Convincing with Your Examples and 30-Second Commercial

Look at the job listing and make a list of your qualifications. Before you walk into an interview, it helps to be very clear about what you offer and why you're the best person for this job. Once you are clear, select your best examples and stories for this interview. Your goal is to give the interviewer confidence, along with some examples about you that the interviewer

---

 You, Online

Learn About Your Interviewer

Use social media tools to learn about your interviewer, not just the company. Search for your interviewer on LinkedIn®, Facebook, and Twitter. You just might learn something you have in common that will help build positive rapport during the interview. Talk about these items if relevant conversation or questions arise:

- Alma mater: Did you go to the same school, college or high school?
- Hometown or state: Did you grow up in the same town or state?
- Previous job experience: Have you worked in the same company or do you know someone that worked in their same company in the past?
- Volunteer/organization experience: Do you share a common interest in a community, nonprofit, or association?

Start by saying, "I viewed your profile on LinkedIn® or from your Twitter feed and saw that we have . . . in common." This opening lets them know you did your research but doesn't get too personal. Having something in common with the interviewer creates the feeling that you already belong. It furthers your likeability and positive rapport with the interviewer—both of which are critical to a successful interview that leads to a follow-up interview or offer.

can use to convince other people in the company that you are a good fit for this job.

Review your Personal Brand Statement and tailor your 30-Second Commercial to each employer so that it matches the requirements of this job. For example, if the job description lists computer skills first, talk about your computer skills first. Use the wording and terms used in the job requirements. Practice saying it in several ways so that it rolls off your tongue smoothly in conversation. Here are things you can do to be convincing:

- **Be authentic**. Make sure your 30-Second Commercial represents you authentically. Don't "sell" what you can't deliver.

- **Include measurable accomplishments**. The key to an effective 30-Second Commercial is to provide examples of your capabilities. Pick the items that best fit the needs expressed by the interviewer. Example: "I can see that *xyz* is the most crucial challenge to your company. My skills can alleviate those problem areas because of my specific *xyz* experience."

- **Focus and polish the content**. Your aim is to prepare a brief, polished summary of your qualifications. The heart of your message should emphasize how you can benefit the employer. It is your interview "billboard" saying "Here's what I can do for you." This helps the interviewer focus on the strengths you have to offer.

- **Be ready for any situation**. Practice delivering the 30-Second version, a 45-second version, and a 15-second version. Weave your commercial into the interview—perhaps a longer version first, followed later by a shorter one. Don't overdo it, however; twice is probably enough.

- **Don't bore your audience**. Observe the situation so that you know when to stop talking. Watch for signals that the interviewer wants to ask a question or move on to a different topic or wrap the interview.

Be Ready for an Offer

Your goal is to get a job offer, but few people think ahead about how to respond when the offer actually is extended! How will you respond if they offer you the job on the spot? There are three basic options: yes, I'd like to think about it, or no. Keep your answer short and sweet. Here are some examples:

- Thank you for the offer. I am happy to accept it.

- I am very excited about your offer. Once we work through the details, I look forward to being part of the team. ("Details" includes such things as compensation, contract, and start date.)

- I am very excited about this offer. When do I need to make my final decision? (This is a good answer if you have additional interviews pending.)

- I appreciate the offer, however, based on what I learned about the job in this interview, I'm not sure it is a good fit for me. May I have some time to think about it further? (Don't burn your bridges just yet. Think it over.)

If you want this job, and they offer it, what will you say if they say they want you to start immediately—today or next week? Plan your answer in advance. If you already have a job, it is common to say that you need to give your current employer two weeks' notice. What if the interviewer or recruiter says they are interested in you but can't make an offer for several months? A good response is to let the interviewer know that you would be very interested to hear from them when they are ready. They know, without your telling them, that they are taking a risk that you might accept another job while waiting for their offer. However, the old adage don't burn your bridges is a good one to remember at this point. It is not uncommon for a person to take another job and then discover it wasn't what was expected. When the delayed offer comes to you several months later, you might actually be in a position to take it!

© Minerva Studio/Shutterstock.com.

CAUTION
Avoid Interview Disqualifiers

Any one of these blunders during an interview could cost you the job:

1. Don't be late. It's hard to count all of the negative messages that being late sends—lack of respect, lack of genuine interest, personal disorganization, and on and on.

2. Don't be abrupt or discourteous to anyone you meet.

3. Don't sit down until the interviewer invites you to; waiting is courteous.

4. Don't bring anyone else to the interview; it makes you look immature and insecure.

5. Don't invade the interviewer's personal space by reading anything on the desk or putting anything on it.

6. Don't touch your cell phone or get distracted by other technology during an interview. Make sure your phone is on silent.

BE PHYSICALLY PREPARED FOR THE INTERVIEW

You have already practiced being mentally and emotionally prepared, that is, you have prepared what you will say and practiced body language that will convey that you are interested in the company and confident that you are the right person for the job. Now it's time to prepare the physical elements of an interview. This includes three things: reviewing the **Interview Preparation Checklist** with portfolio items or marketing materials that you can show to an interviewer, assembling an Interview Survival Pack to help you look and feel confident, and a final practice run with your props to ensure you can move smoothly through your interview.

Show portfolio items that highlight your hands-on experience in the areas that count the most. Do not use every item for every interview.

Review the Interview Preparation Checklist

Before each interview, review the Interview Preparation Checklist in advance. Select items from your Master Career Portfolio that relate to this particular job and job qualifications. Be selective; don't take everything. Put these items in a professional-looking binder or small attaché case. (A regular briefcase is overkill.) If you have more than 10 pages, use labeled folders to organize your materials so you can quickly find what you need during the interview. It may be a good idea to print or copy this checklist and use it before each interview.

Interview Preparation Checklist
General Job-Related Materials from your Master Career Portfolio

☐ A copy of the job posting or description

☐ Your resume—copies for the interviewer(s), yourself, and an extra

- ☐ Portfolio materials and job-related samples of your work
- ☐ Certificates, licenses, transcripts, and related documents
- ☐ Letters of recommendation (for this job or this specific type of work)
- ☐ Lists of references (general endorsement of your character, knowledge, and skills)
- ☐ Business or contact cards, if you have these

Marketing Materials from your Master Career Portfolio

- ☐ A copy of your targeted 30-Second Commercial (for your use only)
- ☐ A reminder list of examples and stories you can tell (for your use only)

Organizing Materials

- ☐ A notebook with questions you can ask during the interview (see Chapter 10)
- ☐ A businesslike pen—not too cheap, expensive, flashy, or quirky
- ☐ A note pad on which to take notes (ask permission to take notes before doing so)
- ☐ Your appointment calendar (If you use your smartphone, turn the sound off before you even walk in the building!)
- ☐ A list of the names, titles, and phone numbers of people related to this interview

Create a set of portfolio items and marketing materials prior to every interview that is tailored to that particular job description. Organize these documents in a professional-looking file, binder, or portfolio. Many of the items you've assembled in the About Me and Master Career Portfolio section of your Career Builder Files will be a good candidate to bring to the interview.

Prepare an Interview Survival Pack

Feeling in control is one way to keep your cool in interviewing situations. If you can anticipate situations ahead of time, you can more effectively manage them. Prepare an Interview Survival Pack to help you. It should be in a small zippered pouch. It will contain items such as these:

- Personal hygiene items (toothpaste and toothbrush, comb, deodorant, tissues)
- Spare stockings or tie (in case of snags or stains)
- A Tide™ stain kit or similar product to take care of unexpected spills and stains
- Cash, coins, or credit card for parking or a bus
- A written map or directions to get to the interview
- A backup plan in case you need your smartphone and it fails or loses its charge
- Your normal "cure" for a headache or upset stomach
- Whatever else you need to look, smell, and be your best no matter what

While preparing your Interview Survival Pack, think through the entire interview event, not just the conversation with the interviewer. For example, if you're riding a motorcycle or bike, what will you do with your helmet? If there's two feet of snow on the ground, how will you carry your shoes into the building and where will you put your boots?

Also think through your attire. Select an outfit that fits well, is clean and pressed, and is appropriate for this interview and the weather. Make sure all the buttons and zippers are in good repair. Choose shoes that are shined, clean, comfortable, and suitable for the job and interview. If you are in a factory, do not wear sandals or open toes shoes. Ladies, leave behind that beloved ancient handbag you take everywhere, instead opting for a simple professional bag or attaché. If rain is in the forecast, take an umbrella and wear a raincoat—you do not want to walk into an interview dripping wet! Wear effective deodorant, but go easy on the after-shave lotion, cologne, or perfume. Be immaculately groomed from head to toe.

Find It Fast

Your interview can come up fast! Here's a guide to the main topics so you can do a rapid review:

Using Your Marketing Materials

Use the marketing materials and portfolio items you've assembled using the Interview Preparation Checklist wisely, especially the job-related samples of your work. Before an interview, arrange the items in priority order based on the best examples of your work related specifically to the employer's needs. Ask if the interviewer would like to see samples from your portfolio before you display anything. Even if the interviewer prefers not to review them, having samples of your work with you makes a good impression and conveys that you are professional and organized.

During the interview, you may still have an opportunity to offer a portfolio sample if the topic suggests it. Simply turn to (or take out) the appropriate portfolio items that demonstrate your qualifications. This tangible evidence of abilities often gives candidates a winning edge in competing for a job. When employers ask questions about your resume, you can use your portfolio items to support your responses. Do not misrepresent yourself in the portfolio items; the work must be your own. Be prepared to provide copies of the work if requested to do so.

It's a mistake to rely only on your portfolio items to convince an interviewer of your qualifications. The focus of the interview is still on you. Your personal appearance, your body language, and your verbal communication skills are essential. The portfolio items are visual aids to support your qualifications. Using the Interview Preparation Checklist, for each interview, select the items to match

Real World Scenario 11-2 Walter was interviewing for a job as a marketer and had just been asked the question, "What's an example of a time when you received negative feedback? How did you handle it?" Walter had used his Interview Preparation Checklist to assemble the right marketing materials for the interview and this was the perfect opportunity to use it. He pulled out a *before and after* sample of branding work he had done as part of a project for a course. He showed his initial ideas and how they improved dramatically with the feedback he received. He highlighted how he incorporated the feedback and pushed the ideas further. By following the Interview Preparation Checklist, he was able to show how he handled negative feedback to create an even better final solution. Even though he didn't predict using his marketing materials for this question, it worked out perfectly.

What versatile samples will you include as you follow the Interview Preparation Checklist? How can you use your assembled marketing materials to highlight your skills and experience?

the specific employer and job. Be prepared to tell the story related to each item. Do not use every item for every interview.

▶ **CAREER ACTION**

Complete Worksheet 11-5

Do Your Homework Before Every Interview, page 301

Last-Minute Preparations

Even if you prepared well in advance of the interview, there are still a few things that can only be done at the last minute. Add to this list based on your own unique situation.

- Look at the Interview Critique Form in Career Action Worksheet 11-4 to remind yourself how you will be judged, and to recall what you learned from your practice

- Call someone from your Career Network for a last-minute morale boost before heading to the interview.

- Check the weather and the traffic, so you can be prepared and on time.

- On the day of the interview, take the time to look your best. Eat well and be rested, immaculately groomed, and appropriately dressed (Chapter 9). Consider the effects of coffee or other stimulating drinks prior to an interview and whether it is a good idea or not.

- Start using positive, assertive body language (Chapter 9), even as you travel to the interview.

- Use your voice well—what you say and how you say it (Chapter 9). Taking a few deep relaxing and refreshing breathes before an interview does wonders for good vocal control.

- Review how to wrap up an interview in your favor (next page).

- Silence your phone before you go into the building for the interview.

Now that you are ready to interview like a Pro, here is some last-minute advice: "Make up your mind to have a good time and *then* go to the party." Approach your interviews the same way and see how a positive attitude can strengthen your performance. Remember that the interview is a two-way process; you are there to learn about the company as much as they are there to learn about you. Try positive visualization and other techniques for managing stress to help you perform at the top of your game.

▶ **CAREER ACTION**

Complete Worksheet 11-6

Get Physically Prepared for Success with Interviews, page 303

Using Your Marketing Materials

To capture an interviewer's attention early in the interview, refer first to a portfolio item that represents one of your most outstanding accomplishments or makes a point about your key qualifications. Use a strong item toward the end of the interview to leave a favorable last impression.

Practice using the marketing materials you've assembled using the Interview Preparation Checklist so that your delivery will be smooth. Have a friend give you a mock interview so that you can practice referring to your marketing materials at key points during the interview. Here is an example:

The interviewer asks, "How important do you think it is to keep up with changing technology?"

Destiny replies, "I think it is very important, and I regularly attend industry group meetings to update my software skills." She provides a brochure for a talk about Mobile Applications that she recently attended at a local chapter meeting of BDPA (Black Data Processing Associates). "Being part of BDPA is one way I stay up to date," she says.

© iofoto/Shutterstock.com.

CLOSE THE INTERVIEW IN YOUR FAVOR

Whether it's a practice interview or the real thing, be proactive and professional by influencing how the interview ends. For your own sake, clarify what to expect next in the process. Leave a positive impression by restating your qualifications and by closing the interview skillfully.

Clarify What to Expect Next

Before you leave the interview, clarify:

- What, if anything, you should do to follow up.
- When a decision will be made.
- How the interviewer prefers you to follow up (by phone, by letter, by email, or in person).

The following sample dialogue shows how to get this information.

Clarifying these details underscores your image as a professional who understands the importance of following through after important meetings.

Use Your Clincher

As you near the close of an interview, make a point of leaving your interviewer with a clear picture of how you fit the job. Bring the interview full circle by asking a question similar to this example in a courteous tone: "Would you please summarize the most important qualifications you're looking for in filling this position?"

Run the short version of your 30-Second Commercial to restate your skills, experience, and other assets that meet the employer's needs. This important clincher gives you one last chance to market yourself and your qualifications. People remember best what they hear first and last.

Following Up

You: When should I expect to hear whether I am selected for the position?

Interviewer: We'll notify all candidates of our decision within two weeks.

You: Do you mind if I check back with you?

Interviewer: I prefer that you don't until we notify you.

OR

Interviewer: No, I don't mind.

You: How would you prefer I contact you?

Interviewer: Please call my assistant.

Close the Interview Skillfully

Some candidates lose the race for a job by not clearing the final hurdle: closing the interview skillfully. Don't let your posture, attitude, or verbal and nonverbal communication slip for even a moment. Use the following techniques to close an interview skillfully:

- Watch for signs from the interviewer that it's time to wrap up the interview. Signs include the interviewer asking whether you have any further questions, tidying up papers on the desk, pushing the chair back, or simply sitting back in the chair. Heed the cue. Don't make the interviewer impatient by droning on at this point.

- Ask the interviewer to notify you when a candidate has been selected. Imply that this is not the only job you are considering: "By what date will you make your decision on this position? I'd appreciate knowing within the next two weeks so that I can finalize my plans."

- Before you leave, determine any follow-up activities the interviewer expects from you. If a second interview is arranged, check your calendar to make sure you are not scheduled for another interview at that time. Then write down the date, time, place, and names of all of the people who will be interviewing you. If you are expected to provide additional information, credentials, references, or work samples, make a note and verify what you are supposed to do and by when before you leave.

- If you're seriously interested in the job, say so! Just as in effective sales, the person who asks is the most likely to receive. Interviewers are impressed by candidates' expressions of interest; candidates who directly express their interest strengthen their position. Offer a simple statement—for example, "I'd be pleased to be a part of this organization" or "After talking with you, I'm convinced that this is the job I want, and I believe my qualifications would be an asset to the Acme Corporation. Please consider me seriously for this position."

- Finally, as you leave, remember to use the interviewer's name: "Thank you for interviewing me, Ms. Carpenter."

- If you haven't been given one, ask the interviewer for a business card. You'll need the interviewer's contact information so you can send a thank-you note.

- Be conscious of using positive body language. Keep your shoulders back and your head up when you stand and give a warm smile and a firm handshake. Once you leave the interviewer's office, you are still interviewing. Thank the receptionist or assistant by name and add a brief parting greeting.

Review Figure 11-1 on page 279 to reinforce your understanding of the areas that employers consider most important during an interview. With all your preparations, you will interview like a pro!

Chapter Checklist

Check off each item you can do. Reread sections in this chapter to help you complete the checklist.

☐ Schedule two practice interviews to improve my performance and confidence (an interview with someone in my Career Network and an interview with an employer in my target field). ❶

☐ Ask interviewers to evaluate my practice interviews. ❶

☐ Summarize every interview and evaluate my performance. ❶

☐ Prepare for interviews by learning more about the company and interviewer. ❷

☐ Have my examples ready to demonstrate how I am qualified and a good fit for this job. ❷

☐ Prepare my response if I am offered the job. ❷

☐ Assemble portfolio items and marketing materials using the Interview Preparation Checklist. ❸

☐ Put together my Interview Survival Pack. ❸

☐ Prepare physically for interviews to reduce my stress level and to appear organized. ❸

☐ Use strategies to wrap up interviews in my favor. ❹

Critical Thinking Questions

1. How have you used the success strategies described in Chapter 1 (maintain a positive outlook, set goals, manage your time, be proactive) to prepare for and participate in a practice interview? Which strategies are most useful? ❶

2. Why is it important to prepare for and perform in a practice interview as if it were the real thing? ❶

3. How can you let an interviewer know that you are interested in the company? Why does this matter? ❷

4. What is the value of customizing your 30-Second Commercial for each interview? ❷

5. What would you tell your friend to do to reduce his or her stress level in the days before an interview? The day of the interview? ❸

6. What advice would you give your friend about wrapping up the interview skillfully? ❹

Additional Resources

For data files, career resources, and more, visit www.cengagebrain.com.

Trial Run

Reflect on Your Job Search Journey

If you are using the chapters in order, you are likely to have found some job leads, applied for jobs, and had at least one practice and/or real interview. In this Trial Run, you take stock of your job search strategies.

Set aside at least two hours for this look-back and assessment. You will need this book, your Career Builder Files, and some blank paper. Find a quiet place to do this work. You can also work with a partner or in groups of three. Spend at least one hour evaluating each person's materials and progress in planning the next steps.

Remind yourself of the key points in Chapters 1–11 by looking at each of the Chapter Checklists and your Career Action Worksheets. Evaluate each area of your own job search thoughtfully and honestly.

	What have I accomplished?	What advice or activity in the book has been most helpful?	Where are the gaps?	What advice or activity in the book (that I haven't done) could I apply?
Example: *Find job openings (Chapter 6)*	*Everyone knows I'm looking for a job; contacts in Ashland & Paducah*	*Very prepared for network meeting with Ms. Garcia; sent her thank-you note*	*Need job leads in small businesses; ask Anil and Jean how they found their jobs*	*Look at trade group sites and Chamber of Commerce sites*
Prepare (Chapters 1–3)				
Create Your Resume (Chapters 4 and 5)				
Apply for jobs (Chapters 6–8)				
Shine at Interviews (Chapters 9–11)				

Develop a plan for each area:

	What is the most important activity (or activities) I could do in this area?	**What is my plan?**
Example: *Apply for jobs*	*Attend spring job fair at Campus Career Center (CCC) to find jobs and apply for them*	• *Research companies @ fair* • *Post resume at CCC job fair page* • *Ask Mrs. Heldman about my Master Career Portfolio; more examples?* • *Review my Interview Preparation Checklist and make sure I am not missing anything* • *Ask Mrs. H if I should schedule 2nd practice interview* • *Look for more job fairs online*
Prepare		
Create your resume		
Apply for jobs		
Interviews		

This page is intentionally blank.

▶ *CAREER ACTION WORKSHEET*
11-1 Arrange a Practice Interview ❶

Schedule a practice interview with your Career Network with (an interviewer and an observer if possible). Use the sample questions in Chapter 10 as a guide for your practice session. You can make a copy of them for the "interviewer." Be sure to include some difficult or stress questions that you want to rehearse. Encourage the interviewer to expand on the questions, if possible, tailoring them to your job target to give you relevant interview practice. If possible, arrange to have the practice interview video-recorded. If you can't find someone to interview you in person, you can use Skype or other video-conferencing technology. You may want to practice using this technology if you are participating in a video interview. If possible, make a copy of Career Action Worksheet 9-1 "Body Language Self-Assessment" and use it to assess yourself after the practice interview ask the observer for additional feedback following the practice interview.

This page is intentionally blank.

▶ *CAREER ACTION WORKSHEET*

11-2 Participate in a Dress Rehearsal Interview ❶

Contact an employer in your career field and ask for help with a course assignment. Ask the employer to conduct a practice interview and complete the Interview Critique Form (Career Action Worksheet 11-4).

1. Dress appropriately.

2. Take a copy of the Interview Critique Form with you and ask the interviewer to evaluate your performance by completing the form during or after the interview.

3. After the dress rehearsal interview, evaluate your performance using Career Action Worksheets 11-3 and 11-4.

4. Within two days of the dress rehearsal, send a thank-you letter to the person who gave you the interview.

This page is intentionally blank.

▶ *CAREER ACTION WORKSHEET*
11-3 Summarize and Evaluate Your Interviews ❶

Summarize every practice and real interview as soon as possible to avoid forgetting important details.

Duplicate and use this worksheet for your own evaluation and follow-up plans. Answer the questions as completely as possible.

Name of Company _____ Date of Interview _____

Location of Interview _____

Name(s) and Title(s) of Interviewer(s) _____

Phone Number _____ Email _____

Summary Activities and Questions

On a separate sheet of paper, write every question you can remember being asked during the interview. Take your time and be thorough. Do this before answering the following questions.

1. Based on the knowledge you gained in your interview and research, which of your qualifications would be the greatest asset in this job? Which of these qualifications should be reinforced with the prospective employer in your follow-up?

2. List any questions you think you answered inadequately. Write out the best possible answer to each question. Use additional paper as needed.

3. Did you forget to provide important information that demonstrates your qualifications for the job? Explain in detail.

4. What questions did you intend to ask but forgot or didn't have a chance to ask? Write them out now.

5. How could you have presented yourself more effectively?

6. In what area(s) do you think you performed the best in your interview? Why?

7. In what area(s) do you think you performed poorly? What steps can you take to improve?

8. Describe information you learned about the interviewer that may be helpful in establishing greater rapport in the future (for example, philosophy, current working projects, personal interests or hobbies, or mutual goals).

9. Is there any point of confusion that needs to be clarified for the employer? Explain.

10. Are you scheduled for another interview with the company? If so, record the date, time, place, and name(s) of the interviewer(s).

11. Record any other activities you offered to follow up on or were specifically asked to follow up on by the interviewer (for example, provide references, transcripts, certificates, or examples of work).

12. How does the interviewer prefer you to follow up (by phone, by letter, in person)?

13. When did the interviewer indicate the hiring decision would be made?

Add your completed work to the "About Jobs" section of your Career Builder Files.

▶ *CAREER ACTION WORKSHEET*

11-4 Interview Critique Form ❶

Give copies of the Interview Critique Form to the people who help you in practice interviews. You can also ask them to look at your completed Career Action 11-3 and offer suggestions. Before you give this form to someone, complete the first two lines below.

Name of Company _____ Date of Interview _____

Location of Interview _____

Position Applied For _____

To the Interviewer: Please check the rating in each category that reflects your opinion of the job candidate's performance. If you can add comments, it would be very helpful.

Documentation (resume, cover letter, employment application)

☐ Excellent   ☐ Very Good   ☐ Good   ☐ Needs Improvement

Comments or suggestions (optional): _____

Attitude (interested in position, self-confident, likable, pleasant tone of voice, smiling)

☐ Excellent   ☐ Very Good   ☐ Good   ☐ Needs Improvement

Comments or suggestions (optional): _____

Appearance (generally neat and tidy, appropriately dressed, alert, good hygiene)

☐ Excellent   ☐ Very Good   ☐ Good   ☐ Needs Improvement

Comments or suggestions (optional): _____

Job Qualifications (education, skills, and experience suitable for position; good personal attributes; human relations capability; dependable; punctual; industrious)

☐ Excellent   ☐ Very Good   ☐ Good   ☐ Needs Improvement

Comments or suggestions (optional): _____

Verbal Communication (speaks clearly with positive tone, uses proper English, avoids slang or repetitive words, emphasizes assets, is courteous, uses name of the interviewer)

☐ Excellent   ☐ Very Good   ☐ Good   ☐ Needs Improvement

Comments or suggestions (optional): _____

Nonverbal Communication (positive, assertive body language, good eye contact, does not fidget)

☐ Excellent ☐ Very Good ☐ Good ☐ Needs Improvement

Comments or suggestions (optional): _____

Listening (does not interrupt or respond too quickly, asks to have a question repeated if necessary, takes time to think through important questions, calmly endures silence)

☐ Excellent ☐ Very Good ☐ Good ☐ Needs Improvement

Comments or suggestions (optional): _____

Enthusiasm (demonstrates interest and energy through verbal and nonverbal communication)

☐ Excellent ☐ Very Good ☐ Good ☐ Needs Improvement

Comments or suggestions (optional): _____

Please summarize any other observations you made during the interview, including several things that were done well and one thing that needs improvement.

Add your completed work to the "About Jobs" section of your Career Builder Files.

▶ *CAREER ACTION WORKSHEET*
11-5 Do Your Homework before Every Interviews ❸

Each time you receive a new job interview, use this form as soon as you can to help you prepare for this interview. Check off items you have completed and answer the questions.

Understand the Job Posting. Make a copy of the job description, and do the following:

☐ Circle words in the job description that are new to you or unique to this company.

☐ Look up the meaning of unfamiliar words in the job description to ensure you know what they mean for this career field and this company. Write the meaning on the job description.

☐ Number each job skill requirement (1, 2, 3, etc.), and on a separate piece of paper, write the numbers and a brief description of how you meet these qualifications. Outline your examples and stories related to this job that can give the interviewer confidence that you are qualified. Attach the separate pages to this worksheet.

Understand the Company. Find the company website (or Wikipedia page) and answer the following questions:

☐ When was the company started?

☐ Who are the owners/leaders of this company?

☐ What is the major product(s) this company provides?

☐ Where is the company located? Is there more than one location?

☐ What is the company's stated mission or purpose?

☐ Does the company state its values or principles? If so, write them here or attach a copy.

☐ How might you work the information above into your interview discussion?

Identify Current Events for the Company. Do a general search on the company's name and the name of the top leaders or owners, then answer these questions:

☐ How recently was this company in the news?

☐ Is the news about this company generally favorable or not?

☐ What does this news tell you about the company?

☐ How might you be able to use this news in an interview discussion to demonstrate that you are the person they want for this job?

Learn about your interviewer. Try to find out the name of the person who will interview you. Do a general Internet and social media search on this person, and answer the following questions.

☐ What do I have in common with this person? Neighborhood? Schooling? Hobbies or Interests?

☐ Is this person someone who can offer me the job directly? Or is he or she someone who will recommend me to others?

☐ Is there a connection between this person and me? A mutual acquaintance? A friend of a family member or networking contact? If so, describe the connection.

☐ How might you use your knowledge of the interviewer in the interview discussion?

Add your completed work to the "About Jobs" section of your Career Builder Files.

▶ *CAREER ACTION WORKSHEET*
11-6 Get Physically Prepared for Success with Interviews ❸

Make a list of at least five portfolio items or marketing materials that you might include by reviewing the Interview Preparation Checklist. Many of these will come from your Master Career Portfolio.

To do this, read two or three job descriptions that you found earlier (see Chapter 6), and list items that demonstrate your qualifications for several of the job requirements. (For example, if you want to work as a cook or chef, include a sample menu, recipes, a nutritional analysis, and a cost analysis.) Be sure to include samples and examples of your career-related work and your transferable skills. (For example, if the job requires "superb customer service," include a thank-you note you received about your service, or a service award, or a letter from a person who recommends you for your attitude toward excellent service.)

1.

2.

3.

4.

5.

Optional: List other portfolio items you might want to bring to an interview, but be careful not to bring too many.

Add your completed work to the "Master Career Portfolio" section of your Career Builder Files.

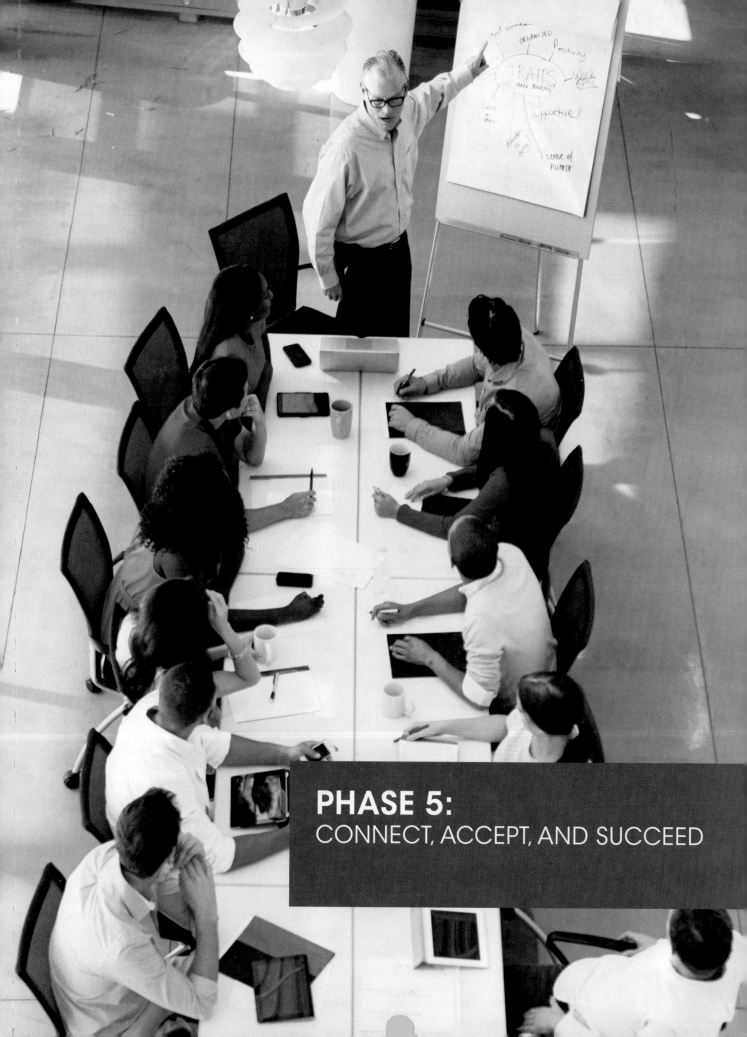

PHASE 5:
CONNECT, ACCEPT, AND SUCCEED

Connect, Accept, and Succeed

PART 5 This part provides tips for what to do after interviews to help you get the job and succeed in your career.

GINA ARENS

Owner, Little Sonoma Fine Wines

ADVICE FROM THE EXPERT

Gina Arens had a wide variety of experience working in all aspects of retail operation before starting her own fine wine retail store. She learned from the ground up what it takes to manage store operations, including purchasing, inventory management, marketing, sales, and supervision of staff.

From her experience of working with and managing new employees, her advice for succeeding at a new job is to "take time to learn and understand the business processes and procedures. Meet and exceed expectations that are set for you." She says the fastest way to appear unprofessional is to "show up to work with an untidy appearance and treat customers in a rude manner," whether these customers are internal or external.

If you do have problems adjusting, organizations will help you improve job performance. Gina says for performance improvement, she will try to "meet and discuss on a regular basis and have someone work with the person to try to improve their understanding, skills, and performance." Additionally, timeliness is an important focus for performance. "We try to address performance immediately (good or bad) rather than wait for annual reviews." For new employees, the organization enables success "by providing training and enrichment opportunities from seasoned employees and knowledgeable vendors."

When it comes to long-term success, Gina says, "Those who are promoted demonstrate a high level of commitment to the company. They are dependable, trustworthy, and hardworking. They are creative thinkers who solve problems and increase business in innovative ways." While promotion is demonstrated through talent, employees who are laid off or fired often make simple errors such as being "not dependable, not honest, and not productive." Often, they "may have lacked the skills we initially thought they had to do the job."

It's important to be cautious on the job as well. The office grapevine can often get you in trouble. Gina's advice is to "stay out of it! Be careful of people who try to draw you into commenting about other employees. You should never say anything about anyone that you wouldn't say to them directly. That includes electronic communication as well!" Another area that often poses issues is building a relationship with your manager. Gina especially highlights the need to be "careful about being critical of current business practices because you could be insulting your boss who initiated these practices and get off on the wrong foot with your relationship."

To make an impact at your job, Gina says, "Watch, listen, and learn before you start trying to reinvent the wheel. Try to understand why things are being done a certain way before making suggestions to do things differently. When you do, you will be able to address the objections that may come up and may just see some change happen!"

PLAN for Success

Most successful people keep a calendar of activities and a running list of tasks they have committed to do. Make *Your Career* a part of your calendar and task list.

- Read the outcomes on the first page of Chapters 12 through 14 and jot down a target date for completing each one. Allow extra time for those that require more than just reading.

- Now make several calendar appointments with yourself to do the reading, homework and projects for this class. Consider your other commitments (for other classes, work, home) as you plan to make Your Career happen for you!

TALES FROM THE JOB SEARCH

Molly Cramer's major in leadership studies required an internship experience, and she learned of an ideal opportunity through word of mouth. She says, "A family friend had participated in the internship program and raved about the experience she had. I then searched online to learn how I could apply." Her proactive approach led to her paid internship at the JVS Cincinnati Career Network, helping members of the community search for sustainable employment.

Molly prepared for her first "real" interview by researching the organization and reading about its staff on LinkedIn®. She then "did a quick brain storming session of questions I thought the interviewer would ask me. I enlisted a friend to ask me the questions, listen to my responses, and give me feedback."

MOLLY CRAMER
Sophomore, University of Richmond, Psychology and Leadership Studies Major

Molly's professional behavior and work habits had a positive effect on her workplace. She says, "I think I contributed to the organization because I brought a can-do attitude and executed a task—organizing a job fair—that would not have been accomplished without a capable intern."

Molly's advice to others is to "establish positive relationships with your supervisors, coworkers, and other personnel. You never know whether an internship could turn into a job down the line, so make every effort to be friendly and professional with everyone."

She now believes "there is nothing more fulfilling than helping others." Helping others find employment was deeply satisfying for Molly. "I know that whichever path my career takes, I will find a way to help others in the process," she says.

OVERVIEW

After the interview, take steps to help you get job offers, understand what the offers really mean, negotiate the contract if needed, and respond to job offers professionally as you continue to make your career happen successfully.

OUTCOMES

1 Describe how to follow up after interviews.

2 Evaluate job offers.

3 Demonstrate how to respond to job offers professionally.

CAREER ACTION WORKSHEETS

12-1: Follow Up After Interviews, page 325

12-2: Internet Research on Salary Information, page 327

12-3: Salary and Benefits Planning Sheet, page 329

12-4: Plan for Dealing with Job Offers, page 331

WHERE ARE YOU ON THE JOURNEY?

PHASE 1: Prepare for the Journey
- *The Job Search Journey*
- *Know Yourself to Market Yourself*
- *Picture Yourself in the Workplace*

PHASE 2: Create Your Resume
- *Plan Your Resume*
- *Write Your Resume*

PHASE 3: Apply for Jobs
- *Find Job Openings*
- *Write Job Applications*
- *Write Effective Tailored Cover Letters*

PHASE 4: Shine at Interviews
- *Know the Interview Essentials*
- *Prepare for Your Interview*
- *Interview Like a Pro*

PHASE 5: Connect, Accept, and Succeed
- *Stay Connected with Prospective Employers*
- *It's an Iterative Process*
- *Take Charge of Your Career*

Something that is seen repeatedly is more easily remembered. Be seen by your prospective employers—in their email, in their workplace, on their phone. Be pleasantly persistent.

PHASE 5: Connect, Accept, and Succeed

Step 1, *Stay Connected with Prospective Employers*

You are in Phase 5, *Connect, Accept & Succeed*, at step 1, *Stay Connected with Prospective Employers*. Your goal in this chapter is to identify professional ways to ensure prospective employers remember you, admire your persistence, and want you to join their workforce. Then, when the job offer comes, evaluate the offer and, if appropriate, negotiate to make the offer just a bit better.

FOLLOW UP AFTER THE INTERVIEW

Interview follow-up can increase your chances of getting the job, yet many candidates don't bother to do it! Interviewers often view follow-up by a job seeker as a proactive step that shows initiative and interest.

Good follow-up reinforces your qualifications and helps you stand out favorably from the competition. Be patient during this stage of the job search. The hiring process takes longer than you want it to take, and often, longer than even the employer expects.

The key to follow-up is timely action: evaluate your interview performance and send follow-up messages to the interviewer.

Evaluate the Interview

At the earliest possible time, summarize and evaluate your own interview performance in writing. Use Career Action Worksheet 11-3. Keep in mind how interviewers tend to evaluate job candidates during interviews, as shown in Figure 11-1 on page 279. This evaluation will help you do the following:

1. **Enhance your positives**. Note what you did well, and look for ways to reinforce these positives in your follow-up actions.

2. **Diminish your negatives**. Note what you forgot to say or did not express as well as you liked. These are areas you might be able to address or fix in your follow-up interactions.

3. **Follow up on commitments**. Did you agree to send something to the interviewer or the company? Did you agree to make a phone call or do something online? Maybe it was as simple as sending your business card or providing a current phone number for one of your references. It is critical that you complete each

commitment on or ahead of schedule and communicate that you have completed the follow-up.

4. **Plan your schedule for follow-up**. The last two questions in the evaluation are about how the interviewer wants to be contacted and the timing for a hiring decision. These will impact your next step of mapping out your follow-up strategy.

Doing your evaluation immediately after the interview is critical. Don't even wait an hour or until the next morning. Why? Because it is too easy to forget little things that will make a difference. So do your evaluation immediately, then review your worksheet the next morning and add anything else that comes to mind. Then start implementing your follow-up strategy.

Plan Your Follow-Up Strategies

Look at question 11 on your completed Interview Evaluation, from Career Action Worksheet 11-3. This question is about follow-up activities. Do these immediately. If you told the interviewer you would do something, consider this your promise. Keep your promises. This demonstrates your ability to follow through, and is a crucial trait that employers look for.

Complete your interview evaluation promptly because some items might be best addressed in your follow-up thank-you note. Your thank-you note should be sent within a few days of the interview. The sooner, the better. See Figures 12-1 and 12-2 for examples of thank-you notes. You should write a thank-you note to every person who interviewed you. The letters can be basically the same, but try to vary each one by highlighting something specific each interviewer said in case the recipients compare notes.

Look through your interview evaluation notes for items that you want to follow

Figure 12-1 Brief Thank-You Letter

2440 Observatory Boulevard, Apartment 34
Reno, NV 89511

July 2, 20—

Ms. Stephanie Nolan
Manager, Auditing Staff
Wyatt & Berkowitz Public Accountants
1410 Quarrier Street, Suite 700
Reno, NV 89503

Dear Ms. Nolan:

Thank you for the opportunity to interview for the Staff Auditor Level 1 position with you and your team. Your invitation to join the first hour of the weekly staff meeting made me feel especially welcome—and sent me to the library to brush up on the finer points of the state's tax credit program for employers who train welfare recipients!

I feel I have a good understanding of the requirements for the position, and I am very interested in joining your team. I look forward to the possibility of working with you. Please call me any time this week at 775.555.1537

Sincerely,

Max Wu

Max Wu

(775).555.1537 | MaxWu@email.com | linkedin.com/in/MaxWu

up on—information you need to clarify or reinforce with the employer, questions you want answered, areas of weak performance and suggestions for improving them, and specific actions you need to take. Jot down notes on how you might address these. Making a table, like the example shown in Figure 12-3, can be helpful.

Determine what method of follow-up is most appropriate for each item. Then, with each follow-up interaction, decide which items you can include from your list. You may not be able to cover all of them, so be selective.

If you remembered to ask the interviewer how they wanted you to follow-up, honor the interviewer's preferences and use that method. If you forgot to ask, send a follow-up letter or email rather than make a phone call, as these are currently viewed as less intrusive methods of communicating. If the interviewer approves of follow-up phone

Figure 12-2 Longer Thank-You Letter

3493 Huntington Heights
Denver, CO 80202
August 23, 20—

Mr. Frederick J. Gray Wolf
Normandy Copiers, Inc.
3500 Main Street
Boulder, CO 80302

Dear Mr. Gray Wolf:

The enthusiasm you shared this afternoon for the customer-centered philosophy behind the new Normandy Print Center is contagious! I know from experience how satisfying it is to break new ground and to achieve results that exceed all expectations. The Normandy management system sounds unique, innovative, and challenging.

During our meeting, we discussed how I could contribute to your marketing plan, but we didn't have time to talk about store operations. While I managed the parts and service operations of Renaissance Business Systems, our team achieved and maintained a production efficiency rate that consistently placed us in the top 5 percent of the 160 shops nationwide. Sales of maintenance contracts increased every year I was in charge, and we had the lowest return rate for products of all the centers.

Thank you for talking with me about the new opportunities at Normandy Print Center. The company will be a great success in Boulder, and I would like to contribute to that success. As we agreed, I will call you next Thursday, but you can reach me before that at 303.555.0171.

Sincerely,

Francesca Elena Valdez

Francesca Elena Valdez

calls, use that method. A phone call is more personal and lively and gives you quicker feedback. If you call, you should also follow up with a letter or an email because it serves as a reminder of you.

This is a good time to double-check your voicemail message to make sure it is business appropriate if someone calls you. If you do miss a call from a prospective employer, be sure to return the call within 24 hours.

Now plan when you will do each follow-up. Figure 12-4 shows a sample schedule. Be ready to change your timing based on how the interviewer and employer respond.

Figure 12-3 Example List of Interview Follow-Up Items, Noting Options for Follow-Up

What needs follow-up	How I might follow up
Reinforce that my experience training others on the JR-equipment can help them as they bring on additional staff	• In my thank-you note • Email • Phone conversations • Send copy of trainer certification as attachment to thank-you note
Forgot to say I really like fixing equipment, and studied the manuals on this	• During any interaction, say, "I like it when I can see the equipment manuals so that I can teach myself how to fix the equipment."
Need to know what their vacation plan is so I can take my annual mountain camping trip with my high school friends	• Wait until an offer is made • See if the answer is on the online site or on GlassDoor.com

Figure 12-4 Scheduling and Spacing Follow-Up Interactions

Follow-Up Items	Timing/Method
Send thank-you note	Today/physical card sent by U.S. mail
Send items requested by interviewer 1. List of my references 2. Copy of my training certificate 3. Email address of college instructor 4. My availability for pre-employment test	Tomorrow/by email (note: send scan of training certificate by email, and then send a hard copy by U.S. mail a few days later with an extra follow-up letter)
Tell them about my additional experience that we didn't discuss.	For critical skill: Today in thank-you note For nice-to-know-about skills: Include in email if I don't hear from them within a few days of the date for a hiring decision
Improve my 30-Second Commercial to be more specific to the company's biggest challenges as described in today's interview	Follow-up interviews
Clarify that I taught myself about the topic I could not respond to during the interview	Today/in thank-you note
Take a drug test	This week, schedule an appointment at their preferred lab; mark calendar to confirm results are sent and received (call the lab, email the company to confirm)
Follow-up on "Did I get the job" (ask if there is any update on the hiring decision and can I provide any additional information to help them with this decision)	Only after the date for a hiring decision has passed/ phone call (note: be prepared to leave a voicemail message too)

This might mean more communications upon their request, or a different method of communicating (for example, more email attachments instead of physical mail), or fewer communications. If the responses to your follow-up messages is something like "We will get back to you next month, as stated in the interview," that is a clear message to back off and let them run their internal process. Don't contact them again until a few days after the stated date.

Make all your follow-up messages brief and polished. Include only the most important questions or information. Be respectful of interviewers' time. Consider what their schedule might be. For example:

- Mondays and Fridays can be the busiest business days, so call on another day.

- Just before lunch and just before the end of the workday are usually inconvenient times.

- Different industries have different busy periods. Financial firms might be very busy at the end of the month. Tax firms are busy from January until April 15, and perhaps around July 1. Restaurateurs are busiest at meal times and when produce shipments are delivered.

In every follow-up interaction, be sure to include some form of your Personal Brand Statement or one of your 30-Second Commercials that are customized for this job and employer. Your personal brand should always be clear and reinforce the job requirements. When a first interview goes well, the prospective employer may request one or more follow-up interviews and request that you take pre-employment tests. Start now to plan for these. A review of Chapter 10 can help you prepare.

Planning is just a way of thinking through what might happen in the future and dreaming up ways to respond. When you plan, you are always more prepared to be at your very best.

Connect with Your Career Network Again

If a member of your Career Network is influential with your prospective employer, contact him or her to ask for additional support. A friendly follow-up call from this person to the employer could tip the scales in your favor.

An alternative to the follow-up call by a network member is a letter of recommendation from one or more people who can confirm your qualifications. Some employers routinely request letters of recommendation from former employers, managers, or supervisors of applicants. Arranging to have such letters sent on your own demonstrates initiative—another benefit for you.

> **CAREER ACTION**
> **Complete Worksheet 12-1**
> Follow Up After Interviews, page 325

EVALUATE JOB OFFERS

"We'd like to offer you the job." Those are the words every job seeker wants to hear. Because the decision to accept or reject a job offer affects your long-term career plans, consider this important decision carefully. Take your time to consider the job offer and stay away from accepting a job offer on the spot.

Consider the following factors when you evaluate a job offer:

- **The salary or wage:** Does the salary or wage match your education and abilities and is it comparable with that of the competition? Does the potential for increases exist?

Successful Follow-Up Phone Call

If your interviewer gave the go-ahead for a follow-up call, you can set yourself apart from the competition with a well-timed, well-prepared phone call.

- **Begin with a greeting and self-introduction.** "Hello, Ms. Nabavi. This is Greg Bell."

- **Demonstrate courtesy.** "Is this a good time for you to talk?" Call only during business hours. Pay full attention on the call; no multitasking.

- **Identify the position for which you interviewed and the date.** "I want to thank you for meeting with me yesterday to discuss the data processing systems analyst I position."

- **Provide important information you omitted.** "After reviewing our meeting, I realized that I hadn't mentioned some pertinent information regarding my (education, work experience, qualifications, certification, other)." Concisely give the specifics.

- **Reemphasize your qualifications.** If necessary, give a short, targeted version of your 30-Second Commercial, emphasizing precisely how your qualifications can benefit the employer.

- **If necessary, ask questions to clarify any points that were not covered adequately.** For example, a clearer description of the job responsibilities or clarification of work relationships.

- **Thank the interviewer, express your interest, and encourage a speedy hiring decision.** "Thank you again for the interview. I look forward to learning of your hiring decision soon. I believe we could benefit each other, and I'd be pleased to be a part of Mississippi Central Power Company."

© oliveromg/Shutterstock.com.

- **Entire compensation package**: This includes everything from the base wage to health insurance, education benefits, and retirement savings plans.

- **Career development opportunities:** Will you have adequate opportunities for professional growth (through training, increased responsibilities, and opportunities for advancement)?

- **The job itself:** Is the scope acceptable? Is the work interesting to you? Does the job fit into your work preferences (see Chapter 3) and long-term career goals?

- **Expense considerations:** If you have to relocate, will the company pay all or part of the moving costs? What is the cost of living in the new location?

- **The job market:** Are jobs in your field plentiful or in short supply?

- **The company and personnel:** Do you feel comfortable with the organizational structure and the people you met? Do the company's stated values and ethics align with yours?

The company expects you to have questions and may have a standard process for giving you the information you need to make an informed decision. This is the time to ask all those questions. You may be given access to a website for job candidates, or a member of the hiring committee or the human resources department may contact you.

Be sure you understand all of the conditions of the job before you decide whether to accept the offer. If you have several offers, it often helps to make a chart so that you can compare the offers more visually. Selecting your next job based on a gut feeling alone has led more than one person to regret their choice. Be thoughtful, and engage your Career Network to help you look at the offers objectively. However, in the end, you are the one who must decide to accept or reject a job offer.

Negotiate a Good Compensation Package

Put yourself in a strong position to negotiate your compensation package by doing your research.

Become knowledgeable about the going salary ranges and the types of benefits

⮞ You, Online

Stay Connected

Staying connected with prospective employers is easier than you think! Use social media not only to stay informed but to maintain a personal connection with interviewers and employees you met during your interview:

- Make sure to follow the company on LinkedIn® and follow its Twitter feed if you haven't already.
- Connect with everyone you met—interviewers, possible team members, hiring managers, and recruiters—on LinkedIn®.
- Mention latest company news or details from interviewers' profiles in your follow-up emails if the information adds value.
- Make sure to include your own LinkedIn® profile in your email signature when you send follow-up emails.
- Continue to stay on the company's social media radar by posting updates on your profile and commenting on discussions and updates shared by your new connections.

CAUTION Background Checks

©iStock.com/DRB Images, LLC.

A background check is a consumer report that employers use to screen potential employees. In addition to confirming your education and work history, employers may request a consumer report from a credit reporting bureau to check your social security number, credit payment record, driving record, or criminal history.

This type of background check is common for jobs that require government security clearance, but it may be used for any job.

Before employers can get your consumer report, they must have your written consent, however. You always have the option of withdrawing your application if there is information you do not want to disclose.

The best way to prepare for a background check is to be truthful on all employment forms, maintain good credit, know what your references are going to say about you, and obtain copies of your personnel files from past employers. If necessary, get a copy of your credit report from a credit bureau and dispute any incorrect information.

Real World Scenario 12-1 Lee and Rose have both been applying for accounting positions at various companies and comparing notes on the offers they received. Lee was excited because he recently got a job offer for $15,000 more annually than Rose's offer. He encouraged Rose to try to get a job where he is going to work. But Rose has done her homework and knows that her employer contributes to her 401(k) retirement plan and provides a health care package that Lee won't get. When she calculated the annual savings with the better health insurance and considered the long term advantages of the 401(k), the total annual value was $25,000 more than Lee's offer. Plus there are three weeks of vacation instead of two weeks. Rose is sticking with her offer.

What factors are important for you to evaluate when looking at the overall compensation package?

being offered in your field. When you get an offer, take the time to understand the comprehensive benefit package. Don't let one company's high base salary fool you into thinking that theirs is the best offer. Other benefits, such as those listed in Figure 12-5, can have a significant impact on the overall value of the compensation package. Often it is easier to negotiate additional benefits than it is to negotiate wages.

Do be aware that sometimes salary and wages cannot be negotiated. Vacation and benefits may be off the negotiating table too. It often depends on such things as government laws and regulations, company policies, and union contracts. Talk to your network to learn more about what is and is not negotiable. See "Caution: When NOT to Negotiate" for more on this topic.

Research Compensation Trends in Your Field

Here are some places where you can find information about compensation trends:

- Talk with leaders in your field, people who hold positions that are similar to your target job, and are a placement specialists.

Figure 12-5 Elements That May Be Part of a Compensation Package

Consider the following as elements of comprehensive compensation package:
- Wages or salary
- Performance reviews, raises, bonuses, profit-sharing opportunities
- Health, dental, and prescription insurance
- Retirement savings opportunities; companies may offer tax-deferred savings plans—known as 401(k) or 403(b) plans—and will contribute to your retirement savings if you participate in the company-sponsored plan through payroll deductions
- Vacation, holidays, personal, and sick days
- Flextime
- Onsite resources such as day care, gym, and cafeteria
- Lifestyle benefits such as maternity/paternity leave beyond government-required minimums, elder-care services, domestic partner benefits, and family-care leave of absence
- Relocation and business travel reimbursement, including personal use of loyalty points for hotels and airlines
- Flexible Spending Accounts; in addition to insurance programs, a Flexible Spending Account allow you to set aside pretax income to pay for medical expenses and dependent care, and can lower your income taxes
- Insurance such as disability insurance, and long-term care insurance

- Search the Internet for salary and benefits information. Glassdoor.com, the BLS *Occupational Outlook Handbook*, and other sites list salaries for specific companies and roles. Salary.com has a salary wizard tool that can be used as well.

- For part-time or contract jobs, use the full-time wage as a starting point. For part-time jobs, calculate the equivalent pay by dividing the full-time wage into an hourly rate and multiplying by the hours you expect to work. For contract jobs, divide the full-time wage by 2,080 hours, the average hours worked by contractors in a year.

- Ask your school's career services office for assistance.

- Check the websites of associations in your career field.

Some employers provide printed job descriptions that include a fixed salary listing, while others offer salary information on their websites. A job listing may include a salary range, or the salary may be open. You may be able to find the range or approximate salary for a position from the employer's human resources department. Some employers, however, don't give out this information. They may give you only the bottom of the range—rarely the top figure. Having a general idea of the range can help you evaluate a job offer.

Before you accept the job offer is the best time to negotiate the terms of your employment.

Salary Negotiation Tips

To obtain the strongest bargaining position, postpone discussion of compensation until you receive a job offer. Instead, focus on your qualifications. If the question of compensation comes up earlier, refocus the conversation using the following tactics:

- **If the interviewer brings up the subject of compensation before you are prepared to discuss it,** delay the topic by saying, "Actually, I'm more interested in learning about the position, than in talking about salary today. Could we discuss the position a little more?"

- **If the interviewer asks what salary you want, a good response is, "What figure or range is the company planning to pay?"** This gives you a starting point for negotiation. If it's higher than you expected, you help yourself by not stating a lower figure first. If it's lower, you now have a place to begin negotiations.

- **If the interviewer presses for your salary requirement, refer to your research.** "The national average for a person with my experience, education, and training is $ _____. Considering cost-of-living factors, I would expect a salary in the range of $_____."

Whenever possible, let the interviewer bring up the topic of salary and benefits. These conversations are usually best held after you get an offer, or, at the earliest, during a second interview. Here is a sample dialog.

Joan: Thanks for coming in for a follow-up interview. Mick, the hiring manager, is looking forward to meeting you.

Juan: Thanks for asking me back, Joan.

Joan: Before we go to meet Mick, I'd like to talk with you about the compensation package. Let me ask you, what was your salary at your last job?

Juan: I am looking at jobs that are in the $60,000 to $70,000 range. And I'm looking for more than my current two weeks of vacation each year. I understand from reading the materials you sent that the compensation package is much more than just salary. Can you walk me through what a total package might look like?

Notice that in the above dialog, Juan does not directly answer the question about his salary from the previous job. As you negotiate, realize that you don't have to give direct answers to every question asked. Instead, keep the focus on your goals. When negotiating salary, use the following strategies:

- **Begin salary negotiations** by asking questions such as: "Thanks, is this the firm job offer?", "Is this negotiable?", and "Is this the base wage only?" These questions confirm you have received an official offer and indicate your interest in negotiating the full compensation package, not just salary or wages.

- **Aim for a salary that equals the peak of your qualifications.** The higher you start, the higher the offer is likely to be. State your requirement in arrange (upper twenties, mid-thirties), making it broad enough to negotiate. Don't specify a low end; if you do, the employer will likely select it.

- **Discuss the entire compensation package** during the discussion of salary. Your total take-home pay is greatly influenced by all benefits such as those listed in Figure 12-5. Review the offer package thoroughly and take the time to calculate the actual take-home pay after taxes. In some cases, a low salary is offset by low insurance premiums with high benefits coverage or pre-tax savings accounts such as the Health Savings Account option. In others, you may want to negotiate a higher salary due to the high cost of insurance, retirement benefits, lack of vacation, cost of living in that area, and so on.

- **Ask about the criteria used to determine compensation increases and the frequency of salary reviews.** Good benefits and salary increases can offset a lower starting salary. Directly ask, "How and when will I be evaluated, and is there a possibility of increase based on that evaluation?"

- **While discussing salary, return to your assets.** Review all of the benefits and qualifications you have to offer the company.

- **Once you state your salary range, do not back down,** particularly if you think it is equal to your qualifications. Base your range on careful research. The employer will respect your confidence in the quality and worth of your work.

- **Do not discuss any other sources of income and do not whine about your expenses.** Stay focused on the negotiation.

- **Stick to the facts.** Ensure you understand when benefits will start, such as health insurance. If your previous insurance will run out prior to start of your new benefits, consider requesting your new employer cover any extension costs as a part of negotiations.

- **If the salary offer is made in a letter and the salary is too low, arrange an appointment to discuss it right away.** Bargaining power is far greater in person than it is by letter or phone.

- **If the salary isn't acceptable, state the salary you would accept** and close by reaffirming your interest in the company and the job. If the interviewer says, "I'll have to think about your requirements," wait one week; then call back. You may receive a higher or compromise offer. If the interviewer gives you a flat "no," express regret that you were unable to work out a compromise. Restate your interest in the job and the company; then send a follow-up thank-you letter within two days. This could swing the decision in your favor.

© Stuart Jenner/Shutterstock.com.

CAUTION
When NOT to Negotiate

There are some instances where you should not negotiate salary. You should always maintain the perception that you are acting in good faith and with integrity. Consider the following situations as times when not to negotiate the base wage offered:

- Do not negotiate just for the sake of negotiating. If you are happy with the offer and it meets the typical range for your role, review all the other benefits thoroughly, negotiate on these points if needed, and then accept the offer graciously.

- If a salary range was previously shared and you accepted the range, do not negotiate outside of the range. If you had accepted the range prior to doing adequate research or because you wanted to continue the process, you cannot go back on your acceptance of the salary range. This can result in removal of the offer.

- Do not negotiate salary without sufficient justification prepared.

- Do not negotiate salary if the range the company is sharing is vastly different from what you want. This will waste both parties' time.

Recall that outside of base wages, there are both costs, such as health insurance premiums, and benefits, such as paid vacation, that ultimately factor into how much you are earning. Consider negotiating in other areas if base wages are non-negotiable.

As you negotiate, consider the people and use your emotional intelligence to help you get a better compensation package. Here are some things to consider:

- **Be likeable**. The people you are talking with are more likely to work harder to maximize your package if they view you as a person they like.

- **Be attainable**. This is not a time to play hard to get. Communicate with body language and your words that you are seriously considering accepting this position provided the negotiations are satisfactory. Make sure you are not wasting their time.

- **Understand their side**. The employer has constraints. Try to understand what they might be. It can be a legal issue, a union contract, or a concern about setting a precedent for all employees.

- **Know the decision maker**. Often you are talking with someone who cannot make the ultimate decision. In some cases it might be the HR department, other times it is the hiring managers. Frequently it is someone higher in the company or even the legal department.

- **Know when to stop**. Pay attention to the mood of your contact. If they appear tired, frustrated, or seem to have other work to attend to, suggest that both of you take a break, and think about this for a day or a week. You never know; the answer might be different on a different day.

> ▶ *CAREER ACTION*
> **Complete Worksheet 12-2**
> Internet Research on Salary Information,
> page 327

> ▶ *CAREER ACTION*
> **Complete Worksheet 12-3**
> Salary and Benefits Planning
> Sheet, page 329

RESPOND TO A JOB OFFER PROFESSIONALLY

A job offer may be made in person by phone, face-to-face, or in writing by email or letter. If the offer is made in writing, you have more time to think it over carefully and less emotionally than you do if it's made in person. Respond to the offer quickly so that you don't jeopardize it in anyway.

If the offer is made by phone or in the interviewer's office, request time to think it over. You may want to discuss the job offer conditions with a member of your Career Network and family.

It's in your best interest to take at least one day to consider the advantages and disadvantages of the job offer. This gives you time to understand fully the compensation package and address any remaining questions you have.

Important: Be sure that waiting one day won't be an imposition or affect the job offer. Don't put yourself in the position of returning the next day to accept the offer only to find that someone else has the job.

When the Answer Is Yes

If you accept the job offer verbally, follow up immediately in writing. Summarize your understanding of the conditions of the offer and state the position title, starting date, salary, and other pertinent items. (Your employer may do the same, but this helps ensure mutual agreement about all of the conditions of the offer.) If a formal contract is given, review thoroughly, sign, and return. Request your new employer to provide you next steps and what to expect so you can come prepared to your first day on the job.

If you are waiting to hear about more than one offer, tell the other companies you interviewed with that you have accepted a job. You may deal with these people in your new job or you may want to contact them in the future regarding employment.

Contact your references and other people who helped with your job search to tell them about your new job and thank them for their help. People you thank are more likely to help in the future when you seek a new position or advancement in your career.

When the Answer Is No Thanks

If you decide this is not the job for you, first notify the employer by phone if possible. Then politely decline the offer in a letter, thank the employer for the job offer, and wish the employer future success.

> ▶ *CAREER ACTION*
> **Complete Worksheet 12-4**
> Plan for Dealing with Job Offers, page 331

Real World Scenario 12-2 Jonas received his first job offer after three long months of searching for a job. He was so excited, he almost accepted it on the spot! But then, he remembered he was waiting for a response from another interview he had recently gone to. He asked for a few days to consider the offer and went home. He contacted the other possibility and let them know that he had received an offer. He made sure to share he was still interested in hearing the decision and they agreed to provide a decision in the next 48 hours. Two days later, Jonas had two offers to consider! He compared the full compensation package from both and began his negotiations.

What items can you clarify or negotiate when you take time to review your job offer?

MAKE IT A HABIT
Be a Gracious Winner

A job search certainly takes a lot of work, but it is not a paying job. The time will come when you need to stop looking for a job and start working at one. Your final decision about accepting a particular job may well be influenced by economics—the need to earn a living.

If a job offer meets most of your requirements but is not your first choice or is not a perfectly logical career step, you may still decide to accept it. If so, take the job with a determination to excel. It is an opportunity for you to establish your reputation—while at the same time taking home a regular salary.

Accept the challenge and view it as preparation for the next step in your career development.

©iStock.com/nyul.

Chapter Checklist

Check off each item you can do. Reread sections in this chapter to help you complete the checklist.

- [ ] Use my interview evaluation (Career Action Worksheet 11-3) to make my interview follow-up plan. **1**

- [ ] Make a strategic plan to follow up after every interview. **1**

- [ ] Involve my Career Network in helping get a job offer after the interview. **1**

- [ ] Consider all aspects of a job offer—the job and company, the compensation package (salary and benefits), growth opportunities, etc. **2**

- [ ] Conduct research about salary ranges and trends. **2**

- [ ] Develop a strategy for salary negotiations. **2**

- [ ] Accept or decline a job offer professionally. **3**

Critical Thinking Questions

1. What would you say to a friend to convince them to complete their own interview evaluation as soon as possible rather than wait a day or two? **1**

2. How might a thank-you note sent to interviewers make a difference in getting a job offer? List three or more ideas. **2**

3. List five reasons a lower salary/wage offer might be better than a higher salary/wage offer. **2**

4. If economic conditions require you to accept a job that is not exactly what you are aiming for, how can you best approach the new job? What are the benefits of doing so? **2**

5. What is an appropriate response when an interviewer asks what salary you are looking for during your initial interview? Would the response change if you'd been given an offer? **2**

6. Base your answers to the following questions on your salary research: (a) What is the entry-level salary for the job you are seeking? (b) What salary range do you plan to seek in your job search? (c) What is this range based on? **2**

7. Why is it important to act professionally when turning down a job offer? **3**

Additional Resources

For data files, career resources, and more, visit www.cengagebrain.com.

Trial Run

Study the Local Economy

Pay scales and benefit packages are affected by larger economic issues. Divide into four teams and research the employment conditions in your area. Use anecdotal information and your own observations and check the websites of the local newspaper, business journal, chamber of commerce, and television stations.

Start by having a class discussion about what you want to learn from your research. For example:

- How have the students in this class been affected by economic changes?

- What can older workers tell you about past economic down turns or economic bubbles?

- What is the relative impact of national and local factors?

- What is the local unemployment rate? How has it changed in the last two years?

- How long do people report taking to find a new job in their field? Are people changing fields or taking contingency jobs?

- What are the elected officials predicting? What are business leaders predicting?

- What advice do you have for your community leaders?

Team 1. Research the two or three largest employers in your area. How have they been affected by the national economy? Have there been layoffs? If so, have these jobs been shifted to other parts of the country or to other countries or eliminated altogether? Have programs been put in place to attract more people into certain fields of work or into an area that needs more workers?

Team 2. Research the local stores or branch offices of national companies. What is the reason behind any new storefront openings or closures; for example, did the national company close low-performing stores, or has its business model changed to focus on suburbs rather than cities? How many people have lost their jobs? How many new jobs have been created?

Team 3. Research small, locally owned retail businesses. Have any small businesses near your school closed? Have new businesses opened? What has happened in the neighborhoods you live in?

Team 4. Research locally owned service businesses. Include companies that provide services to consumers (such as drycleaners and nail salons) and business-to-business companies (such as janitorial services and restaurant supply companies).

This page is intentionally blank.

▶ *CAREER ACTION WORKSHEET*
12-1 Follow Up After Interviews ❶

After an interview, you will follow up at least once, and likely several times. Think about a real or practice interview you have done, as you write the drafts and scripts below. (Use a separate page or file for your work.)

PART A: Draft a thank-you letter.

PART B: Write a script for your follow-up phone call to provide additional information.

PART C: Draft a follow-up email to kindly request information about the job opening now that the date for filling the position has passed.

PART D: Ask someone to review and comment on your letter, script, and email. Revise them based on their comments and feedback.

Add your completed work to the "About Jobs" section of your Career Builder Files.

This page is intentionally blank.

▶ CAREER ACTION WORKSHEET

12-2 Internet Research on Salary Information ➋

PART 1: Compare the websites PayScale.com and Salary.com. Use one site's salary calculator to compute the average salary for a field of your choice for two cities in different parts of the country where you might consider working. Look for difference in cost of living. What are some other factors to consider? Print the results.

PART 2: Visit the *Occupational Outlook Handbook* at the Bureau of Labor Statistics site and complete the following steps, recording your work on a separate page or file.

1. Select a title that closely matches your occupation.

2. Summarize the wage ranges for the occupation and the expected education and experience.

3. Find the wage ranges plus education and experience for at least five more occupational titles that are either similar or that interest you.

PART 3: For additional salary information, check out the valuable "Salary Info" section at the JobStar website. Take at least one quiz or read one article. Record what you learned on a separate page or file.

Add your completed work to the "About Jobs" section of your Career Builder Files.

▶ *CAREER ACTION WORKSHEET*
12-3 Salary and Benefits Planning Sheet ❷

Contact two employers in your field to learn about the salary ranges and benefits they offer for the type of job you are seeking. Ask the following questions.

PART 1: Negotiating Salary and Benefits

Does this position have a fixed salary or a salary range?

If the salary is fixed, would you tell me the amount?

If the salary is in a range, would you tell me the range?

Is the salary negotiable?

What criteria are used for determining the salary for this position?

Are salary raises awarded for excellent job performance? If so, what criteria are used in this process?

What is included in the typical complete compensation package (salary and benefits)?

PART 2: Summary of Strategies for Negotiating Compensation

Review the strategies in the section "Negotiate a Good Compensation Package." On the back of this page or in a separate document, summarize, in your own words, the tactics you plan to use when negotiating a compensation package (salary and benefits). List any additional tips you have found in your Internet or other research.

Add your completed work to the "About Jobs" section of your Career Builder Files.

This page is intentionally blank.

▶ *CAREER ACTION WORKSHEET*
12-4 Plan for Dealing with Job Offers ❹

Respond to the following.

1. List factors you should consider when evaluating a job offer. Be thorough in your answer. You may want to talk with a member of your Career Network, a placement counselor, or both. Address the factors that are specific to your personal Job Search Journey, as well as general factors.

2. Explain how you can best respond to a job offer made in person:

a. If you think you want the job

b. If you are sure you want the job

c. If you don't want the job

3. How can you best respond to a job offer made by phone?

4. List the follow-up steps you should take when accepting a job offer.

5. What should you do to reject a job offer in a professional manner?

Add your completed work to the "About Jobs" section of your Career Builder Files.

Dealing with Disappointment

OVERVIEW

Getting a good job often requires more than interviewing with one company; it may take several tries before you land the job you want. Think of it as a learning experience as you continue on your Job Search Journey. Chapter 13 highlights practical strategies for recharging your motivation, managing a rejection notice, and trying new angles to land a top job.

OUTCOMES

1 Develop strategies for increasing your chances of getting interviews.

2 Develop strategies for improving your interview performance.

3 Explain strategies for managing a rejection notice.

CAREER ACTION WORKSHEETS

13-1: Internet Research on Handling Job Search Rejection, page 343

13-2: Action Plans for Improving Your Job Search Campaign, page 345

WHERE ARE YOU ON THE JOURNEY?

PHASE 1: Prepare for the Journey
- *The Job Search Journey*
- *Know Yourself to Market Yourself*
- *Picture Yourself in the Workplace*

PHASE 2: Create Your Resume
- *Plan Your Resume*
- *Write Your Resume*

PHASE 3: Apply for Jobs
- *Find Job Openings*
- *Write Job Applications*
- *Write Effective Tailored Cover Letters*

PHASE 4: Shine at Interviews
- *Know the Interview Essentials*
- *Prepare for Your Interview*
- *Interview Like a Pro*

PHASE 5: Connect, Accept, and Succeed
- *Stay Connected with Prospective Employers*
- ***It's an Iterative Process***
- *Take Charge of Your Career*

Just like in the fable of Goldilocks and the Three Bears, some jobs may be 'too hot or too cold,' some may be 'too soft or too hard,' and, as you continue your search, you will find the one that is 'just right' for you.

PHASE 5: Connect, Accept, and Succeed
Step 2, *It's an Iterative Process*

You are in Phase 5, *Connect, Accept, and Succeed*, step 2, *It's an Iterative Process*. Your goal in this chapter is to turn any rejection notices you might receive into tools to help you improve and move forward on your Job Search Journey. Sometimes it takes a few iterations to get your message right or to find those jobs where you are the best fit for the position.

Persevere for Success

No one is right for every job. The right person for a job doesn't always get the job. The best prepared and most determined person often does, however. While you may be partly responsible for an initial rejection, you have the power to turn the situation to your favor. All of the strategies in this chapter have been used successfully by other job seekers to win a good job offer, despite previous rejections.

IF YOU DON'T GET INTERVIEWS

OUTCOME 1

There are many reasons you may not be getting interviews. If you have applied for more than 10 jobs and not received a response, it may be time to rethink your strategy.

More Sources

You may need to use more sources. The Bureau of Labor Statistics has compiled data showing that people who use many resources for finding job leads find jobs faster than people who use only one or two resources. If you are relying on Monster and Craigslist for job leads, look at the many sources of leads in Chapter 6 and expand your search options. In a 2010 survey of people who had been laid off in the last year, 21 percent found jobs through job sites and an additional 22 percent found jobs through "personal referrals." Reconnect with your Career Network—so you can tap into a full 50 percent more jobs you may be qualified for. Remember, people hire people they have a connection with. Use the tactics in Chapter 6 to tap into your Career Network positively and effectively to supercharge your job search.

Right Jobs

It could be that you are applying for the wrong jobs. It could be that you are applying for jobs that do not match your qualifications. Look carefully at the requirements for several jobs you have applied for. If your skills and qualifications are at the low end of the requirements, this could explain why you aren't getting interviews.

Fewer Applications.

You may be applying for too many jobs or through a method that has too many applicants, such as an online job board. Job sites make it easy to respond to job listings, and employers get more applications this way than through other sources. A more effective, personal way to reach prospective employers is through your Career Network. Alternatively, focus on fewer jobs that are a great fit for you and your qualifications, and follow up with cover letters and phone calls. Review tips for follow-up from Chapter 12.

Real World Scenario 13-1

Stewart was having a hard time with his Job Search Journey. He was trying to balance school, a part-time job, and family commitments while trying to apply for jobs. His initial strategy was to submit his Job Application Package for five openings every week and to go to a career-related event once a month. After two months, he still hadn't heard back from any companies. He was getting frustrated, especially after he noticed that he spent an average of an hour on each application. He stepped back and reflected on his strategy. He decided instead of spending five hours per week on applications, he would spend two hours at an event or conducting Career Network interviews per week and two hours applying to more targeted job opportunities. Stewart started getting responses with his new strategy!

How can you become more strategic in how you spend your time during the Job Search Journey? How can you increase the probability that the actions you take will deliver the opportunities you are looking for?

MAKE IT A HABIT
Counter Rejection with Success Strategies

To counter natural feelings of rejection, the best approach is taking immediate positive action.

- Maintain a positive attitude.
- Evaluate your performance, your Personal Brand Statement, and your Job Application Package.
- Connect with your network for support. Update your contacts list.
- Plan your next job search steps and follow through. Keep moving forward and don't spend too long looking back!

Taking a short breather helps renew your energy and enthusiasm. Allow yourself one day—but no longer—to do something you enjoy and to relax. Then jump back into your Job Search Journey. Rejection is not an excuse for giving up.

Review Chapters 2 and 3, including your Career Action Worksheets with your self-analysis forms (talents, skills, qualifications, special accomplishments, and personal attributes). Visualize yourself performing successfully in your next interview and on your new job. Make a conscious effort to think and act positively and to use positive self-talk and affirmation statements.

© Jupiterimages/Stockbyte/Getty Images.

Customized Packages

You may need to spend more time customizing your resume and cover letter to match the requirements in the job listing. Convince the hiring committee that you are interested in *this* job and *this* company.

Refreshed Resume

You may need to give your resume a face-lift. Print a copy of your master resume and compare it with sample resumes online. Review Chapters 4 and 5 for improvement ideas. For example, highlight and count the action verbs and keywords and make sure you are using them effectively. Request feedback on your resume from your Career Network contacts, such as people who are already in the job you would like.

If these strategies do not seem to help, get professional assistance to reenergize your job search. Make an appointment with a career counselor to get a professional appraisal of your job search strategy and recommendations for new strategies. Work with a resume adviser to make sure your resume stands out in appearance and content.

IF INTERVIEWS DON'T LEAD TO JOB OFFERS

Getting an interview indicates that you were one of the top applicants for the job. Every time you make it to the next stage in the job application process, take a moment to celebrate. Getting interviews is a positive sign—it means your resume, application, and network are working for you.

Most people have several interviews with multiple companies before they are offered a good job. Each company may have a process that includes multiple rounds of interviews.

Take what you learned from each interview to the next one, and use it in your favor. Getting a top-notch job is a full-time job that usually requires several interviews and some rejections.

If you receive a rejection, always ask the interviewer for feedback so you can learn and improve. Try to get a detailed answer. If you weren't the right fit, why? What else were they looking for? See Outcome 3 for more on this topic.

Also consider your interview performance. Do any of these items apply to you?

☐ Was not physically prepared for the interview (on time, well groomed, had copies of Job Application Package, body language, etc.)

☐ Was not mentally prepare for the interview (hesitated over many answers, didn't prepare questions to ask the interviewer about job, forgot interviewer's name, etc.)

☐ Did not show awareness of the company's current situation or industry issues

☐ Did not convince the interviewer that there is a match between qualifications and job requirements

☐ Did not give well-thought-out examples that showed in concrete, measurable way show previous work helped a previous employer

☐ Did not build positive rapport with the employees and support staff

☐ Answers were too long or rambling; gave too many details

☐ Said something negative about a previous employer

☐ Did not convince the interviewer that there is a match between you and the culture of the company

To improve your interview performance, take these actions:

• Review and use Career Action Worksheets 11-3 and 11-4 to evaluate your performance and recall interview details.

• Make notes about the ideal answer to each question you were asked.

• Video-record yourself answering the questions to provide practice and a chance to see how you look to an interviewer.

The Bad Interview

Some interviews are not good; in fact, some are grim. After learning the details of a job, you may be convinced that you don't want it. The interviewer may be inept at interviewing, making it difficult for you to perform well.

Do not stop trying. Do your best to be professional in every interview. You can always learn something beneficial or use the opportunity to polish your interviewing skills.

Never give up *during* an interview. Besides being unprofessional, it could cost you a future reference or a good job lead from the interviewer.

© yanugkelid/Shutterstock.com.

CAUTION It Isn't Always About You

An application for a job can go flat for reasons you cannot control. Be careful about taking rejection personally. Instead, consider these possible alternatives:

- The company may implement a hiring freeze before the position is filled, or the decision maker may decide that the department doesn't need to fill the position.

- The hiring committee may be told to give preference to current employees and local applicants, or they may already know who the "best candidate" is.

- For political reasons, the person who interviewed you may want to defer to the candidate that another member of the committee recommends.

- The last job search may have backfired, and the hiring committee may decide that none of the candidates is a perfect fit.

- The hiring committee may decide, or be told, to postpone the job search. Overall, fewer jobs are filled in May and June, at the close of the current fiscal year.

- The committee may get applications from overqualified applicants and decide to redefine the job responsibilities.

Taking something personally only serves to hurt you—it demotivates you and makes it more difficult to be positive about the next opportunity that comes your way.

- Ask at least one person you do not know well to give you a mock interview.

- Follow the advice in Chapter 10 to prepare for different types of interviews and interview questions.

- Remember what you learned from interviews and use it the next time.

- Do your homework before the next interview!

- Review tips in Chapter 12 about what to do between interviews.

Winners in all fields agree: Perseverance is a major factor in their success. When they meet an obstacle, they find a way around it.

STRATEGIES FOR BETTER OUTCOMES

After receiving a rejection notice, don't take it personally. Instead, take action!

If you're not sure why you were not selected for the job, call the interviewer and ask for an honest evaluation. You may very well learn that the selection had nothing to do with your interview performance or job qualifications. If you are aware of the perceived shortcoming based on the interview or your Job Application Package, it can help to prepare a strong written clarification that you can refer to while making this follow-up call.

The interviewer may be willing to tell you if they consider you to be lacking in any area of skill, training, or experience. This information may be the starting point for an update of your skills or interviewing technique before your next interview.

Some employers are reluctant to offer specific opinions and are justifiably cautious about being sued by job applicants for unfair hiring practices. Even if you don't get concrete help, express your thanks. Remember, if an employer had one job opening, it is possible that they will have another in the future.

Prepare and Respond

If the interviewer is willing to evaluate your performance and make suggestions for improvement, listen carefully and take notes. Accept the concerns expressed, even if you disagree with the observations or opinions. The important point is that they represent problem areas in the interviewer's perception of you.

Real World Scenario 13-2 Larissa had one goal in mind for the Interview stage of her Job Search Journey: follow-up. Whether she was okayed to move forward to the next round of interviews or if she was rejected, she made sure to follow up in a timely fashion. If she received a positive response, she made sure to follow-up with a thank you and relevant details to reinforce her qualifications and fit. If she received a negative response, she made sure to follow up with a thank you and two quick questions about what she could do to improve her performance next time and whether the interviewer had any possible referrals for other opportunities he or she could share. Larissa felt like following up was the most positive way to deal with any situation the Job Search Journey brought her way.

What is a positive way you can handle any rejection you receive?

If you like the company and you want the job, be prepared to *briefly* clarify your qualifications or clear up any misunderstanding. Use a friendly tone and do not react defensively. Remember that you asked for the opinion. If the interviewer seems receptive, explain that you didn't convey your qualifications as completely as you had planned and suggest that you meet once more to review them. Handled well, this approach demonstrates confidence, competence, and assertiveness and can even give you a second chance, if the job is still open or another position becomes available.

Consider Other Departments

Emphasize your enthusiasm for working for the employer and ask whether you are more qualified to fill another position. This strategy encourages the interviewer to give you more consideration and may land you a "hidden job."

Ask for a referral to another employer. Employers are impressed by candidates who demonstrate initiative and confidence. If you project confidence and competence, you greatly increase your chances of convincing others of your potential.

Don't Be Afraid to Reapply

If you don't get a job with a preferred employer now, don't give up. You never know how close you were to being hired. You might be at the top of the list the next time an opening occurs. You'll have the advantage of being known by the employer because a known applicant saves valuable time in recruiting. Stay in touch with the recruiter, HR resource, and interviewer.

Keeping your name in front of the employer can put you first in line for the next opening. One way you can do this is by calling the interviewer every couple of months just to check in. Keep the phone call brief and polite. Your purpose is to keep your name at the top of the list of applicants.

Be Persistent

Be persistent in pursuing your preferred job. Stay focused on your goal and consider all of the factors that may affect the status of the position. Changes in business conditions may affect the status of your target job. Consider how these changes may also present new opportunities to you as a job seeker.

Many companies keep applications in their active file for a specific period of time. If you are interested in a position with a particular company, find out their policy for keeping applications active. You may need to call a prospective employer periodically to keep your application active and to remind the company that you are interested in new job openings.

 CAREER ACTION

Complete Worksheet 13-1
Internet Research on Handling Job Search Rejection, page 343

 CAREER ACTION

Complete Worksheet 13-2
Action Plans for Improving Your Job Search Campaign, page 345

 ## You, Online

Don't Vent on Facebook!

So you found a great company, you got an interview, and you did your absolute best but still didn't get the job. Rule 1—don't take it personally! And whatever you do, don't air your disappointments on a social media site.

When you're frustrated, it's only natural to turn to your social network for moral support, but it's best to keep your venting local and off the computer. What airs on Facebook doesn't always stay on Facebook—or on Twitter or YouTube or anywhere else online. Keep your negative comments to yourself.

Don't assume that just because you didn't get the job the company didn't like you. Perhaps you weren't right for the position, but who's to say you won't be a perfect match for the next opening? Keep your options open and your bridges intact. Leaving things on a positive note shows professionalism and an optimistic outlook—traits that employers appreciate. Here are some steps to take after an unsuccessful interview:

- Write a positive Facebook status update about your experience, mention how you'd like to be considered for future opportunities, and tag the company in the text.
- Send out tweets commending the company on a great interview process.
- Write a note of thanks to everyone who interviewed you. If you don't have their email addresses, search for them on LinkedIn® and Facebook.

Chapter Checklist

Check off each item you can do. Reread sections in this chapter to help you complete the checklist.

- ☐ Take concrete action to recharge my motivation and improve my chances of getting interviews. ❶
- ☐ Re-evaluate your job search strategy. ❶
- ☐ Improve my interview performance so that I get job offers. ❷
- ☐ Ask each interviewer to evaluate my performance so that I can identify any areas that I can improve. ❸
- ☐ Ask for referrals to other departments within the company. ❸
- ☐ Reapply at a later date and call back periodically to check the company's hiring status. ❸

Critical Thinking Questions

1. Which strategies will you use to improve your chances of getting an interview? ❶

2. What specific steps will you take to improve your interview performance? ❷

3. If your friend got a rejection notice after a job interview, what three things could you say to encourage your friend to continue on the Job Search Journey? ❷

4. What can you gain from seeking an evaluation of your interview performance from an interviewer who did not hire you? ❸

5. If all of your efforts fail to result in a job offer, what last request should you make of an interviewer? ❸

Additional Resources

For data files, career resources, and more, visit www.cengagebrain.com.

Trial Run

Write Yourself a Letter

The search for a new job is challenging and often frustrating. This activity may help you put things into perspective and renew your energy.

Take written notes during each part of the activity.

The activity starts in the present day. Jot down words and phrases that describe the general business climate in the country and your community and the key issues in your career field and in your own career.

Think back five years and repeat the activity. Break into teams of people with related career interests. Take notes during the discussion. Reflect on the changes in your career field. How many of the changes were deliberately planned for and implemented? How many changes were unexpected? How did the larger business environment affect your industry? What things that seemed small five years ago turned out to have big consequences? What big things turned out not to be so big after all?

In teams or as a class, project ahead five years. Take notes during the discussion. What changes do you predict in the general business environment and in your career fields? Where do you expect the most changes? How confident are you about these predictions? What are the implications of these changes for the public and for the people working in the field? If what you expect and what you hope for are far apart, what can you start doing to bring them closer together?

Think about these discussions for a few days and reflect on your own career five years ago and five years from now. Write yourself a letter to be opened in five years:

- Describe the circumstances leading to this letter: this assignment, your work situation today, your current plans, recent setbacks, and so on.

- Record your predictions about your situation in five years.

- List helpful actions and "attitude adjustments" you have decided today to take. Be specific about your plans so that in five years, you can judge how well you succeeded.

- Include anything else in your letter that you believe you will enjoy reading in five years or that you believe will be helpful to reflect on.

Put the letter where you will find it or give it to someone who can mail it to you.

This page is intentionally blank.

▶ *CAREER ACTION WORKSHEET*
13-1 Internet Research on Handling Rejection During a Job Search ❶❷❸

Search the Internet for additional tips on persevering after being rejected for a job. Use the search phrase *job search persistence* or *rejection* or go to job sites and blogs you bookmarked in earlier research. What speaks to you? Summarize your findings below, on a blank sheet of paper, or in a text file.

Add your completed work to the "About Me" section of your Career Builder Files.

This page is intentionally blank.

▶ *CAREER ACTION WORKSHEET*

13-2 Action Plans for Improving Your Job Search Campaign ❸

To assess your progress and develop improvement plans, take a look back at your Job Search Journey so far. Answer the following questions, including specific action plans you will take to improve your job search to get the results you want. Check off each item as you complete the actions.

☐ **Self-Analysis** After reviewing your self-analysis activities in the Career Action Worksheets from Chapters 2 and 3, have you overlooked anything important that supports my Job Search Journey? (List the items and describe any needed research or changes.)	
☐ **Your Network** Have you checked with your Career Network members to find out whether they have any new job leads? (List them here and follow up immediately.)	
☐ **Tailored Resume** Could your resume be tailored to a new job target? How could it be improved? Who could do a good job of helping you with it?	
☐ **Reconnect** Should you make additional phone calls/ personal visits or write additional letters to prospective employers? (List details on a separate sheet of paper and begin following up today. Don't put off these actions.)	
☐ **Cover Letters** Could your cover letters be improved? How could they be strengthened? Who can give you advice?	

☐ **Follow-Up** Have you followed up on the cover letters and resumes you have sent? Have you followed up on all job leads? Have you followed up on every interview? (List any follow-up needed in these areas.)	
☐ **Research** Have you done thorough research on your current job leads—enough to talk intelligently and persuasively about how you would fit in with the company? (List any research that must be completed.)	
☐ **More Sources** Have you tried a broad range of job sources? (Refer to the list of suggested job sources in Chapter 6. List any you could use now.)	
☐ **Reapply** Should you reapply with any employers? If so, when?	
☐ **Search Time** Have you scheduled your job search on your daily and weekly calendars?	

Add your completed work to the "About Me" section of your Career Builder Files.

Take Charge of Your Career

OVERVIEW

Chapter 14 has guidelines for succeeding in a new job and growing your career long term. Successfully onboarding to a new job includes developing good work habits and building relationships. As you adjust to and become a master at your new job, you can consider growing your career through pursuing advancement, seeking new challenges, and transitioning to even more fulfilling roles.

OUTCOMES

1. Develop strategies to onboard quickly to your new job.
2. Explain how to build successful relationships.
3. Describe ways to manage your career.
4. Identify signs that it is time to change careers.

CAREER ACTION WORKSHEETS

14-1: Planning Your Work, page 367

14-2: Learn About Your Job Checklist, page 369

14-3: Learn About Your Organization Checklist, page 371

14-4: Internal Resource Network Map, page 373

14-5: Prepare for Advancement, page 375

WHERE ARE YOU ON THE JOURNEY?

PHASE 1: Prepare for the Journey
- *The Job Search Journey*
- *Know Yourself to Market Yourself*
- *Picture Yourself in the Workplace*

PHASE 2: Create Your Resume
- *Plan Your Resume*
- *Write Your Resume*

PHASE 3: Apply for Jobs
- *Find Job Openings*
- *Write Job Applications*
- *Write Effective Tailored Cover Letters*

PHASE 4: Shine at Interviews
- *Know the Interview Essentials*
- *Prepare for Your Interview*
- *Interview Like a Pro*

PHASE 5: Connect, Accept, and Succeed
- *Stay Connected with Prospective Employers*
- *It's an Iterative Process*
- ***Take Charge of Your Career***

Landing the job is just the beginning. The opportunities to grow are limited only by your ability to dream big.

PHASE 5: Connect, Accept, and Succeed

Step 3, *Take Charge of Your Career*

You are in Phase 5, *Connect, Accept, and Succeed*, at step 3, *Take Charge of Your Career*. Your goal in this chapter is to start your new job and grow your career successfully.

ONBOARD QUICKLY TO YOUR NEW JOB

All workers who start new jobs have one challenge in common: adjusting to the new workplace and the new job. This adjustment includes learning to perform specific tasks, learning how your job relates to the business as a whole, learning to work with others, and understanding the formal and informal rules and ways of doing things. Mastering these elements takes time, effort, and training assistance from your employer.

Don't expect to achieve top efficiency or have a high impact overnight. It doesn't happen because everyone has a learning curve prior to contributing at the capability level expected for your role's responsibilities. Experiencing some anxiety while trying to learn so much new information and so many new procedures is normal. Maintaining enthusiasm, an eagerness to learn, and a positive attitude will help you adjust successfully. The attitude you want to display to your new employer is "I'm ready to take on the challenge. I'm excited to be here. You made the right choice!"

The following steps will help you adjust to a new job quickly and set yourself up for long-term success.

Project a Positive, Competent Image

From Day 1 on the job, your goal is to project and maintain a positive, competent image. Transition yourself from the "looking for a job" mindset to the "I got the job!" mindset. Even though you are new on the job, your immediate manager and new coworkers should walk away from every interaction with the perception that you are willing, able, and excited to succeed on the job.

Prepare for your first day by getting into the right mindset. Your image projects from three sources: your inner confidence, your outward appearance, and your verbal and nonverbal communication.

- **Your inner confidence:** Project a positive "can-do," ready to learn attitude. Remember, they hired you because they believe in your ability to get the job done. At the same time, don't start making suggestions on Day 1 of what could be done better or assume you already know everything. Review and practice the tips on self-esteem in Chapter 1, "Maintain a Positive Outlook," on page 11.

- **Your outward appearance:** Plan to show up on time, or even a bit early, on the first day. Prepare the night before with the right clothes, lunch, and transportation. Try to ensure you know where to go and who you will meet first. Bring any forms or additional information requested. Review Chapter 9, "Dress for Success," on page 226.

- **Your verbal and nonverbal communication:** If you project a negative attitude—insecure, bored, unenthusiastic, unfriendly, too passive—through your speech, appearance, and actions, you will be perceived negatively, even if your work is excellent. Maintain friendly, interested language and posture. Review Chapter 9, "Use Positive Body Language," on page 226.

In addition, developing and displaying good work habits also contribute to a competent image. Be ready to do the following:

- Show up to work on time or early, and avoid absenteeism. Always communicate unavoidable absences and avoid surprising your immediate manager.

- Practice punctuality for meetings, deadlines, and assignments. Value others' time and hold yourself accountable to meet goals. Don't procrastinate.

- Keep your work area neat. Organize your space so what you need is easy to find.

- Plan how you will use your time. Don't rely on your immediate manager to keep you on track. Start Day 1 with a planner or other means to keep track of assignments and milestones.

Projecting a positive, professional, and competent image from Day 1 gives you a competitive edge. For example, if you make an error, your professional image may influence people to view the error as a part of learning rather than a sign of incompetence. If you start your relationships on the right foot, coworkers and your immediate manager will be more willing to help you succeed, and your learning curve will be accelerated.

▶ *CAREER ACTION*
Complete Worksheet 14-1

Planning Your Work, page 367

The First Weeks, Step by Step

Once you have the right mindset to approach your first day at work, quickly ramp up your skills and knowledge within the first week and month on the job. During a job interview, you learn general information about the position and the job duties. To perform the work, you need more detailed information. Ask questions during your first month, especially during your first week, to learn about the following four areas: your job, skills/processes needed, your organization, and your key relationships.

Learn About Your Job

First and foremost, you must gain a complete understanding of your role, including what the basic tasks are, what success and poor performance look like, and what you need to accomplish the tasks. When you meet with your immediate manager and even peers who are in similar roles, make sure to ask and understand the following:

- **Basic equipment:** Make sure you receive all the equipment you need to perform your job as soon as possible. Even if this may be your employer's job to do for you, sometimes you have to proactively ensure everything is in place by contacting administrators and HR resources yourself.

- **Job description:** Ask for a job description if you don't already have one. A job description typically identifies the specific duties and responsibilities of the job, the skills and competencies required, the equipment and tools to be used, the expected outcomes and contributions to the organization, and the relationship of the position to other positions within the company.

- **Success measures:** Ask your immediate manager (your main customer, who will be responsible for evaluating your performance!) what success looks like for your job description, as well as what it would look like to go "above and beyond." How can you excel? How does your role help your immediate manager achieve success? How does your role help the organization achieve success?

Career Action Worksheet 14-2 provides a detailed checklist of questions to ask to learn about your job.

▶ *CAREER ACTION*
Complete Worksheet 14-2
Learn About Your Job Checklist, page 369

Learn What Skills and Processes You Will Use

As you learn more about what your job entails, you will also discover what skills are needed and what processes govern your role. Some work processes may directly enable you to get your job done quickly, while other process may be in place to help you succeed and ensure compliance in the workplace with federal or local regulations and laws.

- **Training:** Ask about any training you will receive. Your employer expects you to have the basic knowledge and skills you need to do your job, but you may need additional training for certain tasks.

- **Technology and standard procedures:** Most roles have certain procedures and systems they must use when performing key tasks. The tasks may also require the use of particular software or technology. Ensure you receive training materials and step-by-step guides for any technology and standard procedures that are critical for performing your role.

- **Policies:** Most organizations have a written **employee handbook** that covers policies and procedures such as work hours, the probationary period for new employees, pay and benefits, and rules about using employer equipment and email. Learn the rules and follow them.

- **Performance evaluation:** Ask how and when your job performance will be evaluated. See "Prepare for Your Performance Evaluation" on page 358.

- **Confidential information:** You have a moral and legal obligation to protect internal employer information that is considered confidential. Ensure you understand what confidential information you will encounter in your role and what procedures to follow to protect such information. When you are hired, you may be required to sign a nondisclosure agreement that defines the type of information that may not be shared with outsiders and the penalties for violating the agreement. Employers dismiss and often sue employees who are found to have leaked confidential information, even if done accidentally.

Learn About Your Organization

Becoming a great employee who is recognized and rewarded often comes from developing a deep understand of how your role contributes to the employer's success. When you first join a new organization and start a new job, you have a great opportunity to ask as many questions as you want—because it is expected! Learn as much as you can about your employer, including:

- **Organizational and departmental values, mission statement, and goals:** Take the time to understand how your role aligns with not only your department's goals but also the broader employer's goals. Understand what business results are measured and what business results your work directly contributes to.

- **Employer culture:** In addition to concrete business metrics, every organization has a unique personality and culture that is expressed in many ways, from the employer's mission statement to the way employees dress for work. To enhance your success, learn and adhere to the culture's values, including the expected work ethic and the customs and rules for interacting with coworkers and customers. Many of the elements that make up "how things are done" are not spelled out. Observe your coworkers and ask a trusted coworker for advice.

- **Products or services, industry, and competitors:** What business is your organization in? What products and services do they offer to customers? Who are they competing with? What products and services are you working on in your role?

- **Future vision:** Request the latest annual report and organizational targets for the next year and next five years if available.

- **Employer history:** Understand the major changes that have shaped your employer.

▶ *CAREER ACTION*
Complete Worksheet 14-3
Learn About Your Organization Checklist, page 371

Learn About Key Relationships

Similar to finding a job, succeeding in a job often hinges on knowing the right people. Furthermore, in a job, it is even more important to spend time developing and building these relationships. Below are the relationships that are important to establish during onboarding in your first weeks. In Outcome 2, you will learn in detail how to build those relationships over the life of your career.

- **Immediate manager:** Your immediate manager guides and designs your work plan, measures your performance, and enables you to deliver results.

- **Immediate coworkers:** Your immediate manager may have multiple direct reports in similar roles to you. You may or may not work directly with these coworkers on projects and assignments.

- **Team members:** Who will you be working with to deliver results, if any? Your role may be very individual. In other roles, for assignments and projects, you may have team members that report to other immediate managers in your organization.

- **Internal customers:** Who does your work impact when you deliver tasks and results? These are your internal customers.

- **Coaches or mentors:** Who will be training you initially? Who can you go to when you have questions? Coaches and mentors may be informal and people who, in your initial introductions, showed interest in helping you find your way around and learn your role. They may also be formally assigned by your immediate manager. You may also ask your immediate manager for coaches and mentors if you'd like help and don't know who would be a good resource.

- **HR/administrative support:** Who do you go to when you have questions on benefits and policies? Who do you go to when you need equipment or technical support?

- **Leaders:** Who is your immediate manager's boss? Who are the top leaders in the organization?

Create a map of your network using Career Action Worksheet 14-4.

▶ *CAREER ACTION*
Complete Worksheet 14-4
Internal Resource Network Map, page 373

BUILD GREAT WORK RELATIONSHIPS

OUTCOME 2

The ability to interact well with immediate managers, coworkers, suppliers, customers, and others is a critical skill in every workplace. There are very few roles that do not involve some kind of dependency on others to succeed. Your work is guided and reviewed by your immediate manager, is impacted by others' contributions to your tasks, and contributes to others' success as well. While it isn't necessary to be close friends with everyone at work, do not underestimate the importance of developing effective relationships at work.

Develop a Good Relationship with Your Immediate Manager

A good working relationship with your immediate manager is essential because you need your immediate manager's advice, help, and general understanding to do your work and because ultimately, your immediate manager determines your performance review, rating, and career growth. Depending on your job, you may have day-to-day personal contact with your immediate manager or only occasional direct contact. When you are first hired, however, you can usually count on spending time together. Do not act flustered if you don't understand everything that is being explained about your job. Don't be afraid to ask many questions to ensure you thoroughly understand. At the beginning of your job, this is expected and shows you are motivated to be successful at your new job.

Your immediate manager's key responsibility is to ensure that his or her group produces the assigned amount of work on time and within acceptable levels of quality. To build a strong relationship with your immediate manager and perform well, consider the following strategies:

- **Deliver as expected.** When you receive an assignment, ensure you understand what high-quality results look like and that you have the resources you need to complete the task. Realize that delivering your results contributes to your immediate manager's goals as well. Find out what your immediate manager needs to meet the group's or department's goals and do what you can to provide it.

- **Learn your immediate manager's work style.** How does your immediate manager like to be communicated with? How often does he or she like status updates? Where do your styles align and where do they differ? Inform your manager how you best work and consider as much as possible what works best for him or her.

- **Balance priorities.** If you get a new assignment that will mean not meeting your deadlines for other work, ask your immediate manager which work should be completed first.

- **Resolve problems.** Before you approach your immediate manager about a problem, demonstrate your initiative by thinking of possible solutions. Even though your problem may seem like the biggest priority on your list, your immediate manager has many more priorities, so make it easy for them to help you. Offer your own ideas, but don't press for your opinion or ideas if other people have information that you didn't. Always do your best work to support the final decision, no matter whose idea it was.

- **Suggest improvements.** If you find a faster way to do your work—without cutting corners or having a negative effect on someone else's work—use a cautious approach. A process that may seem inefficient or that is different from the method used in your previous job may serve a purpose that is not immediately apparent to you. If you think a technique could be improved, request a meeting with your immediate manager to clarify the reasons for using it. Asking thoughtful questions is a good strategy for opening the discussion. Once you understand the reasoning behind the current process, if you still have ideas for improvement, move forward with sharing your suggestions.

- **Ask for feedback regularly.** Ideally quarterly, ask your immediate manager directly whether your performance is meeting expectations or if you need to improve. Ask for specific recommendations for improvement as necessary so you can make noticeable changes prior to your annual performance review. Learn to take feedback well—any feedback is valuable, whether it is negative or positive. Don't react defensively or blame others. Accept the criticism professionally and make improvements. To learn from your mistakes, ask for suggestions about how you can improve the situation. If you don't think the criticism is justified, tactfully present evidence that supports your opinion. If your employer or immediate manager continually criticizes you unfairly, particularly in front of others, request a meeting to discuss the reason for this behavior. If the criticism continues even though you make the recommended improvements, consider seeking assistance from a mentor or HR, before considering a position in another department or looking for a new employer.

By doing all of the above, you earn trust. Trust can make or break your relationship with your immediate manager. A trusting relationship depends on open and honest communication. Avoid surprises with your immediate manager and keep the focus on what will help you deliver the results you have been tasked to do.

Develop Good Relationships with Your Coworkers and Team Members

The way you relate to the people you work with will influence your career success as much as the quality of your job performance— no matter how skilled or educated you are. Studies repeatedly verify that job failure is most frequently the result of poor interpersonal skills (behavior and attitude), not lack of skill.

- **Learn the roles and priorities of the coworkers and team members you work the most closely with.** Understanding their barriers to helping you and how you can help them achieve their goals will enable you to succeed and build positive relationships.

- **Get to know your coworkers.** Be friendly and approachable; do not get a reputation as a loner. However, maintain stable emotions in the workplace, leaving your personal problems at home.

- **Treat people the way you want to be treated.** Help others accomplish their assignments, compliment them on work well done, critique their work tactfully only when necessary, and listen to what they have to say. This behavior encourages others to treat you the same way.

- **Be accountable for your own work.** Check your work so that no one else has to correct it. Meet your deadlines and deliver outstanding work. Don't make excuses or complain about your workload.

- **Stay out of office politics.** Don't take sides when coworkers disagree about something that is not directly related to *your* work. Gossip is not harmless; misinformation and half-truths can damage a person's reputation and career. Develop a reputation for being discreet and courteous—your coworkers will respect you, and it's a good business decision. Don't look for problems or hold grudges.

- **Respect the work environment and culture.** Turn off your cell phone and conduct conversations privately, not over the tops of cubicles or while standing in front of someone's cubicle.

To be an effective employee (and for your own advantage), be aware of organizational politics. Every organization has formal and informal politics. Learn who is respected— or even feared. These people often influence office politics. Learn to deal with them successfully. First impressions are not always accurate, so take time to observe and learn office politics. Avoid affiliating with "complainers" who are not in harmony with your employer's philosophy.

Develop Good Relationships with Internal Customers

You may work in a department where you do not interact with the people or organizations that keep your employer in business by

Real World Scenario 14-1 Mia was assigned to a project with a coworker she didn't know if she would get along with. In the past, the coworker often complained about assignments and accused others of not doing their fair share. Mia decided to take a different approach and try to set the relationship up for success from the beginning. Prior to her first meeting, she took a look at the work and determined what she thought a fair split would be based on time and her personal strengths. When she met with her coworker, she started by saying, "I haven't really gotten a chance to know you since I started here. Mind if I learn a little more about your time here?" She allowed the coworker to share her story and then they talked about the project at hand. She asked open-ended questions such as "What work would you most like to do?" and listened to the answer. It turned out that there were some items they agreed on and some they didn't. Mia first acknowledged where they agreed and then assertively explained her reasoning on the items they didn't. She made sure to document the final agreement and shared her approach with their immediate manager. She planned to keep her immediate manager informed on the status of the project and ask for help if needed.

How can you handle a difficult relationship with positivity and assertiveness?

buying its goods or services. Nevertheless, you have internal customers—the people or groups that depend on your department (or on you) to help them get their jobs done.

If you work in the marketing department, for example, the product development group is your customer because it depends on you to develop effective marketing campaigns. Get to know who your internal customers are, what their needs are, and how they depend on you or your group; then go out of your way to provide great service.

Diversity in the Workplace

As you build relationships, it's important to respect diversity and use your communication skills to build bridges instead of creating divisions. Diversity is important in the workplace because it increases adaptability, allows for greater ability to meet diverse customers' needs, and increases the variety of solutions and ideas available. Do not exclude anyone or treat anyone differently because of factors such as race, gender, age, religion, or physical ability. People from a different background may have a different approach or understanding of tasks than you. It's important to keep in mind that often there is no wrong or right answer.

People have different communication styles, including you! Even in the same culture, people have different communication styles. They process information differently, approach problems differently, want information given to them differently, and socialize differently. Learning the different styles of the people you deal with and adapting your style accordingly can be an important tool in resolving disputes and avoiding conflicts in the workplace.

Ethnicities in a diverse workplace often translate into working from a different set of assumptions of what is appropriate versus inappropriate in the workplace. For example, perceptions of time may be different between a person of an Indian background versus Hispanic background versus American background. Communication styles may be different—Europeans often have a much more direct style, and Asians may have a more subtle approach.

Gender has also been discussed heavily in the workplace. Perceptions of leadership skills and communication ability often differ based on gender. It's important to recognize there is often no right way of approaching work and that each approach has its own benefits.

MAKE IT A HABIT
Be a Lifelong Learner

Rapidly changing technology and a global economy have created a fast-changing world. Jobs and careers will continue to evolve. To have a successful career and distinguish yourself from the pack, you must keep your skills up to date, keep growing your network, and be prepared to learn new skills quickly. In short, you must make learning a lifelong pursuit.

There are many ways to continue learning and avoid being left behind. For example:

- Finish your college degree if you haven't already done so.
- Keep your licenses and certifications up to date. Expand you options by getting new certifications for your profession.
- Take continuing education courses.
- Use the resources of your professional association or industry trade group. Join the local chapter and attend meetings, subscribe to newsletters, and read blogs.

- Use free online training resources for software and for business topics such as teamwork and marketing.
- Follow industry experts on Twitter. Join LinkedIn® groups that relate to your career field.

In all of these ways, you will also grow your network and meet people you can learn from and help. Share what you learn with your immediate manager and team. Your commitment to education and training will help you achieve career success.

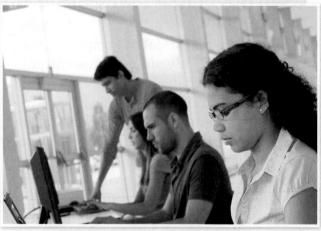

© Goodluz/Shutterstock.com.

Another trending diversity topic is generations in the workplace. For the next 10 years, we will have four generations working side by side in the workplace. These four generations span over 75 years of cultural influences and events that create traits and expectations in the workplace. A more tenured employee may have a certain way of doing things that a younger employee may need to understand. A younger employee may have different expectations given the state of the workplace today that an older employee may need to understand.

An important skill to develop when interacting in a diverse environment is active listening. Wikipedia defines **active listening**

as a "communication technique that requires the listener to understand, interpret, and evaluate what (s)he hears." It is listening with the goal of understanding fully what the speaker intends and is a powerful tool for gaining information and solving problems.

In a conversation, give the other person your full attention. Focus on what is being said, look directly at the other person, and do not interrupt. Acknowledge that you are listening using body language such as nodding. Once the person has shared his or her message, rephrase what you heard in your own words. Ask questions to show the other person that you want to understand. A good rule of thumb is to listen twice as much as you talk. You do not have to agree on all items. However, you must be willing to respect disagreements and honor all viewpoints. Try to find at least one thing you can agree on and start from that point to move forward. Again, acknowledge that it is okay for someone to approach a task differently than you may approach it.

MANAGE YOUR CAREER

Work takes up a large portion of the average adult's time. Use the following techniques to maximize the time you spend on work.

Learn About Your Compensation and Benefits

Take the time to learn about employee benefits and take full advantage of those that can help you save and invest your money, in both the short term and long term.

Enroll in benefit programs, including health, disability, and life insurance, at the start of your employment and update your benefit selections according to your employer's schedule (usually annually). Your employer subsidizes costs of these benefits, so generally it's more affordable than buying these benefits on your own. If your new position doesn't have all of the benefits you had hoped for, you may need to make alternative plans for health and disability insurance. These are available through professional organizations, credit unions, auto clubs, and alumni groups.

If you are fortunate to have a job, you owe it to yourself and to the people who depend on you to *get into the habit of saving money.* No matter how little, save money and deposit into a savings account out of every paycheck you earn.

Small savings add up. For a week or two, keep track of (1) how much you spend on food and (2) where you spend this money. Then make some of these changes and see how much you can save: eat dinner at home more often, make your own coffee, take your lunch to work twice a week, stay away from vending machines, and/or fill plastic water bottles with filtered water from your kitchen sink.

Finally, it is *never* too early to start saving for retirement, so take advantage of any savings and investment plans that your employer offers. Because you save your own money and often get contributions from your employer, this is one of the best ways to save for retirement. Depending on your plan, the amount you put aside can reduce your taxable income, the gains aren't taxed until you retire, and you may draw from the plan to pay for your education or buy a home.

You should also get investment and retirement savings advice from a financial planner or an investment banker who can help you establish an individual retirement account (IRA) if desired. Some companies offer access to advisers for their employees. Do your research on the opportunities your new employer offers!

Earn Your Advancement or Promotion

If you like your employer and want to advance in your career there, find out what it takes to get promoted or gain advancement. To grow in your career, you do not always have to move up. You can also move across to another role that may grow you in different ways than your career role. By mixing a variety of roles *laterally and vertically*, you will have a rich, satisfying career with new opportunities, growth, and recognition.

- **Tell your immediate manager that you are willing to take on new responsibilities.** Negotiate your work plan to include stretching goals or tasks that you are interested in. Demonstrate your ability to handle new responsibilities by acting professionally, working hard, and successfully taking on challenges on the job.

When Douglas first signed the job offer, he didn't realize there would be so many opportunities to take advantage of with his new employer. He always had a bank account, but now learned about two investments accounts he would like to set up for retirement planning. He also wanted to set aside money specifically for his daughter's college education. He didn't know where to start but he thought it wouldn't hurt to ask. So he asked his HR resource and his immediate manager for help. The HR resource took time to explain to him the different ways the employer incentivized establishing various accounts. His immediate manager gave him contact information for a financial advisor. Although Douglas knew it would take additional time and research, he wanted to set himself up for long-term success from the start of his new job.

What opportunities are you not taking advantage of that would jump-start your career success?

- **Learn about the new responsibilities you would have.** That way, your immediate manager will know that you are ready to be promoted because you understand the duties of the new position and can be trusted to become productive in that position quickly. For insight, talk to a mentor or employees who currently have the position you would like. If possible, talk to your immediate manager and take on projects that allow you to learn these new responsibilities or offer to help someone with their work in the role you are targeting. Often, if you can already do the job at the next level, it makes it easy for an immediate manager to promote you into that position.

- **Find a mentor.** A mentor is someone inside or outside your organization who can advise and coach you—someone who is respected and knowledgeable in your field. Seek advice from mentors who are experienced in the areas you need to improve. Don't limit yourself to just one mentor. Look for people who are sensitive to your concerns, who help you learn new skills, and/or who take time to explain organizational dynamics. Strive to meet your mentors' expectations for your performance.

- **Increase your visibility.** Get involved in organizational committees and cross-team projects in which you can excel. Meet people outside your direct line of management. Show extra initiative and demonstrate leadership. Develop your speaking abilities. Having multiple people who can positively speak on your behalf can really help you get a promotion or new role—think of these people as internal references, similar to the references you enrolled during your Job Search Journey.

- **Show initiative.** Personal initiative is a major factor affecting your immediate manager's opinion of your suitability for taking on more responsibility and being promoted. When you finish your assigned duties, don't sit and wait for more work to be assigned. Find an appropriate task to perform on your own, notify your immediate manager that you are ready for another assignment, or ask how you can help someone else. Think creatively about better ways to do your job. Then research and plan how to implement your ideas.

- **Maintain documentation.** Keep track of positive feedback you receive from internal and external customers on work you have delivered. You can use these as support when discussing opportunities for promotion.

Always display the qualities that your employer perceived in you when you were hired. Make your employer glad that he or she chose you.

- **Expand your knowledge and skills.** Identify your greatest working strengths and interests and build on them. Take advantage of all training in these areas. Become known for your special expertise. This will help focus your career in a direction that best suits you and will expand your career opportunities.

  - Stay current in your job and industry knowledge.

  - Get involved in professional groups, training, and education.

  - Learn all phases of the organization, its goals, and how each job is designed to meet the overall goals.

- **Suggest ways to improve work procedures.** There is a right time, place, and method for presenting your ideas or suggestions to your immediate manager. Don't complain or criticize. Learn by observing how others present their ideas. Explain (and show) how your idea can improve a problem area (a cheaper vendor for office supplies, for example) and offer it as a suggestion for consideration. Do not try to bulldoze your ideas through.

- **Use subtle self-promotion techniques.** Sometimes it's not enough to perform well; you must also make your superiors aware of your achievements—without bragging. Focus on your experience, not on yourself. Whenever you talk with coworkers and immediate managers, be positive and enthusiastic about your job and your projects. Speak with confidence about your experience and accomplishments, but avoid making too many "I" statements.

▶ **CAREER ACTION**
Complete Worksheet 14-5
Prepare for Advancement, page 375

Prepare for Your Performance Evaluation

Learn how and when you will be evaluated on your job performance so that you know where to focus your efforts to achieve a good evaluation. This will also help you avoid overlooking an area that is important to your employer.

Find out how heavily the employer weighs each performance area so that you can concentrate on the most important ones. If you don't receive this information with your other employment documents, ask your immediate manager or HR resource to explain the evaluation process.

If your employer uses an informal method of job evaluation, ask what is considered good job performance and what criteria are used in determining promotions and raises. This will provide you with guidelines for your successful performance. As you become more knowledgeable about your job, show initiative by setting your own goals and deadlines for improving performance and growing in the job.

©iStock.com/MichaelDeLeon.

Adapt to Changes in Your Employer and Industry

Your working life—the period of time in your life when you work—will last about 55 years, and maybe longer. Over the course of your working life, changes will occur in the organizations you work for, in society, in your industry, and in every industry. Keep an open, flexible attitude toward changes at work. Don't make yourself obsolete through stubborn resistance; you may miss an open door to a career development opportunity.

Expect differences (some major) between the way your employer conducts business and the methods you learned in school or on another job. While schools often teach theories, employers interpret and apply theories and techniques (often developing their own) to accomplish specific work goals and tasks. Changes in technology make some textbook theories obsolete. Personalities also influence work methods.

Continually update your skills and knowledge through education and training. Request training and if you are not able to participate, find informal ways to stay up to date using the Internet or outside of work resources such as professional associations. You are living in an economy that is based increasingly on knowledge and service and less on manufacturing and goods.

IS IT TIME FOR A CHANGE?

A job involves performing a designated set of responsibilities and duties for a specific employer. A career encompasses a family of jobs. Your career is your life's work. Thus, *high school history teacher for Washington High School* is a job and *teaching* is a career. Similarly, *evening wear salesclerk for the After Five store* is a job and *retail sales* is a career.

You, Online

Keep Your Career on Track with Social Networking

Building a career is not just something you do between jobs. It should be something you think about even when you're happy in your work. It's important to keep your skills sharp, to stay up to date in industry advances, and to keep yourself relevant in the field. Social media sites are ideal for ongoing career networking and development because they are free or low cost and require little investment of time. There's really no excuse not to take charge of your career online!

- Keep your LinkedIn® profile updated and check in regularly to expand your network as you meet people in your line of work. Request recommendations from coworkers who can attest to your proficiency and professionalism and join groups that relate to your career field.

- Subscribe to email updates and newsletters for top industry blogs. Don't be afraid to comment on articles that interest you and share your own knowledge.
- Do periodic searches on Twitter using industry-specific keywords. Respond to and retweet interesting tweets you find. Share articles you've discovered using Twitter and establish yourself as a knowledgeable professional.

If social media participation is encouraged, show your support for your employer by speaking well of the employer and its personnel, products, and services. Speaking negatively about an organization harms its reputation and may result in your being fired. Never post negative remarks about your employer online.

Many people don't understand the difference between a job and a career. As a result, they spend a great deal of time and money changing careers when they only need to change jobs. In other cases, people change jobs repeatedly and continue to be dissatisfied because they're not in the right career. Most people change jobs at least eight times during their working lives. With changes in technology and in people's values and interests, it's also common for people to change careers at least once during their lifetime.

If you realize that your current employment situation is no longer satisfying, consider whether the dissatisfaction is with your career or with the specific job. If you're unhappy with your immediate manager but enjoy your work, for example, you may need to change jobs. If you don't enjoy the type of work you do, however, you may want to consider a career change.

Think Carefully Before Changing Jobs

You may want to consider a job change if:

- Your current employer can't offer you job growth or advancement
- A poor economy requires layoffs or an entire class of jobs is being shipped overseas in an offshoring trend
- You want to move to a new location
- Your department is dissolving
- Your philosophy and values conflict with those of your current employer
- You want a new challenge

Give any change of job serious thought and planning. A job may look good, but without proper research, you could find yourself in a situation that is as bad as or worse than your current one. Evaluate your current job by asking yourself, "Is there room for advancement, or are other important opportunities available?" If the answer is no and you will not be happy staying in your current position, you have strong grounds for considering a new employer. If the answer is yes, there may be advantages to staying with your current employer.

Seeking advancement or growth with your current employer can offer many advantages, including the following:

- Staying is less risky because you are already established and don't need to repeat the process of adjusting to new surroundings and people.
- Your reputation for job stability is better if you stay rather than move frequently from one employer to another.
- In outsourcing and offshoring situations, some employers recognize the value of keeping their best employees. They may offer you retraining opportunities and help you transition out of a vulnerable position.
- You won't lose accumulated benefits such as vacation time, retirement, and profit sharing.
- If your current job offers important benefits such as healthcare coverage and life insurance, it can be risky to give them up. With today's rising cost of benefits, some employers are finding it too expensive to provide extensive coverage. When considering a job change, always consider benefits in conjunction with rewards and compensation.

Alternatively, changing employers can also offer many advantages, including the following:

- You increase your job engagement and motivation by becoming involved with new challenges, surroundings, and people.
- A job change may result in quicker advancement than you could achieve by seeking a promotion in your current organization.

Take Stock of Your Situation

Accepting a job or changing jobs is a big decision! On average, Americans who are fully employed spend 2,000 hours per year at work. When you consider a job offer, think about your current situation and your goals for the future.

If You Have a Job:

- Are you sure you want to change jobs?

- Why do you think the new job is a better opportunity?

- Does the work sound as interesting as you thought it would?

- Is the new job in a more stable industry or with a more stable employer?

- Will you have more opportunities for advancement or more interesting work?

- Do you like your future immediate manager and future coworkers?

- Does the new job have better benefits?

- Have you hit a plateau in your current job?

If You Are Not Working:

- How long have you been looking for a job?

- How much longer can you afford to look for a job?

- How many jobs have you applied for without getting an interview?

- How many interviews have you had without getting a job offer?

- What is the job market like where you live?

- Are you willing to take the risk of declining a job?

- What is your backup plan if you decline a job?

Ask a career professional and a trusted member of your network (or both) for help weighing the pros and cons of your decisions.

© pan_kung/Shutterstock.com.

- You gain knowledge, broaden your experience, and increase your Career Network, expanding your career growth opportunities.

- You start with a clean slate as you develop your reputation for good job performance.

Strategies if You Want to Change Jobs

Before you quit your current job, make sure you follow these strategies:

- Reconnect with your network. To achieve the greatest levels of career success, stay in touch with your contacts so that you are ready the next time you want to pursue a career goal.

- Try to avoid quitting your job before you have a new one. If possible, complete your job change while you are still employed. Because being employed is current proof that you do a job satisfactorily, you're considered more employable when you're currently working.

©iStock.com/4x6.

CAUTION
Think Like a Free Agent

An employer and an employee are partners in a contract that must work for both parties. A job may be temporary, so think about your options and be prepared to take the next step in your career. Being able to adapt to change is also a valuable life skill. If you lose your job and cannot find a full-time position, you may need to consider a series of part-time jobs until you find full-time employment. One of your achievements in this course is your Master Career Portfolio. You may also need to develop a "portfolio career"—a career made up of a variety of jobs and activities that capitalize on your strengths and provide an acceptable level of income. These may include part-time jobs, temporary jobs, contract work, and maybe even a hobby that that you can turn into a home-based business.

- Do your current job to the best of your ability through your last day on the job. You're most likely to be remembered by how well you performed at the end of your employment. This can greatly influence the quality of future references from your current employer.

- Update your Master Career Portfolio before you leave. Assemble samples of your work and documentation of your achievements that are pertinent and exemplary. Update your resume. Ask your coworkers and immediate manager to recommend you on LinkedIn®. Add documents from each job you hold, such as your job description and performance evaluations. Print copies of emails commending your work and forward them to your personal email account.

- Plan for an orderly and efficient transition of your responsibilities to the person taking your place. If you are asked to help train your replacement, be as thorough as possible, taking care to explain your duties clearly and completely.

- Give your current employer at least two weeks' written notice before you leave your job. This is common courtesy and is important in maintaining good standing with your employer. Giving less notice is considered unprofessional. You should submit a formal letter of resignation.

- Resign professionally. Make every effort to leave your current employer with good feelings; do not leave in anger or with hostility no matter how dissatisfied you might be. Throughout your career, references from your past employers will be requested each time you seek a new job. If possible, request a letter of recommendation prior to your last day.

Changing Careers

If, after thorough consideration, you decide that you aren't happy in your work and that a change to another job in the same field would not bring satisfaction, you may want to consider a career change. Ask yourself the following questions:

- **Have I changed positions several times only to find that I'm still unhappy?** Repeated changes of employment that don't improve your job satisfaction may indicate a career problem, not a job problem.

- **Are my problems the result of personality or philosophical conflicts with my immediate manager or coworkers?** If so, it's likely that you need a new employer rather than a new career. The exception occurs when the types of people usually found in your career field, regardless of the organization, don't fit your personality or philosophy.

- **Am I unhappy with the work environment?** If you don't like working at a desk, for example, decide whether this is common to your career field or only to your job. Would you prefer outdoor work? You may want to look at other careers if your career doesn't provide the opportunity for the type of work you want. Is your problem with the work environment common to the career or only to some jobs in the career field?

- **Am I constrained in expressing my values?** Again, is this a function of your job or your career?

- **Is my position interesting?** What are your interests? Are you unable to satisfy them in your career or just in your current job?

- **Am I frustrated that I'm not using my skills and abilities?** Is this a job-related or career-related problem?

Even if you determine that your unhappiness is related to your career rather than your current job, you still have to weigh the pros and cons of making a career change. Rarely can you just jump into another career without making sacrifices, such as taking a cut in pay. You need to evaluate the advantages and disadvantages and decide whether you're gaining more than you're losing.

Reassess Your Situation

First, determine what alternative careers fit your interests and abilities. Study the options to decide which career you think is the best fit. Apply the strategies in Chapters 2 and 3. Then after you have selected an alternative career, find out what additional education or training you need, how long it takes to prepare for the field, and what it will cost. Also determine whether the education or training is available nearby and whether you can get the necessary skills while continuing your current job or if you need to return to school and/or relocate.

Be Realistic

What are the job opportunities in the new field? Are the jobs in a desirable location, and will the pay meet your requirements? Be aware that when you change careers, you often have to start over at the entry-level salary.

What kind of risk taker are you? Are you willing to give up the security of your current position and career and take a chance? Do you expect to be significantly more satisfied in the new career? In the final analysis, decide whether the probable advantages of a new opportunity sufficiently outweigh the disadvantages and whether you are willing to assume any risk involved.

You must also be prepared to discuss your decision persuasively with prospective employers who may question whether you will be happy with such a career change. It is important to convey to employers that you have considered and planned for this change carefully and that you believe the advantages outweigh the disadvantages.

Congratulations! You've come to the end of the Job Search Journey and the beginning of a career. You've done a great deal of work in the activities in *Your Career: How to Make It Happen*. The advice and cautions you have learned and the documents you have created can help you stay ahead of the competition throughout your career. Save the work you've done in this class—you'll be glad you did.

Chapter Checklist

Check off each item you can do. Reread sections in this chapter to help you complete the checklist.

☐ Transition my mindset from finding a job to confidently starting my career. **❶**

☐ Create a plan for my first weeks at work that include learning about my new role, skills needed, organization, and resources. **❶**

☐ Able to discover what success looks like for my role, from my immediate manager's point of view and from the organization's point of view. **❶**

☐ Identify who makes up my network at work. **❶**

☐ Know what is needed to build and develop long-lasting relationships at work. **❷**

☐ Understand how to work well and communicate with my immediate manager. **❷**

☐ Maximize my compensation and benefits to support my life and career. **❸**

☐ Expect changes in the workplace to occur and be flexible and adaptable when faced with changes. **❸**

☐ Take steps to become—and be seen as—promotable. **❸**

☐ Stay in contact with network members and add to my network. **❹**

☐ Evaluate whether it is time to change jobs. **❹**

☐ Evaluate whether this career is the best fit. **❹**

☐ Keep good records of job duties and accomplishments in every position and be prepared to begin a job search quickly and efficiently. **❹**

Critical Thinking Questions

1. What differences are there in mindset, habits, and approach between finding a job and starting a job? **❶**

2. What five things can you do to master a new job? **❶**

3. Why is it important to develop many positive relationships at work? **❷**

4. Why is it important to know how your performance will be evaluated? **❸**

5. Who is responsible for the growth of your career? What are five things you can do to help yourself stay satisfied? **❸** **❹**

6. Why is it essential to adapt to change? How can you demonstrate that you are flexible and adaptable? **❸**

7. What additional training or course work could you take to increase your knowledge and skills? **❸**

8. Why should you be very careful when considering changing jobs or careers? What are the potential consequences? **❹**

Additional Resources

For data files, career resources, and more, visit www.cengagebrain.com.

Trial Run

Follow Your Leader

Every field has thought leaders or leading organizations. For example, in accounting, every year there is a CPA Practice Advisor Thought Leader Symposium. Do an Internet search on your career path. Who are some of the thought leaders or award winners in your career of choice? Pick two thought leaders and review their bios. Take a look at their LinkedIn® profiles and social media feeds. Answer the following questions for each leader:

Question	Leader: _____	Leader: _____
1. Did they have multiple job or career changes?		
2. How did each job or career change contribute to their successful position today?		
3. What values and strengths do they have and/or admire?		
4. What surprised or inspired you about their career path?		
5. From your review, summarize how they achieved success in their career.		

This page is intentionally blank.

▶ *CAREER ACTION WORKSHEET*
14-1 Planning Your Work ❶

Most successful people have a written plan. Start your new job with a solid plan. Update your plan as you learn more on the job. Check off the following planning items as you put them in place during your first days at work.

Your organization systems: Starting a new job requires new organization systems.

☐ **Get a system.** Before your first day, get prepared by selecting some type of planner to organize your workweeks: a spiral-bound planner, the planner in your email program or some other planner on your computer, or a planner app on your smartphone.

☐ **Determine priorities.** Determine your priorities and plan your work around them. Ask your immediate manager and coworkers what tasks are most vital to the successful operation of your department. Prioritize your work based on their answers.

☐ **Form daily habits.** At the beginning or end of the day, take 5 or 10 minutes to plan the day's work. On paper or online, make a list of the things you need to do that day.

☐ **Diligently record.** Record appointments, meetings, assignments, deadlines, and reminders. Enter important tasks and dates as soon as you learn of them so that you don't forget to enter them later. Consider using one color for work obligations and another color for personal obligations.

Block off time to work on larger projects and longer-term assignments so that you don't end up having to do them all at once and miss deadlines for your ongoing work. For example, if you are giving a presentation at a meeting on Thursday, block off time to work on the presentation on Monday, Tuesday, and Wednesday. Make larger projects achievable by listing the smaller steps you need to do. Using to-do lists is a powerful, yet simple way to help you manage and achieve milestones in a large project. Here are some helpful approaches to to-do lists:

Manage Large Projects Well

- Put the most important tasks at the top of the list (tasks that need immediate attention or completion).

- List the tasks as you think of them and then label them A (most important tasks), B (tasks to do after you complete the A tasks), and C (tasks with no specific deadline).

- Beside each task, write the deadline for completing it and the amount of time you think it will take. Be realistic about time requirements, especially when you are new on the job, and ask your immediate manager or a coworker for advice.

- Group similar tasks and complete them in one block of time. This focuses your attention and enhances task performance. For example, schedule one block of time to prepare documents and another to place phone calls.

Reassess Priorities

As new tasks are assigned, periodically review your priorities with your team or immediate manager. Here are questions that you can ask to make the conversation go smoothly:

- Here are our top priorities as I see it for the next week. Do you agree with these?

- Help me understand what has changed that might impact our (or my) priorities.

- If this is our (or my) new set of priorities, can we change the due dates on these other items? If not, what additional resources can we get to assure we have capacity to meet the deadlines and the new priorities?

Add your completed work to the "About Jobs" section of your Career Builder Files.

▶ CAREER ACTION WORKSHEET
14-2 Learn About Your Job Checklist ❶

Use this worksheet as a template to ask questions and note answers as you learn about your role and the skills needed to perform your best.

✔	Question/Task	Notes/Findings
	Obtain a copy of your detailed job description	
	Obtain and discuss your work plan with your immediate manager	
	What are the primary individual assignments you will be spending the majority of your day on?	
	How is success measured for each assignment?	
	What tools will you need to complete each assignment?	
	Who will you interact with for each assignment?	
	How is success measured for your overall role?	
	What knowledge and skills are critical for you to deliver each assignment?	
	What gaps do you have in the knowledge needed to deliver each assignment?	

✔	Question/Task	Notes/Findings
	What training do you need to close each gap in knowledge? (Include both formal classroom training and informal training such as shadowing others along with coach, mentor, and immediate manager guidance and feedback)	
	What is the expected timeline for gaining the knowledge? Put formal trainings on your calendar and note the expected time it should take for informal training to be completed.	
	When are you expected to be a fully functioning, high-performing employee? What is the expected length of onboarding time?	
	Have I filled out all the necessary HR paperwork and reviewed it carefully?	
	Do I have all the equipment necessary to do my job and access my work environment? (computer, phone, uniform, tools, security badge, etc.)	
	Have I been added to the appropriate lists for internal email conferences, information distribution, project teams, etc.?	
	Have I understood all employer policies, including confidentiality procedures, performance, payroll, vacations, and benefits?	

Add your completed work to the "About Jobs" section of your Career Builder Files.

▶ CAREER ACTION WORKSHEET

14-3 Learn About Your Organization Checklist ❶

Use this worksheet as a template to ask questions and note answers as you learn about the organization and how you will play a role in helping the organization succeed.

✔	Question/Task	Notes/Findings
	What is the organization's mission?	
	What are the organization's values?	
	What is the organization's vision? (generally future focused in comparison to the mission statement)	
	What are your direct department's vision and measurable goals?	
	How does your role contribute to meeting your department's goals?	
	How does your role contribute to meeting your organization's goals?	
	What is the organizational structure? What are the different departments and levels that make up the employer?	
	What are the products and services my organization sells? What is my role in these products and services (or details about one specific product/service you will be working on)?	
	Who does my organization compete with in the marketplace?	

✔	Question/Task	Notes/Findings
	What is the history of my organization? What major changes has my organization been through?	
	Take a tour of the building.	
	What is the culture of your department? What is the dress code? What is the level of formality in the workplace? How hierarchical is the culture? How balanced are work and life? Do people bring their personality to the workplace? How well do people know one another?	
	Learn common acronyms and phrases used to describe the work.	

Add your completed work to the "About Jobs" section of your Career Builder Files.

▶ *CAREER ACTION WORKSHEET*

14-4 Internal Resource Network Map ❷ ❸

Fill out the map below by adding the names of key relationships important to the success of your work. If you have any gaps, try to learn who the right people are in your workplace and start building relationships with them.

It may be helpful to ask your immediate manager, department administrator, or HR resource for an organization chart of your department. Also, you can create your own organization chart using PowerPoint or other Microsoft Office tools. Templates for org charts are available online.

Add your completed work to the "About Jobs" section of your Career Builder Files.

This page is intentionally blank.

▶ CAREER ACTION WORKSHEET
14-5 Prepare for Advancement ❸ ❹

Career Action Worksheet 14-5 is a sample job performance rating form that is representative of the forms used by many companies. Typically, your immediate manager will rate your performance in the left column. If you don't have the performance template for your job, use the template below to help you think through the assessment process.

For this Career Action Worksheet, there are several parts:

A. Rating: Rate yourself in the left column. Assign yourself a score of 1 to 3 with 1 representing high performance and 3 representing low performance. Then chose two or three categories where you would like to do even be even better. Next, list action items that will help you improve your performance.

B. Overall: Consider your overall performance. Use an *X* to mark what you think your performance is. Mark with an *M* what you think your manager might rate you. Consider why this difference might exist and what you can do to ensure you both view your performance similarly.

C. Short Term: What would you like to be able to do in the short term, say, 6 to 18 months from now? A good goal is to become advancement-ready. Advancement is defined here based on your personal goals—whether that means being promoted, working more independently, moving laterally to another department or function, or becoming a master in your existing role. With your manager and/or mentor(s), list a few things you can focus on that will help you achieve your short-term goals.

Part D. Long Term: What would you like to be able to do in five to seven years? Again, with your manager and/or mentor(s), determine what things you can start doing now to meet this goal. Have a serious discussion about the probability of this goal becoming a reality, and if they view you as capable of even more or would advise you to take a different route. The primary value of this section is the discussion between you and others.

Part E. Manager's Summary: This is where your manager writes her or his viewpoint and signs it. You too may be asked to sign it. Be clear on whether you are signing to say "I agree" or "I have read this."

Rating*	Performance or Behavioral Category	Action Items
	ABILITY TO ACQUIRE AND USE INFORMATION AND FOLLOW INSTRUCTIONS (Uses initiative in acquiring, interpreting, and following instructions and using references)	
	INTERPERSONAL SKILLS (Is tactful, understanding, and efficient when dealing with people)	
	BASIC SKILLS (Is proficient in reading, writing, mathematics, listening, and verbal and nonverbal communication)	
	JOB SKILLS (Demonstrates command of required knowledge and skills)	
	THINKING/PROBLEM-SOLVING SKILLS (Generates new ideas, makes decisions, solves problems, and reasons logically)	
	ABILITY TO COOPERATE WITH OTHERS (Works well with team members and under supervision, exercises leadership, and works well with people of diverse backgrounds)	
	QUANTITY OF WORK (Does required amount of work)	
	QUALITY OF WORK (Does neat, accurate, complete, and efficient work)	
	GOOD WORK HABITS (Maintains good attendance and punctuality, is dependable, and follows safety/work procedures)	
	ATTITUDE (Demonstrates enthusiasm, interest, and motivation)	
	TECHNOLOGY (Works well with technology— tools, computers, and procedures)	
	PERSONAL QUALITIES (Demonstrates responsibility, initiative, self-confidence, integrity, and honesty; practices good self-management; sets and maintains goals; exhibits self-motivation; and is cooperative)	
	LEADERSHIP SKILL (Demonstrates leadership and ownership of role)	

* Use a rating of 1 to 3, where 1 is best and 3 is not acceptable. Note that at many companies 80 percent of people are typically rated as average (or 2).

Overall Evaluation of Performance and Behavior

Your immediate manager will provide an overall rating of your performance based on the organization's rating code (shown here as Outstanding, Very Good, Good, Acceptable, or Unacceptable).

_____ Outstanding   _____ Very Good   _____ Good   _____ Acceptable   _____ Unacceptable

Employee's Short-Term Goals (List your short-term job or career goals here, and actions you and your manager can take now to help you reach each goal.)

Short-Term Goal	Action Items

Employee's Long-Term Goals (List your long-term job or career goals here, and actions you and your manager can take now to help you reach each goal.)

Long-Term Goal	Action Items

Suggestions for Improving Performance or Behavior (While a typical performance evaluation will not have the right column "Action Items," there usually is a section for suggested actions to improve your work performance or behavior.)

General Comments About Employee's Job Performance (Your immediate manager will also add any other appropriate comments to describe the quality of your work performance.)

Signature of Immediate Manager (This is where your immediate manager would sign your performance evaluation.)

Note: Save your performance review documents to provide insights and reminders about where you have been on your career journey, where you are now, and where you might go next.

Add your completed work to the "About Me" section of your Career Builder Files.

This page is intentionally blank.

Succeeding in the Job Search Journey Using Social Media

Overview

The appendix has step-by-step guidelines for using social media during the job search. The guidelines correspond with each phase of the Job Search Journey. For more, see the *You, Online* features located in each chapter.

OUTCOMES

1. Leverage social media at the start of the Job Search Journey.
2. Share your resume online.
3. Network and find job leads using social media.
4. Prepare for interviews using social media.
5. Manage your ongoing social media presence.

It's not what you know, it's who you know.

OUTCOME 1 — LEVERAGE SOCIAL MEDIA AT THE START OF YOUR JOB SEARCH JOURNEY

Phase 1 of the Job Search Journey, *Prepare for the Journey*, was about creating organization systems for your journey, creating your Personal Brand Statement and goals, and exploring possible careers. Now, with your Personal Brand Statement and 30-Second Commercial in hand, you are ready to use social media to help you prepare for the journey.

Social media is a critical tool for your job search. Recruiters, employers, and job seekers like social media because it helps match a high volume of job seekers to the many companies with opportunities. *Social media* refers to websites and applications that let users create and share content virtually. Statistics reported by JobVite and Career Builder in 2014 highlight the importance of social media in the Job Search Journey:

- 94 percent of recruiters use social media to find candidates. 39 percent of employers use social media for recruiting and hiring.[1]
- LinkedIn®, Facebook, and Twitter are the top social media sources for candidates, respectively. 89 percent of all recruiters report having hired someone through LinkedIn®.[2]
- 51 percent of employers have passed on a candidate due to inappropriate social media activity.[3]

Social media is a crucial component that will increase your chances of landing a job. You can use several social media tools. Choose based on the amount of time you

---

[1] http://blog.capterra.com/top-15-recruiting-statistics-2014/
[2] http://blog.capterra.com/top-15-recruiting-statistics-2014/
[3] http://shar.es/1gI1Uo

have, but at a minimum ensure you maintain a profile on LinkedIn®. This appendix looks at LinkedIn®, Twitter, and Facebook, with a greater focus on LinkedIn®, but choose the tool that is most used and useful for your industry. Talk to people in your Career Network who are in your industry about their opinion on the current best social media tool for you.

Establish Your Brand on Key Social Media Sites

Start preparing now for Your Job Search Journey by sharing your Personal Brand Statement online. Here's how to get started on LinkedIn®, Twitter, and Facebook.

LinkedIn®

Start by building your LinkedIn® profile, where your personal brand can come to life. Word choice is very important because LinkedIn® is *search engine optimized*, meaning that LinkedIn® enables its search engine by focusing on keywords contained in your profile. The better keywords you use, the more likely that your profile will show up in the search results for recruiters and prospective employers. **Think about what words people will use to search and find you, instead of thinking of what words you use to describe yourself.** See Figure App-1 below for an example. Here are tips for each section of your LinkedIn® profile.

- **Headline:** The headline is located under your name and summarizes your brand and expertise in short phrases, ideally using search engine–optimized keywords, separated by a comma or a vertical separator. There's even a link to search what others in your industry are using as their headline to get ideas. This headline is critical because it shows up under your name in search results and should be compelling enough that viewers are enticed to click and view your profile.

- **Industry:** By specifying the industry you belong to, you name your competition in the job market. Make sure your choice is accurate.

- **Summary:** This section is the first set of text viewers see of your profile. It is critical that it contains a compelling summary of your professional story, incorporating industry-wide keywords, and is more than 40 words. A great way to start your summary is by using your Personal Brand Statement. You can also upload documents and videos to your summary. If you have filmed your 30-Second Commercial, this is a great place to include it.

Figure App-1: Image of LinkedIn® Profile Page

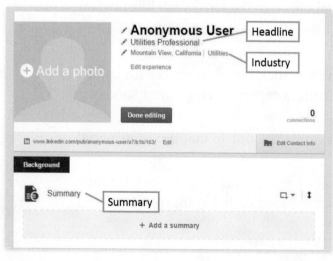

- **Photo:** No one takes a LinkedIn® profile seriously unless it includes a photo. Photos help build trust, and help people recognize and remember you when you are meeting face to face. Choose a high-quality, high-resolution headshot photo with a neutral background in which you are wearing professional clothing.

Twitter

On Twitter, your personal brand shines through in your 140-character profile description and through the network you follow. To *follow* means to sign up to receive the tweets of another Twitter user. A person who signs up to receive your tweets is your *follower*.

- **Profile description:** Use a concise version of your Personal Brand Statement to describe your abilities and goals. Also include relevant hashtags by placing the symbol # before a phrase. A *hashtag* is a way to track conversations between users by organizing and grouping tweets on similar subjects. For a specific topic, for example, for the field of technician, you can search #technician and see profiles and comments related to the topic of technician.
- **Your network:** Spend some time researching the thought leaders, leading companies, and top publications in your field. Carefully choose who to follow and what content to *retweet*, the act of forwarding another's tweet, because recruiters look at this as a reflection of your personality and interests.
- **Your personal thought leadership:** Twitter users build recognition and following by developing a specific expertise. You can create quality tweets and share content about the expertise areas you want to be known for.

Facebook

Facebook is primarily a personal social media site, instead of professional. However, because of its personal nature, the high quality of connections has proven to help many people gain jobs. Create and reinforce your Personal Brand Statement over time on your Facebook profile by sharing industry-related content and status updates. Tell your network about your job search through positive, clear status updates. Categorize your relationships by using the drop-down menu next to an individual's name and adding them to a specific list, such as Close Friends, Acquaintances, or Work Related, so that you can target your status updates as needed.

Check Your Online Image

You may already have an online image or brand on the Internet. It is common for employers and recruiters to search for you online. Search for yourself on the Internet. What do you see? Clean up items that do not reflect well on you. If you are hard to find, such as you have a common name or share a name with a famous or infamous personality, figure out how to help employers and recruiters find the "real you" online.

Explore Careers Using Social Media Tools

LinkedIn® Groups is a great tool for exploring careers, where you can search and join groups related to your field and interests. Consider these tips:

- Join groups that are relevant to your career field and job search.
- Contribute your expertise to discussions.

- After participating in a few discussions, consider starting discussions with direct questions such as "What tips do you have for finding a job in this field?" and "What are the greatest challenges in this job area?"
- Request 15-minute Career Network meetings, as described in Chapter 6, through starting a discussion.

Through the Twitter hashtag feature, follow industry conversations. If you're interested in nursing, for example, do a daily check of #nursing to stay abreast of relevant articles and hot topics.

As you expand your network and research these fields, reflect on what you like or dislike about what you've learned. Use what you learn to become more targeted in your job search.

SHARE YOUR RESUME ONLINE

In Phase 2, you created your resume. Now share it online in the most effective ways as you complete Phase 2 of your Job Search Journey.

Post Your Resume on Social Media

Both LinkedIn® and Facebook let you share your resume with your online network.

Finish building your LinkedIn® profile by copying and pasting the parts of your resume into the Experience, Organizations, and Education sections. Then consider the Skills section of the profile. As you add relevant skills, note that if a skill is common among users, it will appear as you are typing. Be sure to choose common skills because these skills are optimized for searchability. When your network endorses your skill set, LinkedIn® organizes the skills based on those that have the most endorsements. Fill in your Honors and Awards using the information you collected in your Career Builder Files.

On your Facebook profile, fill out the Work and Education portion of your profile by cutting and pasting materials from the materials you already created in Chapter 5 of this book.

Create a Personal Resume Website

With today's technology, setting up a website is easier than ever. There are both free and paid options that walk you through setting up a site that showcases you, your resume, and, if appropriate, your portfolio. There are several categories of personal sites.

- **Simple landing page site:** This is a single page site that showcases your basic information, including an *about* section and links to your social media profiles. Consider About.me, Enthuse.me, and Strikingly websites to help you create a powerful landing page.
- **Full website:** A full website provides you with several different pages, including a blog, portfolio, resume, and more. A *blog* is a website with articles you've written listed in reverse chronological order. Several popular options that offer both free and premium templates to help you build your site are Weebly, Wix,

and SquareSpace. Each has step-by-step documentation and makes it easy for you to manage your site without a lot of computer technical knowledge.

- **Infographic sites:** A new trend has emerged where a visual site is created based off your LinkedIn® profile. They translate your profile into a visual history that can be grasped quickly. A site like this may be useful if you have a long career history and want to "boil down" a lengthy resume to its essentials. Sites to consider for this include Vizualize.me and Re.vu. See an example in Figure App-2.

Figure App-2: Example of an Infographic of a Profile

Having your own website is a great addition to your marketing materials and allows you to more easily control the information about you that is visible on the Internet. In contrast, social media profiles have to be monitored for what your network was contributing to your profile. Your website can also be listed on your business card and resume when networking.

NETWORK AND FIND JOB LEADS USING SOCIAL MEDIA

Ninety-three percent of recruiters look for mutual connections they may have with potential candidates on LinkedIn® and report finding 60 percent of their best quality candidates through referrals.[4] Networking is a key source of job leads, and mastering networking online is central to the Job Search Journey. In Phase 3, *Apply for Jobs*, the focus was on networking, cover letters, and job applications. Now learn how to network using social media to help you in Phase 3 of your Job Search Journey.

Leverage Your Existing Social Network

Your existing social network can be a very powerful resource to help you find job leads if you express your goals and needs clearly.

On LinkedIn®, your summary should state your job search goals. To **connect** with someone on LinkedIn®, you request admittance into an individual's LinkedIn® social network. A user who is accepted is a *connection*.

Look through the profiles of people in your network. Is there anyone who could have relevant connections in your field? Send a private message to those people and request their help in your job search. Alternately, request recommendations for work you have done previously. Be specific when requesting recommendations by suggesting specific skills or abilities that you would like the recommender to highlight. This makes it easier for the writer, and ensures you get the

---

[4] JobVite's 2014 survey. https://www.jobvite.com/wp-content/uploads/2014/10/Jobvite_SocialRecruiting_Survey2014.pdf.

recommendation you want. **Ensure each experience in your profile has at least one recommendation.** Also, ask people to endorse your skills.

On Facebook and Twitter, post status updates that share information and demonstrate thought leadership in your career field. Ask directly and specifically for connections that would help further your job search. On Twitter, ensure you are retweeting others' content as much as sharing your own in order to build quality relationships.

Expanding Your Social Network

The LinkedIn® Groups and Companies features offer several opportunities for you to expand your social network to include more connections.

- Join the top five largest membership groups in your field or industry in your local area, your region, and, finally, at the national level. Everyone who is in a group with you is automatically accessible to become a *first-degree connection*. The higher the number of members in a group you have joined, the larger your network can become.

- Look for people who have posted great discussion topics in your groups. Request to add them to your connections and set up a Career Network meeting with them.

- Use the search function to find companies you would like to work for. Then, on the company page, look at the section How You're Connected. Request to be added as a connection to relevant employees or those who you have a mutual connection with.

- Respond thoughtfully to posts a company has posted or relevant discussions in Groups. You never know who will see your comments and request to be connected with you!

On Twitter, expanding your social network is easy because you can follow anyone. There is no "application process" where a user may not accept your follow. Follow relevant thought leaders, professional associations, companies, and publications in your field. Retweet content you find interesting. Reply and start conversations using the hashtag feature as appropriate.

Finding Job Leads

Most social networks have a job search feature.

- **LinkedIn®:** Use the drop-down menu next to the search field to search for jobs. When you find a job you're interested in, you typically have the option to apply through LinkedIn® or the company site. Sometimes, you can even see the recruiter who posted the job and follow up with him or her directly. LinkedIn® Premium Membership allows you to message people you may not have access to otherwise, as well as access information such as wages or salary range for a specific job. Additionally, you can view how you compare to other applicants for the job and apply with more confidence.

- **Twitter:** Many companies have job-related Twitter *handles* that you can follow for the latest updates on jobs. *Handles* refer to Twitter usernames, which are preceded by the @ symbol.

- **Facebook:** You can *"like"* a company's page and engage through its posts. To *like* on Facebook refers to recommending content or demonstrating agreement that is then shared with your social network. See who in your network works at companies of interest. Keep up to date on new job openings through the company's page.

Outside of these formal approaches for finding job openings, keep in mind that most jobs come from referrals. Stay focused on building quality relationships as you engage on social media.

PREPARE FOR INTERVIEWS USING SOCIAL MEDIA

Social media can also be a great source of information when you are researching for a job interview. In Phase 4, *Shine at Interviews*, you learned how to interview well. Now learn how social media can help prepare you for interviews in Phase 4 of your Job Search Journey.

When you get a request for an interview, use your LinkedIn® connections to help you set up Career Network meetings with existing employees at that company in order to gain insights into the interview process. You can also learn about the interview process through sites such as Glassdoor.com.

You can learn a lot about companies' culture through the brand they present on social media. Pay attention to the words they use on their postings. How informal are they? What are their values? What are the hot topics at the company?

Pay attention to employee profiles on social media channels. What sort of background did they use in their profile photo? What is the level of professionalism presented? These sorts of details can help you understand what to expect when entering their company atmosphere for an interview. However, even if a company appears quite informal, during the interview stage, present yourself more formally. It is better to be overdressed and over courteous. You can always adjust via your language, tone, or attitude if it's clear they have a more open, relaxed atmosphere. Cultural fit is a key qualification. Eighty percent of recruiters on LinkedIn® and 50 percent on Twitter look for cultural fit when evaluating candidates.[5]

Be careful about sharing information about your interviews on your social media profiles. Never announce which companies offered you an interview. While it is nice to celebrate, steer clear of doing so online until you have accepted a job offer and have started working at your new workplace. Sharing specifics beforehand is a red flag to most recruiters and HR resources. You might harm your chances of moving forward. Share your joy privately until your job search is complete.

MANAGE YOUR ONGOING SOCIAL MEDIA PRESENCE

When you accept a job offer and start work at your new workplace, don't forget the strong social media presence you have built! As you wrap up Phase 5 of your Job Search Journey, job in hand, learn about the importance of maintaining and

---

[5]JobVite's 2014 survey. https://www.jobvite.com/wp-content/uploads/2014/10/Jobvite_SocialRecruiting_Survey2014.pdf.

managing your social media presence. There are two keys: manage communication about your new job and stay active in your field's community.

As you communicate about your new job, stay away from negative comments about any company. Learn about your new company's social media policy to avoid any potential HR or legal issues. When in doubt, do not engage in conversations about your company online. Some companies may encourage conversation, while others may prefer that you engage only on the internal social network. Here are some basic guidelines to keep in mind:

- **Don't trash your boss or complain about your job online.** Many people have found themselves unemployed after this infraction. Even if you haven't "friended" your boss, you never know who in your network has, and your post will almost certainly get back to your employer.
- **Don't release private information** you learn on the job or through any of your accounts. An EMT lost his job after tweeting about a call he went out on. Even though he didn't use the patient's name, the tweet was detailed enough that it constituted a violation of the patient's privacy and resulted in the EMT's termination.
- **Don't post offensive photos or comments** that will reflect poorly on your company. Your employer has a right to protect the company's name and reputation.
- **Don't publish articles about your company without permission** from your public relations or communications department. To maintain the company's brand, most have an approval process that you'll want to go through.

Stay active in your career field's community by continuing to share quality content and listening to thought leaders. There are several benefits to taking the time to maintain your social network:

- You may learn new information that you can bring to your workplace.
- Your passion for the field and personal growth will help you stand out as an employee and could propel you toward career growth in the future.
- Your social network will still be active if you need to find a job in the future.
- Try to give back to others who are looking for jobs.

Make sure to thank those who helped you in your job search and let them know where you landed.

Social media is an essential part of today's job search. If at any time you have a question, don't hesitate to search the Internet to find the answer. Being informed and connected will help you land the job of your dreams!

My Career: Making It Happen

This guide contains helpful reminders and tips to help with your job search. Tear it on the perforation and use it to complete job applications and prepare for interviews.

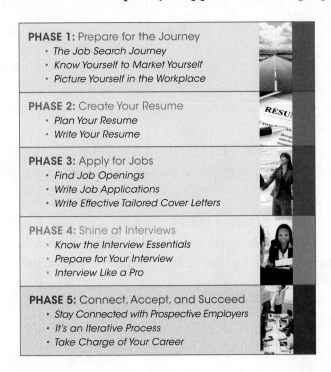

PHASE 1: Prepare for the Journey
- *The Job Search Journey*
- *Know Yourself to Market Yourself*
- *Picture Yourself in the Workplace*

PHASE 2: Create Your Resume
- *Plan Your Resume*
- *Write Your Resume*

PHASE 3: Apply for Jobs
- *Find Job Openings*
- *Write Job Applications*
- *Write Effective Tailored Cover Letters*

PHASE 4: Shine at Interviews
- *Know the Interview Essentials*
- *Prepare for Your Interview*
- *Interview Like a Pro*

PHASE 5: Connect, Accept, and Succeed
- *Stay Connected with Prospective Employers*
- *It's an Iterative Process*
- *Take Charge of Your Career*

PHASE 1: PREPARE FOR THE JOURNEY

A. Organize Your Job Search by setting up your Career Builder Files using these three parts:

- **About Me:** This section contains a collection of records, awards, information about you, your thoughts about jobs and your career, and drafts of your Personal Brand Statement.

- **About Jobs:** Use this section to track job leads, contact information for people you talk to, your research about career fields and job listings, and your draft job applications and resumes.

- **Master Career Portfolio:** In this section, collect documents you will share with others, especially during interviews, such as your final resume and job applications, samples of your work, cover letters, and thank-you notes.

B. Assess and Market Yourself by creating a Personal Brand Statement based on your skills and strengths.

Personal Brand Statement Formula

1. What one or two words describe what you do in general terms? (examples: thinker, doer, innovator, educator, caring person, organizer, actor, designer, worker)

2. What are you known for? (examples: delivering results despite challenges, balancing multiple priorities, being driven to finish tasks, knowing the right flavor combination, having an eye for color)

3. What sets you apart from your peers? (examples: speed, thoroughness, kindness, gentleness, logic)

I am a _____ that _____.

Recall there is a difference between transferable skills and job-specific skills.

- **Transferable Skills** are basic skills and abilities that can be applied to many different types of work. Examples: Computer and technology skills • Multi-tasker • Project Manager • Skilled at Customer Service • Public Speaker • People Manager • Researcher • Skilled at Analysis • Negotiator • Problem Solver • Teach others • Use resources wisely • Write clearly

- **Job-Specific Skills** are skills needed to do a particular job. These may often have a certification or license. Examples: Take blood pressure • Operate a forklift • Frame a house • Drive a truck or vehicle • Create a balance sheet • Give a customer a manicure • Train a police dog • Repair a dented fender

C. Explore Career Fields using your Career Network and websites provided by federal and state agencies such as those linked to the U.S. Bureau of Labor Statistics (BLS) or state business needs. A good example is the CareerOneStop website.

PHASE 2: CREATE YOUR RESUME

A. Plan Your Resume

RESUME OUTLINE:

   i. Contact Information
  ii. Professional Profile
 iii. Qualifications
 iv. Work Experience
  v. Education
 vi. Optional Sections
     • Related Experience
     • Military Service

B. Write Your Resume

a) Use this guide to evaluate your resume:

Rating Scale: 1 to 4 (1 = not really; 2 = sometimes/somewhat; 3 = usually; 4 = definitely)

_____ 1. The Objective or Profile includes the job title or required abilities specified by the employer.

_____ 2. Qualifications contain keywords that match requirements for the job.

_____ 3. Qualifications are relevant to the stated job objective. Major strengths are included. Each job listing contains the employer's name and address (city and state) and job title.

_____ 4. Each job listing describes responsibilities and specific, measurable accomplishments.

_____ 5. Job descriptions use power words and keyword nouns that support the objective.

_____ 6. If work experience is limited, relevant paid and nonpaid internships and volunteer or other pertinent activities are included.

_____ 7. The applicant emphasizes courses, internships, degrees, certificates, and so on that best support the objective.

_____ 8. The overall GPA or GPA in the concentration area is included (if impressive).

_____ 9. The applicant emphasizes involvement in professional and other organizations that support the job objective.

_____ 10. Relevant awards, achievements, and offices held are included.

_____ 11. The overall design is appealing.

_____ 12. The resume tells a personal, compelling story.

_____ 13. The content is correct (grammar, spelling, and punctuation).

NOTE: The Internet offers up-to-date resume templates.

b) Use ACTION VERBS or power words that clearly describe your scope of responsibility and convey a sense of accomplishment:

Accelerate	Discover	Order	Repair
Advise	Distribute	Organize	Report
Analyze	Edit	Originate	Represent
Approve	Eliminate	Oversee	Research
Arrange	Enforce	Participate	Resolve
Assemble	Establish	Perform	Respond
Assist	Evaluate	Plan	Retrieve
Audit	Examine	Prepare	Review
Budget	Expand	Present	Revise
Build	Expedite	Prioritize	Schedule
Change	Forecast	Process	Select
Collaborate	Formulate	Produce	Sell
Collect	Generate	Program	Serve
Communicate	Handle	Promote	Set up
Complete	Identify	Propose	Solve
Compute	Implement	Protect	Specialize
Conduct	Improve	Prove	Start
Control	Increase	Provide	Streamline
Coordinate	Influence	Publish	Structure
Create	Install	Purchase	Study
Customize	Instruct	Raise	Supervise
Delegate	Integrate	Receive	Support
Deliver	Lead	Recommend	Teach
Demonstrate	Maintain	Reconcile	Test
Design	Manage	Record	Track
Detect	Monitor	Redesign	Train
Develop	Motivate	Reduce	Update
Diagnose	Obtain	Reinforce	Upgrade
Diagram	Operate	Reorganize	Write
Direct			

Use KEYWORDS include job titles, specialized skills and tools, industry buzz-words, jargon, acronyms, and words and phrases in job descriptions and ads. Employers and resume scanning software look for keywords that indicate the person is qualified for the job. Review the websites and publications of companies and professional associations in your industry.

PHASE 3: APPLY FOR JOBS

A. Find Job Openings by conducting effective career networking meetings using the directions below.

1. Identify at least two people in your career field.
2. Call or email the person and ask for a 30-minute meeting to learn about his or her job and discuss your job search.
3. Prepare for the meeting. Note the following questions and remember to bring your resume and business cards:

Conversation starters

- What drew you to this career field?
- Is this your first job in this career field?
- How long have you worked at your company?

Job and career questions

- What is your typical workday like?
- Which parts of your job do you find most challenging? Most enjoyable?
- What is the culture like at your workplace/in this career field?
- What is a typical career path at your company?
- What do you wish you had known when you started your career?
- What changes have you seen in this field? What changes do you anticipate?

Career advice

- What advice do you have for someone looking for a job in this field?
- Does my job goal seem realistic and achievable?
- Do you recommend any additional training or certifications?
- What professional or other associations do you recommend joining?
- What publications or websites do you recommend?
- Who else would you recommend I speak with? When I call, may I use your name?

4. Follow-up and evaluation—send a thank-you note or email to the person you met with as well as the person who helped you get the meeting. Summarize what you learned, evaluate your performance, and store your notes in your Career Builder files.

B. Write Job Applications

CAUTION: Save, Save, Save

When applying online, Internet or technical issues can easily derail your application process. You may have spent the time to fill out the full application and at the last screen, run into a page load issue. You may have painstakingly typed in the answer to a difficult question, only to accidentally hit the Back or Refresh button. To avoid the risk of losing your entered data:

- Keep an open Word document or add to your existing plain text document. Copy and paste any new content you are entering into this file throughout the application process.
- If the application site has a "Save Application" functionality, use it frequently.
- Fill out job applications in a place where high-speed Internet is available.

Save passwords and other relevant information in case you need to go back and edit your application.

C. Write Cover Letters Below is a sample cover letter on which to base your own.

TAYLOR WHITAKER

10806 Delaware Avenue | Camden, NJ 08105
[856] 555.0195 | taylor.whitaker@email.com
Linkedin.com/in/taylor.whitaker

January 10, 20–

Mr. Gary Whaley
District Sales Manager
Computeriferals Company
1 Computer Way
Camden, NJ 08102

Dear Mr. Whaley:

Computeriferals has earned my respect. I have used and repaired peripherals from most of the leading manufacturers in my studies as a Business Systems/Computer Repair major and in my job as a sales representative at ComputerChoice. I know you build quality products, and I want to sell quality products—Computeriferals.

Careful review of my qualifications and the requirements of a sales representative at Computeriferals suggest that I am well qualified for a sales position with your organization.

Your Requirements	My Experience
• Ability to handle multiple prospects	• Expanded customer base from 137 to 183 accounts in the past year—a 34% increase
• Proven ability to meet sales goals	• Increased yearly sales from $743,000 to $1,236,000—exceeded goal by 66%
• Ability to expand sales in existing accounts	• Negotiated a new $250,000 service contract for an existing client with five locations
• Strong communication and follow-up skills	• Attained 100% customer retention through a service-first approach and frequent communication

The expanding market for Computeriferals presents an appealing challenge. Even if you have no current sales openings, I would appreciate meeting with you to discuss your requirements. My resume is enclosed for your convenience. I will call next week to request an appointment, or you may reach me at the contact information above. Thank you for your time.

Respectfully,

Taylor Whitaker

Taylor Whitaker

Enclosure

PHASE 4: SHINE AT INTERVIEWS

A. Prepare and Practice before the interview, by doing these things: Research the company's website and search for them in the news • Know where you're going (address, location, maps, offices) • Research your interviewer • Review the interview preparation checklist • Practice your stories • Complete any pre-interview tests • Prepare and practice your body language • Check your appearance • Remember to use business etiquette • Practice good verbal skills.

B. Take Pre-Employment Tests and other screening tests and interviews. For each of these, do the following: Be prepared • Focus on why you are interested in working for the prospective employer • Be professional, courteous, and friendly • Be factual in your answers, as well as be brief yet thorough.

C. Interview Like a Pro using the following checklists before, during, and after your interviews.

INTERVIEW PREPARATION CHECKLIST

General Job-Related Materials from Your Master Career Portfolio

- ☐ A copy of the job posting or description
- ☐ Your resume—copies for the interviewer(s), yourself, and an extra
- ☐ Portfolio materials and job-related samples of your work
- ☐ Certificates, licenses, transcripts, and related documents
- ☐ Letters of recommendation (for this job or this specific type of work)
- ☐ Lists of references (general endorsement of your character, knowledge, and skills)
- ☐ Business or contact cards, if you have these

Marketing Materials from Your Master Career Portfolio

- ☐ A copy of your 30-Second Commercial (for your use only)
- ☐ A reminder list of examples and stories you can tell (for your use only)

Organizing Materials

- ☐ A notebook with questions you can ask during the interview (see Chapter 10)
- ☐ A businesslike pen—not too cheap, expensive, flashy, or quirky
- ☐ A note pad on which to take notes (ask permission to take notes before doing so)
- ☐ Your appointment calendar (If you use your smartphone, turn the sound off before you even walk in the building!)
- ☐ A list of the names, titles, and phone numbers of people related to this interview

DURING THE INTERVIEW: Be prepared for the type of interview you will be participating in:

Screening Interview • Computer-Based Interview • Campus Interview • Phone Interview • Video Interview • Behavioral Interview • Panel Interview • Team Interview

Common Questions

General Interview Questions:

1. Why do you want this job?
2. What type of work do you enjoy most?
3. What are your strongest skills?
4. Are you a team player?
5. What are your long-term career goals, and how do you plan to achieve them?
6. Do you have a geographic preference? Are you willing to relocate?
7. With what type of manager have you had the best relationships?

Behavioral Questions:

1. Describe an accomplishment that demonstrates your initiative.
2. Tell me specifically about a time when you worked under great stress.
3. Describe an experience when you dealt with an angry customer or coworker.
4. Give me an example of your ability to adapt to change.
5. Explain what problems you have encountered. How did you overcome them?

Answering Behavioral Questions:

6. Describe the situation. (What)
7. Explain the actions you took. (How)
8. Describe the outcomes. (Importance)
9. Summarize what you learned from the experience. (Insights from you)

Character Questions

1. How would you describe yourself?
2. What rewards do you look for in your career?
3. What accomplishment are you most proud of, particularly as it relates to your field?
4. Do you work well under pressure?

Stress/Difficult Questions

1. Why do you think you are the best candidate for the job? *or* Why should I hire you?
2. Why do you want to leave your current job?
3. Why have you held so many jobs?
4. What is your greatest weakness?
5. Have you ever been fired from a job?
6. Does your current employer know you are planning to leave?

CLOSING AND FOLLOWING UP AFTER THE INTERVIEW:

Questions You Should Ask:

1. Do you have a training program for this position? If so, will you describe it?
2. Can you tell me about the duties and tasks of this position on a typical workday?

3. May I have a copy of the written job description?

4. Will the responsibilities of this position expand with time and experience on the job? Can good performance in this job lead to opportunities for career growth?

5. Can you tell me about the people I would work with? To whom does this position report?

6. Do you need any more information about my qualifications or experience?

7. When will you be making your hiring decision? What does your hiring process and timeline look like? May I call you if I have additional questions?

Before you leave the interview, clarify:

- What, if anything, you should do to follow up.
- When a decision will be made.
- How the interviewer prefers you to follow up (by phone, by letter, by email, or in person).
- As you near the close of an interview, make a point of leaving your interviewer with a clear picture of how you fit the job.
- Run the short version of your 30-Second Commercial to restate your skills, experience, and other assets that meet the employer's needs.
- Watch for signs from the interviewer that it's time to wrap up the interview.
- Ask the interviewer to notify you when a candidate has been selected.
- Before you leave, determine any follow-up activities the interviewer expects from you.
- If you're seriously interested in the job, say so!
- Finally, as you leave, remember to use the interviewer's name: "Thank you for interviewing me, Ms. Carpenter."
- If you haven't been given one, ask the interviewer for a business card.

PHASE 5: CONNECT, ACCEPT, AND SUCCEED

A. Stay Connected with Prospective Employers by evaluating your interview performance, planning your schedule for follow-up, and sending prompt thank-you letters. Evaluate job offers based on the entire package, including how well they fit your long-term career goals. Respond to job offers professionally, whether accepting or declining.

B. Develop Strategies for increasing your chances of getting interviews, improving your interview performance, and managing a rejection notice.

C. Take Charge of Your Career over the long term by onboarding quickly to your new job; building successful relationships; managing your career path; and assessing when the time is right to change jobs and/or careers.

A

About Jobs one of the three portfolios that make up your Career Builder Files: contains information about job leads, contact information for people you talk to about jobs, your research about career fields and job listings, and your draft job applications and resumes.

About Me one of the three portfolios that make up your Career Builder Files; contains a collection of records, awards, information about you, your thoughts about jobs and your career, and drafts of your Personal Brand Statement.

action verbs in a resume and cover letter, concrete verbs and phrases that reflect very specifically the action taken to meet a goal (for example, *build, prepare,* and *test*).

active listening a communication technique that requires the listener to understand, interpret, and evaluate what he or she hears; listening with the goal of understanding what the speaker intends.

applicant is a person who is applying for a job.

application a form with a set of questions used to collect information about a job applicant's skills, qualifications, and experience.

assertive behavior the ability to express oneself and to stand up for one's point of view without disrespecting others.

B

behavioral interview an interview technique in which the interviewer asks questions aimed at getting the applicant to provide specific examples of how he or she has successfully used the skills required on the job.

board interview see *panel interview.*

business etiquette expected professional behavior in the workplace based on courtesy, manners, and customs.

C

campus interview an on-site interview generally scheduled through a school's career center.

candidate a person who is being considered for a job, and typically has been offered an interview.

career encompasses a series of jobs in the same occupation or profession, either with the same company or with different companies.

Career Builder Files a filing system for collecting, organizing, and updating career and job search information with three sections or portfolios called *About Me, About Jobs,* and *Master Career Portfolio.*

Career Network the people you can contact who might support you in career-related situations.

Career Network meeting a meeting set up by you to discuss career-related topics with anyone who is currently in your Career Network or who might be a good addition to your network.

character questions interview questions asked to learn about the applicant's personal attributes, such as integrity, personality, attitudes, and motivation.

chronological a traditional resume format used to showcase work experience, skills, and a career progression.

code of ethics written guidelines for employees, managers and vendors to follow; based on a company's ethical standards and values.

cold lead an opportunity for a job found through an impersonal source such an online or offline job board; when pursuing the lead, the person on the receiving end is unknown to the job applicant.

combination a resume format that uses features of both a chronological and skills-based resume format in order to emphasize the match between the job seeker's skills and a position's requirements.

compensation both tangible and intangible benefits an employee receives from an employer for work provided to the employer.

Compensation may include a salary, wage, benefits (such as medical benefits, vacation, schooling training, sick days) overtime pay, and bonuses.

competencies the skills and traits that employers look for during job interviews and expect employees to demonstrate on the job.

computer-based interviews time-based interviews in which applicants log on to a password-protected website with instructions on how to complete the interview; often consist of 50 to 100 multiple-choice and true/false questions.

connect as used on the LinkedIn® social media site, indicating a trusted contact who is a first-degree connection.

cover letter a letter of inquiry or introduction that introduces a job seeker to a prospective employer.

E

employee handbook a written handbook that covers an organization's policies and procedures such as work hours, the probationary period for new employees, pay and benefits, and rules about using company equipment and email.

ethics guidelines or accepted behavior about what is right or wrong.

G

gatekeeper the person standing between you and the employer, usually an administrative support person, receptionist, or human resources staff member.

general information questions interview questions asked to obtain factual information.

H

hidden jobs job openings that are not published and that a job seeker must uncover; studies show that 80 to 85 percent of job openings are hidden.

I

immediate manager the person who directly supervises or manages an employee's work and development, often called a supervisor, boss, or manager (differs from *one-up manager,* who is the boss's boss),

interview Preparation Checklist a checklist of items to complete prior to an interview to ensure that you are ready to succeed during the interview.

J

job a role that involves performing a designated set of responsibilities and duties for a specific employer

Job Application Package the documents needed when applying for a job, including a job application, cover letter, and resume; may also include your business card and copies of a few select samples of your work from your career portfolio.

Job Search Journey describes a typical job search as five phases with several steps within each phase.

Job Search Journey Map a graphic model showing the phases and steps of the Job Search Journey.

job target a desirable job or job description; can be further classified as a *stretch target* (hard-to-get "dream job"), *current target* (ideal for you right now), or *contingency target* (easy to get and for which you are overqualified).

job-specific skills skills and technical abilities that relate to a specific job.

K

keywords in a resume, terms that represent the job qualifications and industry-related terms a company has programmed into the resume scanning software to search for; also used in applications and cover letters.

L

Long-term goals targets for achievements that will take a long time to accomplish, such as greater than 6 months.

M

Master Career Portfolio one of the three portfolios that make up your Career Builder Files. Contains documents you will share with others, especially during interviews, such as your final resume, job applications, samples of your work, cover letters, and thank-you notes.

master resume the finalized generic version of a resume that a job seeker uses for networking and distributes at job fairs; also the foundation for customized resumes.

N

networking developing relationships with people who can help in forming job search strategies and in finding strong job leads.

O

objective in a resume, a concise statement of the job seeker's immediate employment goals.

P

panel interview an interview in which the job candidate speaks with more than one person at a time.

Personal Brand Statement a statement that summarizes the unique benefits you offer to an employer; the foundation for 30-Second Commercials and other marketing tools.

personality test a pre-employment test used to determine whether a job applicant's personal and behavioral preferences are well matched to the work involved.

phone interview a cost-effective technique for screening job candidates

plain text cover letter a text file (.txt) version of a cover letter that has no formatting (no bold, no tables, no bullets, etc.) and is used as the source file for the cover letter in online applications.

plain text resume a text file (.txt) version of a resume that has no formatting (no bold, no tables, no bullets, etc.) and is used as the source file for online applications.

positive behavior purposely acting with energy and enthusiasm.

positive visualization purposely forming a mental picture of one's successful performance and recalling the image frequently.

positive thinking making a conscious effort to be optimistic and to anticipate positive outcomes.

proactive approach a focus on solving problems, taking positive actions, and taking responsibility for one's actions. Compare with *reactive approach.*

Professional Profile a two-sentence section of the resume that states your job target or objective and the Personal Brand Statement.

Q

qualifications in a resume, a bulleted list of skills that highlights why the job seeker is the ideal candidate for the job.

R

reactive approach a focus on problems and on avoiding difficult situations. Compare with *proactive approach.*

references people who are willing to vouch for a person's qualifications and recommend that person to prospective employers.

resume a brief one- or two-page document that details a job applicant's qualifications for a job.

S

screening interview an interview used to identify qualified candidates for the next level of interviews and to screen out candidates who do not have the basic qualifications for the job.

search engine optimized (seo) method used by online search software to assure that the most relevant information is listed first.

self-esteem belief in one's abilities and worth.

Short-term goals targets for achievements that are expected to be accomplished in a short time, such as tomorrow or next month.

skills test a pre-employment test used to test for the skills needed for a job.

social media The tools and platforms people use to publish, converse, and share content online.

social networking sites Online places where users can create a profile for themselves and then communicate with others using social media tools.

stress questions interview questions asked to determine how the job candidate performs under pressure and whether he or she is good at making decisions, solving problems, and thinking under stress.

structured interview interview technique using a predetermined set of questions for all candidates so that candidates can be more easily compared.

T

team interview an interview given by a group of several employees; the applicant meets individually with each person; after the interview, the team members meet to discuss the applicant's performance (also called a Day Visit).

transferable skills abilities that can be applied in more than one work environment; the basic skills and attitudes that are important for many types of work.

U

unstructured interview an interview approach that is conversational in tone; used to get to know candidates and assess their fit with the company and the job.

V

values deeply held beliefs about what is important.

video interview uses two-way video to conduct a "face-to-face" interview over the Internet.

W

Warm Introduction personal introductions to a prospective employer and possibly a job opportunity, often when a job opening isn't actually posted.

web resume a resume formatted in HTML and posted on the Internet.

WHI method a way to describe what you have done: what, how, importance; in other words, describe what you did, how you did it, and why the result you achieved was important to the business or organization.

work experience in a resume, the section that lists the job seeker's employment history; jobs are listed in chronological order starting with the most recent job.